# QUESTIONS & ANSWERS:
# CRIMINAL PROCEDURE I & II
# (POLICE PRACTICES AND
# PROSECUTION)

# QUESTIONS & ANSWERS: CRIMINAL PROCEDURE I & II (POLICE PRACTICES AND PROSECUTION)

## Multiple Choice and Short Answer Questions and Answers

## Second Edition

**LEWIS R. KATZ**
*John C. Hutchins Professor of Law;*
*Director of the Master of Laws in U.S. and*
*Global Legal Studies Program*
*Case Western Reserve University School of Law*

**NEIL P. COHEN**
*Distinguished Service Professor of Law and W.P. Toms Professor of Law*
*University of Tennessee College of Law*

ISBN#: 978-1-4224-1744-7

---

NOTE TO USERS

To ensure that you are using the latest materials available in this area, please be sure to periodically check the LexisNexis Law School web site for downloadable updates and supplements at www.lexisnexis.com/lawschool.

---

Editorial Offices
121 Chanlon Rd., New Providence, NJ 07974 (908) 464-6800
201 Mission St., San Francisco, CA 94105-1831 (415) 908-3200
www.lexisnexis.com

MATTHEW♦BENDER

# ABOUT THE AUTHORS

**Lewis R. Katz** is the John C. Hutchins Professor of Law and Director of the Master of Laws in U.S. and Global Legal Studies Program at Case Western Reserve University in Cleveland, Ohio. He has taught criminal law and procedure since 1966. Professor Katz is the author of numerous law review articles, treatises for practicing lawyers and judges in New York and Ohio, and Know Your Rights, a practical guide for ordinary citizens. Professor Katz participated in two landmark cases: he co-authored an amicus curiae brief in *Terry v. Ohio*, 392 U.S. 1 (1968), which authorized and set limits on police stops and frisks, and he served as trial counsel for the plaintiffs in *Cleveland Board of Education v. LaFleur*, 414 U.S. 632 (1974), which established the right of pregnant women to continue teaching in public schools.

**Neil P. Cohen** is a Distinguished Service Professor of Law and W.P. Toms Professor of Law at the University of Tennessee College of Law in Knoxville. He teaches evidence and criminal law and procedure. Professor Cohen is the author or editor of nine books and numerous law review articles. These publications include treatises on evidence and criminal procedure and a casebook on criminal procedure. He has also participated in drafting state rules of criminal law, criminal procedure, and evidence. His practice experience includes both criminal defense and prosecution. Professor Cohen has received many awards for teaching, scholarship, and public service. His memberships include the American Law Institute.

# PREFACE

This book will assist your learning and exam preparation in criminal procedure courses and for the bar exam. The subject matter of the book extends to all major subjects covered in criminal procedure courses. Some schools divide criminal procedure courses into Criminal Procedure I (police practices) and II (prosecution). This book includes the material in both courses. The book consists of multiple choice questions and answers, and short essay questions and answers for both courses.

The Criminal Procedure I materials cover arrest, search and seizure, interrogation, identification, suppression issues, and entrapment. Questions 1 through 143, and the practice final exam for Criminal Procedure I can be found in Questions 303 through 322.

The Criminal Procedure II materials cover discretion to prosecute, bail, complaint, initial appearance, preliminary hearing, grand jury, plea bargaining, joinder and severance, motion practice, discovery, time limitations, jurisdiction and venue, trial, double jeopardy, and postconviction remedies. Questions 144 through 302, and the practice final exam for Criminal Procedure II can be found in Questions 323 through 343.

We suggest that you answer the questions before consulting the answers. It will aid your learning if you answer the questions on your own and then study the answers. Further, our "short answers" are likely longer than you will find in other volumes in the series. The reason is that the types of questions that will best prepare you for the exam are rarely susceptible to one-paragraph answers. In the end, we have tried to balance brevity with the need to provide the student with realistic, useful questions. Our practice has been to err on the side of usefulness, resulting in somewhat longer discussions. While the answers to our short answer questions vary in length, none is more than three paragraphs. And, unless otherwise indicated, the question can be answered in one paragraph (up to 12 sentences). Do not fret if your answer comes in slightly longer or shorter than our answer. As long as the substance is the same, we would give full credit on an exam. If your answer is longer, however, our answer may show how to convey the same substance in fewer words. On time pressure exams, such brevity can be an asset.

Professor Lewis R. Katz
Case Western Reserve University
School of Law
Cleveland, Ohio
September 2009

Professor Neil Cohen
University of Tennessee
College of Law
Knoxville, Tennessee
September 2009

# Table of Contents

*QUESTIONS*

# Table of Contents

# Table of Contents

# Table of Contents

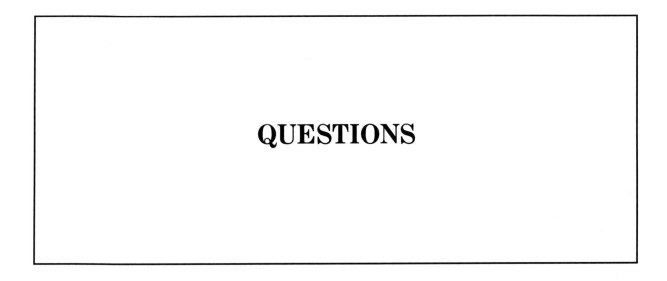

# QUESTIONS

Arnold Arnstein, a gambler, was the target of local prosecutors as well as the local U.S. Attorney for several years. After a federal grand jury investigated Arnstein for two years without returning an indictment, local prosecutors filed a multi-count Bill of Information charging Arnstein with conspiracy to engage in multiple gambling operations. Arnstein sought to have the Bill of Information dismissed, demanding, instead, his Fifth and Fourteenth Amendment right to a grand jury Indictment. The trial judge, denying the motion to dismiss, pointed to the state statute that authorizes charges to be initiated by Indictment or Bill of Information. Arnstein was convicted of all charges and appeals ¶ challenging the state's failure to accord him his Fifth and Fourteenth Amendment right to indictment.

1. The Court of Appeals will

(A) reverse the conviction because all of the rights contained in the Bill of Rights have been applied to the states through the Fourteenth Amendment, and Arnstein was denied the right to a grand jury Indictment.

(B) reverse the conviction because charges involving infamous crimes must originate with a grand jury.

(C) affirm the conviction because the Fifth Amendment right to grand jury indictment was not incorporated into the Fourteenth Amendment.

(D) affirm the conviction because the failure to secure a grand jury indictment is harmless error.

Paula Pickett was one of several hundred demonstrators arrested at a political convention in Denver (Minneapolis, take your pick). She was charged with trespass, a first class misdemeanor, carrying a potential six month jail sentence. Pickett's lawyer demanded a jury trial because of the political nature of the charges. The request was denied because state law guarantees a right to trial by jury only for offenses carrying a penalty of more than six months in jail. Pickett was tried by the court, convicted and sentenced to six months in jail (170 days of the jail sentence were suspended). Pickett appealed, claiming that her Sixth Amendment right to trial by jury was violated.

2. How should the court of appeals rule?

(A) The court will reverse the conviction because the Sixth Amendment guarantees that in all criminal prosecutions the accused shall be accorded a jury trial.

(B) The court will reverse the conviction because the Sixth Amendment guarantees a right to a jury trial in all serious offenses.

(C)   The court will affirm the conviction because the Sixth Amendment right applies only to trials in federal courts, and the states are free to institute their own procedures.

(D)   The court will affirm the conviction because the Sixth Amendment guarantee applies only to serious offenses carrying possible jail or prison sentences greater than six months.

The defendant was arrested and taken to jail for making an illegal left turn. The arresting officer knew the defendant from prior traffic stops and had followed the defendant until she made the illegal turn. Incident to the arrest, the officer searched the interior of the vehicle and found a small quantity of marijuana. The trial court rejected the defense motion to suppress the marijuana, holding that the Fourth Amendment does not bar a custodial arrest for a minor traffic offense. On appeal the state Supreme Court reversed the conviction on the grounds that state law mandates that a police officer issue a summons for a minor traffic offense and does not, then, allow the officer to conduct a search of the vehicle. The state Supreme Court held that the officer violated both the United States Constitution's Fourth Amendment and the state constitution when she arrested the defendant. The state has appealed to the United States Supreme Court.

3.  Will the United States Supreme Court reverse the state Supreme Court?

ANSWER:


Change the facts in Question 3 and ask what if the state Supreme Court ignored the state's prohibition against custodial arrests for minor traffic offenses and upheld the conviction under the authority of *Atwater v. City of Lago Vista*, 532 U.S. 318 (2001), that an arrest for a minor custodial offense does not violate the Fourth Amendment. The defendant appealed to the U.S. Supreme Court.

4.  Will the U.S. Supreme Court reverse the state conviction for failing to hold that the arrest was unreasonable?

    (A)  The U.S. Supreme Court will reverse the conviction because the state's interpretation violated the state constitutional provision.
    (B)  The U.S. Supreme Court will reverse the conviction because the state Supreme Court violated the Fourth Amendment command against unreasonable searches and seizures.
    (C)  The U.S. Supreme Court will affirm the conviction and refuse to implement the state constitution.
    (D)  The U.S. Supreme Court will affirm the conviction because it does not violate the Fourth Amendment.

Neighbors complained about a woman shooting a horse on her property and that the dead horse remained on the property. A humane officer drove to the property to investigate. The officer walked up the driveway and when no one answered the door, she walked farther up the driveway (allegedly looking for someone to talk to) toward a barn 50 feet from the main house. The barn and the house are served by the same driveway. The officer knocked on the side of the barn but no one answered. She heard moaning from within and peered into the barn — without entering — and saw a Shetland pony in a stall. The animal appeared to be emaciated, dehydrated, and starving. The defendant was charged with cruelty to animals and sought to exclude all evidence concerning the condition of the animal as the fruit of an illegal search and seizure.

5. Should the court grant the motion to suppress?

    (A) The court should grant the motion because the barn is within the curtilage of the house.

    (B) The court should deny the motion because the barn is outside the curtilage of the house.

    (C) The court should deny the motion because the barn is not entitled to the same protections as the house.

    (D) The court should grant the motion because the barn was entitled to the same privacy protection as the house.

A police officer and a drug dog were patrolling in front of a bus terminal. The officer observed the defendant in the bus station presumably change directions when the defendant saw the officer and her dog enter the bus station. The officer, now determined to talk with the defendant, walked quickly up to the defendant and directed her drug dog to sniff him. The drug dog placed its nose in the vicinity of the suspect's waist and groin area and then sat down, indicating the presence of drugs. After the positive indication from the dog, the officer arrested and searched the defendant and found drugs on his person. The defendant was and charged with illegal possession of drugs and sought to exclude all evidence seized from his person as the fruit of an illegal search and seizure.

6. How should the court rule?

    (A) The defendant was seized illegally prior to the dog sniff and the drugs are the fruit of the illegal seizure.

    (B) The defendant was illegally seized prior to the dog sniff and the drugs were seized incident to the lawful seizure.

    (C) The drugs were seized incident to the lawful arrest of the defendant following the dog sniff.

(D)   The drugs were seized incident to a legitimate *Terry*-stop.

Police had Tony Soprano under surveillance. At night, the police used night vision goggles to maintain their surveillance. On the night in question, police saw one of Tony's lieutenants deliver to Tony money in a canvas bag with Wells Fargo Bank imprinted on it. The money was given to Tony in his darkened family room, and the agents then watched Tony store the bag in a bin used to store duck food in his backyard. It was a dark night: no moon, no stars. Without the night vision goggles, the police would not have been able to see the transfer of the money in the house or its storage in the backyard. After observing Tony receiving and then storing the money, the officers learned that the lieutenant whom the police observed give Tony the money was the suspect in a bank robbery of a Wells Fargo branch in Monmouth earlier that day. Based upon their observations, the police secured a search warrant and seized the money in the storage bin next to Tony's pool. Tony's lawyers claim that the search warrant was invalid because the probable cause was based upon a Fourth Amendment violation.

7.  Did the police violate Tony's Fourth Amendment rights by using night vision goggles to monitor his activities?

    (A)   The police violated Tony's Fourth Amendment rights by using the night vision goggles.
    (B)   The police did not violate Tony's Fourth Amendment rights by using night vision goggles.
    (C)   The police violated Tony's Fourth Amendment rights by training the goggles on the home, but they did not violate the Fourth Amendment by training the goggles on the backyard.
    (D)   The police did not violate Tony's Fourth Amendment rights because he took no steps to protect his privacy.

Police escalated their surveillance of Tony Soprano by pressuring Tony's small internet server, nornj.net, for a list of email addresses of persons who sent emails to Tony as well as a list of email addresses of persons to whom he corresponded. This information was challenged during a federal prosecution of Tony as a violation of the Fourth Amendment.

8.  Did the police violate Tony's Fourth Amendment rights by securing those email addresses without a warrant?

    (A)   Tony had a reasonable expectation of privacy in the email addresses.
    (B)   Tony did not have a reasonable expectation of privacy in the email addresses.
    (C)   The police violated the Fourth Amendment by demanding the information without a search warrant.
    (D)   The police did not need a search warrant because the internet server voluntarily turned over the information.

The defendant is a 1L student who is trying to finance his legal education by selling drugs at the law school. One evening, while studying at home, the defendant answered a knock on the door to find a classmate. The defendant and the classmate are not particularly friendly, although the defendant knew that the classmate lived in another building in the same apartment complex. The classmate said he dropped by to ask for help with a Criminal Law question. The classmate is a former police officer, a fact which the defendant did not previously know. The classmate had been asked by a former police colleague to befriend the defendant and find out whether the defendant is, in fact, dealing illegal drugs. The defendant answered the classmate's question while standing at the door, but when the classmate feigned ignorance and prolonged the discussion, the defendant reluctantly invited the classmate into his apartment. During the discussion about mistake of fact and law, the defendant offered the classmate a beer. The defendant went into the kitchen to retrieve two beers, and the classmate followed. There, on the kitchen counter, the classmate observed a large supply of glassine envelopes, a scale, and sticking out from under aluminum foil a white powdery substance. After consuming the beer, the classmate left the apartment and notified his former police colleague. A search warrant was obtained that evening and, armed with the warrant, police searched the apartment and found the white powdery substance which turned out to be cocaine. The defendant was charged with possession for sale of an illegal substance.

9. Is the evidence seized with the search warrant admissible in the prosecution's case-in-chief at trial?

ANSWER:

Change the facts in Question 9. What if the classmate was wearing a wire when he entered the defendant's apartment and it was transmitting his conversation directly to the police? Assuming that the classmate did not see the drugs in the kitchen, but after the two discussed mistake of fact and mistake of law, the classmate pretended to divulge the real reason for his visit: that he had heard of the defendant's sideline and wanted to purchase a quantity of marijuana. The defendant responded that he was out of marijuana temporarily but could help the classmate with cocaine which he had plenty of in the apartment. This conversation was transmitted to the police who obtained the warrant and found the cocaine while executing the search warrant.

10. Will the use of the wire change the outcome of the defendant's motion to suppress the evidence?

   (A) The evidence is inadmissible because a wiretap requires a search warrant.
   (B) The evidence is admissible because the police had probable cause to conduct the investigation and did not need a warrant.
   (C) The evidence is inadmissible because it was secured through fraudulent means.
   (D) The evidence is admissible because it was acquired by the police with the consent of one of the parties to the conversation.

Again change the facts in Question 9. The classmate saw no contraband during his visit to the defendant's apartment nor was he able to lure the defendant into discussing his drug dealing. After a fruitless discussion that lasted half an hour, the defendant ended the visit by telling his classmate that he had cases to read quickly because he had an appointment in an hour. Disappointed that he could not help his friends on the police force, the classmate hid behind a wall down the hall from the defendant's apartment. About an hour later, the classmate observed the defendant leave his apartment and enter the elevator. Confirming that the elevator had reached the lobby, the classmate broke into the defendant's apartment and searched it. In the defendant's bedroom closet the classmate discovered a large supply of illegal drugs and paraphernalia. He notified his friend on the police force of what he had found. The officer did not ask the classmate how he had made this find but used the classmate's information as coming from an unnamed reliable informant. A search warrant was issued, and the drugs were found in the closet. After his arrest, the defendant became suspicious of how the police found out about him. At a hearing on a motion to suppress, the defendant and the police found out how the classmate acquired the information which provided the probable cause for the search warrant.

11. Should the evidence obtained with the search warrant be suppressed?

   (A) The evidence is not admissible because it was found by a police agent during a break-in of the defendant's apartment.

   (B) The evidence is admissible because the break-in was not committed by a police officer.

   (C) The evidence is inadmissible because the officer should have named his informant and explained how the informant obtained the information in the application for a search warrant.

   (D) The evidence is admissible because probable cause may be based upon information provided to the police by an unnamed informant.

Change the facts in Question 11. The judge, after the suppression hearing on the defendant's Motion to Suppress, was upset at the police behavior for using an agent who broke into the defendant's apartment. Instead of ruling on the defendant's motion, she dismissed the charges over the protest of the prosecuting attorney. The state appealed.

**12.** How should the court of appeals rule?

ANSWER:

A search warrant was issued for the home of a suspected drug dealer. In the affidavit accompanying the warrant, the officer described the varied suspected illegal activities of the drug dealer. The short affidavit claimed that the target was engaged in multiple crimes and was the head of a notorious gang plaguing the city proper. The affidavit contained no additional facts. The judge issued the warrant authorizing the officer to search the target's residence for evidence of any felonies. Police executing the warrant found evidence of drug dealing, loan sharking, and violent crimes. A multi-count indictment was brought charging the target with violation of multiple statutes involving illegal drug trafficking and loan sharking.

13. Is the search warrant valid?

   (A) The search warrant was invalid because it was vague and did not instruct the police to search for evidence of specific offenses.
   (B) The search warrant was valid because the affiant presented sufficient evidence to search for multiple offenses.
   (C) The search warrant was invalid because there was no probable cause.
   (D) The search warrant was valid because the police had established the notoriety of the target.

Police sought a warrant to search the hotel room of Emile Savoca who police believed was a serial robber. The robberies had occurred over an unspecified period of time. The warrant authorized a search of Savoca's hotel room for evidence of the seven robberies, listing the victims and locations of the seven robberies, but not the dates. During the search of the hotel room, police found objects taken from five of the seven robbery victims. Prior to trial, the defense claimed that the warrant was invalid and sought to exclude the evidence.

14. How should the court rule?

ANSWER:



Los Angeles police intercepted a Federal Express package containing cocaine, which was addressed to the defendant in Dayton, Ohio. The LAPD sent the package to Dayton police, who sought a warrant in anticipation of a controlled delivery of the cocaine. A search warrant was issued authorizing the Dayton police officer to search the defendant's home following the controlled delivery of the package. The package was delivered to the defendant, and police searched the home seizing the package. A motion to suppress was filed in the case.

**15.**   How should the court rule?

(A)   The court should suppress the evidence. When the warrant was issued the magistrate did not have probable cause to believe that the evidence was presently at the house to be searched.

(B)   The court should not suppress the evidence. When the warrant was issued the magistrate had probable cause to believe that the evidence would be at the house when police executed the warrant.

(C)   The court should suppress the evidence because the police caused the package to be delivered to the defendant's house.

(D)   The court should not suppress the evidence because police knew what was in the package and had possession of the package when the warrant was issued.

A confidential, reliable informant phoned Detective Roberts to tip him off that Angel Smith, a major drug dealer in Metropolis, had just received a large shipment of marijuana and cocaine at his home. The informant, an employee of Smith, was present when the drugs arrived. Detective Roberts prepared the following affidavit:

> The affiant, Detective Roberts, has good cause to believe that a large quantity of marijuana and cocaine is presently at the home address of Angel Smith, whom the affiant and other police know is operating a major drug distribution out of his home. Whereupon, affiant requests a warrant issue for the search of Angel Smith's home for marijuana and cocaine.

The magistrate issued the warrant and Detective Roberts executed the warrant and found exactly what he was looking for in Angel Smith's home. Smith was charged in connection with the warrant, and the defense filed a motion to suppress the evidence found during the search.

**16.**   Should the court grant the motion to suppress the evidence?

(A)   The court should deny the motion to suppress because Detective Roberts conducted the search in good faith reliance on the warrant.

(B)   The court should grant the motion to suppress because Detective Roberts failed to inform the issuing magistrate about the informant's identity.

(C)   The court should deny the motion to suppress because there was probable cause to support the warrant.

(D)   The court should grant the motion to suppress because the judge lacked probable cause to issue the warrant.

Change the facts in Question 16. After reading the affidavit, the magistrate told Detective Roberts that the affidavit was insufficient and that she could not issue the warrant based upon such limited facts. Detective Roberts, then, told the magistrate about the unnamed informant and that the informant had been present when the drug shipment arrived at Angel's apartment. The conversating was not recorded, and Detective Roberts was not under oath when he provided the additional information. The magistrate then issued the warrant authorizing the search. Prior to trial, Angel's attorney moved to suppress the evidence.

**17.** How should the court rule?

    (A)   The warrant was invalid because the affidavit on which it was issued was inadequate.

    (B)   The warrant was invalid because the issuing magistrate could not consider evidence not contained in the affidavit.

    (C)   The warrant was invalid because the supplemental testimony was improperly considered.

    (D)   The warrant was valid based upon the affidavit and the supplement information provided in chambers by Detective Roberts.

On a June evening, as the defendant and a companion exited a private residence and entered the parking lot of a YMCA, they were approached by two plainclothes officers. The officers were driving in an unmarked police vehicle. The defendant was gingerly carrying a brown paper grocery bag with the words "Kash'n Karry" and "Loaded with Low Prices" printed on the outside. Neither officer knew the defendant or his companion. One of the two officers, Officer Thomas, exited the vehicle and, without identifying himself, asked defendant to "Come here a minute." The defendant did not respond and kept walking. When Officer Thomas identified himself as a police officer, the defendant threw the sack he was carrying onto the hood of his own car and turned to face Thomas who was approaching. Officer Thomas asked the defendant what the bag contained; the defendant did not respond. Officer Thomas then rebuffed defendant's attempt to protect the bag, pushed defendant's hand away and opened the bag. Officer Thomas discovered drug paraphernalia within the bag and promptly arrested the defendant. The defendant was charged with possession of drug paraphernalia. Prior to trial, the defense moved to suppress the evidence found in the bag.

**18.** How should the court rule on the defense motion to suppress the evidence?

    (A)   The evidence should not be suppressed because the police had reasonable suspicion to stop the defendant and make sure he was not armed.

    (B)   The evidence should not be suppressed because the officer had probable cause to arrest the defendant for obstructing a police officer, and the evidence was found incident to the arrest.

    (C)   The evidence should be suppressed because the evidence was not discovered incident to a lawful *Terry*-stop.

    (D)   The evidence should be suppressed because it was not discovered incident to a lawful arrest.

A police officer walked into a bar where there had been numerous prior drug sales. The officer observed Hill, whom the officer knew, sitting at a table with two individuals who had previously been arrested for drug transactions. As the officer approached the table where Hill was seated, Hill moved his hands to his lap and then stood up and moved toward the door to leave the bar. The officer stopped Hill, made him show his hands which were empty, and then searched him finding a quantity of drugs in his pocket. Hill was charged with illegal possession of drugs. The defense moved to surpress the drugs found on Hill's person.

**19.**    How should the court rule on the defense motion to suppress the evidence?

ANSWER:

A police officer patrolling a downtown neighborhood late on a Sunday night, observed Edwards and a companion walking down the street in front of the post office. The officer believed that the two men had turned on to the sidewalk from the post office driveway. The officer observed few other people in the vicinity and none as close to the post office. Three minutes later, dispatch informed the police officer that a silent alarm within the post office had sounded. The officer turned on his light and stopped Edwards and his companion. The officer arrested Edwards. Prior to placing the two men in the police car, the officer searched them finding paint chips in Edwards' pocket. Those paint chips were later traced to the window of the post office which had been jimmied open causing the alarm to sound. Edwards was charged with attempted burglary of a federal facility. Edwards' attorney moved to suppress the evidence because the officer did not have probable cause to make an arrest.

**20.**    Should the evidence be suppressed?

     (A)    Edwards' presence in the vicinity of the post office provided probable cause for the arrest, and the evidence was seized incident to the lawful arrest.

     (B)    Edwards' presence in the vicinity of the post office was not enough to rise to the level of probable cause, and the evidence was seized incident to an unlawful search.

     (C)    Edwards' presence in the vicinity of the post office was sufficient to justify a *Terry*-stop, and an officer may conduct a search prior to placing a suspect in a police car.

     (D)    Edwards' presence in the vicinity of the post office was sufficient to justify a *Terry*-stop, but the officer had no authority to search Edwards.

Police officer Abner Rottweiler was driving in a Metropolis black and white when he received a radio call that Ike Newton had just robbed a convenience store and was driving a purple Chevrolet Cavalier eastward on W. 44th Street. Rottweiler intercepted the Cavalier and arrested Ike Newton. Rottweiler searched Newton and his car and found drugs in the trunk, nothing else. Rottweiler summoned the canine unit, and the dog alerted to the presence of more drugs in the driver's side door. When the door was dismantled, a large quantity of marijuana was found in the hollow area under the driver's side window. The radio dispatch relied upon by Officer Rottweiler was based upon information provided by Officer Relay. Relay had received an anonymous tip about the robbery. Newton was charged with possession of illegal drugs, and the defense has moved to suppress the drugs.

**21.**    Are the drugs admissible?

ANSWER:

A mother contacted the FBI after becoming alarmed about her child's online activity. The FBI used the child's existing Internet profile as a teenage boy to contact the defendant via chat-room and email as part of an ongoing investigation of people who used the Internet to lure children into sexual relationships. Once in contact with the defendant, the FBI used an undercover child pornography business to send him email messages with price sheets for explicit videos. The defendant corresponded regularly via email with the government's fictional child pornography distributor, Jake's Photo Service; Jake's wrote in one of those email correspondences that it was "updating its inventory" and that it had "more German titles, more action boys, game boys, explosion boys & boys collection." The defendant responded with an order for videos via email but asked the mail order house to hold up shipment because he was going to be out of the country in Mexico for eight days to "play with the boys."

On his return to the country, customs agents found a video camcorder and three undeclared videotape cassettes in the defendant's luggage. The defendant allowed the customs agents to view the videotape cassettes, at least one of which appeared to contain images of child pornography. The defendant was allowed to proceed. A few days later, federal and local law enforcement officers executed a search warrant at the defendant's residence seeking child pornography in various forms. The officers found a child pornography videotape titled "Jap Boys/Mexican Boys," hidden in the basement ceiling, which depicted children between the ages of 10 and 15. The officers also found a large quantity of computer related items such as diskettes, zip disks, and a computer monitor. The defendant sought suppression of the tapes and computer drives containing child pornography because there was not adequate probable cause to issue the search warrant.

22.   Should the evidence be suppressed?

   (A)   Yes. The search warrant was based upon evidence secured when government agents intruded on the defendant's privacy by pretending to be the young boy.

   (B)   Yes. The search warrant depended for probable cause upon the films screened by the customs officers.

   (C)   No. The FBI properly used email messaging with the defendant to build the case for probable cause.

   (D)   No. There is no expectation of privacy in email communications.

Jack Turoff, retired with little to do, lives in a three story walk-up apartment building with six apartments. Jack kept close tabs on his neighbors. His immediate neighbor, James Sanford, who shares the second floor hallway with Jack, has attracted Jack's attention. Jack, through the key hole in his door, observed many people visiting Sanford day and night. Few of the visitors ever entered Sanford's apartment. Instead, they knocked on the door and talked to Sanford briefly, and then handed Sanford something. Sanford shuts the door while the visitor waits. Sanford returns a moment or two later. Turoff has observed Sanford pass his visitors a small object; Turoff has also heard Sanford's visitors refer to reefer, weed and mucah. Finally convinced that Sanford is selling marijuana, Turoff visited the 108 Precinct and spoke with Detective Smith. On the basis of his conversation with Turoff, Detective Smith immediately obtained a warrant to search Sanford's apartment. When the police arrived at Sanford's apartment and told him what they were searching for, Sanford turned over a large quantity of marijuana. The police continued to search and, in a closet, found additional marijuana. Prior to trial, the defense moved to suppress the evidence seized from Sanford's apartment.

**23.**   Should the court suppress the marijuana?

ANSWER:

**24.**   In the facts in Question 23, assume that the search warrant was valid, Should the court suppress the child pornography?

   (A)   The child pornography should be suppressed because the search warrant did not authorize a search for anything other than drugs.

   (B)   The child pornography should not be suppressed because it was discovered in plain view.

   (C)   The child pornography should be suppressed because once the police had the marijuana they should have discontinued the search.

   (D)   The child pornography should not be suppressed because the warrant authorized a search for marijuana and evidence of any other crimes.

Detective Roberts submitted the following affidavit with an application for a search warrant.

> The affiant, Detective Roberts, has good cause to believe that a large quantity of marijuana and cocaine is presently at the home address of Angel Smith, who the affiant and other police know is operating a major drug distribution out of his home. This information comes to us from a reliable, confidential informant who was present at Smith's home three days ago when the drugs were delivered. The informant has provided reliable information three times in the past which led to three successful convictions. Whereupon, affiant believes that a large quantity of marijuana and cocaine will be found now at Angel Smith's residence and requests that a warrant issue for the search of Angel Smith's home for marijuana and cocaine.

Prior to submitting the affidavit and the warrant to the magistrate, Detective Roberts contacted another informant who had purchased on several occasions both marijuana and cocaine from Smith with police buy-money. Roberts directed the informant to attempt another purchase from Smith. Several hours later, the informant called Roberts and told him he had gone to Smith and tried to purchase marijuana and cocaine, and that Smith told him that he was out. Detective Roberts went ahead and submitted the affidavit to the magistrate without informing the magistrate of the information received from the second informant. The warrant was issued, and during the subsequent search Roberts seized quantities of marijuana, cocaine, and magazines containing child pornography that were discovered while searching for the drugs. Prior to trial, Angel Smith learned of the second informant who told Smith what he had told Detective Roberts. On the basis of that information, a motion to suppress was filed.

25. Should the motion to suppress be granted?

ANSWER:


At the conclusion of the suppression hearing in Question 24, the prosecutor argued that even if the court finds that the perjury was material and the redacted affidavit lacked probable cause, the evidence should not be excluded because the police reasonably relied upon the warrant.

26. How should the court rule on the reasonable reliance claim?

   (A) The court should deny the suppression motion because the evidence is admissible under the good faith exception to the exclusionary rule.

(B) The court should deny the suppression motion because, even without the perjured statement, there was adequate probable cause to support the warrant.

(C) The court should grant the suppression motion because the good faith exception to the exclusionary rule is not applicable in the face of police perjury in the affidavit.

(D) The court should grant the suppression motion because, without the perjured statement in the affidavit, there was no probable cause to support the warrant.

A magistrate issued a search warrant based on probable cause that evidence of a major stolen jewelry operation would be found at Carl Smith's residence. The probable cause established that Smith was the city's major fence for stolen jewelry and was running the business out of his home. The warrant ordered police to search the residence and Carl Smith, the occupant of the residence. Police went to execute the warrant at Smith's residence and at Smith's place of employment, a major insurance underwriter. The officers found evidence of the fencing operation at Smith's residence. At the same time, officers went to Smith's place of employment and searched him, finding in his pocket found a large diamond ring which turned out to be stolen. A motion to suppress the ring was filed.

27. Should the ring be excluded from evidence at Smith's trial?

(A) No. The warrant ordered that Smith's person be searched, and police were complying with the terms of the warrant.

(B) No. A search warrant's order is global. The validity of the execution should not turn on where Smith happened to be at the time of the search.

(C) Yes. The search warrant did not specify that Smith could be searched at his place of employment.

(D) Yes. Probable cause did not exist to believe that Smith would have the evidence sought anywhere but at his residence.

Lester Scott lived in a triplex apartment building on Elm Street. Also living in this building was his son, Arthur. Lester and Arthur are very close. Various pieces of evidence led police to conclude that the son committed a robbery/shooting, attempted murder and murder. For instance, 9mm shell casings found at each of the three crime scenes matched shell casings which an informant brought to police after watching the son shoot his 9mm handgun which ejected the casings into a field. Also, prior to his death, the murder victim confessed that he and the son committed the robbery/shooting. A search warrant was issued to search both Lester and Arthur Scott's apartments and the son's vehicle for "a 9mm auto-pistol and other instruments or fruits of these crimes, all of which is evidence of [murder, attempted murder and robbery]." Just prior to the execution of the search warrant, police arrested Arthur Scott in his automobile and found a 9 mm automatic pistol in his car. During the execution of the search warrant, police discovered in Lester Scott's apartment four grams of cocaine in a box for a video tape. They also found in Lester Scott's apartment approximately $17,000 in currency and $1,500 in food stamps in a bag. Some ammunition was also confiscated. Lester Scott was charged with illegal possession of drugs and food stamps. Scott's lawyer moved to suppress the drugs, currency and food stamps.

28. Should the trial court grant the motion to suppress?

ANSWER:

Probable cause was established that the defendant, Jon Peters, transmitted two images containing child pornography from a computer in his home. A warrant issued ordering police to search Peter's home and to seize the computer and the two files and visual depictions in any format or media of minors engaging in sexually explicit conduct. During the search of the computer, police opened many files on the defendant's computer finding multiple images containing child pornography. The defense argued that police had probable cause only to search the two files specified in the warrant.

29.  Should the files other than the ones specified in the warrant be suppressed?

   (A)  No. Probable cause existed, and the warrant authorized a search of other files for images of child pornography.

   (B)  No. Where a warrant authorizes a search of a computer, during the execution of the search police may search all files stored on the computer.

   (C)  Yes. There was no probable cause to search the computer for anything other than the two files that had been intercepted.

   (D)  Yes. Once the police found the two files, they were required to terminate the search.

Police executed the search warrant described in Question 29 at midnight. The search warrant did not authorize a nighttime search or a no knock entry. When they arrived on the scene, officers knocked on the door and entered immediately. They ordered Peters out of bed, and conducted the search described in Question 29. Peters' attorney moved to suppress the evidence.

30. Should the evidence be suppressed?

   (A) Yes. The Fourth Amendment requires that a search warrant be executed during daytime hours and that police knock and announce their presence prior to entering to execute the warrant.

   (B) Yes. The failure of police to adhere to the Fourth Amendment requirements that a search warrant be executed during daytime hours and that police knock and announce their presence prior to entering to execute the warrant should shock the conscience of the court and lead to suppression of the evidence.

   (C) No. The warrant was supported by probable cause and the failure to conform the execution of the warrant to Fourth Amendment requirements did not render the search illegal.

   (D) No. Evidence on a computer may be easily destroyed and deleted; the need to prevent the destruction of evidence created an exigency allowing police not to adhere to Fourth Amendment requirements for execution of searches,

When police arrived at 1424 Main Street to execute a search warrant seeking drugs and drug paraphernalia, they found present in the house and on the porch five teenagers in addition to the suspected teenage dealer who is a resident. The police refused to permit the five non-resident teenagers to leave the home, forcing them to sit on the floor in the living room. After a substantial quantity of drugs were found in the home and the resident teenager was arrested, the police asked the other five teenagers if they had any drugs on them. Two of the teenagers responded that they did, and police arrested the two and on their persons found small quantities of illegal drugs. Parents of the three teenagers who were not arrested brought a § 1983 civil rights action claiming that the three were illegally detained.

31. Were they illegally detained?

ANSWER:

Following the arrests of the two non-residents in Question 31, their lawyers filed a motion to suppress the drugs found in their pockets.

**32.**   Should the evidence be suppressed?

(A)   No. The teenagers volunteered the information that they had drugs in their pockets which provided probable cause for their arrest and search.

(B)   No. Police may search any person found on the premises during execution of a valid search warrant.

(C)   Yes. Police may not search persons who are present during execution of a valid search warrant.

(D)   Yes. The two were in custody when they were asked if they had drugs in their pockets; consequently the admission and search were the fruit of unwarned custodial interrogation.

Police operating with a valid search warrant searched John Broadley's dormitory room. An officer also searched the connecting shared bathroom. The bathroom door to John's neighbor's room, Tom Kimberling, was open. The police officer could see into Kimberling's dorm room. From the threshold to Kimberling's room, the officer saw on the top of a dresser against the far wall a stack of loose marijuana and rolling papers. The officer walked into Kimberling's room and seized the contraband and arrested Kimberling. Kimberling's lawyer moved to suppress the marijuana. The prosecuting attorney claimed that the marijuana was in plain view.

33. Should Kimberling's motion to suppress be granted?

   (A)  No. The contents of the room were in plain view.

   (B)  Yes. The contents of the room were in plain view but the officer did not have authority to enter the room and seize the contraband.

   (C)  No. A dorm room is not the same as a home or apartment and is subject to unannounced inspections for contraband.

   (D)  Yes. The contraband was not in plain view because the officer did not have the authority to look into the adjacent room.

A young man walking in a poor neighborhood called police and reported that he had been mugged and that his overcoat had been stripped from his back. The man told police that the mugger had run immediately into an adjacent small apartment house. Police entered the apartment house and knocked on the open door of a second floor apartment. Frances Todd answered the door and, when told that the police were looking for a grey overcoat, invited the officers into his apartment to look for the coat. Police opened the coat closet near the front door. The overcoat was not in closet, but an officer saw what appeared to be a very expensive camera hanging on a hook in the closet. The officer opened the leather case of the camera and wrote down the serial number on the bottom of the camera. While still in Todd's apartment, the officer called into headquarters to inquire about the camera. He learned that the camera had been stolen during a home burglary in another part of town. The officers seized the camera and arrested Todd. Todd's attorney has filed a motion to suppress the camera.

34. The motion will be

   (A)  denied because Todd had consented to the search and the camera was in plain view.

   (B)  granted because the officers could not lawfully look for anything but the overcoat.

(C)   denied because the officer had reasonable suspicion to believe that the expensive camera was stolen.

(D)   granted because the officer did not have probable cause to believe that the camera was stolen and could not open the case to look for the serial number.

Police officers driving through a high crime area of the city at 1 am, noticed the defendant leaning into a car. When the officers drove around the block and returned, the defendant remained on the street corner but the car was gone. As the officers stopped the car, the defendant walked away from the corner. The officers confronted the defendant and patted him down. In the defendant's outer jacket pocket, the officer felt two cylindrical objects. The officer reached into the pocket and retrieved the two objects containing crack cocaine. The defendant was charged with possession and moved to suppress the bottles of crack cocaine. At the suppression hearing the officer testified that he did not believe the object was a weapon but did believe that it was glass vial used to carry crack cocaine.

**35.**   How should the court rule on the motion to suppress?

ANSWER:

Joe Descarte jaywalked while crossing a busy intersection in the financial district on his way to a job interview. He was stopped by a police officer who intended to write Joe a ticket for jaywalking. Joe explained to the officer that he had an important job interview and was too busy to stop but offered to leave his driver's license with the officer. Joe's attitude annoyed the officer, and the officer arrested Joe who missed his interview. Jaywalking is a minor misdemeanor in the state, carrying a penalty of a $100 maximum fine and no jail sentence. State law authorizes a police officer to arrest or issue a summons for any misdemeanor offense. Following the arrest, the officer searched Joe and found the remnant of a marijuana cigarette in the pocket of Joe's suit. Joe is charged only with possession of a controlled substance, also a misdemeanor. Joe's attorney filed a motion to suppress the evidence.

36.  How should the court rule on the motion to suppress?

   (A)   The court should grant the motion because a custodial arrest for an offense that carries no jail penalty violates the Fourth Amendment; the search was not incident to a lawful arrest.

   (B)   The court should grant the motion because, even though the arrest was lawful, the search of Joe's person on the street for jaywalking violated the Fourth Amendment.

   (C)   The court should deny the motion because the arrest did not violate the Fourth Amendment, and the evidence was found incident to a lawful arrest.

   (D)   The court should deny the motion because the evidence would have been inevitably discovered during a lawful inventory search at the police station.

Officers James and Conway spent a good part of the past year engaged in a public corruption investigation. After a long period of spinning wheels, James and Conway were able to convince Arthur O'Malley to turn state's evidence on his supervisor, Jack Turoff, in the city construction agency. O'Malley provided extensive information about a kick-back arrangement run by O'Malley and Turoff. City construction contractors paid them both hundreds of thousands of dollars. James and Conway have concluded, and their superiors have concurred, that they have probable cause to proceed. Nothing further happened for two months. On December 21, James dropped Conway at the airport who was leaving town to spend Christmas with his children. James spotted Turoff heading towards the departure terminal. James intercepted Turoff and arrested him. James then searched Turoff's carry on luggage and found five large checks made out to Jack Turoff from large construction companies working on city projects. The defense moved to suppress the checks.

37. The motion will be

   (A) granted because the warrantless arrest was illegal where police had more than ample time and opportunity to secure an arrest warrant.
   (B) granted because the warrantless arrest was illegal without exigent circumstances to justify dispensing with the warrant requirement.
   (C) denied because the warrantless arrest was legal based upon exigent circumstances.
   (D) denied because the warrantless arrest was valid even absent exigent circumstances.

A police officer walking through a trailer park saw through the window of a trailer Oliver Morris, a man the officer knew to be the subject of several outstanding arrest warrants. The officer walked up to the trailer door to monitor Morris through the window of the door. Morris saw the officer and walked out of the room. The officer opened the unlocked front door of the trailer and followed Morris into the bedroom and arrested him. On the night stand in the bedroom, the officer saw an automatic weapon, illegal in the state, which he seized. Morris told the officer that the weapon belonged to his girlfriend, Peg, the owner of the trailer who was not home. Peg was charged with possession of an illegal handgun. Her lawyer filed a motion to suppress the handgun. The state counters that the weapon was in plain view when it was seized.

38. Should the motion to suppress be granted?

   (A) The weapon should be suppressed because the officer was not legally present in the bedroom when he seized the weapon.

(B)   The weapon should not be suppressed because exigency supported the officer's entry of the trailer when Morris saw that he had been spotted.

(C)   The weapon should be suppressed because Peg had standing to challenge the seizure of the weapon.

(D)   The weapon should not be suppressed because Peg, who was not present at the time, did not have standing to challenge the seizure of the weapon.

Police officers found a car in a ditch. Several people were standing around the ditch when the officers arrived. They told the officers that the driver was "drunk as a skunk" and had lurched out of the car and then walked down the road. The officers checked the registration and learned the identity of the vehicle owner. They drove to the owner's house which was nearby. When they arrived at the owner's home, the officers entered and went to the bedroom where they found the defendant, the vehicle's owner, asleep in bed. The officers arrested the defendant for driving under the influence of alcohol and took him to the police station where a blood alcohol test showed that the defendant's level was significantly above the legal limit. The defendant was charged with misdemeanor D.U.I. and has moved to suppress the evidence of the blood alcohol test.

**39.**   Is the evidence admissible?

ANSWER:

Police officers had an arrest warrant for Tom Feola. When they went to Tom's house, his mother informed them that he was not at home. She told the officers that Tom was at his girlfriend's house. The girlfriend lived with her father. She provided the officers with the name and address of Tom's girlfriend. The officers went directly to the girlfriend's house, entered and arrested Tom. During the arrest of Tom at his girlfriend's home, the officers saw, sitting on the table in the room where police seized Tom, a magazine containing child pornography. Tom's girlfriend told the officers that the magazine belonged to her father who was not at home, and that her father is weird. Police seized the magazine and charged the father with illegal possession of child pornography. The father's attorney moved to suppress the magazine.

**40.**   How should the court rule on the motion to suppress?

ANSWER:

Jerry Bach was arrested on Thursday evening while trying to purchase a baggy of marijuana on a city street. He made several calls from the jail over the next few days to friends to bail him out; none was home. Sunday evening, Jerry's girlfriend, Trish, was picked up also trying to buy drugs. She was very strung out. During her booking, she informed the booking officer that she was the girlfriend of a very important person. When encouraged to tell the officer the identity of her boyfriend, Trish told him an earful. She told the officer that Jerry was personally responsible for fifty percent of the bad mortgage loans in the city which had resulted in an epidemic of foreclosures. On Monday afternoon, detectives alerted by Trish's information interrogated Jerry, who had been in jail since Thursday without a court appearance. The officers read Jerry his *Miranda* warnings. By Thursday, seven days after his arrest, Jerry confessed to making multiple fraudulent loans. Friday morning, at a preliminary appearance, Jerry was arraigned on the drug charge and on charges arising out of the fraudulent loans. The defense filed a motion to suppress the confession.

41. Is the confession admissible?

    (A) The confession is admissible because it was voluntary.

    (B) The confession is admissible because the interrogation followed Miranda warnings.

    (C) The confession is inadmissible because the defendant was not provided counsel.

    (D) The confession is inadmissible because it was the product of an illegal detention.

On May 22, on I-475 in Genesee County, Michigan, the defendant, Marcus Harvey, was one of two passengers in a 1988 Chevrolet automobile that had no front bumper or right front headlight. Police officers clocked the car exceeding the speed limit by three miles per hour. The officers stopped the vehicle for speeding and equipment violations and because, as one officer later testified at the suppression hearing, "[t]he vehicle that I observed with the defective equipment was very similar in appearance and profile to several other vehicles that I have stopped which ultimately ended in arrests of drug traffickers." When the driver of the car was unable to produce a driver's license, he was asked to step out of the car. He admitted that his license was suspended. He was arrested for driving with a suspended license, and police searched him, finding a rock of crack cocaine in his jacket pocket.

The driver gave conflicting stories about the car's ownership, but the vehicle registration that he produced showed that one of the passengers, Marcus Harvey, to be the owner. Neither Harvey nor the other passenger could produce a driver's license (Harvey's license had been suspended also and the other passenger had never obtained a license) or any other form of identification. Both passengers were ordered out of the vehicle and were patted down for weapons by the officers; no weapons were found. Following the policy of their police department, the officers impounded the car and conducted an inventory search. Because none of the occupants had the key to the vehicle's trunk, the officers removed the back seat in order to inventory the trunk and found a pair of men's sweat pants. In the pockets of the sweat pants, the officers found 78 rocks of crack cocaine and six live .357 magnum revolver cartridges. Also in the trunk, police found a bulletproof vest. At this point the officers pried open the trunk and found a .357 magnum six-shot revolver.

One of the police officers admitted on cross-examination during a suppression hearing that one of the reasons he stopped the car was because "[t]here were three young black male occupants in an old vehicle." The officer also testified that "[a]lmost every time we have arrested drug traffickers from Detroit, they're usually young black males driving old cars." The stop and search parallels "Pipeline," a federal program which provides economic incentives to local police to make stops and searches as in this case.

42. The evidence found during the search of the vehicle is

   (A) inadmissible because it was the fruit of a pretext stop.
   (B) inadmissible because a reasonable police officer would not have made the stop for such minor traffic and equipment violations.
   (C) admissible because police had probable cause to search the car.
   (D) admissible because the stop was lawful.

Police received a tip from an undercover police officer that members of the "Breakaway" gang who had committed a series of burglaries and armed robberies were holed up in Jonathon Break's home located in woods at the outskirts of the city. Police immediately went to Break's home and entered the home without an arrest or search warrant. The police entry caught Break unawares; he had been asleep on a couch in the front room closest to the door. Police handcuffed Break and looked into the room adjacent to the front room and in the closet in the front room. No one was hiding in the adjacent room or in the closet. However, in the closet they saw a number of automatic weapons and ammunition. They seized the weapons. A test of one of the weapons matched a bullet found in the body of a person who had been murdered six months earlier, unrelated to the recent series of burglaries or robberies. Break was charged with that murder. Break's attorneys filed a motion to suppress the automatic weapon and the subsequent ballistic test on the ground that police illegally searched the closet without a warrant.

43. Was the search of the closet lawful incident to Break's arrest?

(A) The warrantless search of the closet was illegal because Break was in custody and could not have reached the weapons in the closet.

(B) The warrantless search of the closet was illegal because police could have secured the premises and obtained a search warrant.

(C) The warrantless search of the closet was legal because police may check areas adjacent to the room where the arrest took place to protect their safety during their departure from the home with the arrestee.

(D) The warrantless search of the closet was legal because they had probable cause to believe that weapons and the proceeds of the burglaries and robberies were on the premises.

After seizing the weapons, the police officers swept the entire house for Break's confederates. During the sweep, a police officer opened a small cabinet hanging on the wall in the basement. Police found inside the cabinet additional guns and a large quantity of stolen jewelry. Break has filed a motion to suppress the items found in the cabinet.

44. Are the items found in the cabinet admissible?

ANSWER:

## SEARCH OF A PERSON INCIDENT TO ARREST

On November 15, Elliot Freeman was observed by a police officer speeding while driving through an intersection. As the officer pursued the automobile, she observed Freeman make an illegal right turn on a red light. After stopping Freeman's automobile, the officer spoke to Freeman and determined that Freeman was intoxicated. The officer arrested Freeman for driving while intoxicated. At the scene, and prior to taking Freeman to the police station, the officer patted down Freeman to determine if he had a weapon or contraband on his person. The officer felt objects in Freeman's pocket which she knew was not a weapon. Nonetheless, she reached into Freeman's pocket and retrieved a glassine bag of cocaine and removed from Freeman's shirt pocket a vial of cocaine. A number of pills of various kinds and some drug paraphernalia were also recovered from Freeman's pockets. Freeman was charged with illegal possession of cocaine, Prior to trial, the defense filed a motion to suppress the contraband.

**45.** Is the contraband found in Freeman's pockets admissible?

    (A) The evidence is inadmissible because the officer knew when he reached into Freeman's pockets that he was not carrying a weapon.

    (B) The evidence is inadmissible because the search should have been conducted as an inventory search at the police station.

    (C) The evidence is admissible because the officer had probable cause to conduct a search of Freeman's person once he felt the objects in the pocket.

    (D) The evidence is admissible because it was a lawful search incident to arrest.

Change the facts in Question 45. Once the officer had stopped Freeman's car, she ordered Freeman to exit the vehicle. The officer observed Freeman stumble and slur his words as he got out of his car. The officer ordered Freeman to empty his pockets and place the contents on the hood of the car. The officer seized the contraband which Freeman placed on top of the car. Freeman was then arrested and charged with a drug abuse offense. Prior to trial, the defense moved to suppress the evidence.

**46.** Is the contraband admissible at Freeman's trial?

    (A) The evidence is admissible because it was seized incident to a lawful custodial arrest.

    (B) The evidence is admissible because it was seized incident to a lawful traffic stop.

    (C) The evidence is inadmissible because a search incident to arrest may not precede the lawful arrest.

    (D) The evidence is inadmissible because a police officer may not search the person of a motorist stopped only for a traffic offense.

An undercover police officer saw Franklin Pierce give a passerby a small object after the passerby gave Pierce folded currency. The officer knew that Pierce had prior convictions for selling illegal drugs. As the officer approached Pierce to arrest him, the officer observed Pierce reach into his pocket, remove several small objects, and place them in his mouth. The officer ran up to Pierce and grabbed his testicles and twisted them until Pierce opened his mouth and spit out its contents. The officer handcuffed Pierce and retrieved the objects that he spit out; those objects were several rocks of crack cocaine. Pierce is charged with possession and sale of crack cocaine. His attorney moved to suppress the evidence retrieved from Pierce's mouth because of the excessive force used by the police officer.

**47.** How should the court rule?

ANSWER:

Congressman Lamont Cranston, known as "the Shadow of the Congress" because of his many absences, was arrested for bribery in his home yesterday morning. Mrs. Cranston admitted the police who had an arrest warrant. She showed the police into Cranston's library where he was seated in his pajamas behind a big beautiful roll top desk. Cranston rose when the police entered, but the officers told him to remain seated. Police handcuffed Cranston behind his back and in his desk chair. Police then searched the desk drawers and found correspondence addressed to Cranston from a contractor from his hometown who was charged with bribery. The officers looked inside the already opened envelopes and found $180,000. Cranston's lawyers have filed a motion to suppress the envelopes and their contents.

48.    How should the court rule on the motion to suppress?

   (A)   The court should deny the motion because the search was incident to a lawful arrest with a warrant.
   (B)   The court should deny the motion because the police had probable cause to believe that evidence of bribery would be found at Cranston's home.
   (C)   The court should grant the motion because police should have sought a search warrant in addition to an arrest warrant.
   (D)   The court should grant the motion because the search did not fall under the search incident to arrest exception to the warrant requirement.

Let's change the facts in Question 48. When the police entered Cranston's study to make the arrest, they saw enormous piles of cash on top of the desk in front of where Cranston was seated. Additionally, cash was sticking out of the partially closed center-top drawer. The police handcuffed Cranston and moved him from behind the desk to a nearby sofa. The police officers, next, seized and catalogued the cash on top of the desk and sticking out of the drawer. They then searched the desk and found the incriminating letters containing more cash. At a contentious suppression hearing, the state argued that the presence of all that cash created exigent circumstances to justify a search of Cranston's entire library and desk.

49.    Is the government's argument correct?

ANSWER:

Following Cranston's arrest in his library, he told police that he did not wish to be photographed entering the police station in his pajamas. The police officers allowed him to change his clothing but accompanied him into the bedroom. When Cranston reached into a top dresser drawer to grab a pair of sox, the officers opened the drawer farther and saw a corn cob pipe and a baggy containing marijuana. Cranston was also charged with illegal possession of a controlled substance. His attorneys filed a motion to suppress the marijuana and paraphernalia seized from the dresser drawer.

50.  Should the court grant the motion to suppress?

   (A)  No. The search of the dresser drawer was incidental to the arrest.
   (B)  No. The search of the dresser drawer was justified by exigent circumstances.
   (C)  Yes. Police had no authority to enter the bedroom; Cranston's wife could have secured the clothing.
   (D)  Yes. The search of the dresser constituted an invasion of Cranston's privacy and police should have secured a search warrant.

Police answered a 911 call with no one on the other end and received a busy signal when they repeatedly tried to call back. Officers dispatched to the scene found a sheet blocking the view through a screen. The officers banged on the door. After a couple of moments, the defendant answered the door by poking his head around the sheet. The defendant appeared surprised by the presence of the officers and very nervous. The defendant denied calling 911. When police asked if they could come in and look around, the defendant said no. The officers entered without his permission. They walked through the entire house and found marijuana sitting on top of a dresser drawer and child pornography in the dresser. The defendant was charged with drug abuse and possession of child pornography.

The defense moved to suppress the marijuana and the child pornography.

51. Should the court suppress the marijuana?

   (A) Yes. The entry of the home without the defendant's consent was an illegal search.
   (B) Yes. The police should have asked the defendant whether anyone else was present.
   (C) No. The marijuana was in plain view when police entered to search for anyone who needed help.
   (D) No. The police had probable cause to search the house when the defendant was uncooperative.

52. Is the child pornography found in the dresser drawer admissible?

   (A) Yes. The child pornography was found while police searched for anyone in need of assistance.
   (B) No. Police illegally extended the search for a person to the dresser drawer.
   (C) Yes. When police discovered the marijuana in plain view, they had probable cause to search the house for other contraband.
   (D) No. The police had no authority to enter the house.

Four officers who responded to a call regarding a loud party heard shouting from inside the house and saw two juveniles drinking beer in the backyard. They entered the backyard and saw through a screen door and windows a fight taking place in the kitchen where four adults were trying to restrain a juvenile. The juvenile broke free and struck one of the adults in the face. An officer testified that he saw the victim of the blow spitting blood into the sink. The other adults continued to try to restrain the juvenile. The police entered the house and eventually got the attention of the persons in the house. The fight stopped immediately. The officers arrested the adults and charged them with contributing to the delinquency of a minor, disorderly conduct and intoxication.

**53.** Did the police enter the house lawfully?

ANSWER:

Frank Sheppard fled from an arresting officer following a drug sale. Police believed that Sheppard was hiding out in his apartment. They banged on the door of the apartment but no one answered the door. Sheppard was seen by police officers from a fire escape right outside the apartment. When Sheppard saw the officers on the fire escape, he ran into a back bedroom and closed the door. The officers opened the window, climbed into the apartment and opened the front door for other officers. They entered the back bedroom with weapons drawn and arrested Sheppard. Additional drugs were found in the back bedroom. Sheppard's defense attorney moved to suppress the evidence. The state argued that exigent circumstances existed to allow police to enter the apartment without a warrant from the fire escape because they feared that Sheppard was getting a gun or destroying evidence.

**54.** Did the police enter the apartment lawfully?

(A) Yes. The police were in hot pursuit of Sheppard when they entered the apartment without a warrant.

(B) Yes. Exigent circumstances justified the warrantless entry of the apartment.

(C) No. Police may not rely upon exigent circumstances of their own making to justify a warrantless entry to arrest or conduct a search.

(D) No. Police needed an arrest or search warrant to enter the premises to search for a weapon or contraband.

A police officer patrolling at night saw a car legally parked with a person dressed in hospital scrubs slumped in the driver's seat. No one else was in the car. The officer banged on the front window but was unable, at first, to rouse the slumped-over driver. The officer, calling for back-up assistance and an ambulance, continued to bang on the window of the parked car. Before assistance arrived, the person in the driver's seat moved and slowly began to respond to the knocking on the window. Finally aroused, the person in the parked car rolled down his window. He explained to the officer that he had just finished working a 24- hour shift at the hospital and fell asleep after he parked his car a block from his home. The officer ordered the driver out of the vehicle. Once awake, the driver exhibited no signs of intoxication. The officer reached under the driver's seat and felt a gun. He removed it. When the driver told him that he did not have a permit to carry a loaded gun in his car, the officer arrested the driver.

55. Did the officer have the right to look under the driver's seat where he found the gun?

    (A) Yes. The search was a limited protective search for weapons.

    (B) No. The officer had no reason to disturb the driver who was parked legally.

    (C) Yes. The search was part of the officer exercising a caretaking function.

    (D) No. The search exceeded the officer's authority under the caretaking function.

Peter Laval was a very successful mortgage broker whose lifestyle plummeted along with the economy. He had been trying to make do by serving as a middleman for a major drug dealer. Laval sold and delivered substantial quantities of drugs to mid-level sellers. Late one night Laval was driving along Interstate 95; he was listening to his music on his iPod. Traffic was very light at that hour and Laval was weaving all over the road. Suddenly, he saw a police car behind him signaling him to pull over. The officer observed Laval weaving and wanted to check him for drunk driving. He ordered Laval out of the car and ordered him to perform field sobriety tests. Laval was sober and had no trouble passing the tests. The officer prepared to write Laval a ticket and fed Laval's information into the system. With all of his economic woes, Laval had forgotten to renew his driver's license which had expired four months earlier. The officer arrested Laval for driving without a license, pursuant to state law that authorizes arrests in such cases. He handcuffed Laval and put him in the back of the police car. The officer then searched Laval's automobile and found a large quantity of marijuana in the trunk of the vehicle. Laval had expected to deliver the marijuana that evening, but the first delivery took much longer than anticipated and Laval had postponed the second delivery until the following morning. The police officer seized the marijuana and charged Laval with possession for sale of a very large quantity of marijuana, a felony with a mandatory ten-year prison sentence. Laval's lawyer moved to suppress the marijuana found in the trunk of the vehicle.

56. Is the marijuana admissible at Laval's trial?

   (A) The marijuana is admissible because it was found incident to a lawful custodial arrest.
   (B) The marijuana is admissible because it was found during a search under the automobile exception to the warrant requirement.
   (C) The marijuana is inadmissible because the arrest of an unimpaired driver for a traffic offense is unlawful under the Fourth Amendment, and the subsequent search is tainted by the illegal arrest.
   (D) The marijuana is inadmissible because the search of the trunk was unlawful.

Peter Paul and his wife were out on the town. Peter got drunk but insisted on driving home over his wife's objection. She asked him several times to stop the car and let her drive, but Peter refused. About four blocks from their home, Peter was stopped by a police officer who observed the car swerving from one lane to the next. Peter was arrested and placed in the backseat of a back up police car and taken to the police station for booking.

Peter's wife, a licensed driver who was not drunk, asked if she could take the car home. She told the officer that she would go to the police station in the morning and bail out her husband. The officer told her that he would let her take the car when they were finished at the scene. The officer then searched the interior compartment of the automobile. In Peter's briefcase which was on the back seat of the vehicle, the police officer found a large packet of counterfeit Megabucks tickets and a dozen picture postcards depicting children involved in sex acts. After the evidence was seized, and the trunk was searched where no other evidence was found, the officer permitted Peter's wife to take the car and drive it home. Peter is charged with possession of stolen property and possession of child pornography. The defense filed a Motion to Suppress the evidence found in the car.

57.  How should the court rule on the Motion to Suppress?

  (A)  The evidence should be admitted at trial because the search was incident to the lawful arrest of the driver.
  (B)  The evidence should be admitted at trial because the search was a valid inventory search of the vehicle.
  (C)  The evidence should be suppressed because the search was not a valid search incident to arrest.
  (D)  The evidence should be suppressed because it was not recovered during a valid inventory search of the vehicle.

Frances Van Buren was arrested a month ago for driving under the influence. After Frances was sober she was released from jail on her own recognizance. After she failed to show up in court for her arraignment on the charge, a bench warrant for her arrest was issued. A sheriff's deputy went to Frances' home to arrest her. No one answered the door. The deputy parked across from Frances' house and waited for her to arrive home. The officer saw Frances park her car on the street, exit the car and lock it. As Frances started walking towards her house, the deputy arrested her. The deputy searched Frances and took her car keys. He then opened the car and, under the front seat of the vehicle, found a hand gun. It is illegal in this state to carry a handgun in a car without a permit, and Frances did not have one. A charge of illegal possession of a weapon in an automobile was added to the D.U.I. charge. The defense moved to exclude the gun from evidence at Frances' trial.

58.  How should the judge rule on the motion to suppress the gun?

ANSWER:

Officer Trapper saw the defendant run a red light. After stopping the car, the officer walked up to the driver's window and instructed the driver to lower the window so that she could observe the driver and ask for the driver's license and registration. As soon as the window was lowered, Officer Trapper detected the odor of burnt marijuana and observed the end of a single burnt roach in the car's ashtray. Officer Trapper ordered the defendant out of the vehicle and made him perform field sobriety tests which the defendant passed satisfactorily. Possession of a small quantity of marijuana is a minor misdemeanor in the jurisdiction; police may not arrest for minor misdemeanors. Prior to writing tickets for the red light and marijuana offenses, the officer searched the defendant's car. The officer found no additional contraband in the driver's compartment, but in the trunk of the vehicle the officer discovered several opaque-wrapped packages the size of bricks. The officer opened one of the bricks and found that it contained marijuana. Officer Trapper arrested the defendant. The car was removed to the police station where the remaining bricks were opened without a search warrant. The remaining bricks also contained marijuana. Additional quantities of marijuana were discovered in the doors of the vehicle. The defense filed a motion to suppress all of the marijuana found in the car.

59. The marijuana found by Officer Trapper at the scene of the stop is

    (A) admissible under the automobile exception to the warrant requirement.
    (B) not admissible under the automobile exception to the warrant requirement.
    (C) admissible under the search incident to arrest exception to the warrant requirement.
    (D) not admissible under the search incident to arrest exception to the warrant requirement.

We can change the facts in Question 59. For the purposes of this question, assume that the state Supreme Court in this jurisdiction has held that discovery of a small quantity of marijuana in the driver's compartment provides adequate probable cause to search the entire vehicle.

60. The evidence found during the warrantless search of the vehicle at the police station is

    (A) admissible because it was found incident to a lawful custodial arrest.
    (B) admissible because it was found during a search under the automobile exception to the warrant requirement.
    (C) inadmissible because once the driver was arrested and the car towed to the police station there was no justification to search the car without a warrant.

(D)  inadmissible because the search of the trunk was unlawful.

A police officer monitoring speeding on a highway received a radio report to be on the look out for a 1971 purple Volkswagon van containing two men who had just robbed an electronics store and made off with a 42 inch Sony television. The officer saw the purple van and stopped it. At the time of the stop, the driver was alone in the van. The officer ordered the driver out of the car, patted him down for weapons, and placed him in the back of the police car. The officer opened the back doors of the van. There was no television set in the van. On the floor, however, was a soft leather briefcase. The officer opened the briefcase and found two small film canisters. In one canister the officer found a small quantity of marijuana and, in the other canister, the officer found a developed roll of 35 mm film. The officer shined the flashlight on the negatives and saw pictures of a small, naked child. The defendant was charged with possession of an illegal substance and possession of child pornography.

**61.**   Are the items found in the canisters admissible in evidence?

ANSWER:


For a year, Officer Larry Welby had been investigating Marcus van Buren, reputed to be a major link between several gangs engaged in drug trafficking in Metropolis. A member of Van Buren's gang called Welby and told him that he just left Van Buren's house. The snitch told Welby that Van Buren was on to Welby and was packing his luxury SUV to leave Metropolis with over half a million dollars in cash, the proceeds from his drug trafficking. Metropolis is situated on the U.S.-Canada border; Welby put out an all points bulletin for Van Buren's Cadillac Escalade. Within minutes of the stop of VanBuren's Cadillac just twenty minutes from the border crossing, Welby made it to where VanBuren was stopped. In the Cadillac with Van Buren was his wife and in the back seat, Mr. and Mrs. Frankel, a notable society and influential Metropolis couple. The VanBurens and the Frankels were ordered out of the Cadillac. All of the luggage in the rear of the SUV was placed on the side of the road. Mr. and Mrs. Frankel's luggage was clearly tagged, and the Frankels protested Welby's intention to search their luggage. In the VanBuren's suitcases, Welby found a substantial quantity of cash, and in the Mr. Frankel's suitcase Welby found a large packet of marijuana. Mr. Frankel was charged with illegal possession of marijuana. His attorney moved to suppress the marijuana.

**62.**   The marijuana found in Mr. Frankel's suitcase is

(A)  inadmissible because Officer Welby did not have probable cause to believe that Frankel was involved in Welby's illegal trafficking.

(B)  admissible because Officer Welby had probable cause to search the Cadillac.

(C)  inadmissible because the Frankels were illegally seized and the search was fruit of the illegal seizure.

(D)  inadmissible because the officer had probable cause to arrest everyone in the car, and the search was incident to the lawful arrest.

Change the facts in Question 62. Police had ample probable cause to arrest Van Buren, but they had delayed and continued the investigation until Officer Welby received the tip that Van Buren was about to flee with the huge amount of cash proceeds from his illegal drug business. The tip also indicates that, in addition to the cash, Van Buren would be leaving with a large cache of illegal drugs, and that Van Buren would be carrying both in a large footlocker. Welby and other officers sped to Van Buren's house to arrest him before he left. Just as they arrived at VanBuren's house, the officers saw Van Buren leave the house carrying a footlocker. Welby arrested Van Buren on the sidewalk and seized the footlocker that was padlocked with a Master lock. Incident to the arrest, Welby searched Van Buren and found the key to the padlock on his person. Van Buren was handcuffed and placed in the back of a police car. Welby unlocked the footlocker and found $500,000 and a large cache of drugs.

**63.** The search of the footlocker was

   (A)  lawful incident to VanBuren's arrest.
   (B)  lawful because the officers had probable cause to believe that evidence would be found inside, and exigent circumstances prevented them from getting a warrant.
   (C)  not a lawful search incident to arrest because the footlocker was not within VanBuren's control when it was searched.
   (D)  not a lawful search incident to arrest because police did not have probable cause to conduct a search.

Add the following facts to Question 63. When the police arrived at Van Buren's house, they saw him leave carrying the footlocker. They did not arrest him immediately. They followed him for a couple of blocks. They presumed that he was heading towards the Greyhound bus terminal. As Van Buren made his way to the bus terminal carrying his footlocker, a car pulled up alongside Van Buren. The driver got out and helped Van Buren place the footlocker in the trunk of the vehicle. Van Buren got in the passenger seat of the car, and the two drove off. The police officers turned on their lights and the car in which Van Buren was riding was pulled over to the side of the road. They arrested Van Buren and searched the vehicle. In the trunk of the car they found the footlocker. They seized the key from Van Buren, and after handcuffing him and the driver and placing them in the back of the police car, the officers opened the footlocker and found the drugs. Prior to trial, the defense moved to suppress the cash and the drugs found in the footlocker that was seized from the trunk of the car.

**64.** Are the cash and drugs admissible?

ANSWER:

The defendant was arrested for shoplifting while trying to leave Target. The arresting officer asked the defendant where his car was parked. The car was in a large lot that serviced Target and other stores in a shopping complex that was open 24 hours a day. The officer called for a tow truck and then inventoried the vehicle before it was towed. During the inventory, the officer found a handgun in the glove compartment. The defendant was charged with improperly handling a firearm in a vehicle, in addition to the shoplifting charge. The defense moved to suppress the handgun.

65.  The handgun is

(A)  inadmissible because the impoundment and inventory were illegal.

(B)  inadmissible because the defendant should have been issued a summons and allowed to drive the car away from the scene of the arrest.

(C)  admissible because the impoundment and inventory were legal.

(D)  admissible because the defendant was in custody and the inventory was incident to a lawful arrest.

Tina Mesa's car was totaled following an accident in Metropolis, and she was taken to the hospital by ambulance from the accident scene. Tina was cited for failing to yield during a turn. Her car was blocking traffic. Metropolis police regulations require that prior to towing, police must inventory the contents found in the car's unlocked compartments and containers. In the glove compartment, the officer found a diamond watch that turned out to be stolen; in the trunk of the vehicle behind the spare tire, the officer discovered an opaque-wrapped brick-size package which the officer opened and saw that it contained marijuana. Tina was charged with receiving stolen property and possession of a large quantity of marijuana. The defense filed a Motion to Suppress the objects found in the vehicle.

66.  How should the court rule on the Motion to Suppress?

(A)  The watch and marijuana are admissible because they were found during a lawful inventory of the disabled car's contents.

(B)  The watch is admissible but the marijuana is not because the inventory of the trunk was illegal.

(C)  The watch and the marijuana are both inadmissible because an inventory is limited to objects that are visible from outside the car.

(D)  The watch and the marijuana are both admissible because the search was incident to arrest.

# COMPARING DIFFERENT JUSTIFICATIONS FOR SEARCH OF AN AUTOMOBILE

A police officer stopped the defendant's vehicle when she observed the defendant driving very slowly and weaving back and forth across the dividing center line. After ordering the defendant to stop the vehicle, the officer noticed the defendant reaching down to an area between the driver's seat and the gas and brake pedals. The officer ordered the defendant out of the vehicle to take field sobriety tests, which he failed. The officer asked the defendant what he was reaching for in the automobile. The defendant explained that there was a hidden compartment just in front of the driver's seat. The officer ordered the defendant to demonstrate how to open and close the compartment. He did, but the compartment was empty. The defendant was arrested and charged with impaired driving. He pled guilty and was sentenced to 60 days in jail. The vehicle was impounded and held by the police. Sixty days later, when the defendant was released from jail, the state did not contest his petition for return of the vehicle. On the day that the car was to be returned to the defendant, police performed an Ionscan test (device used to detect microscopic particles of drugs) on the hidden compartment of the vehicle that revealed the trace presence of cocaine. The defendant, charged with possession of cocaine, moved to suppress the Ionscan test evidence.

**67.** How should the judge rule on the motion to suppress?

ANSWER:

Police were investigating drug activity complaints in a Metropolis public housing unit. When they entered the hallway, they saw Aldo Glick leaning against the wall in the hallway. Three officers walked over to Glick and began asking him questions. Glick testified during the suppression hearing that the officers did not raise their voices, did not use profanity, and did not draw their weapons. Glick also testified that, at first, he ignored the officers and did not respond to their questions but that they persisted. He started to walk away from the officers but they walked with him. Finally, he engaged them in conversation when he realized that they would not let him ignore them and leave. One of the officers told Glick that tenants had complained that drugs were being dealt in the hallway. The officer asked Glick where he lived. He responded, untruthfully, that he did not live in the building and was just waiting for a friend. They asked to see his I.D., and he fished out his driver's license from his wallet and handed it to the officer. The officer checked the license and told Glick he had lied to them about not living in the building. Glick asked for his license back so that he could go up to his apartment. One of the other officers told Glick that he could have his license back and leave if he allowed them to search his backpack for a weapon. Glick testified that he realized that the officers would not let him leave until he let them search. He handed over his backpack which one of the officers opened and then removed several glassine envelopes containing rocks of cocaine. Glick was arrested and charged with illegal possession of crack cocaine. The defense filed a motion to suppress the evidence seized from Glick's backpack.

68. Are the packets of crack cocaine admissible at Glick's trial?

   (A) The evidence is admissible because Glick consented to the search of his backpack.
   (B) The evidence is inadmissible because Glick was illegally seized at the time he granted consent.
   (C) The evidence is admissible because it was found during a legitimate search for weapons.
   (D) The evidence is inadmissible because it was found during an illegal search.

Police received a tip at 1 a.m. from an anonymous caller that he had overheard a phone conversation on his police scanner of details of a drug sale that was about to take place in the parking lot at a Walgreen's pharmacy. Police rushed to Walgreen's, which they knew was in an area where a large number of drug transactions occurred. The drug store was closed. In the deserted parking lot behind the store, police saw Ethan Cole standing outside his parked, running Jetta. As police exited their vehicle, they saw Cole reach into his jacket. An officer reached in as well and seized a gun tucked in Cole's waistband. Cole was arrested for carrying a concealed weapon. Police searched Cole but did not find any drugs. Prior to Cole's trial on the concealed weapon charge, the defense filed a motion to suppress the gun.

69. The gun is

    (A) admissible because the anonymous tip provided reasonable suspicion to seize the defendant and the search was a lawful frisk.

    (B) admissible even though the anonymous tip was not sufficient by itself to justify the seizure, his presence in the parking lot corroborated the tip and the search was a lawful frisk.

    (C) inadmissible because the officers did not have reasonable suspicion to seize the defendant, and absent a lawful *Terry* stop there could be no search for a weapon.

    (D) inadmissible because the officer reached into Cole's pocket beyond the scope of a legitimate frisk.

Officers from the Metropolis narcotics unit were in an unmarked car patrolling an area known for heavy drug activity. They saw two occupants in an illegally parked car by an open field. The officers circled the block and, on their return, could see only one occupant. The officers pulled in behind the parked car. At this time, the second occupant, a woman, was seen "popping up" in the passenger's side of the front seat, turning and looking back at the officers, and then bending forward. The officers approached the vehicle and ordered the male suspect, Bobo, sitting in the driver's seat, to get out of the car. After Bobo got out of the car, one of the officers found a gun under the front seat on the passenger side. Bobo was charged with illegally carrying a gun in a vehicle.

At the suppression hearing, the officers testified that (1) the area in which the action occurred was an area of very heavy drug activity in which weapons were prevalent; (2) it was nighttime, when weapons could easily be hidden; (3) one of the officers who approached the vehicle in which Bobo was sitting had about twenty years of experience as a police officer and numerous years in the surveillance of drug and weapon activity; included in this experience were about 500 arrests each for guns or drugs city-wide and over 100 arrests in the area in which Bobo was parked; (4) the officer had knowledge of how drug transactions occurred in that area; (5) the officer had observed Bobo disappear from view, reappear when the police car was close, look directly at the officers, and then bend down as if to hide something under the front seat; (6) the officer had experience in recovering weapons or drugs when an individual would make the type of gesture made by Bobo in ducking under his seat; and (7) the police officers were out of their vehicle and away from any protection if the defendant had been armed.

70. How should the court rule on the motion to suppress?

    (A) The officers had reasonable suspicion to make a *Terry* stop and reasonable suspicion to search for a weapon.

    (B) The officers did not have reasonable suspicion to make a *Terry* stop.

    (C) Even if the officers had reasonable suspicion to make a *Terry* stop, the search for a weapon exceeded the frisk allowed under *Terry*.

(D) The officers had probable cause to believe that a drug transaction had occurred and, therefore, probable cause to search the car.

Officer Carbonari was investigating reports of drug sales on a street corner. Carbonari watched Willie Warble for several minutes, as motorists and pedestrians engaged Warble in very short conversations. Carbonari did not see money or objects change hands. Carbonari drove right up to the corner where Warble was standing. When Warble saw the police car, he walked away from the corner. Carbonari started after Warble, and Warble started running away. Carbonari saw Warble reach into his pocket, while he was running, and throw away several objects. Warble was stopped at the end of the block by Carbonari's partner. Carbonari found the objects thrown away by Warble. Those objects were small glassine envelopes containing small quantities of cocaine.

**71.** Is the cocaine admissible at Warble's trial?

ANSWER:

Evan Kolander runs for exercise every day. Evan is black, and he tends to run in predominantly white neighborhoods in Metropolis at all hours of the day or night. Police tend to stop him and ask what he is doing in the area. Evan considers the police behavior racial harassment, but the officers claim that they are doing their job keeping the community safe. Evan runs without a shirt and in running shorts. No one who sees Evan running could believe that he is carrying a weapon. Metropolis adopted an ordinance making it a minor misdemeanor for any person lawfully stopped not to identify himself or herself to the police. Evan was out running around midnight when he was stopped by the police and asked to identify himself. He refused and was arrested under the Metropolis ordinance.

**72.** Is the arrest lawful?

   (A) Evan's arrest was unlawful because the ordinance violates the Fourth and Fifth Amendments.

   (B) Evan's arrest was unlawful because he was not properly seized under *Terry*.

   (C) Evan's arrest was lawful because the ordinance is a reasonable exercise of the police powers.

   (D) Evan's arrest was lawful because he failed to comply with the statutory requirement.

A police officer stopped Sumner Wells for running a red light. The officer sat behind Wells' car for about five minutes until back-up vehicles arrived at the scene, and then, along with three other officers from the back-up units, with guns drawn, walked up to Wells' car, ordered Wells from the vehicle, told him to lie on the ground and handcuffed him. The primary officer frisked Wells and found a handgun on his person, which turned out to be unlicensed. At the same time as the frisk, one of the back-up officers walked a drug dog around Wells' car. The dog reacted to the presence of drugs in the trunk of the car. An officer took Wells' keys from the car and opened the trunk; inside the trunk was a large quantity of drugs. Wells was charged with illegal possession of a handgun and possession of the large quantity of drugs.

73. The gun is

(A) admissible because the defendant was patted down incident to the traffic stop.

(B) admissible because police officers may take reasonable steps to protect their safety during a traffic stop.

(C) inadmissible because Wells was arrested without probable cause and the weapon was found incident to the illegal arrest.

(D) inadmissible because the state failed to present any facts to justify the use of force and the frisk during a routine traffic stop.

74. The drugs are

(A) admissible because the use of the drug dog provided probable cause for a warrantless search of the automobile.

(B) admissible because the search of the vehicle was incident to the arrest of the motorist for carrying a handgun.

(C) inadmissible because the search was part of the excessive force used during the traffic stop.

(D) inadmissible because there was no reasonable suspicion to justify use of the drug dog to ascertain whether there were drugs in the automobile.

Metropolis police set up a roadblock at the corner of East 55th Street and Central Avenue where a shooting had occurred at the same time two days earlier. Police hoped that someone traveling the intersection would have information about the shooting. The police stopped every car and handed the driver a handbill asking for information about the shooting. David Evans car was in line. When his car reached the front of the line, a police officer asked Evans to roll down his window. As the officer gave Evans the handbill, he noticed that Evans was nervous and his speech slurred. Instead of being waved on, Evans was ordered to the side of the road where another officer ordered him out of the vehicle and told to perform field sobriety tests. Evans failed. Evan was arrested, taken to the police station and given a Breathalyzer exam which reported that his blood alcohol level was over the legal limit. Evan was charged with D.U.I. Evans' attorney moved to exclude officers at the scene of the checkpoint stop from testifying about Evans' condition as well as the results of the breathalyser exam.

**75.** How should the court rule on the motion to suppress?

ANSWER:

The defendant Robinette was stopped by Sheriff's Deputy Newsome for speeding in a construction zone. Before approaching Robinette's vehicle, Newsome had already decided to issue a verbal warning, which was his routine practice. After checking Robinette's driver's license and registration and finding no violations, Deputy Newsome returned to Robinette's vehicle and ordered him out of the car and into the area "between Robinette's car and the deputy's cruiser." Once Robinette was in place, Newsome returned to his car and activated the video recorder in order to videotape their further interaction. Newsome administered a verbal warning regarding Robinette's speed, returned Robinette's driver's license and then said, "One question before you get going: Are you carrying any illegal contraband in your car? Any weapons of any kind, drugs, anything like that?" When Robinette answered that he did not have any contraband, Newsome asked to search the car, which the deputy testified he routinely did "as part of the drug interdiction project." Robinette answered yes, and during the subsequent search of the vehicle, Deputy Newsome found a small quantity of marijuana. The defense moved to exclude the marijuana found in the defendant's car.

76. The marijuana found in Robinette's car is

    (A) admissible because it was found incident to a valid traffic stop.

    (B) inadmissible because the officer should have written the ticket or given the warning and allowed the defendant to leave.

    (C) admissible because the defendant consented to a search of his car.

    (D) inadmissible because the detention was unlawful.

A uniformed police officer entered a crowded tavern to conduct a safety inspection, pursuant to departmental regulation. He counted the number of patrons present. He then asked the tavern owner to show him the legal occupancy permit, which was in the owner's office. The owner led the officer to the office located behind the tavern. The officer read the permit and cited the owner for exceeding the legal occupancy limit and for not having the permit posted in a public part of the tavern as required by statute. The officer also observed from the owner's office that one of the rear exit doors was blocked by cases of beer; the officer also cited the tavern owner for this violation. While writing up the citations, the officer observed a corn cob pipe and marijuana sitting on the owner's desk. At that point, he arrested the tavern owner. The owner was charged with failure to have the occupancy permit posted in the public room of the tavern, exceeding the legal occupancy limit, failure to maintain access to all exits, and drug abuse. The owner's lawyer moved to suppress the evidence.

77.  How should the court rule on the evidence?

   (A)  The evidence is all inadmissible because the officer needed a search warrant to look beyond the public areas of the tavern.

   (B)  The evidence pertaining to the safety violations is admissible, but the evidence of drug abuse is inadmissible because the officer was admitted to the private areas only for the safety inspection.

   (C)  The evidence is all admissible because the tavern owner complied with the officer's request for access to back room.

   (D)  The evidence is all admissible because it was a safety inspection, not a police search for evidence of a crime.

February 1 in Metropolis, is Inter-High School Competition Day. Students in all winter sports and extra-curricular competitions compete in all activities. On February 1, student athletes and club participants from Landrieu High School boarded buses, along with their coaches and club advisors, and traveled to Boggs High School. February 1 also was the day that the authorities at Boggs High School arranged for Metropolis Police Department Canine Units to conduct drug sniffing of all cars in the high school parking lot and all school lockers. Additionally, all students at Boggs were subject to the dog sniffing their persons. When the Landrieu students arrived at Boggs, their backpacks and athletic gear bags were subject to dog sniffing. All Boggs students had to line their bags up in the Boggs hallway as the dog handlers walked their dogs down the line of bags. The dog alerted to four of the Landrieu students' bags. Each of the four bags was searched by a police officer, and quantities of marijuana were found in three of the bags. Following the searches of the backpacks, the students were required to line up and file past the drug dogs. As each student passed a dog, the dog went up to each student, sniffing as it had done to the backpacks and gear bags. The dog stopped and sat in front of a boy who was taken to an office on loan to the police and searched. A small quantity of marijuana was found in the boy's pants pocket. That student and the three in whose backpacks or gear bags marijuana was found were referred to Juvenile Court for a delinquency determination. Attorneys for the four students filed motions to suppress the marijuana.

78.   How should the court rule on the Motion to Suppress?

    (A)   All the evidence should be suppressed because the searches were conducted by police officers, not school administrators.

    (B)   All the evidence should be admitted because students do not have a protected right of privacy in schools because of society's interest in maintaining a safe and drug-free environment in schools.

    (C)   The evidence seized from the backpacks and gear bags lockers should be admitted, but the evidence seized from the boy's person should be suppressed.

    (D)   All the evidence should be admitted because a dog sniff is not a search and once alerted by the dog, there was probable cause to conduct each of the searches.

After the discovery of drugs on students and in their bags, the Metropolis School District adopted Policy 227, which requires all middle and high school students seeking to participate in extracurricular activities or requesting permission to drive to school or park at school to sign, or have a parent sign, a contract consenting to testing for alcohol and controlled substances. The policy defines extracurricular activities as all athletics, clubs, and other activities in which students participate on a voluntary basis, and for which academic credit is not awarded. The policy includes the following statement of purpose: "As representatives of the school district and leaders in their schools, students involved in extracurricular programs and students who drive to school are expected to exemplify high standards by the public and are held in high esteem by other students. Participants in extracurricular programs and those who drive to school are expected to accept the responsibilities accompanying these opportunities."

**79.** Is the school board's drug testing policy valid?

ANSWER:

What if the Metropolis school board policy were extended to require drug testing of all teachers who coach school inter-mural teams and teachers supervising other extra curricular activities? The policy requires termination of any teacher who refuses to take the drug test or who fails the drug test.

**80.** Is the school board policy valid?

(A) The suspicionless drug testing of some teachers is an unreasonable search.

(B) Suspicionless drug testing of teachers and coaches does not violate the Fourth Amendment command of reasonableness.

(C) The testing of student athletes and students involved in extra-curricular activities would violate the Fourth Amendment if not extended to school personnel who travel with the students.

(D) The testing of some teachers and not others violates the Equal Protection Clause of the Fourteenth Amendment.

George Bailey left a hotel room which was under surveillance by police who thought the guest in the hotel room was selling drugs. Bailey was intercepted by the police just after he left the room. Three police officers surrounded Bailey and asked him to empty his pockets. One of the items Bailey took from his pocket was an empty cigarette pack. Police opened the pack and found eight individually wrapped packets of cocaine. George Bailey's attorney moved to suppress the evidence.

81. The cocaine is

   (A) admissible because Bailey voluntarily emptied his pockets.
   (B) inadmissible because Bailey emptied his pockets involuntarily.
   (C) admissible because there was reasonable suspicion to stop Bailey when he left the hotel room.
   (D) inadmissible because police detained Bailey illegally.

After Bailey's arrest, the captain in charge of the precinct where Bailey was booked thought something was fishy about Bailey. The captain ordered two officers to go to Bailey's house to see what they could find. When the officers arrived at Bailey's home, they were met at the door by Mrs. Bailey. They told her that her husband was arrested and asked to search the house. When Mrs. Bailey hesitated, an officer said, we can always get a search warrant if you don't let us in. Mrs. Bailey let the officers in and they searched every room, closets, dressers and the basement. What they found amazed them. They had, apparently, discovered that Bailey maintained a major fence operation in Metropolis. Throughout the house the officers found and seized very expensive jewelry, furs and electronic equipment which had been stolen.

The defense attorney moved to suppress everything found in the house.

82. The evidence found in the house is

   (A) inadmissible because the officers should have sought a warrant before they went to the Bailey home.
   (B) admissible because exigent circumstances justified not getting a warrant.
   (C) inadmissible because Mrs. Bailey did not voluntarily consent to the search of her home.
   (D) admissible because Mrs. Bailey's consent to search the house was voluntary.

Alter the facts in Question 82. When police arrived at the Bailey household, they told Mrs. Bailey that her husband had been arrested. They asked for permission to search the house. Mrs. Bailey hesitated but then agreed. She told the officers that she would consent to their searching her husband's belongings, but said they had could not go into the basement. When the officers began the search, Mrs. Bailey became very nervous. The officers found some of the expensive jewelry and furs in the front closet off of the living room. When the officers went into the Baileys' shared bedroom, Mrs. Bailey ordered them to stop the search and leave the home. The officers did not leave and continued to search the house, including the basement where they found additional stolen jewelry and furs. George Bailey was charged with numerous felony counts of receiving stolen property found during the search of the house. Bailey's attorney filed a Motion to Suppress all evidence found at the house. The state claimed that the evidence found in the basement preceded Mrs. Bailey's order to the police to stop the search.

**83.**   How should the court rule on the motion to suppress?

ANSWER:



Metropolis police received information from an undercover police officer that the officer had purchased illegal drugs from Mrs. Stewart. The police officers went to Mrs. Stewart's home without a warrant. They asked her if they could come into her house and talk. She opened the door and invited the officers into her apartment. While Mrs. Stewart sat in the living room talking to one of the officers and denied dealing drugs from her home, two other officers who entered with the consent, looked through a closet which opened onto the living room and found a large quantity of drugs in the closet. Mrs. Stewart was arrested and charged with possession of illegal drugs with the intent to sell. Mrs. Stewart's lawyer filed a motion to suppress. The officers testified that they had not told Mrs. Stewart that she could refuse to allow them to enter the house and search.

**84.**   What should be the result?

  (A)   The evidence should be suppressed because the police did not inform the defendant of her right to refuse to allow the police officers to enter her apartment and conduct a search.

  (B)   The evidence should be suppressed because the defendant did not consent to a search of the her apartment.

  (C)   The evidence should be admitted at trial because it is irrelevant whether the defendant knew that she could refuse the police entry to her apartment.

  (D)   The evidence should be admitted because the officers had probable cause to conduct a search and could have entered without the defendant's permission.

Police were investigating reports that Dennis, a graduate student, had become a principal supplier of illegal narcotics at the university. Police watched Dennis' movements and carefully went to his rented duplex apartment when Dennis was out and only his roommate was at home. Len, Dennis' roommate, answered the door. Len was reluctant at first to let the police into the apartment, but Len's girlfriend who was also present helped police persuade Len to allow a search of the apartment. Len showed the officers around the apartment. He showed them his bedroom and pointed to Dennis' bedroom. Dennis' bedroom was unlocked and police entered and searched Dennis' belongings. In the closet in Dennis' room, the officers found an army duffle bag which was loaded with drugs. Dennis was charged with trafficking. His attorneys moved to suppress the evidence. The state countered with the claim that the search was legal pursuant to Len's consent.

85. The evidence should be

(A) suppressed because the roommate did not have authority to consent to a search of Dennis' room.

(B) suppressed because the police should have sought the consent of Dennis, not his roommate.

(C) admitted because co-tenants may consent to a search of their entire home including the roommate's private space.

(D) admitted because the roommate waived Dennis' Fourth Amendment rights.

Police were investigating a complaint that Peter Masten had sexually abused his step-daughter. Masten lived with his wife and step-daughter. Mrs. Masten, the sole owner of the shared home, consented to a police search of the house. When they were searching the family room used by all three family members, the officers requested access to a locked file cabinet. Mrs. Masten advised the police that the file cabinet was her husband's and that he had the only key. She granted permission to forcibly open the file cabinet. The officers broke the lock and found sexually explicit pictures of Masten and his step-daughter in the file cabinet. Prior to the defendant's trial, the court denied the defendant's motion to suppress the pictures. The defendant was convicted and appealed.

86. Should the appellate court reverse the trial court's denial of the motion to suppress?

(A) The appellate court should pay deference to the trial court's decision and uphold the conviction.

(B) The appellate court should sustain the trial court's decision because Mrs. Masten, as the sole owner of the house, could consent to a search of the house and all of its contents.

(C) The appellate court should reverse the trial court's decision because they should have sought Mr. Masten's consent to search the cabinet.

(D) The appellate court should reverse the trial court's decision because police could not reasonably rely upon Mrs. Masten's consent to search the file cabinet.

Change the facts in Question 86. Police had probable cause to arrest Mr. Masten on charges related to the sexual assault of his step-daughter. They went to the Masten home to make the arrest without a warrant. When they arrived at the house, Mrs. Masten let them into the house where they arrested Mr. Masten. They asked for permission to search the house, but Masten refused. The officers handcuffed Masten and took him outside and placed him in the police car. The officers then returned to the house and asked Mrs. Masten for permission to search the residence. She granted permission. In the Masten's bedroom closet, police found a box on the shelf that contained sexually explicit photos of Masten and his step-daughter. Masten's attorney moved to suppress the photographs.

**87.** The pictures are

(A) admissible because Mrs. Masten consented to a search the house.

(B) inadmissible because Mr. Masten, the target of the search, had refused consent.

(C) admissible because the search was incident to the lawful arrest of Mr. Masten.

(D) inadmissible because police could not enter the house to arrest Mr. Masten without a warrant.

Martin Postum, a major drug king pin in Metropolis, operates a drug business out of his home where he lives with his wife and three children. Margaret Postum, the eighteen-year-old daughter, has always been a difficult child. She fought with her parents all her life and resisted her parents' attempts to control her behavior and to limit her contacts with friends. She allowed herself to be picked up at a Starbucks by an undercover police officer assigned to investigate her father's illegal business. The officer and Margaret met often, a fact unknown to Margaret's parents. Conveniently, Margaret spent much of their time together complaining bitterly about her parents. She also told the officer details of her father's drug business. According to her information, her mother was not actively involved in the drug business. Margaret often complained that her father made her use her cell phone to give orders in code to drug couriers. Margaret whined bitterly that her father did not interfere with her siblings' cell phones.

After numerous meetings between Margaret and the undercover officer, Margaret declared her love for him. Startled by her declaration, the officer told her who he was. She told him that he could prove what she said was true by allowing the officer to listen to calls she made on her father's behalf from her cell phone. Immediately after their final meeting, with the information provided by Margaret, the police sought an eavesdropping warrant authorizing collection of all conversations on the two land lines leased to the Postum residence and for all cell phone conversations on Margaret's cell phone, and those of her mother, father and two siblings. The application for the warrant did not include facts indicating why this broad wiretap was necessary. The warrant was issued authorizing a tap of all incoming and outgoing telephone conversations on the Postum's land lines, as well as all cell phones leased by members of the household. Police listened to and recorded all phone conversations on the two land lines and five cell phones for a fifteen day period. Conversations regarding the illegal drug trafficking were recorded on all seven lines.

**88.** Is the evidence admissible?

ANSWER:

The defendant Homer Carr was a bank teller who, over a period of two years, embezzled $250,000 from the bank. Carr pleaded guilty to the felony offense, and the trial judge sentenced Carr to a three-year prison term. After six months in prison, Carr was recalled by the court and ordered to serve the remainder of his prison term on parole. One of the conditions of parole imposed by the trial court, and agreed to by Carr, required him to submit, at any time of day, to searches of his residence by his probation officer accompanied by township police. Near midnight on February 20, Carr was awakened by pounding on his front door. He went to the door and found his probation officer with two police officers in tow. The probation officer asked Carr to allow her and the two police officers to enter and search Carr's home. Carr protested the late hour, but the officers pushed by Carr and entered the home. The three officers did a search of every room and closet in the house and of every container in the house. When Carr asked why they were doing this to him, his probation officer answered because they could. In the night stand in Carr's bedroom, the officers found a small quantity of marijuana. Carr was charged with a parole violation and a misdemeanor-marijuana possession offense. Carr's attorney filed a motion to suppress the marijuana. The trial court denied the motion, and after a trial lasting less than two hours, the judge found Carr guilty, revoked his parole, and sentenced him to serve the remainder of the prison sentence. Carr appealed on the ground that the trial court erred when it denied his motion to suppress.

89. What result should we anticipate on appeal?

   (A) The conviction will be reversed because the state failed to establish probable cause to justify the midnight search of Carr's home.
   (B) The conviction will be reversed because the state failed to establish reasonable suspicion to justify the midnight search of Carr's home.
   (C) The conviction will be affirmed because a parolee has no expectation of privacy.
   (D) The conviction will be affirmed because, as a convicted felon, Carr is subject to a search of his person and home at all times.

A Metropolis police officer observed the defendant driving just before the driver passed the city line out of Metropolis into a neighboring suburb. State law prohibits a municipal police officer to arrest outside the territorial jurisdiction of her municipality unless in hot pursuit. The Metropolis police officer, nonetheless, followed the defendant. Five minutes later, the officer observed the defendant driving erratically. The officer stopped the defendant's car to determine if the defendant was drunk. The officer administered field sobriety tests, which the defendant failed, and then arrested the defendant. Prior to trial, the defendant's lawyer claimed that the arrest was illegal and sought to exclude the officer's testimony. The trial court concluded that the officer violated the defendant's

Fourth Amendment rights and excluded the testimony. The state court of appeals reversed the ruling and held the evidence admissible. The defendant appealed to the U.S. Supreme Court.

**90.** How should the U.S. Supreme Court rule?

ANSWER:

Officer Merit accompanied a housing inspector executing an administrative search warrant for a safety inspection because departmental rules require that a police officer accompany housing inspectors at all times during safety inspections. At the house, Officer Merit saw a baggy containing a small amount of marijuana sitting on a dresser. As a result of what he saw, Officer Merit applied for a search warrant, using a boilerplate form providing an exhaustive list of all illicit controlled substances "which he had reason to believe were being concealed based upon his observation" and referring to the place to be searched as a "drug house." During the execution of the warrant, Officer Merit confiscated an additional amount of illegal drugs during an exhaustive search of the premises. The defense moved to suppress the evidence.

91. The evidence is

(A) admissible because Officer Merit's observation of the baggy during the administrative search provided adequate probable cause for the warrant.

(B) inadmissible because the warrant was lacking in probable cause.

(C) admissible because, even if the warrant were invalid, Officer Merit was entitled to rely on the warrant.

(D) inadmissible because the warrant was invalid and Officer Merit could not reasonably rely on the warrant.

Officer Constable submitted this affidavit for a search warrant:

The affiant is a commissioned officer with the Metropolis Police Department. The affiant has been a member of the Department's Narcotics Squad for eleven years. Affiant received tips from two confidential informants who have proved reliable in the past that Morgan Washington, residing at 2204 Main Street, within the city, possesses a large quantity of uncut powder cocaine at his residence and is dealing said cocaine out of his house. Washington, who drives a 2007 Honda Accord, uses the car to transport cocaine. The affiant's investigation has verified the informants' information. A search of Washington's residence two years ago netted a large quantity of cocaine.

The affiant, possessing probable cause, asks this court to issue a search warrant for Washington's residence and automobile.

The magistrate issued the warrant which was executed by Officer Constable. Police seized close to a kilogram of powder cocaine and over 70 grams of 124 crack cocaine. Washington was charged with three first degree felony drug abuse offenses. Conviction of each offense carries a ten year mandatory prison sentence. The defense moved to suppress the drugs found at Washington's home. The state argued that the search warrant was valid, but if not, the drugs are admissible under the good faith exception to the warrant requirement.

**92.** How should the court rule on the motion to suppress?

ANSWER:

A police officer patrolling a public park stopped a group of three young men, frisked them, and found a weapon on one of the suspects. The officer arrested the person carrying the weapon. The defense moved to suppress the weapon. The officer testified at the suppression hearing that he believed it was lawful to search all persons on public recreation grounds.

**93.** The motion should be

    (A)  denied if the trial court finds that the officer acted in good faith reliance on his mistaken belief about the law.

    (B)  denied because persons in a public park have no reasonable expectation of privacy.

    (C)  granted because the officer stopped and frisked without reasonable suspicion.

    (D)  granted because the officer's belief as to the law was unreasonable and would not support an objective reasonable reliance.

The Department of Human Services ("DHS") began an investigation regarding allegations of sexual contact between Donald Dingalong and his fifteen-year-old stepdaughter, Sandra. A social worker from DHS telephoned Carol, Sandra's mother, to tell her that she and the Donald had to appear at the social worker's office for an interview about the allegation. Mrs. Dingalong testified that when she asked what would happen if they failed to go to the interview, the social worker stated that the child would be removed from their home. The social worker testified she did not say this.

Mrs. Dingalong testified that she had not wanted to go to the DHS office and asked that the social worker come to the residence to talk with the family. The social worker insisted that the interview must take place in the DHS office. Mrs. Dingalong testified that she believed, if they did not go to the interview and cooperate, her daughter would be removed from their home.

One day after the telephone call, Donald, Mrs. Dingalong and Sandra went to DHS for the interview. Over the objection of Donald and Mrs. Dingalong, the child was interviewed by the social worker and Police Sergeant Conner. Donald and his wife requested they go with the child, but they were told that the child would be questioned separately. The child was questioned for about half an hour. After the child was questioned, Donald and his wife were questioned. Donald, Mrs. Dingalong, the Social Worker, and Sergeant Conner were present at the interview.

Prior to their arrival at DHS, Donald and his wife did not know that a police officer would be present for the interview which took place in a small private office with the door closed. Sergeant Conner sat very close to the Defendant and his wife. Conner himself testified that he sat facing appellee while questioning him, moving from a position "2–3 feet away to possibly inches from the defendant." Conner also testified that, at one point, Donald backed up his chair, and expressed discomfort at Conner's proximity to his body. Sergeant Conner, who is 6 feet 5 inches tall and weighs 330 pounds, controlled the interview and asked the vast majority of questions. Donald was told he was free to leave and that he was not under arrest. However, he was not given any of the *Miranda* warnings. The interview lasted over an hour.

During the interview Donald made several incriminating admissions. At the conclusion of the interview the family was permitted to leave and return home. A week later Donald was indicted for illegal sexual contact with his stepdaughter.

**94.** Are the statements Donald made during the interview admissible at his trial?

ANSWER:

Carrie Clepto and her two infant children were observed via closed circuit television in a Target store. Carrie was stuffing women's and children's clothing in pockets sewn into the lining of her coat. A store detective, Donald Dick, who had been observing Carrie in the store for weeks, grabbed her at the check out counter and took her to the back room. Dick showed her the store's video tape and triumphantly told her that she was going to prison unless she helped the store identify, apprehend, and convict the ring leader of the gang that had been for a number of months stealing almost daily from this particular Target store. When Carrie hesitated, Dick threatened that Child Services would take her two children from her custody, and she would never regain custody. By now, the two infants were screaming and crying, and Carrie agreed to tell all. She told Dick that, in fact, she was part of a shop-lifting ring that had stolen thousands of dollars worth of merchandise from this Target store over a period of ten weeks. She identified the ring leader and promised to testify against him. Her statement was video recorded. After she made the statement, local police were summoned to the store where the officers arrested Carrie and read her *Miranda* rights.

Carrie was charged with felony theft after she was released on bail and refused to cooperate with prosecutors. Her defense attorney moved to suppress the video tape made at the time she gave her incriminating statement to the store detective.

95. What result?

   (A) The statement is inadmissible because Carrie was not given *Miranda* warnings prior being questioned.

   (B) The statement is inadmissible because it was not voluntary being the result of the threat to take away her children.

   (C) The statement is admissible because she was not under arrest when she was questioned.

   (D) The statement is admissible because the store detective who questioned Carrie was not a government agent.

Officer Charles was a rogue cop. Since he was a child he wanted to be a police officer, but Charles also had a fondness for easy money. He had many opportunities as a police officer to steal drugs and money from drug dealers; he then turned around and sold the stolen drugs to other street dealers. His commanding officers were suspicious of Charles, but they never were able to get proof of his illegal activities.

One night, Charles was stopped for driving under the influence. Charles was quite evidently drunk, and the officer who stopped the car arrested Charles, although at the time he did not know that Charles was a fellow officer. Charles had pulled into a lawful parking space seconds before his encounter with the police officer. Since the car was lawfully parked, the car was not towed.

Charles was transported to the police station where he was identified as a police officer. The arresting officer, without administering the *Miranda* warnings, asked Charles about his service revolver. Charles admitted that it was in the trunk of his vehicle. When officers went to the vehicle to search the trunk for the service revolver, they found a large quantity of drugs and of cash. Officer Charles has been charged with D.U.I., possession of the drugs and possession of stolen property (the cash).

96. Officer Charles' statement about the location of the gun and the evidence found in the trunk is

   (A) admissible because the car was searched incident to the arrest.

   (B) admissible because the public safety exception to *Miranda* allowed the officer to interrogate Charles about the location of the gun prior to issuance of the warnings.

   (C) inadmissible because Officer Charles should have been given the *Miranda* warnings because he was in custody and subject to police interrogation.

   (D) inadmissible because the search of the car was illegal.

Barry Brewster was arrested for drunk driving. He refused to take a Breathalyzer test. He was booked for drunk driving. During the booking proceeding, Brewster was told to stand in a boxed-out area on the floor so that his answers and responses could be captured on videotape.

The videotape captured a stumbling Brewster who spoke with a hesitating and slurred speech. The videotape was strong evidence that Brewster was inebriated when he was brought to the police station. Asked to spell his name, Brewster first misspelled it and then corrected himself. He had similar difficulty with his address. He was then asked for his date of birth and social security number. He was able to recite his date of birth but not his social security number. After he made several unsuccessful attempts at his social security number, the booking officer finally gave Brewster his driver's license back so that he could read his social security number from the license. Asked to recite the alphabet, he got hopelessly mixed up after the letter "e". The booking and fingerprinting took about thirty minutes, during which Brewster never received *Miranda* warnings. Prior to trial, his lawyer moved to suppress evidence about Brewster's responses to the questions asked during the booking.

**97.** The motion should be

(A) granted because Brewster was never advised of his *Miranda* warnings.

(B) denied because booking questions are pedigree questions which need not be preceded by *Miranda* warnings.

(C) granted because Brewster should have been advised of his *Miranda* when he was arrested.

(D) granted as to evidence pertaining to his inability to recite the alphabet, denied as to all of his other answers.

Danny was a small-time Chicago hood who had been in and out of trouble numerous times. He gained notoriety after killing his brother-in-law and escaping justice. The Supreme Court threw out his conviction because incriminating statements he made to police were in violation of his right to counsel. Not too long after that conviction was reversed and Danny went free, he was arrested again.

A police dispatcher sent a patrol car to a retail establishment after midnight where a silent alarm indicated that a break-in was in progress. When the police car pulled up to the store, the officers saw a smashed plate glass window. The officers got out of the car, drew their weapons and shined their flashlights into the store through the broken window. Immediately, Danny came out of the store through the broken window with this hands in the air. He said to the officers, "You've got me this time." They handcuffed Danny and placed him in the back of the police car. An hour later after completing their investigation of the break-in, the police officers returned to their squad car where Danny was waiting to be taken to jail.

During the ride downtown, Danny, without being spoken to by the officers, talked freely about the break-in and about how arresting him red-handed should assure the two officers' promotions. Just before they got to the jail, Danny also told the officers that nothing he told them could be used against him since they had forgotten to give him *Miranda* warnings. Danny's attorney moved to suppress the statements made to the police officers.

98. The statements are

    (A) admissible because they were volunteered.

    (B) admissible because Danny knew his rights and spoke anyway.

    (C) inadmissible because the officers should have administered the *Miranda* warnings when Danny was arrested.

    (D) inadmissible because the officers should have *Mirandized* Danny on the ride to the police station.

The defendant, known as "Hothead" Grant, was arrested for the brutal murder of his girlfriend. Hothead and the victim had lived together for two years. Everyone who knew the couple was aware of their stormy relationship. The two quarreled in front of family and friends, and periodically each would turn up with bruises and bandages. When the victim's body was found in an alley behind their apartment, Hothead was arrested immediately and taken to the police station.

Following his booking, Hothead was told to sit in the seat next to the investigating detective's desk in the police wardroom. That seat was four or five feet away from the public area of the police station. While Hothead sat, the detective ignored him and focused on paper work, presumably about the homicide. However, the victim's family was in the public area of the station, shouting at and threatening Hothead. After about 20 minutes of constant abuse, Hothead turned to the detective and said, "If you take me out of this room, I will tell you how and why I murdered my girlfriend." The detective moved Hothead immediately, and the defendant gave a full confession. After the defendant confessed, he was read *Miranda* warnings, and he signed a waiver and a written verbatim copy of his confession.

The defendant's attorney, prior to trial, moved to suppress the confession.

99. Is the confession admissible?

ANSWER:

Instead of the facts above, consider the following alternative facts. Following Hothead's arrest and booking, he was placed in a jail cell to await a court appearance. Shortly after Hothead's arrival in the cell, another inmate was locked in the cell with Hothead. The two began to trade information about why they were there. While they talked about their criminal exploits, Hothead confessed to the murder of his girlfriend and provided details in response to questions from his cellmate. In fact the cellmate was a police officer pretending to be another detainee in order to pump Hothead about the murder. That police officer will testify at trial about Hothead's admissions obtained in the jail cell.

**100.** The officer's testimony about Hothead's statements is

    (A) admissible because Hothead's statements were not the product of custodial interrogation.

    (B) admissible because the statements were spontaneously made.

    (C) inadmissible because the questioning should have been preceded by *Miranda* warnings.

    (D) inadmissible because the Hotread's statements where the product of deceit and trickery.

Police arrested the defendant and took him to the police station where he was placed in an interrogation room. Detective Kurt Wallender told the defendant that he wanted to talk to him about a burglary that had occurred the night before on the defendant's street. First, Detective Wallender told the defendant, "I have to read you your *Miranda* rights." Wallender told the defendant that he had the right to remain silent, and that anything he said could be used against him in a court of law. Wallender also told the defendant that he had the right to talk to a lawyer for advice before being asked any questions, and that a lawyer "would be appointed if and when you go to court." After asking the defendant if he understood those rights and wished to waive them, the defendant answered affirmatively.

During the interrogation, the defendant admitted committing the burglary. Wallender also asked the defendant about a number of recent robberies, and after some hesitation, the defendant also admitted to committing them.

At trial, the defense moved to suppress the defendant's confession because of the inadequacies of the *Miranda* warnings.

**101.** Is the confession admissible?

ANSWER:

In the facts above, the defense attorney moved to suppress the defendant's statements pertaining to the robberies. The defense motion was based upon the fact that Detective Wallender only informed the defendant that he wished to question him about the burglary.

**102.** The motion to suppress should be

(A) granted because the defendant waived his *Miranda* rights only to questions related to the burglary.

(B) granted because the detective's failure to inform the defendant about the other crimes he wanted to question him about constituted trickery and deceit.

(C) denied because the defendant knowingly, intelligently and voluntarily waived his *Miranda* rights.

(D) denied because trickery and deceit do not affect the quality of a defendant's waiver.

Harlan Stone, a member of a notorious biker gang involved in major drug dealing in Los Angeles County, was arrested in connection with the brutal murder of a police snitch. Even before police were done booking Stone at 10 a.m., a lawyer retained by the gang to represent Stone was demanding to see him. Police told the lawyer to wait until after jail inmates were given their lunch. Following the booking, Detective Svedborg took Stone into an interrogation room. Stone had not seen the lawyer and did not know that a lawyer was asking to see him.

Detective Svedborg read Stone his *Miranda* rights and then asked Stone if he understood the rights and was prepared to waive them. Stone did not respond. A moment later, the detective asked Stone, again, if he was prepared to waive his rights and answer his questions. Stone said, "I guess so." In the two hours that followed, Stone admitted to killing the snitch and implicated several gang leaders who correctly believed that the snitch was feeding information about the drug operation to the L.A.P.D. At the end of the two hours, Stone was informed about the lawyer waiting to see him. Stone made it clear that if he had known that the lawyer was at the jail he would not have answered any questions before talking to him. A pretrial motion to suppress Stone's confession was filed.

103.   The motion should be

   (A)   granted because Stone should have been permitted to see the lawyer retained to represent him.
   (B)   denied because Stone did not exercise his *Miranda* right to counsel.
   (C)   granted because Stone exercised his *Miranda* right to counsel.
   (D)   denied because Stone knowingly, intelligently, and voluntarily waived his right to counsel.

Johnny Dealer was caught on videotape selling crack cocaine to an undercover police officer during a buy and bust operation. Dealer was arrested the next day. Police hoped to turn Dealer into a state's witness against his supplier, who, they hoped, would lead to the next person up the chain. Dealer was interrogated by Officer Krupke who read him the *Miranda* warnings. Krupke told Dealer that he thought they could help each other out, but Dealer said he wanted a lawyer. Krupke asked him, "What for? I can do more for you right now than a lawyer can." Dealer asked the officer to explain, and Krupke told Dealer that he was prepared to go to bat for Dealer and make sure he did little or no time in return for information. Dealer thought about it, and agreed to talk with Krupke, and signed a written waiver of *Miranda* rights. While they talked, Dealer implicated himself in several crimes but got cold feet and was unwilling to talk about his supplier. He told Krupke that if he talked, he'd be a dead man. Dealer's statement resulted in additional criminal charges being filed against him. At trial, Dealer's attorney moved to suppress his statement.

**104.**  What will be the result of the motion to suppress?

ANSWER:

When Freddy Felon was arrested in his home for a string of home burglaries, one of which resulted in the death of the home owner, the arresting officer told Freddy falsely that his fingerprints were found all over the home where the death occurred. The officer did not read Freddy his *Miranda* rights prior to making that statement. Freddy responded, angrily, that he committed the burglary, "but I'm not going to take the fall for the murder." No further comments were exchanged by the officer or Freddy. Freddy was taken from the home and transported to jail. Once at the jail, Freddy was booked and then taken to an interrogation room. A detective assigned to the case was informed of the statement made to the arresting officer at Freddy's home. The detective met with Freddy and advised him of his *Miranda* rights. Freddy agreed to waive his rights and wrote a written confession admitting to the burglaries and the accidental death of the home owner. Prior to trial, the defendant's attorney moved to suppress both confessions.

**105.** Should the confessions be suppressed?

(A) Both confessions should be suppressed because the first was given without *Miranda* warnings and is inadmissible, and the second confession is inadmissible because the "cat was already out of the bag" and the defendant's second confession was the result of the first.

(B) Both confessions are admissible because the first confession was not the product of custodial interrogation, and the second confession was given in full compliance with *Miranda*.

(C) The first confession is inadmissible because it was not secured in compliance with *Miranda*, but the second confession was secured by a different officer in different surroundings following the reading of *Miranda* warnings.

(D) The second confession is admissible because it was secured in full compliance with *Miranda* rules, and the first confession is admissible because, at worst, its admission would be harmless error.

Nate Ramirez was at home around three o'clock in the afternoon and received a phone call from Grimshaw, his accomplice in a murder case who was in police custody at the time of the call. Shortly after the call, a sheriff's deputy wearing a badge and carrying a firearm arrived at Ramirez's home. The deputy asked Ramirez to produce the physical evidence linked to the murder, including the suspected murder weapon and some of the victim's jewelry. According to the deputy, Ramirez was a "little hesitant at first, [and] denied having the articles." After the deputy informed Ramirez that she knew about the phone conversation with the accomplice, Ramirez turned over the items that were in the house and accompanied the deputy to retrieve other items.

Ramirez was then transported to the police station, placed in a small room, and questioned by two other detectives. The entire interrogation at the station was videotaped and is part of the record on appeal. The videotape reveals that the lead detective began the interrogation by questioning Ramirez about how the items came into his possession. When Ramirez initially claimed that Grimshaw gave him the items, one of the detectives told Ramirez: "What I want you to do is I want you to be honest with me. The indication we have is that both you and John [Grimshaw] are involved. . . . I want you to tell me what happened that night. I know you were there. I wouldn't be here if I didn't know that. You know what I'm saying?" After these statements by the detective, Ramirez admitted breaking into the victim's house the night of the murder.

After this admission the second detective suggested that Ramirez be informed of his *Miranda* rights. The detective said: "Why don't you let Nate [Ramirez] know about his rights. I mean, he's already told us about going in the house and whatever. I don't think that's going to change Nate's desire to cooperate with us." Ramirez then asked if he "was like being placed under arrest?" to which the other detective responded, "No, no, I'm just reading your rights at this time." After the *Miranda* rights were administered, Ramirez acknowledged what the detective had read by nodding and stating, "I guess that is what I'm here for." Ramirez eventually admitted his involvement not only in the burglary, but also in the murder. He stated that he was the one who shot the victim and claimed that he was acting at Grimshaw's direction. Only after Ramirez fully confessed to the murder did the detectives belatedly obtain a written waiver of his *Miranda* rights. When Ramirez was asked to sign the waiver of rights form after he had fully confessed, the lead detective asked him to acknowledge that he had not been promised anything or been threatened before giving his statement. Ramirez's response was that the detective had only promised to be his friend.

106.  Are Ramirez's statements admissible?

   (A)  All of his statements are admissible because Ramirez was not in custody.
   (B)  His initial statements are inadmissible because he was not *Mirandized*, but the statements made after he was *Mirandized* are admissible.
   (C)  All of his statements are inadmissible.
   (D)  His statements made at home are admissible, but all of his statements at the police station are inadmissible.

Prior to a planned interrogation, a police detective read the *Miranda* rights to a suspect who had been arrested the previous night. When the detective asked the suspect if she understood her rights and was willing to waive them and answer the detective's questions, the suspect answered: "Maybe I should talk with a lawyer. What do you think?" The detective did not respond to the question, but asked the suspect if she was ready to get down to business and answer questions. The suspect nodded, and the detective began the interrogation which produced answers implicating the suspect in a series of armed robberies.

**107.** Are the answers admissible at trial?

    (A) The defendant's answers are inadmissible because they were secured without a valid waiver of the defendant's *Miranda* rights.

    (B) The defendant's answers are inadmissible because he invoked his right to counsel.

    (C) The defendant's answers are admissible because he did not invoke his right to counsel and then waived his rights.

    (D) The defendant's answers are admissible because the defendant's willingness to answer the detective's questions revoked his earlier invocation of the right to counsel.

Allison Aide, a nursing assistant in a retirement home, was arrested for battering residents in her care. Allison was transported to the police station, booked on the charges, and given *Miranda* warnings. Allison signed a written waiver of rights and agreed to questioning. After about half an hour, the questions became much more difficult and incriminating. At first, Allison did not respond to the tougher questions, sitting in absolute silence. She then answered a few questions. When the officer asked her specifically about her actions with one of the alleged battered victims, Allison replied: "I'd rather not make any other comments at this time." The officer did not press Allison to answer the question, instead he asked her questions about other incidents. Allison answered. The interrogation continued for another hour by which time Allison had confessed to battering four of the residents of the nursing home. Allison's attorney filed a motion to suppress all of her answers to questions after she had informed the officer that she did not want to "make any other comments at this time."

108.   The motion should be

(A)   denied because Allison waived her rights.
(B)   granted because Allison rescinded her waiver.
(C)   denied because Allison continued to answer questions.
(D)   granted because she had the right to see an attorney prior to the resumption of questioning.

Thad Lewing, age 18, was arrested for the purse snatching-robbery and murder of a woman on the street. He had been in trouble as a juvenile for a string of robberies. Lewing matched the description given by a person who witnessed the robbery-murder. Police arrested Lewing at his mother's home. Once at the police station, Lewing was taken to an interrogation room where he was read his *Miranda* rights and signed a written waiver. During the interrogation, when confronted by a detective with information that he had been identified by a witness, Lewing said, "I didn't do it and that's all I'm going to say." The interrogation stopped immediately. Lewing was told to remain in the room. About fifteen minutes later, the detective returned and asked Lewing if he wanted to see his mother. He then visited with his mother for fifteen minutes; she encouraged him to tell the truth. As the mother was leaving, the detective walked back in the room and asked Lewing if he was ready to help himself and admit to the robbery-murder. Lewing agreed to talk. Over the next hour, Lewing answered all of the detective's questions and admitted to the robbery and killing.

**109.** Is Lewing's confession admissible?

ANSWER:

Deputies arrived at the residence of defendant Francis Scott in response to a complaint concerning gunshots in the neighborhood. When Mr. Scott was apprehended, he was lying at the bottom of a small ravine behind his residence. He was handcuffed immediately with his hands behind his back and read his *Miranda* rights. The first officer asked if he wanted to talk. Mr. Scott answered, "No." While being led to a police cruiser Scott made a belligerent remark to a second officer and made further statements, innocuous and noninculpatory, such as "I don't believe this is happening." Mr. Scott was placed in a cruiser for a period of about ten to fifteen minutes.

After fifteen minutes, a third officer took Scott out of the police cruiser. Scott said to him, "This is bullshit." After this statement, the third officer asked whether Mr. Scott had been advised of his rights. Mr. Scott answered, "Yeah." That officer further asked whether he was aware that he had the right to an attorney. Mr. Scott again answered, "Yeah." Then the officer asked him what had happened. Mr. Scott replied that there had been a "hassle." The officer asked with whom. Mr. Scott answered, "Glenda." When asked whether he had shot a gun, Mr. Scott replied that he had shot into the air.

**110.** Are Scott's statements to the officer admissible.

ANSWER:

The defendant was arrested when his girlfriend called police and reported that he raped her. Read the *Miranda* warnings, he told the investigating officer that he wanted to see an attorney. Later that day, the defendant met with the public defender. At the end of their meeting, the public defender told the defendant that he would be back the following evening and instructed the defendant not to talk to the police nor even his cellmate. On his way out of the police station, the defender also instructed the police not to interrogate his client.

The following morning, the investigating officer took the defendant from his cell and told him that now that he had seen and talked with a lawyer, it was time for the defendant to talk to the officer. The defendant agreed to talk to the officer and began answering the officer's questions about the alleged rape. His answers incriminated him.

111. Will the defendant's incriminating statements be admissible at trial?

(A) The defendant's incriminating statements are admissible because the defendant consulted with counsel prior to the interrogation.

(B) The defendant's incriminating statements are admissible because the defendant knowingly, intelligently and voluntarily waived his *Miranda* rights.

(C) The defendant's incriminating statements are inadmissible because they were secured in violation of his *Miranda* right to counsel.

(D) The defendant's incriminating statements are inadmissible because the officer failed to read him his *Miranda* warnings at the outset of the second interrogation session.

Arthur was arrested for drunk driving. During a first court appearance, he pleaded not guilty and an attorney was appointed to represent him. Arthur, unable to make bail and ineligible for release without bail, was being held in jail pending trial. During this time, police received a tip from a reliable informer that just prior to the drunk driving arrest, Arthur had robbed a local branch of the American Savings and Loan Bank and shot and killed the bank's security guard.

Following the tip, police placed an undercover agent in the cell with Arthur to question him about the bank robbery. Eventually, the agent, without giving Arthur *Miranda* warnings, engaged Arthur in conversation, including asking him if he had ever "done" anybody. Arthur ended up discussing the bank robbery and the murder of the guard. He also told the agent that after the bank robbery he got blind drunk to forget about the killing and that's when he got arrested for drunk driving.

Arthur was charged with the robbery and murder of the guard. Before trial on the robbery and murder charges, Arthur's attorney moved to suppress the statements made to the undercover agent.

112. Is Arthur's confession to the undercover agent admissible?

(A) The confession is inadmissible because it was secured in violation of defendant's *Miranda* rights.

(B) The confession is inadmissible because it was secured in violation of defendant's Sixth Amendment right to counsel.

(C) The confession is admissible because even though defendant's Sixth Amendment right to counsel had attached, he volunteered the statement to the undercover agent.

(D) The confession is admissible because it did not violate defendant's *Miranda* rights when he did not know he was talking to a police undercover agent.

113. Will the undercover agent be permitted to testify about Arthur's confession about drunk driving at the trial on that charge?

ANSWER:

The defendant was arrested and charged with robbery of a pedestrian who was walking towards a subway station at night. The defendant was picked up just a couple of blocks from the subway station. He had never been in trouble with the police. Immediately after his arrest, he was transported to the subway stop where the victim said that he was not sure but he thought the defendant was the person who had robbed him.

The defendant was taken to the police station where he was given *Miranda* warnings. The defendant agreed to talk to the police and signed a written form waiving his rights. The interrogating officer told the defendant that he had been identified by the victim so that he might as well confess. The defendant insisted that it was a mistake and that he had not committed any crime. This exchange went on for 11 hours. The officer's partner filled in for him for an hour. During the 11 hours, the conversation changed very little. The officer or his partner insisted that they knew the defendant was the robber, and the defendant insisted, sometimes crying hysterically, that he was innocent. In the morning, at the end of the eleventh hour of questioning, the defendant finally agreed with the officer that he had committed the robbery. The officer read the *Miranda* warnings again and then asked the defendant to sign a written statement of his oral confession. The defendant did so while crying hysterically.

The defendant has now recanted the confession and insists that he is innocent. Without the confession, the victim's shaky identification will not be enough to assure the defendant's conviction.

114.  Is the defendant's confession admissible?

   (A)  The confession is admissible because the defendant waived the *Miranda* rights.
   (B)  The confession is admissible because it was voluntarily given.
   (C)  The confession is inadmissible because it was secured in violation of *Miranda.*
   (D)  The confession is inadmissible because it was involuntary.

The 22-year-old defendant is a first year teacher at a suburban high school who developed a crush on a 17-year old junior at the school. The teacher and student had a sexual relationship that lasted for three months. The student was more sexually experienced than the teacher. Their relationship ended when the student became involved with a classmate. He told his new girlfriend about his prior relationship with the teacher, and word about their relationship spread throughout the high school. When the principal heard about the affair, he notified the superintendent's office and the police. After interviewing the 17-year-old who refused to cooperate with the police on the advice of his parents, the police obtained an arrest warrant for the teacher for rape of a minor and arrested her on a Friday afternoon as she left the school.

The teacher was given *Miranda* warnings, and she waived her rights. The investigating officer told her that if she cooperated and told the truth, he might be able to have the case moved to juvenile court because the victim was still a juvenile. Obviously that was not a possibility, but the teacher was looking for any break she could get. She told the officer that she didn't rape the boy, "We loved each other, and I still love him." She admitted to having had sex with the juvenile over a period of three months. Without the juvenile's cooperation, the defendant's admission was the only evidence the state had. All the prosecution needed was to be able to use the admission to prove the defendant's guilt.

115. The statement is

   (A) admissible because the defendant waived her *Miranda* rights.
   (B) admissible because the defendant waived her *Miranda* rights and confessed immediately thereafter.
   (C) inadmissible because the statement was involuntary.
   (D) inadmissible because the defendant should have been allowed to consult with an attorney and have an attorney present during questioning.

The defendant was arrested and charged with crimes arising out of a home repair con scheme to defraud elderly pensioners. Before a preliminary hearing, she was indicted by a grand jury and then arraigned on the indictment. Just prior to trial, the prosecutor had arranged a lineup. The defendant appeared in a lineup along with five other women of similar height, weight and hair color. The four victims who showed up that morning all identified the defendant as the person who had promised extensive home repairs, got them to give her thousands of dollars in deposits, and failed to do any of the work. Later in the afternoon, three other elderly victims, who had not made it to the morning lineup, were shown a picture of the defendant along with five other women. These three victims also picked the defendant from the photo array. The prosecutor did not notify the defendant's lawyer in advance of the lineup or the photo identification.

116. Is evidence about the lineup identification admissible at trial?

ANSWER:

117. May the witnesses who identified the defendant at the lineup testify at trial and identify the defendant as the perpetrator of the fraud?

ANSWER:

118. Is the pretrial identification testimony of the three victims who picked the defendant out of the photo array admissible at trial?

(A) The witnesses' testimony about the pretrial photo identification is admissible because the Sixth Amendment right to counsel does not attach to a photo array identification.

(B) The witnesses may identify the defendant at trial only if that identification is based upon prior contacts with the defendant other than the pretrial photo identification.

(C) The witnesses' pretrial photo identification is inadmissible because the defendant's attorney should have been notified and given an opportunity to attend the presentations of the photo array to the witnesses.

(D) The witnesses' pretrial photo identification is inadmissible because it was likely suggestive.

Tina, looking out her kitchen window while washing dishes toward evening, saw a man walk into the parking lot of her building, open the driver's door of her neighbor's vehicle, look around, get in, and drive out of the parking lot. Tina explained that while the thief was opening the door, he "did look up and glance like a three-quarter turn." Her view of the car thief lasted less than a minute. She contacted the police who came to interview Tina. She described the individual to the officers as: "Early 20's, about 145 pounds, five eight. He had dark brown curly hair, had a dark blue jacket, and a white shirt underneath and blue jeans." Two weeks later, following a raid on a chop shop where her neighbor's car was found and nine men were arrested, the officers interviewed Tina again and showed her a photo array of nine color mug shots of white males. The purpose of the array was to determine whether Tina could identify the thief who stole the automobile. Before presenting the photos to Tina, the officers permitted Tina to review the actual theft report containing her description of the thief. At the photo array, the officer handed the nine photographs face up in a stack to Tina. Looking at just the fronts of the photographs, she selected the defendant's picture without hesitation. Four of the nine photographs were of four of the people arrested at the chop shop." A fifth picture was of a suspect who was also "wanted in connection" with the shop. The other four photos were fillers. Following Tina's photo identification of the defendant, he was charged with grand theft auto.

Defendant's attorney moved to exclude Tina's trial identification of the defendant. At the suppression hearing, Tina agreed that seven of the nine photos depicted men having straight hair. Of the two remaining pictures, one was of a man who has curly brown hair but who barely had any hair on the top of his head. The ninth photo was of the defendant. The other eight photos were of men who were considerably older than the defendant, and five of the photos were of men who were considerably heavier than the defendant. On cross-examination at the trial, Tina agreed that she had told the officers that the thief's hair was fluffy and worn in an "Afro."

**119.** Tina's trial identification testimony is

(A) admissible because the photo identification was made prior to the time the defendant was charged and his Sixth Amendment right to counsel had not attached.

(B) admissible because Tina's trial identification testimony was reliable; she had no reason to lie.

(C) inadmissible because the defendant had been arrested in connection with the chop shop raid, and his attorney should have been contacted about the presentation of the photo array.

(D) inadmissible because the photo identification was impermissibly suggestive, a fact which tainted Tina's in-court identification.

On December 6 around 6:30 p.m., 11-year-old Melinda had gone to a corner store close to her home on Chamberlain Avenue. The day before it had snowed and the side streets, such as Chamberlain, were still slippery. On her way home Melinda noticed a car following her. The car pulled onto Chamberlain. As Melinda turned the corner onto Chamberlain, a man who was "going down in his pocket" as if to get something walked past her and without a word grabbed her neck from behind and started hitting her. She struggled and screamed as she was thrown into the assailant's car. Melinda's younger sister witnessed the beating and abduction and called to her mother. Mrs. Grissom, who was barefoot, ran outside to the car, and grabbed the locked door of the driver's side of the car in which Melinda had been thrown. Mrs. Grissom hung on to the door while screaming for help and for her daughter to jump from the car. The icy road made the car's wheels spin and slowed its travel, thus allowing Mrs. Grissom to hold on to the door and to pound the window and push the car with her hip so that the car bumped into a parked car.

Melinda followed her mother's shouting, and unlocked the door on the passenger's side and jumped out. The commotion was witnessed by two young men who got the license number of the departing car and gave it to Mrs. Grissom. Melinda was taken to the hospital because her leg had been injured in the fall from the car. Within an hour, the car, a 1993 Buick, had been traced to its owner, the defendant's father. The engine was still warm when the police arrived. The defendant, who was at his father's house, admitted that he had been driving the car. He was read his *Miranda* rights and voluntarily accompanied the police to the hospital, where he was positively identified by Mrs. Grissom and her daughter. He was then arrested.

120. Testimony about Melinda's and her mother's identification of the defendant at the hospital is

(A) admissible because the defendant voluntarily accompanied the police to the hospital.

(B) admissible because the identification was reliable.

(C) inadmissible because it was the result of an illegal and unduly suggestive showup.

(D) inadmissible because the defendant was in custody and his Sixth Amendment right to counsel had attached.

# ENTRAPMENT

In June 1990, the FBI asked Richard Stanton, a previously utilized informant, to contact Manouk, who the government believed was laundering money. Stanton was directed to present himself as a money launderer and narcotics organization pilot with good connections in Belize and other Central American countries. Over time, the FBI's investigation evolved into a "reverse sting" narcotics operation. Manouk introduced Stanton to Andy and George. Eventually, Manouk, Andy and George agreed to purchase five kilograms of cocaine from Stanton's "Colombian" sources. Andy, the intended distributor, was arrested when he picked up the cocaine at a Long Beach Holiday Inn parking lot. All three were charged and convicted.

The government argued that appellants were sophisticated cocaine dealers, with prior distribution experience, who were anxious to establish a distribution network in Los Angeles. In negotiations with an FBI agent who posed as an accountant for the fictitious Colombian drug cartel, appellants spoke in code and, right up to the end, seemed aggressive and self-assured.

Manouk and George claimed that they were entrapped by the government. In particular, they pointed to their testimony that Stanton befriended them, represented himself as a "father figure" who would protect their interests, and that they tried to back out of the deal but were told by Stanton that the "Colombians" were "wild" and withdrawal "would be bad" for them. Stanton, they argued, knew about their financial troubles, pushed the drug deal from the start, and did everything in his power to see it consummated.

Andy testified that he got involved, meeting with Stanton and the FBI "accountant," only because he wanted to help Manouk, who had gotten in over his head. When Manouk and George wanted to pull out of the deal, Andy testified, he told them that he would "take care of this thing" and that "[t]his will end in a good way." His plan, he told the jury, was to pick up the cocaine and call the FBI. When arrested, he was carrying an address book containing an FBI agent's telephone number.

All three defendants were convicted. At trial, Manouk and George attempted to raise a constitutional claim that they were entrapped by the government. The trial court denied the motion and submitted the entrapment defense to the jury which rejected it. They appealed.

**121.** Did the trial court err by not dismissing the charges as a matter of constitutional law?

ANSWER:

Teri ("Blue") Collar, a single mother, lost her job when the Ford stamping plant in her hometown closed. Blue had worked at Ford ever since she graduated from high school seventeen years ago. Blue was now desperate to find employment to support herself and her daughter. At the union hall and at the grocery store, Blue asked everyone she met to let her know of any jobs in town. She said she was willing to do absolutely anything. Two months later, she still had not found a job. At the grocery store, Blue ran into Sally, who had also worked at the Ford plant, and who had for years supplied Blue and others at the plant with small quantities of marijuana. Sally had been caught selling drugs when she sold a kilo of marijuana to an undercover officer. She was so scared of going to prison that she agreed to help the police catch other sellers.

When Blue told Sally that she was still looking for a job, Sally suggested that there was good money to be made selling marijuana. Blue hesitated but then laughed and said that she didn't think it was a good idea. Over the next month, Blue still had not found work and ran into Sally several times who continued to suggest that Blue start selling marijuana. Sally promised to set Blue up with a supplier and a list of contacts who were regular buyers. Blue continued to say no, but after five months of unemployment, had decided to take up Sally's offer when she ran into Sally again. Sally provided Blue with a kilo of marijuana (supplied to Sally by the police) and also provided Blue with a list of regular purchasers. Blue sold an ounce to the first person on Sally's list who was an undercover police officer. Blue was arrested and charged with selling marijuana. She raised the defense of entrapment.

**122.**   Should Blue's defense of entrapment prevail?

    (A)   She will not prevail because Blue has a long history of using marijuana.

    (B)   She will not prevail because Sally only provided a means to commit the crime, not the disposition to commit the crime.

    (C)   Blue will prevail because there was no reason for Sally to believe that Blue would commit the crime before suggesting that she sell marijuana.

    (D)   Blue will prevail because she did not succumb to Sally's offer at first.

The defendant was riding with his girlfriend in her father's car, a brand new Cadillac. A police officer, stopped at a red light next to the Cadillac, decided to follow the car because of the race and youth of the occupants. After following for about a mile, the officer observed the Cadillac fail to come to a full stop at a stop sign. The officer turned on his roof top light and pulled the Cadillac over. When the officer walked over to the Cadillac, the driver said, "I'm sorry, officer. You made me so nervous following us that I did not see the stop sign until I began the turn." The officer ordered the occupants out of the car and searched it. In the back seat of the vehicle, the officer found the defendant's back pack. In the back pack, the officer found a significant quantity of rock cocaine. The defendant was charged with possession with intent to distribute. Defendant's attorney moved to suppress the evidence.

123.   The motion to suppress will be

   (A)   granted because the officer conducted an illegal search.
   (B)   granted because the officer while conducting a legal search of the vehicle did not have authority to search a passenger's belongings.
   (C)   denied because a passenger in a vehicle does not have standing to challenge a search of a vehicle.
   (D)   denied because the search was lawful incident to a valid stop of the vehicle.

Let's manipulate the facts in the previous question. What if, after following the vehicle for a mile, the officer did not observe any traffic violations? At the end of the mile, the officer decided to pull the car over to see if it was stolen. After ordering the occupants out of the vehicle, the officer searched the car and, again, found in the defendant passenger's backpack the quantity of crack cocaine. The defendant's attorney, again, moved to suppress the evidence found in the defendant's backpack.

124.   The motion to suppress will be

   (A)   granted because the officer conducted an illegal search.
   (B)   granted because the search was incident to an illegal stop.
   (C)   denied because the defendant-passenger has no standing to challenge the search.
   (D)   denied because the defendant-passenger has no standing to challenge the stop.

Police arrived at a home during a party to search for illegal drugs. They informed all the guests that they were free to leave as soon as they were searched. The defendant, a guest at the party, stashed his drugs in his date's purse. The police searched the purse and found the drugs; the defendant admitted that the drugs were his. The defendant was charged with illegal possession of narcotics. The defendant's attorney moved to suppress the drugs, but the state countered that the defendant does not have standing to challenge the search.

**125.** Will the motion to suppress the drugs be granted?

ANSWER:

The defendant, Carter, had spent an evening at the home of a casual friend, Sara Thompson. After the party when all of the other guests had left, Carter, a drug dealer, sat at Thompson's kitchen table and cut a kilo of cocaine and divided it into packets for sale. He gave Thompson a small quantity of the cocaine in return for letting him use her apartment. The two then had sex. While Carter and Thompson were having sex, police, who had been following Carter, broke into the house, seized the cocaine on the table, and arrested Carter who admitted that the cocaine was his. Carter was charged with possession of cocaine for sale. Prior to trial, Carter's attorney moved to suppress the cocaine. The state claimed that Carter did not have standing to challenge the search of Thompson's apartment.

**126.** The motion to suppress should be

    (A)   granted because the search of the apartment was unlawful.

    (B)   denied because the police entry was lawful to prevent the destruction of the evidence.

    (C)   denied because the defendant had no privacy interest in the house when he used it to process the illegal drugs.

    (D)   granted because the defendant was a lawful social and sexual guest, and the police could not enter without a warrant.

At the conclusion of a suppression hearing to determine whether evidence secured during the stop of an automobile should be admitted at trial, the judge ruled that the police officer's testimony was credible and the driver and her passenger's testimony were not. The court ruled that the evidence could be used by the prosecution at trial because the defendant had failed to prove that she did not consent to a search of her car. On appeal, the defendant claimed that the police officer's testimony was not believable and that the trial court erroneously applied the law of consent searches.

127.    The trial court's finding that the police officer's testimony was credible and the defendant's and her witness's testimony incredible

    (A)    was erroneous because the one officer's testimony was contradicted by two witnesses.

    (B)    will be overturned by the court of appeals if the court finds the defendant and her witness's testimony to be more credible.

    (C)    will stand because the court of appeals virtually never substitutes its judgment for that of the trial court on a question of fact.

    (D)    will stand because the trial court's finding on a question of fact is not subject to review on appeal.

128.    The trial court's conclusion that the defendant failed to prove that the search was illegal

    (A)    will be reversed on appeal because the conclusion is based upon an erroneous finding of fact.

    (B)    will be reversed on appeal because it is based upon an erroneous conclusion of law.

    (C)    will be affirmed because the trial court's findings are entitled to deference.

    (D)    will be affirmed because the moving party seeks to upset the status quo and bears the burden of proof.

A police officer observed a young man wearing gym shorts and a T-shirt hanging around a street corner late at night, a street corner known to police as a high drug-trafficking location. As the officer approached the corner, the young man turned his back on the officer, crossed the street and walked in the opposite direction. The officer followed. Two blocks from where the officer first observed the young man, the officer ordered him to stop. The young man stopped in his tracks and turned towards the officer. The officer pushed the young man up against the store front, told him to put his hands over his head against the glass and to spread his legs. The officer then reached into the front of the young man's gym shorts and found a clear plastic baggy containing several rocks of crack cocaine.

The defendant was charged with possession of crack cocaine for sale. The defense moved to suppress the evidence seized from the defendant's shorts. At the suppression hearing the officer and the defendant testified identically about what happened the night of the arrest. At the conclusion of the evidence, the trial court denied the motion to suppress, holding that the officer had probable cause to arrest the defendant, and the evidence was found during a search incident to arrest. The defendant entered a conditional plea to the charge and was found guilty. The defendant appealed the conviction claiming that the trial court erred in its ruling.

**129.** How should the court rule on the appeal?

ANSWER:

What if the judge in the previous question had granted the defendant's motion to suppress, and the state elected to appeal immediately from that ruling? The state asks the appellate court to hear its interlocutory appeal so that the evidence would be available to the prosecution at trial.

**130.** Will the appellate court consider the interlocutory appeal?

ANSWER:

Defendant Larry Carter, charged with aggravated trafficking in cocaine, moved to suppress evidence gained from a search of his residence and garage. On February 19, at 10:15 a.m., Officer Lowe testified he was in an unmarked cruiser traveling southbound on Philadelphia Drive approaching West Riverview when he noticed a white Bronco truck parked behind a garage in an alley. Lowe said he observed Larry Carter seated in the driver's seat and he noticed Chris Ross standing by the corner of a garage carrying some type of bundle in his arms. Lowe said Ross switched the bundle from his left arm to his right arm. Lowe said the bundle seemed heavy and was wrapped in something gray. Lowe said he watched Ross get in the passenger seat of the Bronco and Carter then drove the Bronco down the alley and onto Everett.

With back up assistance, Officer Lowe made a "felony stop" on the car; the subjects were ordered out of the vehicle at gunpoint. Officer Lowe looked in the car and saw a bundle lying on the front floorboard and it appeared to be the bundle he saw Ross carrying into the Bronco. Lowe said he unwrapped the gray bundle and found a small package wrapped in brown opaque paper. He unwrapped the package and found two pounds of cocaine. A search warrant was obtained to search Carter's home and garage where Officer Lowe first observed the defendants. The search uncovered a large quantity of cocaine in the garage. Carter was charged based upon the evidence found in the garage. Officer Lowe admitted upon cross-examination that he did not observe Carter or Ross violate any law prior to the stop.

The defendants moved to suppress the evidence found in the car and the garage.

**131.** How should the court rule?

ANSWER:

The defendant, arrested a block away from a jewelry store that had just been robbed, met the description given by the proprietor. Immediately following the arrest, the arresting officers searched the defendant and found a gun sticking out of his pants. They asked him what he had done with the stolen jewelry. The defendant told the police that he discarded the jewelry in the trash container at the corner when he saw the patrol car with flashing lights approaching. One of the officers retrieved the jewelry from the container.

Prior to trial, the defendant moved to suppress his response to the officer's question and the jewelry.

132. How should the court rule?

(A) Both the defendant's statement and the jewelry should be suppressed because the officer failed to give the defendant *Miranda* warnings and the jewelry is derivative of the *Miranda* violation.

(B) Both the statement and the jewelry are admissible because *Miranda* warnings need not be given during a public safety emergency.

(C) The defendant's statement is inadmissible because of the *Miranda* violation, but the jewelry is admissible.

(D) The statement and the jewelry are inadmissible because the defendant's statement was involuntary and taints the derivative evidence.

The defendant was the manager and only employee of a rare coin shop. The absentee owner of the shop reported to police that seven sets of rare coins had disappeared from the shop over a period of seven days. After store closed each day, the owner would enter the shop, go over the books, remove the proceeds of the day and check the inventory. He began to notice that the coins were missing.

Police followed the defendant home one day. As the defendant unlocked his apartment door and entered, the police followed before he was able to shut the door. The officers searched the defendant and the apartment, finding one set of coins on the table by the doorway where the defendant put down what he was carrying. The police took the defendant to the police station. After he was booked, the police read the defendant his *Miranda* rights and he confessed to stealing from his employer. Prior to trial, the defendant moved to suppress his confession.

133.    How should the court rule?

   (A)    The warrantless entry of the defendant's apartment was justified by exigent circumstances to prevent the destruction of evidence; therefore, the confession secured with *Miranda* warnings is admissible.

   (B)    The warrantless entry of the defendant's apartment was a Fourth Amendment violation, and the confession is inadmissible because it is the fruit of the poisonous tree.

   (C)    The warrantless arrest of the defendant was without probable cause, and the confession is inadmissible because it is derivative of the Fourth Amendment violation.

   (D)    The warrantless entry of the defendant's apartment to make an arrest was a Fourth Amendment violation, but the confession is not derivative of that violation.

The defendant was arrested during a dragnet arrest of young black men after a woman reported that she had been robbed by a young black man. Fourteen people were arrested and presented to the robbery victim in a series of lineups. She identified the defendant as the perpetrator who had robbed her in broad daylight as she exited a Giant Eagle supermarket. The defendant was charged with robbery, the principal witness against the defendant being the robbery victim. The defendant's attorney moved to suppress the victim's courtroom identification testimony as the fruit of an illegal arrest. The court denied the defense motion. The victim testified and identified the defendant in the courtroom. The victim testified that she had ample opportunity to view the defendant during the robbery. The defendant was convicted and appeals.

134. How should the court rule on appeal?

   (A) The in-court identification of the defendant was legal even though his presence in court was derivative of an illegal arrest.

   (B) The in-court identification of the defendant was legal because he was lawfully arrested following the lineup identification.

   (C) The in-court identification of the defendant was illegal because it was derivative of an illegal arrest.

   (D) The in-court identification of the defendant was illegal because it was derivative of an illegal lineup.

Police executing a valid search warrant at the home of a mob kingpin entered the home without knocking and searched the home finding the evidence listed in the search warrant. The defense moved to suppress the evidence found during the search. Police officers testifying at the suppression hearing did not offer any reasons for failing to knock, announcing their identity, and waiting for the occupants to open the door.

135. How should the court rule on the motion to suppress?

   (A) The motion to suppress should be granted because the judge issuing the search warrant did not authorize a no-knock entry, and the police violated the defendant's Fourth Amendment rights.

   (B) The motion to suppress should be denied because, even though the police violated the defendant's Fourth Amendment rights, the evidence was seized pursuant to a valid search warrant.

   (C) The motion to suppress should be granted because there was no exigency to justify the no-knock entry.

(D)  The motion to suppress should be denied because the Fourth Amendment does not require police to knock and announce themselves and wait before entering to execute a valid search warrant.

Police obtained numerous reports that Coca Mary was selling marijuana out of her first floor duplex apartment. One of the reports came to the police from an established informant who advised the police that he had purchased a large quantity of marijuana from Mary. The police maintained a watch on the apartment and observed an unusually high number of people come to the porch of the house, knock on Mary's door, and engage in a momentary conversation which might be consistent with drug transactions.

The officer running the informant instructed him to break into Mary's apartment while she was at work to determine if the apartment contained a large amount of marijuana and its location. The informant reported back to the officer that he was inside the apartment and found a closet full of marijuana and other drugs right off the front entry. The police then obtained a search warrant for Coca Mary's apartment, and found the closet full of drugs when executing the warrant. Coca Mary has been charged with possession for sale of marijuana and other drugs, an offense that carries a mandatory prison sentence. The defense filed a motion to suppress the drugs found in the closet.

**136.** How should the court rule on the motion?

ANSWER:



The defendant was stopped for suspicion of drunk driving when police officers observed his vehicle weaving in traffic. The officers ordered the defendant out of the vehicle. It became evident during roadside sobriety tests that the defendant was not operating the vehicle under the influence. While one officer administered the sobriety tests, the other officer searched the vehicle and in the trunk found a quantity of illegal drugs. The officers arrested the driver. In the jurisdiction, illegal weaving does not authorize a custodial arrest. At the suppression hearing, the state claimed that the drugs should be admitted under the inevitable discovery exception to the exclusionary rule.

**137.** How should the court rule on the motion to suppress?

(A) The motion should be granted because the search was incident to issuance of a traffic summons.

(B) The motion should be denied because the police would have found a sufficient reason to search the vehicle.

(C) The motion should be granted because there was no alternative legal justification to search the vehicle, and the drugs were not discovered under the inevitable discovery exception.

(D)   The motion should be denied because following the defendant's arrest, the vehicle would have been impounded and the drugs inevitably discovered during an inventory search.

In the early morning of May 2, 2008, Chattanooga police officers received an anonymous telephone tip reporting that the residents of 824 Arlington Avenue were selling drugs. In response to the complaint, officers conducted a warrantless search of the residence, which was shared by Akridge and his roommates Kevin Ellison and Tiffany Stewart. During the search of the apartment, officers found marijuana, cocaine, and three loaded semi-automatic pistols. On June 19, 2008, ATF officials interviewed Akridge, Ellison, and Stewart regarding the May 2008 search of their residence. All three admitted to selling crack cocaine and marijuana, and Akridge further admitted to firearms possession and selling drugs from the Arlington Avenue residence, although he later denied making such a confession. Akridge, Stewart, and Ellison subsequently were arrested on June 20, 2008 for drug trafficking and firearms possession.

On June 27, 2008, Stewart executed a plea agreement, not entered of record with the Court until January 5, 2009, in which she pled guilty to a charge of aiding and abetting Ellison and Akridge in drug trafficking. On October 3, 2008, the Government reached a plea agreement with Ellison. At Akridge's trial Ellison and Stewart testified on behalf of the prosecution; the Government also presented a tape of an incriminatory phone call made from the Hamilton County jail by Akridge to his girlfriend. Following a suppression hearing, the trial court granted a motion to suppress all of the evidence found during the search of the house, but denied the motion to suppress the testimony of Ellison and Stewart. The defendant Akridge was convicted and later appealed, challenging the trial court's decision to permit Ellison and Stewart to testify.

138.   How should the court of appeals rule?

(A)   The court of appeals should reverse the conviction because the witnesses' testimony was the fruit of the illegal search of the apartment.

(B)   The court of appeals should affirm the conviction because live witness testimony can never be the fruit of the poisonous tree.

(C)   The court should affirm the conviction because the witnesses would have been inevitably discovered notwithstanding the illegal search.

(D)   The court should affirm the conviction because Stewart and Ellison's testimony was sufficiently attenuated from the illegal search.

Denny Dealer sold small quantities of marijuana along Main Street, which bordered on a university campus. Denny had never been arrested, nor had he any dealing with the police. On Thursday evening as he turned onto Main Street, a police officer grabbed Denny and forced him up against a wall. The officer then searched Denny and found a dozen packets of marijuana concealed in Denny's underwear. Denny was charged with possession with intent to sell.

The trial judge suppressed the evidence found in Denny's underwear as well as the testimony of the police officer who conducted the search. The prosecution produced a few university students who testified to buying small quantities of marijuana from Denny. Denny was called as the principal defense witness. On direct examination, Denny denied ever selling marijuana. He claimed never to have possessed any more than a very small quantity of marijuana for personal use. On cross-examination, the prosecutor began to question Denny about the night of his arrest and the dozen packets of marijuana found on his person. The defense attorney objected to the line of questioning.

**139.** How should the trial judge rule?

(A) The judge should deny the motion and allow the defendant to be questioned about the drugs seized in violation of the Fourth Amendment.

(B) The judge should deny the motion because the defendant had lied while testifying.

(C) The judge should grant the motion because to allow the prosecution to question about the seized marijuana is to allow the government to benefit from its own illegality.

(D) The judge should grant the motion because the evidence was suppressed.

Maria lived with her boyfriend Danny who ran out of their house a sophisticated business buying and disposing of stolen cars. The cars were either sold to area chop shops where they were dismantled and sold for parts or shipped to Canada where they were sold to unknowing buyers. Maria handled all the paper work for Danny. Armed with a valid search warrant, police lawfully entered the home and searched for and seized records pertaining to the stolen car operation. Maria and Danny were both arrested.

At the police station, Maria was questioned by Detective Madden who did not read Maria the *Miranda* warnings. Danny had provided for this eventuality and had instructed Maria that if the police came to the house or she was arrested she should not answer any questions about the business. Nonetheless, during a two hour interrogation, Maria weakened and told Detective Madden about her involvement in the business. She was indicted in connection with the business. The defendants were tried separately.

Prior to Maria's trial, her confession was suppressed. At the trial Maria testified. She admitted to knowing about Danny's illegal enterprise but denied any involvement in his business. On cross-examination, the prosecutor sought to destroy her credibility by asking Maria about her confession. In summation, the prosecutor's strongest argument for conviction rested on Maria's own confession. Maria was convicted and appealed.

**140.** Should the conviction be reversed?

    (A) Yes. A confession secured without *Miranda* warnings is inadmissible for any purpose.

    (B) Yes. A confession secured without *Miranda* warnings may be used only to impeach a defendant's testimony.

    (C) No. The confession was not used until Maria took the witness stand and lied.

    (D) No. The confession was used only to impeach Maria's credibility.

Let's change the facts in the previous question. Detective Madden read Maria the *Miranda* warnings prior to questioning. When Detective Madden asked Maria if she was prepared to waive the *Miranda* rights, she responded no and asked to call the lawyer who had represented Danny in a previous case. Detective Madden ignored her request and began interrogating her as to the business. After two hours, she gave a full confession implicating herself in the criminal enterprise and detailing her role in the business. Once again, Maria elected to testify and deny any involvement in the illegal business. On cross-examination, the prosecutor began to question her about the confession she had given Detective Madden. The defense attorney objected.

**141.** How should the court rule?

    (A) The court should sustain the objection and not allow the prosecutor to use the confession because Detective Madden intentionally violated Maria's *Miranda* right to counsel.

    (B) The court should sustain the objection and not allow the prosecutor to use the confession because it was secured in violation of Maria's Sixth Amendment right to counsel.

    (C) The court should overrule the objection and allow the prosecutor to use the confession because Maria knew her rights and elected to make a statement.

    (D) The court should overrule the objection and allow the prosecutor to use the confession to impeach Maria's credibility.

Change the facts again. Detective Madden did not read *Miranda* rights to Maria. Instead, during the two hour interrogation he banged on the table and shouted at her that she would go away for life if she did not cooperate and confess her involvement in Danny's illegal business. After about an hour and a half, another detective came into the room and whispered in Madden's ear. After the second detective left the room, Madden informed Maria (falsely) that Danny was talking and had told the other detective of Maria's role in the business. Again, Detective Madden banged on the table and shouted at Maria that she was a goner if she did not cooperate. At that point, sobbing, Maria confessed her role in the illegal enterprise. At trial, Maria took the witness stand and lied. On cross-examination, the prosecutor sought to use the confession for the limited purpose of impeaching Maria's credibility. The defense objected.

**142.** Should the court sustain the objection?

(A) Yes. The statement may not be used because of the *Miranda* violation.

(B) Yes. The statement may not be used because it was involuntary and violated Maria's Fifth Amendment rights.

(C) No. The statement may be used for all purposes because Maria elected to testify and then lied.

(D) No. The statement may be used to impeach Maria's credibility because she elected to testify and then lied on the witness stand.

The defendant stabbed a man during an altercation at a bus stop. The defendant ran from the scene but was identified by several witnesses. The victim later died at the hospital. An arrest warrant was issued for the defendant. Several months later, the defendant was driving and rear ended a police car. When the police officer radioed headquarters about the accident, he was informed that there was an outstanding arrest warrant for the defendant. The defendant was taken to the police station, and informed, during booking, why he was arrested. Later after the booking, the defendant was advised of his *Miranda* rights and he asked for a lawyer. At trial, the defendant took the witness stand and testified that he had stabbed the victim in self defense. During cross-examination the prosecutor sought to use the defendant's failure to tell the arresting officer or the booking officer that he had killed in self-defense. The defense attorney objected.

**143.** How should the court rule?

(A) The court should allow the prosecutor to use the defendant's failure to come forward and his subsequent failure to tell the police at any time that he killed in self-defense.

(B) The court should allow the prosecutor to use the defendant's failure to come forward and his failure to tell the police that he killed in self-defense at the time of his arrest; the prosecutor may not use the defendant's silence to impeach him following the arrest.

(C) The court should allow the prosecutor to use the defendant's failure to come forward and his failure to tell the police at the time of the arrest that he killed in self-defense; the prosecutor may not use the defendant's silence to impeach him after he was taken to the police station.

(D) The court should allow the prosecutor to use the defendant's failure to come forward and his silence at the time of and following his arrest until the defendant was given the *Miranda* warnings.

You are the Hazzard County prosecutor in the State of Duke, which follows the Federal Rules of Criminal Procedure. Sheriff Cletus Coaltrain informs you that he has just arrested Cooter, a local mechanic, for various felonies and misdemeanors. Since your office is very busy, you would like to have as few trials as the law allows. Ignore any perceived venue problems.

Cooter has been charged with the following crimes:

    I.   Conspiracy with several customers in Hazzard to commit theft by disguising minor automotive damage so that it would appear to insurance investigators that the vehicle was a total loss.

    II   Illegal dumping of hazardous waste products generated routinely during auto repairs. This is a misdemeanor in the State of Duke punishable up to six months in prison.

    III.   Conspiracy to commit insurance fraud by teaching other mechanics how to disguise motor vehicle damage so it would seem a wrecked car is a total loss and then splitting the proceeds of the scam.

**144.** Which of the above crimes can be joined together at a single trial of Cooter under Rule 8 of the Federal Rules of Criminal Procedure?

    (A)  None of the above; each must be tried separately.

    (B)  I and II.

    (C)  I and III.

    (D)  II and III.

Wilhemina Madison was arrested in connection with a series of four murders committed in the Rockies National Park over a period of two years. Each murder was especially brutal although the only outward similarity between all the cases was that the crimes were committed against hikers who were apparently by themselves at the time of their abduction or murder. Each victim was killed in a different manner: shot, stabbed, strangled, and injected with a toxic poison. All of the victims were eventually found in wooded areas several miles from the scene of their abduction. The FBI has built a complex case of circumstantial evidence for each of the four crimes and the U.S. Attorney has joined all four homicides in a single trial. Thompson's defense attorney has filed a timely motion under Rule 14 of the Federal Rules of Criminal Procedure to have each homicide tried in a separate proceeding.

**145.** You are the judge's law clerk. Your boss has indicated that she is inclined to grant the defendant's motion and has asked you for reasons that she can put into her opinion to justify her ruling granting the severance. Briefly state your reasons to the judge. Do not draft a formal memorandum.

ANSWER:

Relying on a valid arrest warrant, federal drug authorities arrested Max, who had a long criminal record for various drug offenses, as he boarded a train in Boston. At the time of the arrest, authorities found a large cache of heroin in the suitcase Max was carrying and a small pistol in his pocket. Max was charged with two crimes: possession of heroin and being a felon in possession of a firearm.

**146.** If the U.S. Attorney wants to join these offenses in one *trial* under Rules 8(a) and 13, would they survive a Rule 8 motion to sever for improper joinder?

(A) Yes. Officers found the gun at the time of the arrest for the heroin possession and the two crimes are closely interrelated since drug dealers often carry weapons to protect themselves.

(B) Yes. In order to preserve resources, prosecutors can join all charges they have against one defendant in the same trial.

(C) No. Gun possession is an entirely different kind of crime from drug dealing.

(D) No. It would be unfairly prejudicial to include the gun possession count and the drug count in the same trial.

Sarah used a sophisticated computer program to obtain credit card numbers from the computer files of the Belle Boutique #1, an upscale women's clothing store. The local newspaper published a detailed account of the theft. A week later Ken stole credit card numbers from the computer files of Belle Boutique #2, also an upscale women's clothing store and also owned by the same corporation that owned Belle Boutique #1. The two stores used the same, linked computer system and had the same security codes protecting the information in it. This jurisdiction has adopted the Federal Rules of Criminal Procedure in all relevant aspects.

**147.** Which of the following, if true, would be most helpful to the prosecutor if he or she tries to join Sarah and Ken in one trial?

(A) an eyewitness saw Sarah and Ken at a coffeehouse and overheard them talking about defeating some kind of computer security system.

(B) Sarah and Ken both shopped at the Belle Boutique stores.

(C) when Sarah was arrested for the credit card crime, Ken put up the money for her bail bond.

(D) Ken's method of hacking into the computer system mirrored Sarah's in every way, including many details not printed in the paper.

The Anderson's house was burgled while they were on vacation in Europe. Herb and Donald were arrested for the crime when a neighbor saw two men break a window and climb in the house. The neighbor called the police who arrested Herb and Donald as they left the home carrying an envelope with $4500 in it. At a line up, the neighbor clearly identified Herb as one of the two who entered the house and said that she thought that Donald "might well have been the second one."

Herb and Donald each hired a defense lawyer. Herb suspects that Donald may cooperate with the police and implicate Herb, who was the instigator of the burglary and who talked Donald into participating in it. The district attorney seeks to try them together for the burglary. This jurisdiction follows the Federal Rules of Criminal Procedure in all relevant aspects.

**148.** Is joinder proper? If so, what other alternatives are available to Donald's lawyer in pursuit of a separate trial?

ANSWER:

You represent a woman charged in federal court with the illegal purchase of food stamps. The government plans to try your client together with the alleged co-conspirator who sold the stamps to your client. You want a separate trial for your client.

**149.** What standard will you have to meet in order to persuade the court to grant a Rule 14 motion for discretionary severance?

(A) The government has the burden to show that joinder is not prejudicial to either defendant's rights. It must establish that there was no serious risk of actual prejudice to a specified trial right or likelihood that a jury would be unable to make a reliable decision.

(B) The government has the burden to show that joinder is not prejudicial to either defendant's rights. The government must establish that there was no reasonable possibility of prejudice, or of a reasonable uncertainty that a jury might not be able to make a reliable decision.

(C) Your client has the burden to show prejudice. Most courts require that she show a serious or substantial risk that a joint trial would compromise a specific trial right or would prevent the jury from making a reliable judgment of guilt or innocence.

(D) Your client has the burden to show prejudice. She must show a reasonable possibility of prejudice from the joint trial.

Debbi Duncan, a radical anti-industrialist, was charged in federal court with mailing a series of six deadly pipe bombs to factories throughout the Midwest. The bombs were sent every two months. Three of the bombs exploded when opened. Investigators believe that Debbi was in the process of mailing the bombs to a series of locations that when plotted on a U.S. map, would make the pattern of a $ sign. Six bombs were mailed before federal agents arrested Debbi. The U.S. Attorney has sought to try her on all six bombings in one trial.

**150.** Which of the following facts, if true, would most strongly support Debbi's Rule 8(a) Motion for Relief from Improper Joinder of Offenses?

(A)  since each bomb was sent to a factory a long distance from the target of any other bomb, it would be difficult for the defense to adequately investigate each location in time for one trial.

(B)  each bomb was mailed from a different Florida post office.

(C)  each bomb was manufactured differently and had a different kind of detonation device.

(D)  only three of the bombs actually exploded. Regarding the three bombs that did not explode, the federal grand jury only returned misdemeanor charges on those occurrences.

151. In which of the following scenarios is Federal Rules of Criminal Procedure 3's requirements, as amended by case law, of a valid complaint NOT violated?

(A) FBI agent Jones submitted a sworn, signed statement that "Defendant Ramona Smith committed an act of terrorism against the United States" and a federal magistrate judge signed the complaint.

(B) FBI agent Smith appeared before a magistrate judge in a pressing narcotics case. He detailed the essential facts of the case, and the magistrate suggested the charged offense. The FBI agent wrote the statement containing the essential facts of the charge but did not sign it, and hurried back to the U.S Attorney's Office, where the supervising Assistant U.S. Attorney signed a separate statement indicating that she had read Agent Smith's statement. The magistrate judge signed the complaint.

(C) FBI agent Vegas submitted a written, sworn statement to a magistrate judge containing the essential facts and the charged offenses, using language that substantially mirrored the words in the federal criminal law allegedly violated. In court, the magistrate judge cornered an Assistant U.S. Attorney who signed the statement.

(D) FBI agent O'Malley submitted a written statement to a *state* judge because all the federal magistrate judges were at a conference for federal judicial personnel. The written statement contained the essential facts and the charged offenses. Since no U.S. Attorney was available, a secretary signed the name of the United States Attorney for the District. The state judge signed the complaint.

Martin was arrested by federal drug authorities pursuant to an arrest warrant on Second Avenue at 2:00 A.M. on Tuesday, April 2, selling drugs to an informant. The crime and arrest occurred in an area covered by the United States District Court for the Eastern District of State A. Because of budgetary issues, local jails were shut down after 1:00 A.M. and Martin was taken to a nearby federal penitentiary located in the adjoining federal district (the United States District Court for the Western District of State A) inside the same state. As a federal warden of the prison where Martin is housed, you are aware that you are required to take Martin to a judge.

152. Assume that the arrest was made on the basis of a valid arrest warrant issued the day before the arrest and based on a complaint filed by a federal undercover drug agent. Under Rule 5 of the Federal Rules of Criminal Procedure, where and when should you take Martin before a magistrate?

ANSWER:

153. Same facts as question 152 except the crime occurred in the area covered by the Eastern District of State A, but the arrest was ten miles away in the Western District of State A. Where must the initial appearance be held?

ANSWER:

154. Changing the facts, how would your decision be affected if the arrest were made without a warrant?

ANSWER:

A three-year-old chid was killed by a stray bullet as she sat near a living room window in a housing project. The police investigated and arrested "Little Scott" Legus, the son of a very prominent politician. Legus had gone to the housing project to buy cocaine and sell a stolen pistol. He had forgotten to unload the gun, which fired the stray bullet when he handed it to a potential customer.

The victim's mother and a group of residents in the project have demanded that the local district attorney prosecute Legus for negligent homicide. The district attorney, an elected official, looked into the matter and decided not to prosecute since it was 'just an accident, no more."

The mother has obtained the services of a large law firm's *pro bono* team and has filed suit against the prosecutor to force her to file charges against Legus.

155.  The court should

(A)  issue the injunction compelling the district attorney to prosecute Legus in good faith.

(B)  empanel a grand jury and order the case presented to them.

(C)  appoint a special prosecutor.

(D)  dismiss the action.

Claudio was arrested operating a professional gambling location. He was taken to the local jail, then to an initial appearance before Judge Cotton who set bond at $2500. Claudio's counsel explained to him that there were several options for obtaining release from custody.

156. If Claudio will appear as directed for all court appearances and wants to save as much money as possible, which of the following modes of release would cost him the MOST money in the long run?

   (A) cash bond.
   (B) surety bond using a bail bonding company.
   (C) property bond.
   (D) unsecured bond.

Golda is arrested for the federal felony of illegal importation of a restricted animal species. She was taken promptly before a federal magistrate. She has no criminal record. The Bail Reform Act of 1984 discusses many possible options when a federal magistrate deals with a person, such as Golda, charged with a federal offense. The federal judicial officer is given a hierarchy of choices.

157. According to the Bail Reform Act, the option most preferred for Golda is

   (A) release on conditions.
   (B) release on personal recognizance.
   (C) release on secured bond.
   (D) temporary detention.

In assessing whether a person charged with a crime of violence should be released or detained pending trial, the Bail Reform Act of 1984 establishes a standard of proof the judge must use in deciding whether any condition(s) will reasonably assure the safety of another person and the community.

158. What is the standard of proof for this determination?

   (A) probable cause.
   (B) preponderance of the evidence.
   (C) clear and convincing evidence.
   (D) beyond a reasonable doubt.

After a five-year undercover investigation, federal authorities arrested Merriweather for selling and transporting drugs. Merriweather was arrested in her truck and a search revealed three automatic weapons, baby formulas, and a large quantity of cocaine. Her counsel, Marilyn Fogel, has asked the judge to order Merriweather's release pending trial, arguing that the defendant's boyfriend forced her to drive the truck and that she is a mother of two young children who need her to take care of them. Your boss, the Assistant United States Attorney handling the case, has asked you, as a law clerk, for advice on whether the Bail Reform Act of 1984 contains any provisions facilitating detaining Merriweather until the trial.

**159.** Advise your boss.

ANSWER:


You are a federal appellate judge presiding in the appeal of a case involving Carlos Fuentes who is in jail awaiting trial for holding hostages in a federal building at gunpoint. Fuentes was a former police lieutenant who allegedly took the hostages to make the point that his law enforcement colleagues had framed him for embezzling from the police department and killing an undercover police investigator. Fuentes had threatened to "get even with those lying suckers."

At a detention hearing, defense counsel argued that Fuentes should be released until the trial because he has long-term community ties, a steady job, and no criminal record. The federal magistrate judge rejected these arguments and ordered Fuentes to remain in jail until the trial in three months. In giving her judgment, the magistrate judge said, "I believe your client will appear for trial but he is a threat to the safety of the community because this fallen angel seemed pretty comfortable waiving a gun at these civil servants and making serious threats to good people," pointing to several people sitting in the courtroom.

Defense counsel has appealed this decision, based on a prediction of future criminality, arguing its constitutionally infirm since the only reason a person should be detained is a reasonable likelihood that he or she will not appear for trial. Otherwise the presumption of innocence is meaningless.

**160.** How will you rule on the appeal?

ANSWER:


**161.** The United States Constitution deals with the concept of bail in the Eighth Amendment. What practice is barred by this provision?

    (A)   excessive bail.

    (B)   denial of bail.

    (C)   setting money bail on indigent and minorities in violation of the Due Process Clause.

(D) allowing professional bail bonding companies to use excessive force to detain bail jumpers.

(E) all of the above.

(F) only (A) and (B).

You are a district attorney in a small town where a high school teacher, Mr. Farrell, was arrested for having sex with a young woman a few days before the woman turned eighteen. After looking into the case and discovering that the young woman had initiated the sexual experience and clearly consented to it, you take the case to the grand jury with a strong recommendation that the grand jury not issue an indictment. The grand jury took your advice and did not indict Mr. Farrell for statutory rape or anything else.

When the local paper learned of your decision, it began a strong campaign to have Mr. Farrell prosecuted by you "or someone more tuned in to this community. Facing re-election next year, you are now reconsidering your position and have identified four possible options:

    I. Resubmit the matter to a different grand jury.

    II. Do nothing. The grand jury decision acts as an acquittal and further prosecution is barred by the Double Jeopardy Clause.

    III. Seek Mr. Farrell's permission to proceed by information.

    IV. Ask the same grand jury to reconsider.

162.   In a typical jurisdiction with no statutes or rule on point, which of the following statements accurately reflects your choices among the above options:

    (A)  I, III, and IV only.
    (B)  I and III only.
    (C)  I only.
    (D)  II only.

On Sunday at midnight the transit workers began to strike, effectively halting all public transportation in the city. A grand jury has been hearing cases for several months and is nearing the end of its docket. While some grand jurors are unable to get to the federal court this morning because of the strike, many were able to walk or get a ride to the court house and want to continue working on their caseload by hearing witnesses and resolving cases.

163.   Under the Federal Rules of Criminal Procedure, what is the minimum number of grand jurors who must vote to indict in order to return a valid federal indictment?

    (A)  24
    (B)  12

(C)  9

(D)  16

The supply room in a federal court is preparing to order one new notepad for each of the grand jurors in one jury room.

164.  How many notepads must be ordered if the maximum number of grand jurors appear on the day the pads are distributed?

(A)  40

(B)  12

(C)  24

(D)  23

A defense attorney received a copy of an indictment charging her client with wire fraud. She later learned that when witness Hernandez testified, he did so with a Spanish interpreter because he did not speak any English. The defense attorney also learned that the Assistant United States Attorney and a court reporter were present while Hernandez was testifying. Knowing that grand jury proceedings are secret, the defense attorney wants to challenge the indictment because of their presence.

165.  What is the likely result of the challenge?

ANSWER:


166.  In federal courts which of the following DOES NOT remove the defendant's right to a preliminary hearing?

(A)  the defendant is indicted by a grand jury.

(B)  the defendant waives the hearing.

(C)  the defendant requests jury trial.

(D)  the government files a valid information.

167.  Which of the following groups of people are NOT subject to a general obligation of secrecy about grand jury proceedings:

(A)  grand jury witnesses.

(B)  grand jurors.

(C)  grand jury interpreters.

(D)  grand jury court reporters.

168.  Which of the following is NOT specifically authorized to find out some information about which witnesses testified in a specific grand jury proceeding?

(A)  an attorney for the government for use in the performance of her job.

(B)  an investigator assisting a government attorney in the performance of her job.

(C) state government officials investigating violation of state law.

(D) the person indicted in that proceeding.

169. Which of the following is NOT TRUE about a federal grand jury?

(A) the grand jury may consider evidence barred by the Federal Rules of Evidence.

(B) the grand jury may issue an indictment that is sealed by the magistrate judge until the accused is arrested.

(C) the witness's testimony is not tape recorded in order to preserve grand jury secrecy.

(D) the grand jury's voting and deliberations are not tape recorded in order to preserve grand jury secrecy.

170. A Bill of Particulars is

   (A) an itemized statement of amounts owed for professional legal services.

   (B) a request by the government for more details about the defendant's likely defenses.

   (C) a request by defense counsel for additional information about the crimes alleged in an indictment.

   (D) an order by the judge for information about the likely evidence to be used by each side and is designed to assist the court in predicting how long the trial will take.

You are a prosecutor in a jurisdiction that has criminal procedure rules similar to those in federal courts. Your investigation showed that Vito is a member of an underworld crime syndicate and has probably committed a number of extortions and murders. You want to begin criminal proceedings against him without letting him know that you have done so since you have good reason to fear that he may well abscond or kill certain witnesses if he is made aware of the criminal charges before his arrest.

171. You may accomplish this by

   (A) information.
   (B) indictment.
   (C) complaint.
   (D) citation.

Marilyn Shapo is a junior associate in a large law firm who is doing a *pro bono* project by assisting in the representation of several Haitians indicted for smuggling illegal aliens into the United States. The partner for whom you work, who has never handled a criminal case and wonders whether the indictments are valid, has asked you to research the requirements for a valid federal indictment.

172. Your research revealed that a federal indictment need NOT

   (A) be in writing.
   (B) cite the statute allegedly violated.
   (C) be signed by the defense attorney.
   (D) be signed by an attorney for the government.

You are the attorney for a former Wall Street investment banker who has been indicted for committing securities fraud "in connection with seven transactions" he handled while employed at the bank. Your client informs you that over the course of the 25 years he worked at the bank, he was involved in thousands of transactions and the indictment does not indicate what seven transactions are allegedly fraudulent.

**173.**   Why might it be helpful for you to request a Bill of Particulars?

ANSWER:

A friend of yours in the prosecutor's office just told you that the grand jury that indicted your client for a domestic violence related assault did not have before it information that the victim had recanted her statement to the police implicating your client. When you discuss this with the assistant district attorney in charge of your client's prosecution, he says he was aware of the recantation, but he believed that the victim only recanted because the victim relies financially on the defendant. Accordingly, the prosecutor said he did not believe the recantation and did not present it to the grand jury. He assumed you would bring it out during trial.

**174.**   You want to challenge the indictment because of the prosecutor's actions in depriving the grand jury of very relevant evidence. Assess the likely result.

ANSWER:

You work for a subcommittee of the United States House of Representatives and are exploring ways to streamline federal criminal procedure so that victims do not have to wait as long to obtain justice. One possible measure is to reduce the cases where an indictment is necessary because your research has found that the use of indictments may delay a case for 4-6 months.

**175.**   Under current federal criminal procedure, which of the following crimes does NOT have to be initiated by an indictment.

(A)   a crime punishable by life imprisonment.
(B)   a crime punishable by a maximum of 18 months imprisonment.
(C)   a crime punishable by a maximum of 12 months imprisonment.
(D)   a crime that is a felony.

Your client has been charged in state court with an information alleging the felony sale of a controlled substance. A state statute specifically authorizes the use of an information in all criminal cases and your state constitution does not mention a grand jury. You also do federal criminal work and know that federal felony prosecutions routinely involve an indictment, not an information.

**176.**   You want to challenge the state information because your client was not indicted. Assess your chances of successfully challenging your state's use of an information instead of an indictment in this case

ANSWER:

# TOPIC 61
# MOTION PRACTICE

On the third day of a hotly contested criminal trial, the prosecution makes an oral motion to exclude the defendant's mother from the courtroom because of her noisy reaction to prosecution proof. Defense counsel wants to object to the motion.

**177.** Which of the following is LEAST likely to succeed as a basis to have the motion denied:

    (A) the defendant and the public are entitled to a public trial and the court should not exclude a member of the public without excellent cause.

    (B) the motion was not in writing.

    (C) the motion was not filed before trial.

    (D) (B) and (C) above.

You just passed the bar and have opened your own law practice specializing in federal criminal defense. Since you have relatively few clients at this time, you spend your extra time trying to learn the rules of criminal procedure. One of your concerns is motion practice. Your criminal procedure course did not cover the topic but you know how important it is. Your jurisdiction has adopted the Federal Rules of Criminal Procedure. You are now quizzing yourself on your knowledge of motion practice under the Federal Rules.

**178.** Which of the following motions does NOT have to be raised before trial?

    (A) Motion to Admit Victims' Prior Criminal Records.

    (B) Motion to Suppress Evidence.

    (C) Motion to Sever Charges.

    (D) Motion to Dismiss Indictment.

You receive the following memo from the judge who just hired you as her law clerk:

To: New Law Clerk

From: Federal District Judge Neophyte

Re: Motions in Criminal Cases

Dear New Law Clerk,

Since I was appointed to the bench last month, I've been reading over the Federal Rules of Criminal Procedure but am a bit perplexed. I've never handled a criminal case before in my law practice and I couldn't find any rule that talks about specific types of motions that are filed in criminal cases. Please prepare a short list for me of the general types of routine motions I can expect in criminal cases. I know your response will have to be quite general.

**179.**   How do you respond to the Judge's memo?

ANSWER:

You are a federal prosecutor scheduled to try Clem Carter in the near future. The judge has scheduled a Motion Day for next Monday. It is the judge's standing practice to hear all pending motions at one time soon before trial. Because of a large backlog of cases and a desire to use all court time efficiently, the judge hates granting continuances and can be very rude to lawyers who hint that they need one. Late afternoon on Friday, a runner from Carter's lawyer shows up and gives you a new Motion to Suppress Defendant's Confession. You were quite surprised since defense counsel had not hinted that the confession would be challenged.

**180.**   What are your options?

ANSWER:

You represent a client accused of aggravated battery stemming from a fight at a bar on a Saturday night. Your client was undoubtedly inebriated when arrested at the bar. He forcefully resisted the officers trying to arrest him and yelled racial slurs at them.

**181.**   What would be the best way to ensure that those details about the arrest stay out of the subsequent trial?

    (A)   timely object any time you believe a witness or prosecutor is about to broach the subject.

    (B)   at trial, avoid asking questions about the arrest.

    (C)   file a motion in limine to bar any reference to the arrest.

    (D)   nothing — your client's acts relating to his arrest are admissible.

Mary Lawford was convicted of tax evasion in federal court. In a written pretrial motion, her defense lawyer asked the prosecutor to provide the defense with an F.B.I report concerning an investigation of a third person. The prosecutor never responded to the motion and it was not discussed in a hearing or ruled on by the magistrate judge. You are handling the appeal and have raised the government's failure to turn over the F.B.I. Report about the third person's possible involvement in the crime.

**182.**   How should the appellate court treat this motion?

    (A)   arguments raised by the motion are probably waived because no disposition was ever reached at the trial court level.

    (B)   because the F.B.I reports were not introduced at trial, failure to consider the motion is harmless error.

    (C)   the cause should be remanded to the trial court for a hearing on the motion and any effect it might have on the trial outcome.

(D) the appellate court should consider the motion on the merits and attempt to determine if the non-disclosed report would have had any real bearing on the outcome of the trial.

Attorney for defendant has timely filed a series of motions, supported by detailed memoranda of law, and asked the prosecutor several times for her reply to these motions. Assume there has been more than sufficient time for the prosecutor to respond in writing to these motions. At a pre-scheduled "motion day," defendant's attorney moves for a default judgment on these motions because the prosecutor failed to timely object to any of these motions or file any supporting memoranda of law.

**183.** Using the Federal Rules of Criminal Procedure (and not any local rules), the court should

(A) grant all the defense motions as the prosecutor waived any objection for failure to file a timely written response.

(B) scold the prosecutor but grant a one-week continuance and demand that written responses to the motions be filed forthwith.

(C) consider the motions on the merits but refuse to allow the prosecutor to offer any objection or rebuttal on the record.

(D) consider the motions on the merits after hearing any arguments from the prosecutor.

You are a criminal defense lawyer and have a federal homicide trial scheduled to start in a week. As part of your trial preparation, you have compiled a trial notebook. One of the sections in it is entitled "Motions" and includes a draft Motion for Judgment of Acquittal.

**184.** What is the timing for filing this particular motion and when must the federal judge rule on it, under the Federal Rules of Criminal Procedure?

ANSWER:


Donald Deff was represented at trial by Cedric Washington, widely recognized as one of the best criminal defense lawyers in the area. Despite this, Deff was convicted of robbery because the alleged victim made an effective in-court identification. Four days later Washington died in an automobile accident. You have been retained by Deff's family to look into the case. You hired a private detective who found another eyewitness to the crime. The new witness would testify that the robber was at least 6'4" tall (Deff is 5'6") and had long blonde hair (at the time of the crime, Deff had dark brown hair cut very short). You think a Motion for New Trial under Federal Rule of Criminal Procedure 33 would be a good way to vacate the conviction and grant a new trial.

**185.** What is the standard the trial will use in vacating a conviction and granting a new trial under Rule 33?

(A) violation of defendant's substantial rights.

(B) violation of defendant's constitutional rights.

(C)  if the interest of justice so requires.

(D)  if it appears that the defendant was wrongly convicted.

186.  If you choose to file a Motion for New Trial under Rule 33, when must you do so in the instant case involving Mr. Deff?

(A)  within 120 days after the verdict or finding of guilty.

(B)  within one year after the verdict or finding of guilty.

(C)  within three years after the verdict or finding of guilty.

(D)  within ten years after the verdict or finding of guilty.

The Federal Rules of Criminal Procedure specifically provide three types of post-trial motions: Motion for Judgment of Acquittal (Rule 29), Motion for New Trial (Rule 33), and Motion in Arrest of Judgment (Rule 34).

187.  Compare the three motions on the basis of the grounds each recognizes as appropriate to reverse a conviction.

ANSWER:

Terence is being tried for bank robbery. His defense is alibi: he was not at the scene of the crime and can prove it with three witnesses who will testify he was elsewhere. Judge Wright has a crowded docket and wants to speed up Terence's trial. She issued an order limiting each side to one subpoena.

188.    What arguments can Terence make against Judge Wright's ruling that Terence may have only one subpoena?

ANSWER:

189.    In an ordinary criminal case governed by the Federal Rules of Criminal Procedure, who of the following would most routinely issue the subpoena for a defense witness?

    (A)   the presiding judge.
    (B)   the prosecuting attorney.
    (C)   the court clerk.
    (D)   the defense lawyer.

The prosecution in a drug conspiracy case, involving four defendants who are members of a violent gang, wants to subpoena an undercover agent whose identity is not known to the defense. There is some reason to believe that the undercover agent's life could be in jeopardy if the defendant and his violent cohorts found out about the surprise witness before trial. Because the defendant's gang seems to have someone in the court clerk's office who provides the gang with confidential information, the prosecution is afraid that somehow the defendant would learn the name of anyone the clerk's office subpoenaed for trial.

190.    Which of the following is the most sensible outcome under the Federal Rules of Criminal Procedure:

    (A)   the prosecutor should not have a subpoena issued to ensure anonymity.
    (B)   the prosecutor should have the witness subpoenaed but have the clerk's office keep the list of people subpoenaed in a sealed envelope locked in the office vault.
    (C)   the prosecutor should not worry since the subpoenas are issued in blank and the clerk's office will not have a record of the names of people receiving a subpoena.

    (D)  the prosecutor should have the subpoena issued to "John Doe" so no one in the clerk's office will know who is subpoenaed.

Judge Thomas Watt was presiding over a complex murder case when he was mugged while going home after the sixth day of trial. His doctors said he would be hospitalized for at least a week and would need two or three months to recuperate before returning to the bench. Chief Judge Kathy Moore has cleared her schedule so she can preside over the rest of the murder trial.

191.  You are law clerk to Judge Moore. Under Rule 25 of the Federal Rules of Criminal Procedure, what must be done in order for Judge Moore to finish this trial?

(A)  all lawyers must agree that she can conduct the trial.
(B)  Ms. Pettigrove, the defendant, must agree that Judge Moore can conduct the trial.
(C)  Judge Moore must certify that she is familiar with the record of the trial.
(D)  Nothing can be done. Since Judge Moore did not hear the evidence presented in the first days of the trial, there must be a mistrial and the trial must be started all over before a judge who will hear all the proof.

United States District Judge Mohammed Al-Haftiri's life-long wish was granted. He was appointed a federal appellate judge and was expected to start immediately in a city 400 miles away. He had just finished presiding over a stock fraud case where today the jury returned a guilty verdict on all counts against all defendants. A sentencing hearing was scheduled in a month. Judge Al-Haftiri would not be able to be at the sentencing hearing, however, because of his new duties.

192.  Under Rule 25, Federal Rules of Criminal Procedure, what is the correct procedure:

(A)  another federal judge in that district may complete any tasks, including sentencing, since Judge Al-Haftiri cannot be present at the sentencing.
(B)  the trial would have to be conducted again so a new judge could hear all the evidence and impose sentence.
(C)  Judge Al-Haftiri would have to return to the area and conduct the sentencing hearing.
(D)  the maximum sentence that a new judge could impose is that for a misdemeanor; no felony sentence is possible with the new judge.

Scarface Joe, has been charged with a federal felony charge of transporting cocaine across state lines. Scarface Joe is a fan of law and order television shows and remembers a lot of the defendants pleading no contest (or nolo contendere). You are Scarface Joe's attorney. He asks you why he might want to enter a no contest plea, and whether there would be any reason why he could not do so.

**193.** Advise your client.

ANSWER:

**194.** Under Rule 11 on pleas and plea bargaining, what is one of the principle differences between a guilty plea and a no contest (or nolo contendere) plea?

(A) After the court has accepted a defendant's plea but before the sentencing, the defendant has a right to withdraw a nolo contendere plea without providing a reason but cannot withdraw a guilty plea without providing a fair and just reason.

(B) Before accepting a nolo contendere plea, the court is not required to determine voluntariness because it is presumed under the rule. However, the court must determine that a defendant who enters a guilty plea did so voluntarily and free of "force."

(C) The court is provided discretion in informing the defendant of the benefits of a nolo contendere plea during plea negotiations, provided that the defendant's attorney is present. However, the court cannot be involved in a guilty plea negotiation.

(D) A nolo contendere plea is inadmissible in a subsequent criminal or civil trial where the defendant is involved. However, if the defendant accepts a plea of guilty, that plea is admissible in a subsequent trial, assuming the other provisions of the Federal Rules of Evidence are satisfied.

Kimberly Killer was charged with first degree murder in a jurisdiction that has adopted the Federal Rules of Criminal Procedure. The prosecutor realized that a key witness is unwilling to testify. Without telling the defense attorney of this fact, she made a formal offer that "if Kimberly would plead guilty to involuntary manslaughter, then Kimberly would serve no more than three years in prison." Kimberly immediately accepted the deal.

At the sentencing hearing, Kimberly told the judge that she pled guilty to involuntary manslaughter and admitted under oath she committed the crime. The judge accepted Kimberly's plea, then vociferously condemned the prosecutor for downgrading the charge to involuntary manslaughter.

On the record the judge said that he would not accept the involuntary manslaughter charge but would accept the plea to a charge of second degree murder. The judge then rejected the plea agreement limiting the sentence to a maximum of three years and took under advisement the sentence. The judge indicated that a five-year sentence and a ten-year probation "may well be appropriate in this case, but I need to think about it some more."

**195.** What can happen at this point?

    (A) Kimberly can withdraw the guilty plea and stand trial, but her admission of being guilty of involuntary manslaughter is admissible at trial.

    (B) Kimberly can withdraw the guilty plea and stand trial; her in-court admission of killing the victim is inadmissible at trial.

    (C) The guilty plea has already been entered and the judge should now proceed to sentence Kimberly to any sentence the judge thinks is appropriate.

    (D) Because of the doctrine of separation of powers, the plea agreement is between the prosecutor and the defendant; the trial court cannot reject a plea agreement that both sides knowingly and voluntarily decided was an acceptable resolution of the case.

Fred was charged with a series of drug-related crimes. Fred's lawyer and the prosecutor worked out a plea agreement that dismissed a number of the charges in exchange for Fred's cooperation. Consistent with state sentencing law, the agreement specified that the sentence would be between five and nine years in prison, with the sentencing judge selecting the exact sentence. The agreement also contained a provision saying the prosecutor would ask the court to set the actual prison sentence below the five-year minimum if Fred fully cooperated with the government in the prosecution of other persons involved in the drug trade with Fred. Fred entered a guilty plea in open court. Sentencing was postponed until after all subsequent trials were concluded.

Fred testified at several trials and this testimony was instrumental in the conviction of three significant crime figures. Because the prosecutor felt there was some factual inaccuracies in Fred's testimony, however, she did not recommend to the sentencing court that Fred be given the reduced sentence. Fred then moved to enforce the plea agreement and impose a sentence lower than the five-year minimum.

**196.** How should the court rule?

    (A) Conduct a hearing to determine whether Fred fully lived up to the bargain. If so, the deal must be honored and the prosecutor must make a good faith effort to request a sentence below five years or the court must so sentence Fred.

    (B) Deny the motion. Since the sentence had not been imposed, the prosecutor could change her mind at any time as long as it was done in good faith.

    (C) The trial court has no authority to modify or interpret plea agreements; this is a function of the prosecutor because of separation of powers concerns.

    (D) The prosecutor breached the letter and spirit of the plea agreement and the court should honor it by dismissing the charges against Fred, who should not have to relitigate a matter already resolved by contract.

A noted law professor and civil activist has compiled reliable statistics from one jurisdiction that show criminal defendants who undergo a jury trial are sentenced to 35% longer prison terms than those who are charged with the same crime and plead guilty. Armed with these statistics, the professor files a number of federal habeas (or post-conviction relief) petitions arguing this disparity violates defendants' right to a jury trial, equal protection, and due process.

**197.** Based on these data, do you expect an appellate court will mandate many new sentencing hearings?

   (A) Yes, these statistics show that defendants are being punished for exercising their right to a jury trial.

   (B) No, there is no constitutional requirement against having defendants who demand a jury trial serve longer prison sentences.

   (C) No, criminal defendants and their lawyers are well aware of this tendency and take this into account when deciding how to plea. This is merely a part of the process.

   (D) No, an overburdened criminal justice system has to have some sort of carrot to offer to defendants so they agree to plead guilty.

Bobby and Kenny, two brothers, are arrested and charged with several counts of defrauding the federal government. If convicted, Bobby and Kenny could languish in federal prison for many decades. The prosecutor offers Bobby a deal whereby he will plead guilty and only receive a one-year prison sentence in exchange for his testimony against Kenny. Bobby agrees to the deal, but Kenny elects to go to trial. Bobby lives up to his plea agreement and testifies. Despite the substantial evidence and some inconsistent witness testimony, Kenny is acquitted of all charges. Bobby then moves to set aside his guilty plea.

**198.** The court should

   (A) view Kenny's acquittal as evidence that the charged offenses did not occur and set aside Bobby's guilty plea.

   (B) set aside Bobby's plea under the doctrine of fundamental fairness.

   (C) set aside Bobby's plea because Kenny's acquittal sufficiently shows that Bobby's plea was not made voluntarily, knowingly, and intelligently.

   (D) enforce the plea agreement as written.

Jack was charged with several counts of child abuse and could have received a thirty-year prison term. Jack disputed many of the less severe charges against him but, on the advice of counsel, agreed to plead guilty since there was substantial evidence of guilt and juries in the jurisdiction were notoriously unsympathetic to defendants in child abuse cases. Jack immediately directed his lawyer to negotiate a plea with the prosecutor to reduce the prison sentence to the lowest level possible, regardless of the actual sentence.

Consistent with the plea agreement, Jack received a four-year prison sentence and was placed on probation. However, Jack's lawyer did not tell him that a new state law required Jack to register with the local police department wherever he lived or worked in the state for fifteen years after his release. Furthermore, Jack's name, address, and picture would be placed on a state-run website. Upon learning of this new law, Jack sought to have his guilty plea set aside and face a trial, even though if convicted he might receive a thirty-year sentence. Jack's new lawyer argued that his first lawyer provided ineffective assistance by failing to advice Jack of all the consequences for pleading guilty.

**199.** How should the court rule in a jurisdiction that follows the Federal Rules of Criminal Procedure?

(A) Jack, as a citizen, is responsible for knowing about existing laws. His ignorance of this law is his own fault and will not invalidate his plea.

(B) Jack's lawyer should have told him about this law, but failure to do so would not have changed anything and therefore constitutes harmless error.

(C) The court is required to inform Jack of all the foreseeable consequences associated with pleading guilty. Since the court failed to inform Jack about these conditions, this constitutes reversible error and Jack should be allowed to withdraw his plea.

(D) Jack's lawyer had no responsibility to inform Jack of the new law.

Kenny is charged with felony assault for severely injuring a bouncer in a barroom brawl. A few weeks before trial, the junior prosecutor assigned the case offers Kenny a plea agreement where he will serve two years in jail. Kenny's lawyer is furious at this suggestion which he deems inappropriate since the bouncer attacked Kenny, who merely defended himself.

Defense counsel goes directly to the head prosecutor to "talk sense." After a violent argument, the head prosecutor says, "You and your client are gonna pay for trying to go over the head of my assistant." The head prosecutor then reviews the charges against Kenny and discovers Kenny has several other felony convictions that could earn Kenny a mandatory life sentence under the state's "three strikes" law. Kenny is so charged under the three strikes provision, convicted, and given a life sentence. On appeal, Kenny's lawyer argues that the court should set aside the conviction based on prosecutorial vindictiveness, especially since the prosecution had originally offered a mere 10 days in jail.

**200.** How should the court rule?

(A) this fact pattern would shock the conscience of the court, which should overturn the felony convictions and sentence Kenny to two years in jail.

(B) the court should overturn the sentence and allow the defendant an opportunity to accept the prosecutor's original offer of two years in jail.

(C) The court should overturn the conviction. The prosecutor's conduct violates Kenny's right of equal protection and due process, since he is apparently the unfortunate victim of a quarrel between his lawyer and the prosecutor.

(D) The court should uphold the conviction and the sentence. The prosecutor is ordinarily free to seek any charges allowed under the law

Assume that Marybeth works out a deal in which she will plead guilty to one count of the fraudulent use of a credit card and the government will dismiss three other similar charges. She then has second thoughts and wants to withdraw the plea because she would rather take her chances at trial.

**201.** Under the Federal Rules of Criminal Procedure, which of the following is NOT correct:

(A) If the court has not yet accepted Marybeth's plea, Marybeth may withdraw her plea for a "substantial reason that serves the interests of justice."

(B) If the court has accepted her plea but has not yet imposed sentence, she may withdraw the plea if the judge rejects the plea agreement because the judge thinks the additional charges should not be dismissed.

(C) If the court has accepted Marybeth's plea but has not yet imposed sentence, she may withdraw the plea if she can show a "fair and just reason for requesting the withdrawal."

(D) If the court has accepted the plea and imposed sentence, Marybeth may not withdraw the guilty plea. She may only have it set aside on direct appeal or collateral attack.

You are a law clerk to a United States District Court Judge who was just appointed to the federal bench after a long career handling family law matters. Your judge is conducting an arraignment in a federal perjury case. The defendant has just said to the judge, "Your honor. I want to plead guilty and get this nightmare over with, but to tell the truth, I ain't lied to no one, never in my life." Your judge is confused about what to do since the accused has said he wants to plead guilty while, at the same time, denies being guilty of the crime.

**202.** Your judge asks you what are the court's options with regard to the plea.

ANSWER:

Anthony Quinlan faces charges of bank robbery in state court. If convicted he could face a 50-year sentence. Rather than risk this outcome, he has finally agreed to plea guilty and accept a 10-year sentence, but Quinlan absolutely refuses to admit guilt in open court. Defense counsel does not know why Quinlan is so adamant about not confessing to the crime.

The problem is that the state has a statute providing that any person who pleads guilty must testify on the record, under oath, that he or she is in fact guilty of the crime and must also provide enough factual details to satisfy the court that the defendant really is guilty.

Since Quinlan refuses to confess his guilt as required by statute, defense counsel has filed a motion to allow Quinlan to plead guilty without the confession. Counsel argues that the mandatory confession violates Quinlan's Fifth Amendment protection against compelled self incrimination.

**203.** How should the court rule?

ANSWER:

Dora Holwell, a truck driver, is being prosecuted for the interstate transportation of stolen televisions. She wants to plead guilty and accept a favorable plea deal, but she also wants to tell the judge that she is really not guilty because she did not know the televisions were stolen. The judge's practice is to accept "best interests" or *Alford* pleas.

**204.** What will be the effect of this plea?

    (A) defendant is convicted. Evidence of the conviction cannot be used against the defendant at a later civil trial since the defendant denied guilt.

    (B) defendant is convicted but could withdraw her guilty plea at any time.

    (C) defendant is convicted.

    (D) defendant is essentially offering a nolo contendere plea.

Viktor Kote was arrested on a string of kidnaping and murder charges. He was believed to have abducted and murdered three small children. When Kote was captured, police believed that the victims could have still been alive. Kote refused to answer any questions about the crime.

Frustrated and worried about the continued safety of the missing children, the local prosecutor said, "Kote, you'll only do 30 years if you will tell us where everybody else is."

Kote quickly said, "I accept your offer." He then directed police to a wooded hideout where all three victims were found dead.

Outraged and facing growing community anger, the prosecutor indicted Kote for three counts of first degree murder and sought the death penalty. Kote's lawyer argued that a valid plea deal was in place and sued for specific performance of that deal. Prosecutors argued that Kote accepted the deal in bad faith, knowing the victims were all dead.

**205.** How should the court rule?

    (A) the deal should be enforced as stated. Kote adhered to his part of the deal and the prosecutor must do so as well.

    (B) the deal should be voided because of Kote's bad faith "acceptance."

    (C) reject Kote's argument because there was no valid plea deal present.

    (D) the deal should be voided, but the evidence found after Kote's "acceptance" of the deal should be ruled inadmissible.

    (E) Reject the deal since it was never accepted by the court. Until the court accepts it, both sides may withdraw from it.

By local rule, all the judges in this federal district court have adopted one standard "script" used when holding a hearing where a defendant pleads guilty. Judge Pauley, a federal judge in this district, inadvertently brought to the bench an earlier draft version of the plea agreement script that was later revised significantly. Judge Pauley conducted several plea hearings before discovering the error. One of the defendants who entered a plea agreement last week under the outdated script now seeks to withdraw his plea because Judge Pauley used the wrong script.

**206.** Based solely on the limited facts above, which of the following is most accurate:

    (A) all the pleas entered using the unapproved script are unconstitutional and invalid because they violate a local rule.

    (B)  all the pleas entered using the unapproved script are valid under the harmless error doctrine.

    (C)  even though the script actually used was not formally adopted by the trial court, it may still be a valid means by which to take a guilty plea.

    (D)  all the defendants who pled guilty using the outdated script should be given a new hearing where the correct script is used.

Judge Chang was recently appointed to the trial bench. To help her prepare for her first trial, she has made a list of the rights that are waived when a criminal defendant pleads guilty.

**207.**  Which of the following rights should not be on her list?

    (A)  jury trial.

    (B)  confrontation.

    (C)  effective assistance of counsel.

    (D)  self-incrimination.

Emil was just arrested for possession of child pornography. The federal prosecutor has called defense counsel to meet and discuss a possible plea. Since the government's case is very strong, defense counsel is willing to explore all plea alternatives.

**208.**  Under Rule 11 of the Federal Rules of Criminal Procedure, which of the following pleas is NOT specifically authorized?

    (A)  guilty plea.

    (B)  not guilty plea.

    (C)  nolo contendere plea.

    (D)  reserved plea.

Drugs were found in Kyle's house when the police burst into his house after an anonymous call indicated that there were a dozen or so baggies of marijuana in the bedroom closet. The marijuana was found exactly where the caller said it would be. Kyle's lawyer believes that the search was illegal since there was no search warrant. The prosecutor claims the search was valid because of "exigent circumstances," but offered Kyle a wonderful deal that would allow Kyle to plead to a misdemeanor. Kyle would like to plead guilty but also appeal the illegal search, hoping to escape all liability if the appellate court finds the search was illegal.

**209.**  Under the Federal Rules of Criminal Procedure, the best option for Kyle is to

    (A)  take the deal, plead guilty, and hope the appellate court will reverse because of the faulty search.

    (B)  plead not guilty, then appeal the search issue if he is convicted at trial.

    (C)  enter a conditional plea, reserving the right to appeal the search issue.

    (D)  abandon the search issue and take the favorable deal.

Mary Sue was caught red-handed robbing a bank. The prosecutor has offered her a lenient sentence if she pleads guilty, which she wants to do.

**210.** In the Rule 11 guilty plea proceeding in federal court, Judge Blumenthal must do all of the following EXCEPT

  (A)  make sure defense counsel has thoroughly investigated the case before recommending that May Sue accept or reject any plea deal.

  (B)  ensure that the plea is voluntary.

  (C)  assure itself that there is a factual basis for the plea.

  (D)  inform the defendant of the maximum possible penalty, even if that penalty is greater than that to be recommended in the plea agreement.

A maverick federal prosecutor has decided that guilty pleas result in sentences that are too low and therefore compromise deterrence. Accordingly, he has issued an order that bans all plea bargains and anything else that encourages pleas in the district. His goal is to go to trial whenever possible because defendants who are convicted after a trial receive longer sentences than those convicted after a plea.

**211.** Under Rule 11 of the Federal Rules of Criminal Procedure, which of the following procedures is possible only if the prosecutor consents?

  (A)  guilty plea.

  (B)  not guilty plea.

  (C)  conditional plea.

  (D)  nolo contendere plea.

You have been hired as a law clerk for a newly appointed District Judge who is concerned about her lack of knowledge of federal criminal procedure. She asks you to prepare a concise list of the rights a criminal defendant waives when he or she pleads guilty.

**212.** How would you respond?

ANSWER:

A defendant is arrested for various terrorist activities and is prosecuted in federal court for several felonies involving explosives and conspiracy.

213. If all significant federal procedures are followed in their case, which of the following would occur FOURTH:

(A) initial appearance.

(B) arrest.

(C) grand jury.

(D) preliminary examination (also known as a preliminary hearing).

As an intern for the public defender's office, you assist defense attorneys in their representation of indigent clients, some of them having emotional and mental problems. One day, you accompany an attorney to interview a client who was just arrested for homicide. During the interview, the client described his recent trip to the moon where he encountered four sea monsters and he expressed great fear from the hundreds of "trapezoids" who are hiding under his cell bed.

Your boss has asked you and a co-clerk to prepare concise, informal memos on certain procedural issues concerning a possible insanity or mental disability defense. Your assignment is to assess whether Rule 12.2 of the Federal Rules of Criminal Procedure must be satisfied and, if so, what should be done. You are also asked to discuss briefly any benefits from using this Rule and any costs if the rule is not followed. Your co-clerk will research all other issues.

**214.** Draft a short memo responding to your boss's concerns.

ANSWER:


Harry and Gary and twin brothers. Harry was arrested for an attempted carjacking, but claims to be innocent and alleges Gary was the actual culprit. Harry has two witnesses who will testify he was at the movies with them at the time of the carjacking. The prosecution does not know about these witnesses, but has heard a rumor that Harry will offer an alibi defense in the federal trial.

In order to best defend against Harry's likely alibi defense, the Assistant United States Attorney wants to follow all procedures mandated by Rule 12.1 of the Federal Rules of Criminal Procedure..

**215.** Which of the following is NOT necessary if the government wants formal notice of Harry's intended alibi defense and alibi witnesses so it can prove the alibi is fiction:

(A) the government must request in writing that the defense notify the government of an intent to present an alibi defense.

(B) the government must notify the defense of the time, date, and place of the alleged carjacking.

(C) the government must notify the defense of the name, address, and telephone number of each witness the government intends to rely on to establish the defendant's presence at the carjacking.

(D)  the government must disclose to the defense its investigative file showing every contact it made in order to find witnesses to rebut the alibi defense.

Rules 12.1 and 12.2 of the Federal Rules of Criminal Procedure are notice rules that share some common features but have significant differences as well. Read the following features that *could possibly* be shared by both:

   I.   Aimed at preventing trial surprises.

   II.   Triggered by the government/prosecution.

   III.   Authorizes the court to require the defendant to submit to a physical examination if relevant to rebut the defense.

   IV.   If notice required by the rule is withdrawn, the withdrawn notice cannot be introduced as evidence in a later trial against the party who withdrew the notice.

**216.**   Which of the above are common characteristics of Rule 12.1 on alibi defense and Rule 12.2 on insanity defense?

   (A)  only (I) and (II).

   (B)  only (I) and (IV).

   (C)  only (II) and (IV).

   (D)  none is a characteristic of both rules.

You are a law clerk to a trial judge in a jurisdiction that follows the Federal Rules of Criminal Procedure. Your boss has noticed that many lawyers are sloppy with some of the notice rules.

**217.**   Your assignment is to prepare a short memo about the consequences of not following the notice Rules 12.1 and 12.2.

ANSWER:

Ibn Al-Aqqad is a new Federal Prosecutor about to prosecute his first trial. He is preparing his closing argument. The court follows Rule 29.1 and the usual rules concerning closing argument.

218.  Assuming Al-Aqqad wants to take full advantage of the chance to address the jurors, when will he face them to make an argument after all the proof has been presented?

(A)  before defense counsel makes her closing argument.

(B)  before and after defense counsel makes her closing argument.

(C)  after defense counsel makes her closing argument.

(D)  after the jury returns to the courtroom with questions that arose during deliberations.

Carmel Colon's client is charged with four counts of first-degree murder. The defendant has a prior history of violent felonies and drug possession convictions. The defendant testified at trial and the prosecutor brought up his prior convictions to impeach his credibility.

219.   Colon wants Judge Huang to instruct the jury that the defendant's prior criminal history should only be admitted to determine his credibility. Under Federal Rule of Criminal Procedure 30, what should defense counsel Colon do to present the request to Judge Huang?

ANSWER:

220.   When must Judge Huang rule on defense lawyer Colon's request under the Federal Rules of Criminal Procedure?

(A)   before the actual trial during the evidentiary hearing.
(B)   after the prosecution rests and before the defense presents its case.
(C)   before the closing statements.
(D)   after the closing statements.

Judge Huang has informed Ms. Colon that he will not give the requested jury instruction because the instruction was not required by existing law and would confuse the jury. Defense lawyer Colon wants to object to this ruling and preserve the issue for appellate reversal. Her research has located several cases indicating that her requested instruction is permissible.

221.   What must Colon do to preserve the issue for appellate consideration?

ANSWER:

After the Enton Corporation went bankrupt, the federal government charged David Kenneth, the Chief Financial Officer, of deceiving the shareholders and fraud. The trial received widespread media coverage and numerous credible witnesses testified for both sides.

After a week of deliberations, the jury foreperson sent a message to the Judge that the jury was hopelessly deadlocked. The Judge then had the jury return to the courtroom where the foreperson stated that the jury seemed unable to reach a consensus. One juror winked in a flirting way with one of the prosecutors. The Judge then asked counsel whether they wanted an "*Allen* charge."

222.  What is an "*Allen* charge"?

   (A)  a jury instruction urging the jurors to listen to one another and attempt to reach a decision.

   (B)  an opportunity for each lawyer to make a brief statement (called "counsel's charge") to the jurors urging them to resolve their differences and reach a unanimous decision.

   (C)  a small fine imposed on jurors who unreasonably disrupt deliberations and prevent the jury from reaching any verdict at all.

   (D)  a court finding that the jury has been improperly tampered with, and that an immediate adjournment is in effect.

223.  The *Allen* charge has engendered a great deal of criticism. What is the primary argument against its use:

   (A)  it coerces the minority into agreeing with the majority.
   (B)  it coerces the majority into agreeing with the minority.
   (C)  it is unfair to the prosecution because it leads to more defense verdicts.
   (D)  it produces too many hung juries.

You are a new defense attorney for a small firm that specializes in criminal practice. Your boss just gave you your first assignment: to represent client Martha Fellows in a federal preliminary examination scheduled early next week. Fellows is charged with insurance fraud.

224. Which of the following is NOT TRUE about the federal preliminary examination?

(A) it is an adversary proceeding in which a prosecutor and criminal defense lawyer will likely participate.

(B) the accused may testify.

(C) the decision is made by a jury of twelve.

(D) the accused may cross-examine prosecution witnesses.

You have studied Rule 5.1 of the Federal Rules of Criminal Procedure in anticipation of your preliminary examination.

225. Which one of the following provisions is actually in Rule 5.1?

(A) evidence obtained in violation of the Constitution may be admissible.

(B) the prosecution cannot admit hearsay information in violation of Federal Rules of Evidence, which apply in full measure in preliminary examinations.

(C) if the preliminary hearing judge finds no probable cause that the defendant committed the charged offense, the judge should nevertheless order the accused to be continued in custody until the grand jury hears the case because the defendant may abscond before the grand jury can act.

(D) the judge can hold the preliminary examination 30 days after the defendant's initial appearance regardless of whether the defendant is in custody.

You are a judge in a jurisdiction that has criminal procedure rules identical to the Federal Rules of Criminal Procedure. You just heard a preliminary examination in a case involving a rape. The prosecution's position was that the defendant took the drunk victim to her house after a fraternity party and raped her while she was unconscious. The defense maintains the victim consented to sexual relations and was "high" but not drunk when the incident occurred.

226. Which of the following would be the most accurate statement of the law of preliminary examinations?

(A) the standard of proof is probable cause that a crime was committed and that the accused committed that crime.

(B)   the standard of proof is guilt beyond a reasonable doubt.

(C)   despite the effective cross-examination, the defense did not prove that the defendant was innocent.

(D)   the prosecution had to use its best witnesses rather than choosing not to in order to prevent the defense from discovering what their testimony will be at trial.

In a drug possession case, the prosecution calls to the stand a federal agent who planted a listening device in your client's car without a warrant. The agent testifies and reveals what she learned from the recordings of the listening device without having the recordings played in court. The conversation states that your client is to sell a large quantity of drugs to another drug dealer. You believe that the agent's testimony is inadmissible under the Federal Rules of Evidence and was obtained in violation of the Fourth Amendment.

**227.**   Assess the admissibility of the agent's testimony in the preliminary examination.

ANSWER:

Joe is charged with committing terrorist activity for blowing up the office of a credit card company. The bombing was caught on video surveillance by a police camera located in the street. The police investigator viewed the video and thought the suspect looked very much like Joe. Joe's defense is that he did not commit the acts and maintains that someone by the name of Tyler actually blew up the building.

Joe's lawyer filed a motion requesting to review the surveillance videos, and the prosecutor relayed the unfortunate fact that the tape was routinely destroyed by the police for administrative reasons. To save money, the police had long had a practice of erasing their security videos to save storage space and reduce the costs of purchasing blank ones.

Joe has asked that the case be dismissed because of the police misconduct in destroying the tapes that would have shown that Joe did not commit the bombings.

228. Under the United States Constitution, the case will

(A) be dismissed since the police were responsible for destroying evidence that might have exonerated Joe.

(B) be dismissed because the police have a duty to preserve all relevant evidence in a case.

(C) not be dismissed since it is unclear whether the destroyed evidence would have helped or harmed Joe's case.

(D) not be dismissed unless Joe can demonstrate that the police acted in bad faith in destroying the evidence.

You are a prosecutor preparing for a trial next month involving Marvin Green, an accountant charged with embezzling from the aerospace company for whom he worked. During plea negotiations, defense counsel has claimed that her client is innocent and that someone else "set up" Mr. Green to hide the real culprit.

As you review the file, you find a document that you had not noticed before. The item is one sheet of unsigned, undated paper bearing the handwritten words: "Green is innocent. He is being framed by the man who took the money." You ask around and no one in your office and no police officer involved in the investigation knows anything about the document. Of course you do not plan to introduce the item into evidence. Even if it helped you prove guilt (which it does not), you believe it is inadmissible hearsay.

The defense made a formal request under Rule 16 for all documents in the government's possession that are material to the defense.

229. Must you turn this item over to the defense? Why or why not?

ANSWER:

Rule 16 of the Federal Rules of Criminal Procedure allows the defendant wide latitude to request information from the government regarding its case against the defendant.

230. All of the following material needs to be turned over to the defendant upon request except:

(A) defendant's statement to the police before and after arrest in response to interrogation if the government intends to use the statement at trial.

(B) defendant's prior criminal record.

(C) any internal government record in connection with investigating the case against the defendant.

(D) any record of examination of the defendant's physical or mental condition that the government intends to use at trial.

Paul Catolandito was indicted for conspiracy for ruthless mob activities. The indictment stated that Paul had "committed an unknown number of murders for hire in Queenland County between 2000 and 2006." You are defense counsel and are finding it difficult to defend since you know very little about the allegations.

231. Using the Federal Rules of Criminal Procedure, which of the following is most likely to help you find out more about the charges?

(A) bill of particulars.

(B) notice of alibi.

(C) notice of insanity defense.

(D) deposition.

William Dasilva is a defense attorney representing a woman charged in federal court with several gambling violations for running a poker game in a national park's camping ground. Dasilva wants to maximize discovery under the Federal Rules of Criminal Procedure. He notes that he, as defense counsel, cannot initiate all discovery processes.

232. Which of the following processes is begun by an action of the *prosecution*?

(A) notice of insanity defense.

(B) notice of intent to use expert testimony on mental condition.

(C) notice of alibi.

(D) notice of defense based upon public authority.

In a homicide case, the prosecutor just learned that one of her many witnesses has terminal cancer and may not survive the commencement of the trial. You are one of her interns and you suggested that a deposition be taken in order to preserve the testimony, and your supervisor concurs.

233. If you want to use a deposition under Rule 15 of the Federal Rules of Criminal Procedure, which of the following is NOT accurate?

(A) the deposition may be taken only in "exceptional circumstances."

(B) the defendant has no right to be present at the taking of the deposition but has a right to be present in court when the deposition is entered into evidence.

(C) the deposition can be taken only with the court's permission.

(D) the deposition may be used at trial under the Federal Rules of Evidence.

Sara Kam is a criminal defense lawyer representing a key prosecution witness who has been detained by the government to ensure the witness will appear at a racketeering trial scheduled to begin in a month. Kam's client has directed Kam to do whatever she can to have the client released from detention. Kam has suggested that the client be deposed under Rule 15, Federal Rules of Criminal Procedure

**234.** If this material witness is deposed, which of the following is accurate:

(A) the witness must make a formal written motion to be deposed.

(B) the witness must sign the deposition transcript before being released.

(C) the witness may be discharged after being deposed.

(D) all of above.

Judge Crane is presiding over a prolonged white-collar criminal case. The defendant is charged with fraudulently embezzling large sums from two corporations. The defendant was arrested and posted $2 million for bail. Both sides have aggressively pursued discovery under Rule 16 of the Federal Rules of Criminal Procedure.

**235.** Which of the following does the government NOT have to be turn over to the defense pursuant to Rule 16?

(A) a written statement the defendant gave to the police, which is now in a prosecutor's case file.

(B) a written statement the main government witness gave to the police, which is now in the prosecutor's case file.

(C) a copy of the defendant's criminal record, which is in the prosecutor's case file.

(D) written business documents, now in the government's possession, from the corporate victims' files providing strong evidence that the defendant committed the fraud.

Rule 16 of the Federal Rules of Criminal Procedure generally requires reciprocal discovery. The general pattern is that the defense requests certain information from the prosecution, which the prosecution is then obligated to give the defense. This triggers a reciprocal duty by the defense to turn over similar information to the prosecution. However, not all information is subject to this mutual requirement.

**236.** Which of the following is NOT subject to this reciprocity requirement?

(A) written or recorded statement of defendant.

(B) reports of examinations and tests.

(C) documents and tangible objects.

(D) summary of testimony of expert witness intended to be used at trial.

Tovah Siegel is an experienced state criminal defense lawyer but has never handled a federal criminal case. She was just hired to do so and is making a careful study of Rule 16, Federal Rules of Criminal Procedures, which she has been told is the primary discovery device in federal court. She knows that she must turn over certain materials to the prosecution if she makes a request for similar items from the prosecution. Assume she makes all requests authorized by Rule 16 and the government fully complies.

237. Which of the following statements is accurate under Rule 16:

    (A)   Siegel must give the prosecution access to all documents not protected by the work product rule that are material to the prosecution's trial preparation.

    (B)   Siegel must turn over anything, other than the defendant's statements, that is helpful to the prosecution just as the prosecution must turn over materials helpful to the defense under *Brady v. Maryland*.

    (C)   Siegel must give the government access to reports of mental examinations of the defendant if she has the reports in her file and intends to use them in her case-in-chief at trial.

    (D)   Because of the Fifth Amendment's self incrimination clause, Siegel does not have to disclose anything that would tend to incriminate her client.

Federal Rule of Criminal Procedure 26.2, often called the Jencks Rule, requires disclosure of a witness's statement after the witness has testified on direct examination. The purpose of this procedure is to facilitate cross-examination.

238. While Rule 26.2 applies to many proceedings, in which of the following is it inapplicable?

    (A)   sentencing hearing.
    (B)   preliminary hearing.
    (C)   suppression hearing.
    (D)   grand jury proceeding.

Judge Martinez is presiding over a murder trial. The prosecution alleges that the case involved a drive-by shooting motivated by a failed drug operation. Margaret Spotter, who was cleaning her window at the time of the shooting and saw it occur, testified on direct examination for the prosecution that the defendant was the lone gunman. A year ago shortly after the incident, Ms. Spotter provided the police a written statement containing significant detail about the event and the shooter. The prosecutor has Ms. Spotter's statement in her file.

239. Under Federal Rules of Criminal Procedure 26.2 (Jencks act), which of the following reasons would support Judge Martinez's decision NOT to order the prosecutor to provide the defense with a copy of this statement to use in its cross-examination of Ms. Spotter?

    (A)   the statement is in the prosecution's case file that was prepared for the sole purpose of assisting the prosecutor to get ready for trial, hence it is protected by the work product rule.

(B) the defense made no motion requesting this statement.

(C) the statement would not help the accused since it simply supported what Spotter said on direct examination.

(D) Ms. Spotter strongly opposes allowing the defendant to see her statement.

Nicholas Lacken is on trial for trafficking in narcotics. The state relies on a police officer who testified that he received a phone tip from a very reliable and often-used informant who said that defendant Lacken would be selling small baggies of cocaine at the corner of Sixth and Broad Streets at 8:30 PM on July 1st. The officer obtained a search warrant to search Lacken at that time. The warrant was executed and Lacken was found with 17 baggies of cocaine in his coat pocket.

The state does not plan on calling the informant as a witness and refuses to reveal the informant's name, so defendant Lacken has moved to compel the state to identify the informant. The state argues that revealing the informant's name would compromise future investigations and could bring harm or even death to the informant. The defense maintains that the identity of the informant could help the defense locate witnesses and explore the informant's motivation in directing the police to focus on the defendant.

**240.** You are the trial judge considering the motion. How should you rule?

ANSWER:

You are the prosecutor considering charging Christina with auto theft for stealing a used Camaro from the Star Used Car Emporium last month. You discover that last year she was convicted of stealing a used Camaro from the same business. It crosses your mind that perhaps double jeopardy in the fifth amendment may bar the current case.

241.  What is the proper language of the Fifth Amendment double jeopardy provision?

   (A)  "No person shall be convicted twice."
   (B)  No person shall "be subject for the same offense to be twice put in jeopardy of life or limb."
   (C)  No person shall "'be subjected to double jeopardy."
   (D)  No person shall "be tried more than one time for the same crime."

The United States Supreme Court has routinely held that the Double Jeopardy Clause applies to three separate constitutional protections.

242.  Which of the following is NOT barred by double jeopardy?

   (A)  second prosecution for the same offense after an acquittal.
   (B)  second prosecution for the same offense after a conviction.
   (C)  second prosecution for the same offense after a mistrial based on a hung jury.
   (D)  multiple punishments for the same offense.

On the third day of a trial, a spectator approached the defense attorney and said he saw a member of the prosecution team get on the elevator with one of the jurors. While the jury was excused, the judge heard from the defense attorney, who recounted what the spectator had said happened. The judge immediately declared a mistrial over the strong objections of defense counsel.

The prosecutor then asked for a new trial date and the defense attorney argued that double jeopardy prohibited a new trial

243.  What result when, as here, the defendant did not request the mistrial?
ANSWER:

244.  Same facts as above, but assume that the defense counsel requested the mistrial. The defense case had been going poorly and the defense lawyer hoped that she would fare better with a second shot at an acquittal.

ANSWER:

Erik was charged with transporting illegal firearms across state lines, a federal crime, and following a jury trial, he was acquitted. Disappointed by the verdict, the Assistant U.S. Attorney (AUSA) looked over the case file and the applicable statutes. She found that 18 U.S.C. § 922 prohibits an alien from possessing a firearm and Erik is in the United States as a registered alien. Before she goes any further, the AUSA consults case law on double jeopardy.

**245.** Under the *Blockburger* approach to double jeopardy, which of the following is the correct test to determine whether transporting firearms across state lines and "alien in possession of a firearm" are the "same offense"?

(A) are there some common elements in the two crimes?

(B) does each crime require proof of a fact that the other does not?

(C) did the legislature intend for someone to be prosecuted for both crimes?

(D) did the two offenses occur during the same transaction or set of acts?

Edmund Jamison was charged with raping Valery Victim two times on January 1st last year. The first incident occurred at 1:00 a.m. and the second an hour later. Jamison was tried for the first rape and was acquitted. Defense counsel has filed a Motion to Dismiss the second prosecution because collateral estoppel, applicable as part of the double jeopardy guarantee, bars the additional proceeding.

**246.** How should the court rule on the Motion to Dismiss?

ANSWER:

Ilene Gleason was charged with armed robbery and being a felon in possession of a deadly weapon. The crimes occurred when Gleason robbed a jewelry salesman who was carrying $250,000 in diamonds to a customer.

The prosecutor elected to join the two charges in a single indictment and trial. In a short trial the jury found Gleason guilty of both offenses. At sentencing, Gleason's lawyer has argued that double jeopardy bars her from being sentenced for the two offenses. You are the judge.

**247.** What result?

(A) Gleason cannot be convicted or sentenced for the two charges since they occurred at the same moment in time.

(B) Gleason cannot be sentenced for the two crimes because they both require the offender to possess a deadly weapon as an element.

(C) Gleason can be sentenced for the two crimes if the legislature enacted separate sentences for these offenses and intended for both of them to be imposed on the same offender.

(D)  Gleason can be sentenced for the two crimes since, under *Blockburger*, they are not the "same offense."

Brandon Briber was convicted of one count of bribery and was sentenced to two years imprisonment, a shockingly light sentence under the circumstances. He successfully appealed the admission of certain prosecution evidence and was granted a new trial.

While on bond awaiting the bribery retrial in three months, Brandon was convicted of arson for starting a fire in his furniture warehouse to collect on a fire insurance policy. Brandon was then convicted at the bribery retrial and the judge is now considering sentencing him to a five year sentence, three years longer than the sentence imposed at the initial bribery trial. Brandon's lawyer argues that a sentence longer than that imposed at the first trial (two years) is barred by double jeopardy.

248.  A harsher sentence after retrial in a case is:

(A)  illegal because double jeopardy bars a harsher sentence on retrial.

(B)  illegal because equal protection bars a harsher sentence on retrial.

(C)  possible since any sentenced authorized by state sentencing law is permitted if the defendant chooses to appeal a conviction and a new trial is ordered; the appeal is a waiver of double jeopardy protection.

(D)  possible if the defendant's conduct after the first trial justified the increased penalty.

Oliver Stoned was being tried for cocaine possession and jury selection was scheduled to start at 9:00 A.M. that day. At 9:15 A.M. the prosecutor received a note indicating that the only significant prosecution witness was in the hospital and would not be available to testify for at least two months.

The prosecutor immediately made a motion to postpone the trial for four months. The trial judge, a former prosecutor, granted the motion, dismissed all the potential jurors, and scheduled the trial in three months. The defense lawyer moved to dismiss the new trial date, arguing that jeopardy had attached at the first trial and therefore the second trial was barred by double jeopardy.

249.  When does jeopardy attach in a jury trial?

(A)  when the accused is formally arrested.

(B)  immediately after the indictment is signed.

(C)  when the jury is selected and sworn.

(D)  when the first witness is sworn.

Changing the facts, what if Mr. Stoned had waived a jury and opted for a bench trial.

250.  When does jeopardy attach at a bench trial?

(A)  when the defense gives its closing argument.

(B)  when the prosecution rests its case in chief.

(C)  when the court has heard all the evidence.

(D)  when the first witness takes the stand to testify.

Lionel Washington was hired to represent Beverly Lawton who had been convicted of five serious drug crimes. After the conviction, Lawton fired her lawyer and hired Washington to pursue the appeal. Washington prepared an excellent appeal and was successful in having the conviction overturned. The prosecution has now moved to schedule a trial date for a retrial.

**251.** Which of the following grounds for the appellate reversal would bar the retrial?

   (A)  the trial court erroneously admitted evidence that should have been suppressed because of an illegal search.

   (B)  the weight of the evidence was insufficient to convince the appellate court of guilt.

   (C)  the trial judge gave an incorrect jury instruction on reasonable doubt.

   (D)  there was not sufficient evidence of guilt presented at the trial

Sammy Solicit was arrested in Grand Central Station, New York City, New York State, for soliciting a prostitute after he deboarded a train arriving from Connecticut. Soliciting prostitution violates United States law, New York and Connecticut State law, and New York City ordinances. Sammy had been traveling back and forth between New York and Connecticut in order to patronize prostitutes. A local politician, with a strong family values platform, was running for re-election. The politician made frequent campaign speeches, calling for Sammy's prosecution in as many places as possible to "teach the sex fiends a lesson." The local churches and news media have echoed the demand for multiple prosecutions.

Because of this attention, the head New York City prosecutor convened a meeting of representatives of the various jurisdictions whose laws Solicit violated.

**252.** Which of the following sets of places could NOT prosecute Solicit without violating the Double Jeopardy Clause?

   (A)  United States and New York State.

   (B)  Connecticut and New York State.

   (C)  United States and New York City.

   (D)  New York State and New York City.

A defendant was charged with violating federal laws that prohibit hunting and fishing in protected wildlife sanctuaries. The punishment is as follows:

> (b) Punishment — The punishment for an offense under this section is a fine of not more than $10,000, imprisonment for not more than 6 months, or both.
> (c) Mandatory Restitution — Upon conviction under this section, the court shall order restitution in an amount equal to value of the wildlife illegally killed or harmed seriously.

The trial judge rejected the defendant's timely request for a jury trial and convicted him after a short bench trial. He was sentenced to serve six months in prison and fined $700. The defendant appeals, claiming that his Sixth Amendment right to a jury trial was violated.

**253.** You are the appellate judge in this case. On the basis of the United States Constitution, how do you respond to the defendant's appeal?

ANSWER:


Arnold Assaulter has been charged in state court with a misdemeanor count of domestic violence assault. The domestic violence assault statute authorizes a maximum penalty of six-months' imprisonment for conviction of this misdemeanor. However, a federal law makes it unlawful for any person "who has been convicted in any court of a misdemeanor crime of domestic violence to receive any firearm which has been shipped or transported in interstate commerce."

Arnold has filed a demand for a jury, and the district attorney has contested Arnold's entitlement to a jury trial in state court. The district attorney has stipulated that the federal law would effectively prohibit Arnold from possessing any firearm if he is convicted of the state domestic violence assault, thus Arnold would be subjected to an additional adverse consequence of the state conviction.

**254.** Under federal constitutional law, how should the court respond to the request for a jury trial?

(A) Arnold's demand for a jury trial is denied, because a misdemeanor is, by definition, not sufficiently serious to trigger a defendant's sixth amendment right to a jury trial since it signifies that the legislature did not consider the crime a serious one.

(B) Arnold's demand for a jury trial is denied, because a crime carrying a six-month prison term is not by itself sufficiently serious to mandate a jury trial. The denial of any right to bear arms does not change the legislature's determination of a crime's seriousness.

(C) Arnold's demand for a jury trial is granted, because a crime carrying a penalty of six months or more is a "serious offense."

(D) Arnold's demand for a jury trial is granted, because the additional consequence of losing one's right to bear arms reveals the legislature's determination that an offense is "serious," despite only authorizing a six-month prison term.

*Duncan v. Louisiana* is a seminal case in sixth amendment jury trial law.

**255.** What is the primary rationale for *Duncan v. Louisiana's* ruling that a defendant to a serious offense has the right to a jury trial?

(A) to increase accuracy in fact-finding.

(B) to increase public respect for verdicts by multiplying the number of persons deliberating on each case.

(C) to provide a defense against arbitrary law enforcement by including the public in the decision-making process.

(D) to give members of the public insight into the justice system.

**256.** In which case would the defendant be entitled by the United States Constitution to a trial by jury?

(A) an 17-year-old defendant in juvenile court facing a charge carrying a maximum sentence of five years in a juvenile detention facility.

(B) a 22-year-old defendant in adult criminal court facing a charge carrying a maximum sentence of six months in prison and a $750 fine.

(C) a 12-year-old defendant in adult criminal court facing a charge carrying a maximum sentence of 9 months in prison.

(D) a 9-year-old defendant in juvenile court facing a charge carrying a maximum sentence of five years in a juvenile detention facility.

You are prosecuting a defendant charged with bribery. The defendant is a member of the Konrad Church, a small local denomination. During jury selection, you come to learn that one member of the same denomination is on the panel that has been tentatively seated, subject to the parties' exercise of their peremptory challenges. You would like to use a peremptory challenge to exclude the juror because you are concerned she will be prone to side with the defendant.

**257.** May you exclude the potential juror for this reason?

ANSWER:

You are a criminal court judge handling the case of Donnie Defendant, who has been charged with drug conspiracy crimes for which he could be sentenced to a maximum of 20 years in prison. Donnie considers himself to be very intelligent and is proceeding *pro se* in the matter. At the last status conference you informed him of his right to a jury trial, but he said that he wanted to waive a jury and have a bench trial. Satisfied that Donnie knows what he is doing, you are prepared to grant his request. However, the prosecutor objected to the waiver and demanded a jury trial.

The law in your state, which is the same as the Federal Rules of Criminal Procedure, grants prosecutors the power to veto a defendant's waiver of a jury, but you are concerned that the state law may conflict with constitutional or federal law. The prosecutor has presented the following list of reasons why you must order a jury trial.

**258.** Which of the following reasons is INCORRECT regarding waiver of a jury trial?

  (A)  you (the judge) have not adequately investigated whether Donnie's waiver was made intelligently or voluntarily, so you may not properly grant a waiver.

  (B)  a waiver of a jury trial must be made in writing, and since Donnie has not done this, it would be error for you to grant the waiver at this time.

  (C)  even if you grant a waiver, state law allows the opportunity for the district attorney to veto the waiver, and that power does not violate Donnie's right to a jury trial.

  (D)  the state, as a party in the case, has the same federal constitutional right to demand a jury trial that Donnie does — either party can demand a jury, but both must waive it.

Frannie Fire was charged with felony arson in state court, which carries a maximum of 15 years in prison. The state's criminal procedure rules require that a six-member jury be used in all felony trials. Frannie's motion for a twelve-member jury was denied and she was subsequently convicted. On appeal, she is claiming that the trial violated her Sixth and Fourteenth Amendment rights to a jury trial and request a retrial in front of a twelve-member jury.

**259.** You are the appellate judge. How do you respond?

  (A)  her appeal is denied because a six-member jury is constitutionally permissible.

  (B)  her appeal is denied because while a twelve-member jury is constitutionally required, the use of a six-member jury in this case is harmless error because the overwhelming proof of guilt meant that Frannie would have been convicted by a larger jury, anyway.

  (C)  her appeal is granted because Frannie has a constitutional right to a jury trial, and the definition of a jury when the Sixth Amendment was written was a body of twelve members.

  (D)  her appeal is successful since Frannie's constitutional right to a jury trial was violated by the jury of six members. Such a verdict may not be the result of careful deliberation, consistently achieved by a group of people representative of the community at large.

Vinnie Vandal was charged in state court with a misdemeanor count of vandalism, which carries a maximum penalty of nine months in prison. The complaint alleged that he started a small fire in a metal garbage can.

To save money, a year ago the state legislature adopted a criminal procedure rule approving a four-member jury to be used in all misdemeanor jury trials. Vinnie's motion for a twelve-member jury was denied, and he was subsequently convicted. On appeal, he is claiming that the trial violated his Sixth and Fourteenth Amendment rights to a jury trial.

**260.** You are the appellate judge. How do you respond?

    (A)   the appeal is denied because a four-member jury is constitutionally permissible under the sixth amendment for this crime.

    (B)   the appeal is granted because Vinnie's constitutional right to a jury trial for this crime was violated using a four-member jury. Such a verdict may not be the result of careful deliberation, consistently achieved by a group of people representative of the community at large.

    (C)   the appeal is denied because, while a twelve-member jury is proper size, the mistake was harmless error since Vinnie confessed to the crime and lighter fluid was found in his home after a constitutionally valid search.

    (D)   the appeal is granted, because Vinnie has a constitutional right to a jury trial, and the definition of a jury when the Sixth Amendment was written was a body of twelve members.

You are a member of a state legislative committee investigating how to increase the efficiency in the state judicial system, which is suffering from an extensive backlog of pending criminal cases. The committee chair has suggested that a real problem is that a state statute mandates that jury verdicts be unanimous in criminal cases. If the jurors are not unanimous, there is a "hung jury" and the case may be retried, taking up scarce judicial resources for a second trial in the same case. The chair has asked your opinion on the lawfulness and wisdom of changing state law to permit a jury verdict of 10-2 to convict or acquit.

**261.** What is your opinion regarding the jury verdict?

ANSWER:

Daisy Defendant was tried and convicted for murder in Delta County. An ethnic group that is a minority nationwide and forbids its members from participating in elections makes up 60% of the citizens and residents in Delta County. Since the list of registered voters form the entire jury pool, persons of this ethnicity make up only 10% of the jury pool. The entire jury venire of 500 persons from which Daisy's twelve-person petit jury was ultimately selected included 2% of the ethnic group and the twelve-member petit jury that convicted Daisy contained only one jury member who belonged to the ethnic group. Daisy's conviction has been attacked on the basis of this statistical disparity.

**262.** Acting under authority of the United States Constitution, how should a higher court dispose of this attack on Daisy's conviction?

(A) Daisy's conviction should be affirmed, because there is no constitutional guarantee of statistical representation of the community in the jury selection process.

(B) Daisy should be retried, because the composition of the petit jury violated Daisy's right to be tried by a petit jury representative of the community in which the crime was committed.

(C) Daisy should be retried, because the composition of the jury pool and venire violated her right to be tried by a petit jury selected by a process that does not systematically exclude a segment of the community in which the crime was committed.

(D) Daisy's conviction should be affirmed, because the disproportionate composition of the jury pool, venire, and petite jury constitute a violation of the civil rights of members of the severely underrepresented ethnic group; it does not violate any of Daisy's rights.

Susan Corrigan is the defendant in federal burglary case stemming from a break-in at an Army Reserve Armory. She is not happy about her upcoming trial and asks you, her lawyer, when her absence from the trial could prevent it from proceeding.

**263.** You check Rule 43, Federal Rules of Criminal Procedure, and tell her that her absence could prevent a trial in the following circumstance:

(A) the defendant attends all pretrial conferences and hearings, agrees to the trial date, but fails to appear for any part of the actual trial.

(B) the defendant attends all pretrial conferences and hearings, appears for the first day of trial, and disappears after the government presents a very persuasive case to the jury.

(C) the defendant is present at almost all pretrial events, but is excluded from an attorney-only pretrial hearing to determine whether the alleged victim (a minor) is competent to testify. Later, the defendant is present for the trial.

(D) the defendant, a corporation, fails to send any officer or representative to the trial and is represented by the corporation's lawyer.

Harry Darwin is on trial for marijuana possession. He has been convicted on the same charge eight times in the past six years, and the same judge has presided over all of those cases. In an effort to speed up the trial, the judge tells defense counsel that although Harry wants to testify, he "doesn't need to testify. I have heard him testify many times. He is going to say the drugs weren't his. So, I will assume that is what he will say now and so his testimony is unnecessary. I rule he cannot testify because it would be cumulative evidence." The defense counsel objected.

**264.** You are handling the appeal for the defense lawyer. Does the criminal defendant have a constitutional right to testify at the defendant's own trial? If so, what is the constitutional basis for the right?

ANSWER:

Quinn Quiet is on trial and chose not to testify. In closing argument, the prosecutor plans to argue to the jury that the reason Quinn did not testify and deny any of the evidence presented was because Quinn knew he would be committing perjury if did deny them. The judge anticipates the prosecutor may make such an argument, so she has planned to give the jury the following instruction:

> Every defendant has the constitutional right to testify or to not testify. If a defendant should choose not to testify, that decision does not give rise to any interference or presumption against the defendant or about the facts in the case.

> Such a decision to remain silent should never be considered in determining that defendant's guilt or innocence.

In an unrelated case, Tammy Talkie decided to testify on her own behalf. That prosecutor plans to tell the jurors that they should consider the reliability of the witnesses testifying. Specifically, he plans to argue that jury evaluate Tammy's credibility because she, unlike all of the State's witnesses, was able to remain in the court and listen to all of the testimony.

**265.** Which, if any, of these statements would violate the respective defendant's right not to testify under the United States Constitution?

(A) the prosecutor's closing argument in *State v. Quiet* would be unconstitutional.

(B) the judge's planned jury instruction in *State v. Quiet* would be unconstitutional.

(C) the prosecutor's comments in *State v. Talkie* would be unconstitutional.

(D) none of the statements discussed above would be unconstitutional.

Katrina Weiser is being tried for kidnaping. While the prosecution's star witness was testifying, Weiser became irritated and argued with the witness, yelled to the jury that the witness was lying, and shouted out her version of the events. The judge immediately reprimanded Weiser and ordered her to control herself and stop disrupting the trial.

However, a few minutes later Weiser became disruptive again. This time, when the judge ordered her to be quiet, she yelled back, "No, you be quiet! I'll say what I want and if you say different I'll shut your mouth myself!"

The judge told Weiser that she would be held in contempt if she did not behave, and warned that if she did not stop disrupting she would be removed from the courtroom until she could control her behavior. The judge held her in contempt twice for making obscene gestures at him.

Ultimately, after Weiser repeatedly refused to control herself, she was removed from the courtroom. Before she left, the judge told Weiser that she could return if she promised to behave in an appropriate manner. At regular intervals, the judge brought Weiser back into the courtroom and asked her if she would act appropriately. Each time Weiser turned her back on the judge and did not respond. The judge then ordered her removed from the courtroom and the trial proceeded with defense counsel in attendance.

After the closing arguments, the defense moved for a mistrial because Weiser had been denied her constitutional right to be present at her own trial. You are the judge's clerk.

**266.** What advice will you give the judge on the motion for a mistrial?

ANSWER:

The United States Supreme Court has recognized that a judge presiding in a case where the defendant is persistently disruptive has a number of available options.

**267.** Which of the following is NOT one of them, according to the leading case of *Illinois v. Allen:*

(A) find the defendant in contempt of court.

(B) remove the defendant from the courtroom.

(C) bind and gag the defendant.

(D) instruct the jury that it may consider the defendant's courtroom behavior when it assesses his guilt or innocence.

Daniel Defendant was tried for the brutal murder of several elderly persons. The trial in a small court room was highly publicized, and many members of the press and general public attended the trial. Once the seats were all filled, the bailiffs began turning people away, explaining that the courtroom was full and that fire codes prohibited the admission of any more people. Among those turned away were some members of the press, some members of Daniel's family, two members of the victims' families, and others who just wanted to observe. Throughout the trial, as various persons would leave the courtroom, a corresponding number of people were allowed in to take their places. Daniel has appealed his conviction, arguing that his Sixth Amendment right to a public trial was violated since many members of the public were barred from the court room.

**268.** How should the appellate court respond to Daniel's appeal?

ANSWER:


**269.** Which of the following is NOT a legitimate reason for a judge to order that an appropriately narrow portion of court proceedings be closed to the public?

(A) protecting an undercover agent's identity.

(B) protecting a witness or party from grave physical harm or protecting the welfare of a particular crime victim.

(C) protecting national security matters that would be compromised by public hearings.

(D) protecting a defendant from vicious media attacks and public denigration.

Polly Popularity is on trial for a crime that the popular press has been decrying for some time. Not wanting his every decision and ruling to be picked apart and analyzed, the judge has ordered that the trial be closed to the public and the press. Polly has not objected because she thinks a closed trial may benefit her.

The major area newspaper, however, has filed a suit against the trial judge, seeking an injunction against the trial closing. The paper makes two arguments. First, the paper maintains that closing the trial violates Polly's Sixth Amendment right to a public trial. Second, the press argues that closing the trial violates the First Amendment guarantees of freedom of the press and freedom of assembly.

**270.** Which, if any, of these is/are valid ground(s) for the newspaper's demand for an injunction?

(A) the judge's order violates the First Amendment.

(B) the judge's order violates the Sixth Amendment.

(C) the judge's order violates the First and Sixth Amendments.

(D) none of the newspaper's arguments is valid.

Tina Triggerhappy, on trial for second degree murder, has claimed self-defense. While the events leading to the shooting were hotly disputed, the prosecution and defense witnesses all testified that Tina placed a gun in direct contact with Vinnie Victim's head and pulled the trigger three times, fatally shooting Vinnie.

After the close of proof, the district attorney filed Proposed Jury Instruction #1, which reads in part, "Should you find that the State has proven beyond a reasonable doubt every element of the charge of second degree murder, you may nevertheless acquit Tina if you find that she has proven by a preponderance of the evidence the following elements of the defense of self-defense." The statutory elements of self-defense are then listed.

The district attorney also filed Proposed Jury Instruction #2, which states, "A person is presumed to intend the natural and probable consequences of his or her acts." Tina's attorney objected to Proposed Instructions #1 and #2, claiming that both of them unconstitutionally place the burden of proof on Tina.

Afraid that the judge might deny Proposed Jury Instruction #2, the district attorney has filed Proposed Jury Instruction #3 as an alternative. Proposed Jury Instruction #3 reads, "Should you find the following facts to be true: (a) that Tina aimed a loaded gun at a living person, and (b) that Tina then pulled the trigger of that loaded gun, then you may infer that Tina intended to kill." Tina's attorney has lodged the same objection to Proposed Instruction #3.

271.    Assuming that the three jury instructions accurately apply the relevant state law, what is the status of each of the proposed jury instructions under the United States Constitution?

      (A)    proposed Jury Instruction #1 unconstitutionally shifts the state's burden of proof.

      (B)    proposed Jury Instruction #2 unconstitutionally shifts the state's burden of proof.

      (C)    proposed Jury Instruction #3 unconstitutionally shifts the state's burden of proof.

      (D)    all of the proposed jury instructions — #1, #2, and #3 — unconstitutionally shift the state's burden of proof.

You are chair of a legislative subcommittee making recommendations on improving the insanity defense in your state. Two issues are which side should have the burden of persuasion and what should the standard of proof be to establish the insanity defense.

272.    Which of the following is combinations would be permissible under the United

States Constitution:

(A)  placing the burden of persuasion on the government to prove the defendant was sane beyond a reasonable doubt.

(B)  placing the burden of persuasion on the defendant to prove the defendant was insane by a preponderance of the evidence.

(C)  all of above are constitutional.

(D)  none of above is constitutional.

Adam and Bobby conspired to sell counterfeit merchandise in two adjacent counties: Ware and Selle. Both counties are in the State of Ethon. Both Adam and Bobby went to their warehouse in Ware County and picked up the merchandise and transported their load to Selle for resale at small mom-and-pop stores. As soon as they crossed into Selle County, they were arrested at a roadblock after police officers, who were searching for a missing child, discovered that the two were transporting the counterfeit merchandise. Assume that possessing the counterfeit products is a crime under both federal and Ethon law.

273. Under the usual state jurisdiction and venue rules and under Rule 18 of the Federal Rules of Criminal Procedure, which of the following would have jurisdiction to try them for possessing and transporting the merchandise?

   (A)  the United States District Court in the federal district that covered Ware County.
   (B)  the Ware County criminal court.
   (C)  the Selle County criminal court.
   (D)  all of the above.

Michelle Adams was driving her car with her baby secured in the passenger seat in the State of Jefferson. Throughout the trip, the baby cried uncontrollably. When Michelle refueled the car, her baby continued to cry. She took the baby out of the car and shook him violently, then struck him in the head several times with her fist. The baby became quiet.

Michelle then drove into the State of Dickerson, and again shook the wimpering baby to punish it for crying at the gas station. Several minutes later Michelle discovered that the baby was unconscious. She drove to the hospital, where the baby was pronounced dead a short while later. The coroner found that the baby died from "shaken baby syndrome" from the violent shaking that Michelle did in the States of Jefferson and Dickerson.

274. Where is the proper jurisdiction (Dickerson or Jefferson) to try Michelle for reckless murder of the baby?

ANSWER:


Rules 20 and 21 of the Federal Rules of Criminal Procedure specifically authorize a motion requesting a change of venue for certain purposes.

275. Which of the following is NOT true with regard to this motion:

   (A)  the defendant may file the motion to obtain a fair and impartial trial.

(B)  the government may file the motion to obtain a more convenient venue.

(C)  the defendant may move to transfer for plea and sentencing.

(D)  The United States Attorneys in both locales must approve in writing any transfer for plea and sentence.

Defendant Herman, who is in a wheelchair, is being tried for negligent homicide. Since the federal courthouse where the trial is scheduled has extremely poor facilities for the disabled, Herman wants to transfer the trial to another federal district in the same state. There, the modern court house is fully accessible and is only two blocks from Herman's home. The defense counsel now seeks a change venue under Rule 21 of the Federal Rules of Criminal Procedure.

**276.**  Which of the following is NOT required under Rule 21?

(A)  the consent of the government.

(B)  a motion by the defendant.

(C)  ordinarily, the motion to obtain the transfer must be initiated before arraignment.

(D)  the consent of the court.

On March 1st, three years ago, Joan Solan embezzled money from her employee, a local bank. The theft was quickly discovered and she was arrested on March 15th of that year. She waived a formal indictment and an information was filed on June 1st. Trial was to begin on December 1st, three years ago.

On November 15, Solan fired her lawyer and hired Bob Hellerstein who immediately asked for a continuance since he did not have time to prepare for the December 1st trial. The prosecutor agreed to the continuance and trial was again scheduled for May 1st, two years ago.

On April 20th two years ago it was rescheduled because the judge handling the case had a heart attack. Trial was set for September 1st of that year before a new judge.

On August 15th, two years ago, the prosecutor asked for a continuance because a "huge case load simply made it impossible" for him to work up the case. The defendant objected to the delay, but the court granted the continuance and scheduled the case for January 15th, one year ago.

On that date one year ago, the prosecutor asked for a two week continuance since a key prosecution witness had disappeared. The court agreed, though the defendant objected.

When the witness was not located within a week, the prosecutor requested a three month postponement, until April 15th, one year ago, to allow him to clear his docket and to find the witness. The defendant again opposed the postponement, which was nevertheless approved by the court.

On April 14th, one year ago and the day before the trial was scheduled to begin, the court house caught fire and all trials were postponed for six months. The trial was reset for October 18th, one year ago, but was not held because the defendant had the flu. It was reset for July 16th of the current year.

Finally, the trial began on July 16th of the current year. The defendant was convicted of all charges.

277. You are the defense lawyer representing defendant Solan on appeal. Discuss the approach you should take to assert that her constitutional speedy trial right was violated by the extensive delay.

ANSWER:

Defendant Duane Simpson is serving a 10-year sentence in the State of Boerum for armed robbery. Under state law he is ineligible for parole and will have to serve the entire 10-year term. Now after serving three months of the sentence, Simpson's lawyer informed him that he was just indicted in the State of Brooke for murdering his girlfriend, who was mysteriously found dead in her home six months ago.

Simpson maintains that he was playing poker in the back room of a bar when the homicide occurred, but is concerned that he will be unable to locate and obtain the trial testimony of three alibi witnesses if the State of Brooke's trial is not held until he is released from prison in almost ten years.

**278.** Under the Sixth Amendment's speedy trial guarantee, which is correct?

(A) Simpson has no right to have his homicide trial in the State of Brooke held until he can appear in person in that state in about ten years.

(B) Simpson has no right to have his trial held in the State of Brooke because the speedy trial guarantee does not apply to prisoners lawfully incarcerated in another jurisdiction.

(C) Simpson has a Sixth Amendment right to have, upon his demand, the State of Brooke authorities make a diligent effort to bring him to trial in that state.

(D) Simpson has a Sixth Amendment right to have, upon his demand, a prompt trial in the State of Boerum (where he is incarcerated) on the outstanding homicide indictment issued in the State of Brooke.

Kenneth Wilson, who has not been indicted, is arrested for violating federal securities law, a felony, after his energy company failed shortly after he gave an optimistic assessment of his company's status. Kenneth was arrested at an airport with a suitcase and his passport. You are his lawyer and are clearing your calendar so you are free to deal with the future proceedings in the case.

**279.** Under the Federal Speedy Trial Act of 1974, the indictment must be held within how many days after Kenneth's arrest?

(A) 10 days.
(B) 30 days.
(C) 60 days.
(D) One year.

Assume that Kenneth, described in the previous question, is indicted 28 days after his arrest and is now eager to proceed to trial. However, you, Kenneth's defense counsel, have advised him to do nothing until the time period that the trial must be held under the Federal Speedy Trial Act of 1974. The additional time will permit you to investigate this case thoroughly, have your experts carefully examine many pertinent documents, and let you negotiate a possible favorable deal with the prosecutor handling the case.

**280.** Under the federal statute, when must Kenneth's trial be held, absent acceptable reasons for a delay?

(A) within one year of arrest.
(B) within 70 days of the indictment.

(C)   within one year of the indictment.

(D)   any time before the accused's right to a constitutional speedy trial is violated.

Immediately after Kenneth (see previous two questions) was indicted, his case attracted widespread media attention and has become "the" case of the century, since investors lost billions in their retirement savings. The judge handling the case is calculating when the trial must be held under the Federal Speedy Trial Act.

A review of the extensive record in the case showed the following events:

(1)   The defense filed a motion that took the government 60 days to file a response:

(2)   The defense took an interlocutory appeal that was rejected by the appellate court four months later;

(3)   Defense counsel sought and gained the court's approval to conduct a mental examination of Kenneth to determine whether he is fit to stand trial. The examination took 14 days to complete;

(4)   The government obtained another 30 days of extension because the government's evidentiary documents were misplaced in the office.

**281.**   Of the mentioned delays, all of them are to be excluded from calculating the time limitation under the Federal Speedy Trial Act of 1974, EXCEPT:

(A)   the 60 days it took the government to respond to the defense motion.

(B)   the four months needed to resolve the interlocutory appeal.

(C)   the 14 days it took to determine whether Kenneth is mentally fit to stand trial.

(D)   the 30 days it took for the government to locate the missing evidence.

You are a law clerk to a federal judge who is obsessed with keeping a current docket in criminal cases. In order to protect the public from dangerous offenders and to provide victims with a speedy resolution of their cases, your boss is considering adopting a schedule that, whenever possible, would try every defendant within ten days of indictment.

**282.**   Your boss has asked you to tell him whether due process or the Federal Speedy Trial Act places any limits on scheduling cases too quickly. How will you respond?

ANSWER:

Late in the afternoon of December 31st, three years ago, Evelyn had rushed to get home from work so she could get ready for a New Years Eve date. Her light truck crashed into a minivan, causing three deaths. Because she sustained extensive injuries in the collision and was in a coma for two months, her arrest was delayed for seven months, occurring on July 22nd, two years ago.

The grand jury indicted her on December 6th two years ago on three counts of negligent homicide and her trial was scheduled to began on June 30th, one year ago. The trial was postponed three times for various reasons.

It finally began three days ago, but the judge declared a mistrial after a defense witness stated something that was explicitly barred by the judge in a pretrial hearing. The judge scheduled a retrial for February 6th of next year. Defense counsel is exploring whether the statute of limitations has run so that the case must be dismissed.

283. When does the "clock begin to run" for the statute of limitation in Evelyn's case?

   (A)  on December 31st (three years ago) when the accident occurred.
   (B)  on July 22nd (two years ago) when she was arrested.
   (C)  on December 6th (two years ago) when she was indicted.
   (D)  three days ago when the trial began.

The concept of "tolling" is important in assessing whether the statute of limitations has been violated in a particular case.

284. What does it mean that the statute of limitations is "tolled?"

   (A)  the statute has been exceeded.
   (B)  the statute has started to run.
   (C)  the running of the statute of limitations has stopped.
   (D)  the initial event starting the running of the statute of limitations has not yet occurred.

Bob "Pit Bull" Pitler was convicted in federal court of seven counts of conspiracy to traffic in drugs and twenty-two substantive drug offenses. He maintains that the convictions should be overturned because devastating evidence obtained in an illegal interrogation in violation of the Fifth and Sixth Amendments was introduced at his federal trial.

His defense counsel unsuccessfully challenged the evidence in the trial court, then failed in an appeal to the appropriate federal circuit court and the United States Supreme Court refused to consider the case. Defense counsel now wants to pursue collateral relief on the theory that Pitler's federal constitutional rights were violated when the federal court admitted evidence obtained in the interrogation.

285.  Which of the following remedies should ordinarily be used?

    (A)  federal habeas corpus.
    (B)  motion to vacate sentence under 28 U.S.C. § 2255.
    (C)  appeal to the state supreme court in the state where the conviction occurred.
    (D)  state habeas corpus.

After a lengthy trial, Khaleel Mostuma was convicted in State B of smuggling untaxed cigarettes into the state. Defense counsel unsuccessfully objected to jury instructions on the definition of reasonable doubt. Appeals to the State B intermediate and supreme courts also failed. The defense lawyer now will file a federal habeas corpus petition contesting the jury instructions.

286.  Where should the federal habeas corpus petition be filed?

    (A)  in Washington, D.C., where the U.S. Supreme Court is located.
    (B)  in a State B trial court in the judicial district where the trial occurred.
    (C)  in a federal district court in the judicial district where the state supreme court is located.
    (D)  in a federal district court in the judicial district where Mostuma is incarcerated.

287.  Which of the following would preclude a federal court from considering a petition for habeas corpus from a state prisoner?

    (A)  the same claim was presented in a prior federal habeas corpus application.
    (B)  the defendant has not yet completed service of the sentence imposed for the conviction allegedly obtained in violation of the United States Constitution.

(C) the state judgment became final six months ago when the period for direct appeal under state law expired.

(D) the state prisoner's petition alleges a violation of the United States Constitution rather than the constitution of the state where the conviction occurred.

You have been hired to represent Shlomo Blumberg who was convicted in a federal court of seven counts of identity theft for his involvement in a scheme to obtain and use stolen credit card information. At trial another lawyer argued that Blumberg's Fifth Amendment rights were violated by police interrogation at his home. The trial court rejected the argument as did both the state appellate and supreme courts. The trial lawyer also lost a federal habeas corpus petition.

You want to file a second habeas corpus petition presenting a better researched argument that the trial court had made a fatal error in using a jury selection procedure that effectively eliminated elderly citizens from being included on the venire.

288. Which, if any, of the following must you establish in order to have a chance at having the second habeas corpus petition granted by the federal court.

(A) the claim was actually presented in the first habeas corpus hearing, but the federal judge incorrectly rejected it as lacking merit.

(B) the claim was not presented in the first habeas petition because counsel did not discover the jury selection error until after Blumberg was convicted.

(C) the case law that was violated by the jury selection system had been in place over twenty years and the state jury authorities should have been aware of it.

(D) none of above would be helpful.

289. Which of the following is CORRECT about federal habeas corpus:

(A) a habeas corpus petition on an issue that was already rejected in a prior habeas petition shall be dismissed.

(B) any judge on the court of appeals may permit a second habeas corpus petition if the appellate judge finds by clear and convincing evidence that the defendant would have been acquitted had the errors at issue in the second petition not have been made in the trial court.

(C) because of concerns about federalism and separation of powers, a federal judge considering a habeas corpus petition may not issue a stay of state court proceedings but may overturn the result of any such proceedings that conflict with the federal court's ruling in the habeas corpus case.

(D) none of above is correct.

You represent a state prisoner challenging a state conviction. Your federal habeas corpus petition, alleging numerous federal constitutional violations during the state prisoner's trial, was just dismissed by the United States District Judge. You and your client think the court erred in dismissing the habeas corpus petition and you have been authorized to appeal the decision.

**290.** What must you do in order to perfect the appeal to the appropriate federal circuit court?

(A) obtain the permission of the United States Supreme Court.

(B) file a brief in the appropriate circuit court.

(C) obtain a certificate of appealability from the appropriate circuit court.

(D) file a notice of appeal with the District Court that dismissed the petition.

A new client, Carla Fuentes, was recently convicted of arson by a state court jury and was sentenced to five years in state prison. Trial counsel appealed unsuccessfully to the state intermediate appellate court. The state supreme court denied certiorari. When Fuentes' lawyer died suddenly, you were retained to represent her. You are considering filing a federal habeas corpus petition to challenge the state conviction. You begin your study of the huge case file. You know that federal habeas corpus law requires that, in most cases, the petitioner must have "exhausted" available state remedies.

**291.** What must you look for in the file to assess whether this occurred?

ANSWER:

Assume that your review of the file showed that the issue you want to raise in habeas corpus — the validity of a confession — was already raised unsuccessfully by appellate counsel on direct appeal in state court.

**292.** How will this state appellate decision affect your habeas corpus petition?

ANSWER:

Your were appointed to represent, Bethany Doomer, an indigent person convicted of prostitution. Your client is consistently unreasonable and insists that you appeal the prostitution conviction, though neither she nor you can think of a ground to do so. The trial judge conducted an error-free hearing as far as you can tell and the evidence against your client was absolutely overwhelming. Nevertheless, she has instructed you to think up something for the appeal.

**293.** Which of the following is the best course for you to follow as an ethical lawyer:

(A) inform your client that you refuse to file anything in any court.

(B) file an *Anders* brief in the appellate court.

(C) send a letter to the appellate and trial courts informing them that you have withdrawn from representing your client.

(D) file an appellate brief arguing issues that you believe are frivolous but which you present as serious issues, hoping that the appellate court will somehow agree with you.

In 1972 the United States Supreme Court decided *Furman v. Georgia* which invalidated the death penalty.

294.  What part of the Constitution did the *Furman* majority find was violated by the way the death penalty was imposed and carried out:

(A)  the Cruel and Unusual Punishment Clause of the Eighth Amendment.
(B)  due process of the Fourteenth Amendment.
(C)  equal protection of the Fourteenth Amendment.
(D)  Supremacy Clause.

The United States Supreme Court has placed severe limits on who may be given the death penalty.

295.  Which of the following may NOT be executed for murder under the Supreme Court cases:

(A)  people who were under age 18 when they killed.
(B)  mentally retarded offenders.
(C)  people who are insane.
(D)  all of above may not be given the death penalty or executed.

The Supreme Court has also limited the types of criminal involvement that may be the subject of the death penalty.

296.  Which of the following would be a valid crime for a state to sanction by the penalty of death:

(A)  rape of an adult woman.
(B)  rape of a child.
(C)  minor participation in a felony murder where the offender had a reckless indifference to human life.
(D)  major participation in a felony murder where the offender had a reckless indifference to human life.
(E)  All of above.

You were appointed to represent Leland Ferrell charged with the intentional homicide of the dean of his college and facing the death penalty under state law. Your investigation has revealed that Ferrell was sexually assaulted by a priest when he was a young boy and your psychiatrist is prepared to testify that your client is "especially prone to violence against authority figures" because of the incident.

Your client was convicted of first degree murder and you are now in the sentencing phase. You call your psychiatrist as a witness. The prosecutor objects, arguing that the testimony is inadmissible "because in our jurisdiction we have aggravating and mitigating factors. Our legislature has limited the mitigating factors to six topics and your psychiatrist would not address any of them." The judge has asked for your response.

**297.** What argument should you make?

ANSWER:

**298.** Which of the following is TRUE about procedures that must be followed in capital cases:

(A) a state is free to have a judge make the death penalty decision and may dispense with the jury as long as the judge carefully follows state laws on death penalty procedures.

(B) unless waived by the defendant, a jury must decide the facts that will determine whether the state's aggravating and mitigating factors have been established by the parties.

(C) a state may not allow victim's impact statements to be introduced in a capital sentencing hearing because it would appeal too much to the jurors' emotions and may interfere with careful attention to the statutory elements of the crime.

(D) all of above are true.

299. Of the four traditional theories of punishment (retribution, deterrence, rehabilitation, and incapacitation), which is/are NOT designed to decrease future criminal activity:

(A) retribution.
(B) deterrence.
(C) rehabilitation.
(D) incapacitation.
(E) only two of above.
(F) only three of above.

At a sentencing hearing, the judge must accord the right of allocution.

300. What is allocution?

(A) defense counsel may interrogate prosecution witnesses.
(B) the jury has the opportunity to ask the court to clarify jury instructions.
(C) the defendant has the right to address the court concerning the sentence.
(D) the prosecutor, as a representative of the community, gets to express the community's position on the proper sentence.

In *Apprendi v. New Jersey* the United States Supreme Court greatly enhanced the jury's role in sentencing.

301. What is the result of *Apprendi:*

(A) the jury must be allowed to set the exact sentence the defendant will serve.
(B) the Equal Protection Clause requires the jury to make factual findings on sentencing issues that increase the maximum sentence.
(C) if a state's sentencing laws increase the sentence for a prior criminal conviction, the fact of that conviction must be found by a jury.
(D) the jury, unless waived, must make factual findings that increase the penalty beyond the prescribed statutory maximum.

Four years ago the State of Lincoln's legislature was convinced that auto theft was a serious problem that had increased tenfold. To combat this crime, three years ago the legislature increased the penalty for a second conviction for auto theft from a maximum of three years in prison to a minimum of fifty years in prison.

You are an appellate judge hearing the appeal of a defendant who, despite having previously been convicted of auto theft last year, again stole a car earlier this year and was convicted of the second heist. The trial judge sentenced your client to fifty years in prison for second crime. Defense counsel has attacked the fifty-year sentence on the ground that it is cruel and unusual punishment in violation of the Eighth Amendment.

**302.**   What is your response to the argument?

ANSWER:

# PRACTICE FINAL EXAM: QUESTIONS

A police officer and his drug dog walked through the hallways of an apartment house. The departmental policy authorizes officers to walk through the common hallways of apartment houses to detect the presence of illegal drugs. The dog signaled a positive alert in front of apartment 14D. Using the dog alert as probable cause, police secured a search warrant for Apartment 14D and found, during the execution of the warrant, a small quantity of marijuana.

**303.** Is the evidence seized during execution of the search warrant admissible?

ANSWER:

Detective Roberts submitted an application for a search warrant based upon information received from a confidential unnamed informant. After considering the affidavit, the magistrate informed Roberts that the probable cause section was insufficient. The magistrate administered the oath to Roberts and asked him questions to fill out the probable cause. The magistrate recorded Roberts' supplemental testimony. After hearing Roberts' additional information, the magistrate told Roberts and the assistant prosecutor that she was not convinced that the informant really existed. The magistrate ordered Roberts and the assistant prosecutor to produce the informant in chambers the next morning.

**304.** Must the prosecutor produce the informant?

(A) Yes. The prosecutor must comply or forgo the warrant.
(B) Yes. The prosecutor must comply with the order. It does not really matter because the informant will have to be produced at trial.
(C) No. The prosecutor need not comply because the informant's privilege protects the prosecutor from ever having to disclose the informant's identity.
(D) No. The prosecutor need not comply because the judge has no right to that information.

A search warrant ordered police to conduct a search at "210 Centre Street, a four apartment complex, front apartment number 3 on the second floor, belonging to Angel Smith." When police arrived at the 210 Centre Street, they discovered that Apartment 3 was at the rear of the second floor; the name on the door plate read Angel Smith. They entered Apartment 3 and found large quantities of illegal drugs. Prior to trial, the defense moved to suppress the evidence.

**305.** Should the court grant the motion to suppress?

(A)  Yes. The search warrant misdirected the police.

(B)  Yes. A search warrant must particularly describe the place to be searched; here the description was inaccurate.

(C)  No. The search warrant described the place to be searched with adequate specificity.

(D)  No. The police acted in good faith reliance on the search warrant.

Police investigating a street shooting recognized the victim, Charles Todd, who was a major drug trafficker in the upper west side of the city. Todd had been shot execution-style three times in the head. The investigating officers noticed red marks around the victim's throat. Missing from the victim's body was a heavy gold necklace with a crucifix which the victim always wore. The officers speculated that the necklace had been ripped away from Todd's body. Later the same night, police received a tip from an informant who was a regular police source of information about drug trafficking that Todd had been murdered by John Sanford, a competitor whose territory had been encroached upon by Todd's people. Sanford was also known as a major drug dealer in the same part of the city, and the informant said that Sanford was sitting on an enormous cache of drugs.

Armed with the information from the informant, police presented a magistrate with probable cause to believe that Sanford was involved in Todd's murder and requested a warrant to search Sanford's home for the necklace. The officers did not present the magistrate with information about drugs. The warrant ordered police to search Sanford's home for the necklace. The warrant did not command the officers to search for drugs. Prior to entering Sanford's home, the commanding officer instructed the search team to look for the necklace and drugs. Once in the house, police scoured the premises for drugs and the necklace. In several closets on the first floor police found large quantities of drugs. Police then searched the rest of the house. On the second floor of the home, in a child's dresser drawer, police found the necklace. Sanford's lawyer filed a motion to suppress the necklace and the drugs.

**306.**  How should the court rule on the motion to suppress?

ANSWER:

Police officers had a warrant to arrest Tom Feola. When they went to Tom's house, his mother informed them that he was not at home. She told the officers that Tom was at his girlfriend's house. She provided the police with the name and address of Tom's girlfriend. Police went directly to the girlfriend's house, entered and arrested Tom. Tom claims the arrest was illegal.

**307.**  Was the arrest illegal?

(A)  The arrest is legal because the officers had an arrest warrant.

(B)  The arrest is legal because of exigent circumstances since the defendant may have learned from his mother that the police were looking for him.

(C)  The arrest is illegal because police entered a home to search for a non-resident without a search warrant.

(D) The arrest is illegal because police entered without permission or exigent circumstances.

Evelyn Piersall was arrested for drunk driving. The normal procedure in Metropolis is to book drunk driving suspects, strip search them, and then place them in individual holding cells until they are sober, at which time they are released and issued a summons. Piersall was booked and then strip searched by a female police officer. The officer found, hidden in Piersall's underwear, a small bag of marijuana. She was charged with D.U.I. and possession of marijuana, a misdemeanor. Piersall's lawyer has challenged the strip search.

308. Is Metropolis' strip search policy constitutional?

(A) The policy is consistent with Fourth Amendment standards because the standardized policy controls police discretion.

(B) The policy is consistent with Fourth Amendment standards that allow a full search of the person incident to a lawful custodial arrest.

(C) The policy violates the Fourth Amendment because evidence of drunk driving is not likely to be found on the person of the arrestee.

(D) The policy violates the Fourth Amendment because a search of such magnitude must be based upon individualized cause.

A Metropolis ordinance authorized warrantless inspections by police of vehicles in public garages, auto sales lots, junkyards, and other vehicle salvage facilities. The regulatory scheme required proprietors of such establishments to present, on demand, titles or other documentary evidence of ownership in vehicles located on the premises.

The "Cheap Used Cars" lot is located at the corner of Superior and East 118th Street. The owner of the lot was previously convicted in connection with a chop shop operation. Officer Krupke entered the "Cheap Used Cars" sales facility located at the rear of the lot and demanded to see the title for a 1997 Cadillac Eldorado for sale on the lot. When the owner refused Officer Krumpke's demand for the title, he was charged with violating the inspection statute.

309. Is the statute valid?

ANSWER:

Craig is a Mr. Fix-it. He makes his living doing minor repairs for busy people. Generally, a home owner leaves a key under a doormat so that Craig can get in the house when no one is home and attend to repairs. One day, as Craig was fixing a leaky sink in a kitchen, police drove up to the house and rang the doorbell. Police told Craig who answered the door that they wanted to search the bedroom of the family's sixteen year old daughter suspected of involvement with two students who have been threatening classmates. Craig, who is an immensely curious person, identified himself to the police and volunteered to help. He showed them to the girl's bedroom. He also showed the police a key to the room which was sitting on the ledge above the bedroom door. He unlocked the room for the police and let them in. Inside the room, the police found pictures of the girl with the two principal suspects in the case. The girl and the two boys were holding automatic weapons and hand grenades in the pictures. The girl and the two boys were arrested and charged with illegal possession of automatic weapons and hand grenades. School authorities and the police credited Craig with helping to prevent a tragic shooting. The girl moved to suppress the pictures found in her bedroom.

**310.** Are the pictures admissible?

    (A) The pictures are admissible because Craig was the home owner's surrogate and waived the owner's Fourth Amendment rights.

    (B) The pictures are admissible because police could have entered the house to search based upon exigent circumstances.

    (C) The pictures are inadmissible because police could not reasonable rely upon Craig's consent to search.

    (D) the pictures are inadmissible because police must seek the permission to search of the target of an investigation.

Police received an anonymous tip that William Grass was operating a marijuana grow operation from his three acre farm on the outskirts of Metropolis. Two police officers were dispatched to investigate the tip. Officer 1 walked up Grass' driveway and around to the back patio off of the family room of the home. On the patio, Officer 1 observed six marijuana plants growing in pots on the patio. Officer 2 climbed over a locked fence, posted with No Trespassing signs, about 150 yards from Grass' home. Officer 2 walked through a cultivated field which contained tomato plants and corn. At the back of the cultivated area, Officer 2 discovered 100 marijuana plants. Both officers executed affidavits detailing what they had seen and applied for a search warrant. The officers executed the search warrant and seized the marijuana plants from the patio and the field. The defendant was charged with illegal cultivation of marijuana. The defense filed a motion to suppress.

**311.** How should the court rule on the motion to suppress?

    (A) All of the marijuana should be suppressed because the officers relied on an anonymous tip.

    (B) All of the marijuana is admissible because the officers did not violate the defendant's reasonable expectation of privacy.

    (C) The marijuana on the back patio is inadmissible because the officer violated the defendant's living space, but the marijuana in the field is admissible because the defendant has no protected privacy interest in a field.

    (D) The marijuana is inadmissible because Officer 1 violated defendant's privacy in his home and Officer 2 trespassed on to Grass' posted and fenced field.

Abby was stopped for speeding in a school zone during school hours. The police officer ordered Abby out of her car and ran a license and registration check. After the check turned up no outstanding warrants, the officer wrote out a traffic citation. Before handing the completed citation to Abby, the officer searched the motorist and found marijuana and a small marijuana pipe in her pants pockets. The officer arrested Abby. She was charged with possession of an illegal substance and drug paraphernalia. The defense moved to suppress the marijuana and contraband.

312. The evidence is

   (A) admissible under the search incident to arrest doctrine if speeding in a school zone is an arrestable offense in the jurisdiction.
   (B) admissible because the officer has the authority to order a legally stopped motorist from his or her vehicle and to frisk the motorist for the officer's safety.
   (C) inadmissible because speeding is not an arrestable offense and an officer may not search incident to a speeding stop.
   (D) inadmissible because the motorist was not under arrest when the officer conducted the search.

Add the following facts to those in Question 312. When the officer ordered Abby to get out of her car, Abby was very surly, mumbled responses to the officer's questions, seemed to fidget inordinately, and indicated to the officer that she needed to get away from the area immediately. The officer responded to Abby's reaction by ordering her to sit in the back of the police cruiser. The officer frisked Abby before placing her in the back of the cruiser but found no weapon. The officer checked Abby's license and registration and determined that there was no outstanding warrant for her arrest. The officer wrote the traffic ticket and walked Abby back to her car. Before allowing Abby to get in her car, the officer reached into the car and found a gun under the driver's seat. The officer arrested the motorist for carrying a concealed weapon. Prior to trial, Abby's lawyer moved to suppress the gun.

313. The gun is

   (A) admissible because it was found incident to a valid traffic arrest.
   (B) admissible because it was found during a lawful search of the vehicle for weapons.
   (C) inadmissible because the officer did not have probable cause to believe that there were weapons in the car.
   (D) inadmissible because the officer had no authority to search the vehicle once he decided to release to motorist.

Tony O'Malley, an undercover police officer, purchased three rocks of crack cocaine from Tom Dunn, a street vendor. During the purchase, Dunn became suspicious and drew a gun on O'Malley who also drew his weapon. Both fired, and O'Malley was fatally injured. Dunn was also wounded but managed to escape. Later, when Dunn was arrested, he was bleeding and taken to the hospital where doctors were able to stop the bleeding and dress the wound. At the request of the arresting officers, the hospital took Dunn to the operating room where he was anesthetized and had the bullet removed from his leg. The recovered bullet is critical evidence that Dunn was the drug seller who murdered the police officer. Dunn's attorney seeks to suppress the bullet.

314. The bullet should be

   (A) admitted at trial because it is essential to prove Dunn's guilt.
   (B) admitted at trial because it was extracted incident to the arrest of Dunn.

(C)  suppressed because it was seized without prior judicial approval.

(D)  suppressed because the evidence taken from Dunnt's body compels the defendant to incriminate himself in violation of the Fifth Amendment.

Lush, a broadcaster on the F.I.B. Network, was driving home with his girlfriend after dinner at a popular watering hole. Lush had attacked the president non-stop during his three-hour radio show. Feeling very satisfied with himself, Lush had a bottle of champagne with dinner. He continued to lambast the president while driving home, making sure his girlfriend understood and agreed with every point he made. Lush, so engrossed in the conversation, was unaware that he was driving all over the road. A police officer stopped the car; Lush tried to talk the officer out of a ticket. The officer ordered Lush out of the car and insisted that he perform field sobriety tests. Lush passed the tests. The officer, then, noticed that Lush's driver's license had expired. Under state law the officer could have issued a traffic ticket or arrested the motorist for driving with an expired license. The officer was so upset with Lush for persisting in trying to talk him of writing the ticket that he arrested Lush. Lush's girlfriend who had a valid license was prepared to drive the car home. The police officer told her that she could take the car as soon as the officer was finished at the scene. Lush was placed in a back-up vehicle and immediately driven to the police station. The officer searched the entire car. In the trunk, the officer found multiple bottles of prescription drugs in several names. Lush was charged with driving with an expired license and illegal possession of prescription drugs. Prior to trial, the defense moved to suppress the prescription drugs.

**315.**  How should the judge rule on the motion to suppress?

ANSWER:

Guinness Stout drove his Ford pickup along the highway, weaving in and out of his lane, crossing both the lane and edge lines. Sheriff's Deputy Dogood saw Stout at 10:32 p.m. and pulled him over. The officer summoned back-up assistance and ordered Stout from the truck.

Stout called his brother, told him what had happened and asked his brother to come to the scene of the stop and pick him up. Once the back-up officers arrived, Dogood ordered Stout to perform certain field-sobriety tests. Not surprisingly, Stout performed very badly. At 11:15 p.m., Dogood told Stout's brother that he might as well go home and asked Stout to sit in the back of the police car. While walking Stout to the police car, Dogood asked him how much he had to drink. Stout answered, "Only six beers." At no time had Stout been given *Miranda* warnings. One half hour later the Sheriff arrived and notified Stout that he was under arrest.

**316.**  Is Stout's statement admissible at trial?

(A)  The statement is admissible because a traffic arrest is not a custodial arrest and *Miranda* warnings need not be given.

(B)  The statement is admissible because when asked if he was drinking Stout had not yet been arrested.

(C)  The statement is inadmissible because Officer Dogood conducted a *Terry-*

stop on reasonable suspicion of drunk driving which requires *Miranda* warnings.

(D) The statement is inadmissible because Stout was in custody and should have been given *Miranda* warnings prior to any questioning.

Charles ("Big") Deal was arrested and charged with rape. Shortly after the police were notified about the rape, an officer met with the victim to establish the identity of the assailant. The victim provided a description of her attacker. When asked to view slides that were selected by the police according to her description of the assailant, the victim selected Big and later confirmed this identification when she was shown a photo of him. On the day trial began, the police officer and an assistant prosecuting attorney took the victim to the holding cell outside the courtroom where Big was being held prior to the commencement of the trial proceedings. The victim, again, identified Big as her attacker, picking him from a group of five men being held in the cell. This identification took place outside the presence of the defense attorney who was already in the courtroom. The defense challenged the victim's in-court identification. The trial court denied the defense motion to suppress, saying that the victim's in-court identification was not tainted by the holding cell viewing because of the detailed description which she had given the investigating officer shortly after the attack as well as her earlier identification of the defendant from the slide and picture. The defendant was convicted and appealed.

317. Should the conviction be reversed?

(A) The conviction should be reversed because the final viewing of the defendant violated the defendant's Sixth Amendment right to counsel.

(B) The conviction should be affirmed because the witness' in-court identification was independent of the holding cell identification.

(C) The conviction should be reversed because the prosecutor's failure to notify counsel who was present was a purposeful violation of the constitutional rule.

(D) The conviction should be affirmed because the holding cell viewing was casual and not a lineup.

Instructions: All of the remaining five short answer questions are based upon the following facts. Abner and his wife, Lisa, were indicted on multiple counts of mortgage fraud. They were arraigned and appeared with counsel. Abner and Lisa were freed on bail during the pretrial period but failed to show up for their trial. A bench warrant was issued for their arrest. Abner and Lisa were believed to have absconded with records implicating them in the fraud.

George and Laura are friends with Abner and Lisa. George has multiple criminal convictions involving violent crimes and drug trafficking. His most recent arrest had to do with drug trafficking in Metropolis. When George was arrested last week, he was given *Miranda* warnings by Detective Roberts, the head of narcotics investigations. George asked for his lawyer and told police that he would not answer any questions until he saw his lawyer. Detective Roberts did not pursue the interrogation, and George was released without being charged. Laura is suspected of involvement in her husband's illegal operations, but no evidence has ever been discovered to prove that, and she has never been arrested. The police believe that during George's past prison sentences, Laura maintained the drug operation until George's release when he resumed control of the business.

When Abner and Lisa failed to show up for their fraud trial, their pictures appeared in the media. They were captured when they were recognized by a gasoline service station attendant on the outskirts of Metropolis, just miles from the border. The gas station attendant called the Metropolis police who arrived in time to arrest Abner and Lisa.

At the time of their arrests, Abner and Lisa were accompanied by George and Laura, who were unknown to the arresting officers. All four were traveling in Abner's car. All four were ordered out of the car, and Abner and Lisa were arrested as fugitives. The arresting officers knew that Abner and Lisa were believed to have absconded with the business records. Although George and Laura were also ordered out of the car, they were not detained or otherwise hassled by the police. They were free to leave but did not do so because Abner asked George to take possession of his and Lisa's car.

Following the arrest, the police searched the passenger compartment of the vehicle and the trunk of the car. In the trunk, the police found enough marijuana, cocaine, and pills to set up a drug supermarket. These items where contained in separate boxes as well as in suitcases of all four of the persons in the car at the time it was stopped. Each suitcase had a luggage label identifying its owner. George and Laura were arrested following the search. All four were transported to the Metropolis County Jail. Once George and Laura were taken to the police station their identities became known. Detective Roberts was summoned to direct the investigation of the four.

After they were booked, Abner and George were taken to separate interrogation rooms and the women were placed in separate cells. At this point none of the four had been read the *Miranda* rights. The women, in separate cells, found solicitous cellmates, who were in fact jail snitches serving time in the county jail who were also on the police payroll. These women regularly were placed strategically to encounter certain newcomers to the jail and to engage these newcomers in conversation. The women are paid for their testimony and for getting the information. The women engaged Laura and Lisa in the type of general conversation that one would expect between cellmates. The women told Laura and Lisa of their own crimes and sentences and then inquired why Laura and Lisa, obviously women of stature and wealth, were in jail. Both Laura and Lisa responded, making incriminating statements about their involvement in drug trafficking.

Abner and George were interrogated separately by Detective Roberts. Abner never had previously encountered Detective Roberts. However, Detective Roberts had many prior contacts with George, most recently the week before. Abner and George were placed in adjoining interrogation rooms, and Detective Roberts questioned them both about the drugs, moving back and forth between the two rooms in ten or fifteen minute intervals. He did not ask Abner about the fraud charges. Prior to the interrogations, he administered the *Miranda* warnings to both of the men. Both men agreed to waive their rights.

Over the course of the next two hours, Abner and George provided extensive statements incriminating themselves and each other, as well as their wives, in a major drug trafficking operation. Abner admitted to feeling so cornered as a result of the arrest and discovery of the narcotics that he also made statements that were useful in proving his intent to defraud banks and mortgagors in the mortgage fraud operation. He admitted that the profits from the mortgage fraud business were used to help finance the drug operation. Each man admitted that prior to his arrest he was fleeing the country. They were within three miles of the border and escape at the time of the arrests.

Subsequently, all four were indicted on drug trafficking charges. Each will be tried separately; Abner and Lisa also will be tried on the preexisting mortgage fraud charges. Each defendant's attorney filed various motions to suppress evidence.

You are the judge handling the pretrial motions in all of the cases. On each of the following motions, please state your rulings carefully. You are expected to write a paragraph or more indicating the basis of each defendant's claim and the legal basis and the reasoning for your rulings. Where there is more than one ground for a defendant's claim, identify each and rule on each ground separately without reference to the other.

There are five separate questions to answer. The questions pinpoint various issues in a way so that you need not repeat yourself.

318.  George and Laura have moved to suppress the evidence found in their tagged suitcases that were in the trunk of Abner' car. How should the judge rule on the motion and why?

ANSWER:

319.  Laura has moved to suppress the statements that she made to her cellmate. How should the judge rule on the motion and why?

ANSWER:

**320.** Lisa has moved to suppress the statements that she made to her cellmate. How should the judge rule on the motion and why?

ANSWER:

**321.** Abner has moved to suppress the statements that he made incriminating himself on the drug trafficking and fraud charges. How should the judge rule on the motion and why?

ANSWER:

**322.** George has moved to suppress the statements that he made incriminating himself on the drug trafficking charges. How should the judge rule on the motion and why?

ANSWER:

**PART III**

You represent Sally O'Madigan who was arrested for illegal gambling, a felony in your jurisdiction. Your client was caught after an undercover police officer, wearing a recording device, placed a bet with O'Madigan on a pro football game. O'Madigan had approached the officer in a bar and offered to be his bookie. The prosecutor, who hated Irish people because of an incident involving his grandparents, pressed charges to get even.

323.    Which of the following would be your best defense:

    (A)  entrapment.
    (B)  First Amendment.
    (C)  equal protection.
    (D)  due process.

You practice in a jurisdiction that has adopted the Federal Rules of Criminal Procedure.

324.    Which of the following procedures would occur LAST:

    (A)  arraignment.
    (B)  complaint.
    (C)  indictment.
    (D)  preliminary examination.

Fagan was arrested and is in jail for selling drugs to a street thug who "ratted out" Fagan when the thug was arrested and offered a sweet deal to provide police with information about the source of the thug's drugs. The police had long known that Fagan peddled drugs but had no solid evidence until the thug's statement, which convinced the police to launch a serious investigation of Fagan. After a week of surveillance, the police decided to go ahead and arrest Fagan after witnessing him involved in repeated drug transactions on a street corner where drug activity was rampant. The police had probable cause to arrest Fagan but did not bother to obtain a warrant.

325.    Which of the following would be necessary because Fagan had been arrested without a warrant.

    (A)  initial appearance.
    (B)  grand jury.
    (C)  preliminary hearing.
    (D)  *Gerstein* hearing.

Fagan was accorded a bail hearing once counsel was appointed at the initial appearance. The day before the bail hearing Fagan told a cellmate that the "scumbag who ratted on me will never make it to testify at trial."

At the bail hearing, the cellmate repeated what Fagan had said and the trial court denied release on bail pending trial, finding that Fagan posed a danger to the safety of the main prosecution witness. State law permitted pretrial detention to protect the life of potential witnesses.

**326.** The state law authorizing pretrial detention to protect the safety of potential witnesses is:

(A) constitutional under the Eighth Amendment's excessive bail provision.
(B) unconstitutional under the Eighth Amendment's excessive bail provision.
(C) unconstitutional under the Equal Protection Clause.
(D) illegal under the Bail Reform Act of 1984.

Fagan was detained pending trial and a preliminary examination was scheduled in ten days.

**327.** In a jurisdiction based on the Federal Rules of Criminal Procedure, which of the following is the standard that the presiding judge at the preliminary examination will use in deciding whether Fagan's case should go forward:

(A) beyond a reasonable doubt.
(B) clear and convincing evidence.
(C) preponderance of the evidence.
(D) probable cause.

Your client, Sally Meares, was sentenced to federal prison for three years after being convicted of money laundering in federal court. She now seeks release pending appeal.

**328.** Under the Bail Reform Act of 1984, what must your client establish by clear and convincing evidence in order to be released pending appeal:

(A) she is not likely to flee.
(B) she is not likely to pose a danger to the safety of the community.
(C) the appeal raises a substantial question of law or fact likely to result in reversal or a new trial.
(D) all of above.

You are a legislator in a state that is streamlining its criminal procedures. Currently a state statute gives the criminal accused the right to a grand jury hearing for all felonies. The state constitution is silent on the issue. Many legislators want to eliminate the grand jury because a recent study showed that it delayed trials by almost four months and costs several million dollars to fund statewide.

**329.** Can your state legislature constitutionally eliminate the grand jury?

(A) yes, for all crimes except capital crimes where Due Process requires grand jury consideration.

(B) yes, for all crimes.

(C) no, the Due Process Clause requires grand jury approval for all felonies.

(D) no, the Fifth Amendment requires grand jury approval for all crimes unless waived by the accused.

Your client, Chung Foo, is charged with the rape on June 2nd of a four year-old girl who lived two houses away. After discussing the matter with your client, you have obtained an airline ticket, hotel bill, and restaurant bill that would establish that your client was in another town, 100 miles away, when the alleged incident occurred. With the permission of your client, you gave copies of the documents to the prosecutor handling the case and requested that the information be given to the grand jury that would be deciding whether to indict your client. The prosecutor declined to provide this information to the grand jury, which issued an indictment against your client.

You filed a Motion to Dismiss the Indictment for Failure to Provide Exculpatory Information to the Grand Jury.

330. Under the United States Constitution, your motion will be:

(A) granted since the defendant's due process rights were violated.

(B) denied since the accused has no right to have the grand jury consider exculpatory information.

(C) granted because under the Fifth Amendment's grand jury provision, the government must give reliable exculpatory information to the grand jury.

(D) denied because the defendant should have given the exculpatory proof to the judge rather than to the district attorney.

You are a law clerk for United States District Judge Feinberg who has asked you to review a federal indictment that is being challenged as being constitutionally infirm.

331. In assessing the validity of the indictment in a federal case, which of the following is NOT a factor the court must consider:

(A) whether it fairly informs the defendant of the charges to be defended.

(B) whether it protects the defendant against double jeopardy in future prosecutions.

(C) whether it gives the grand jury adequate information to assess whether there is probable cause to indict.

(D) whether it contains the elements of the offense charged.

Jayne and Tyrone decided a quick way to make money is to open a checking account, then neatly write their account number on deposit slips in their bank's lobby. Val Victime went into the bank, got a deposit slip bearing Jane and Tyrone's account number, and deposited $1138 from a social security check into Jayne and Tyrone's account. When Victime's account did not reflect the deposit, bank security personnel quickly discovered the scam and had Jayne and Tyrone arrested. The district attorney has charged them with bank fraud and wants to join them in a single trial since the witnesses against them both are the same people.

**332.**   Under the Federal Rules of Criminal Procedure, is joinder permissible?

(A)   joinder is permissible because they participated in the same transaction.

(B)   joinder is permissible since they were charged with violating the same bank fraud statute.

(C)   joinder is impermissible if either objects to joinder because due process guarantees that each person has the right to his or her own trial.

(D)   joinder is impermissible unless both consent to the joinder.

The state prosecutors' association has drafted a bill to change discovery rules so they are more favorable to the prosecution, which state law has long required to turn over certain materials to the defense. The new rules provide that neither the prosecution nor defense has to provide the other with any discovery at all. Each side is left to its own devices to obtain information needed to prepare for the case.

**333.**   Assess the constitutional validity of the new rule:

(A)   it is constitutional since it treats both sides the same.

(B)   it is constitutional because due process recognizes that a trial is an adversary process and the defendant may obtain a fair trial as long as the rules are not tilted against the accused.

(C)   it is unconstitutional because due process requires significant reciprocal discovery to provide a fair trial.

(D)   it is unconstitutional because the prosecution must turn over information to the defense that would be helpful to either guilt or sentence.

Kathleen Browning robbed the Good Foods Market on January 1, 2006. She was finally arrested on January 1, 2007, indicted for robbery on July 2, 2007, and convicted in a one-day trial on January 5, 2008. She seeks to overturn the conviction.

**334.**   Which of the following theories would MOST LIKELY be viable in reversing the conviction:

(A)   due process because of the one year delay between the crime and the arrest.

(B)   speedy trial because of the six month delay between arrest and indictment.

(C)   statute of limitations because of the six month delay between indictment and trial.

(D)   none of above would be a viable theory to overturn the conviction.

Assume that a rape occurred in Washington County, co-defendant Smith lives in Franklin County, co-defendant Foster lives in Adams County, and the rape victim lives in Jackson County.

**335.**   In the usual case, which of the following is the proper venue for the trial, assuming no defendant has moved for a venue change:

(A)  Washington County where the rape occurred.

(B)  Franklin or Adams County where a co-defendant lived.

(C)  Jackson County where the victim lives.

(D)  all of above.

Mike "Killer" Fossal was the hitman for a drug cartel. After torturing and killing Reynaldo Cruz who sold drugs for a rival organization, Fossal was arrested and charged with capital murder. The local press devoted a lot of publicity to the coming trial, calling it the "trial of the century." Fossal's lawyer wants the press excluded from the trial to prevent the extensive coverage that counsel fears would somehow be communicated to the jury and cause immense prejudice to defendant Fossal. Counsel has filed a Motion to Exclude Press from Trial. The government opposes the motion.

336.  Based on the facts above, the motion will be:

(A)  granted because the defendant has a due process right to a fair trial.

(B)  granted because the Sixth Amendment right to a public trial is for the defendant's benefit and the defendant may waive it.

(C)  denied because the press and public have a First and Fourteenth Amendment right to attend a criminal trial.

(D)  denied because the government is entitled to a public trial and the court may not close a courtroom if the government wants a public trial.

In order to save money, a state legislature is considering reducing the number of jurors in a felony trial to ten but maintaining the requirement that guilt be found unanimously. The state constitution mandates a jury of twelve in felony cases.

337.  The new statute reducing the number of jurors from twelve to ten is:

(A)  unconstitutional in violation of the Sixth Amendment.

(B)  unconstitutional in violation of the state constitution.

(C)  both (A) and (B).

(D)  constitutional since under the separation of powers doctrine, the legislature has the power to establish criminal procedures.

Judge Kathleen Nobuku is presiding over a difficult five-month criminal antitrust case. Both sides have offered substantial proof. State law requires a unanimous verdict for a conviction or acquittal. After three days of jury deliberation, the jury foreperson gave Judge Nobuku a note saying, "We are deadlocked on the case. I do not know if we can ever reach a verdict one way or the other." Judge Nobuku has decided she wants the jurors to continue deliberating but wants to put a bit of pressure on them to reach a verdict. State law gives her much flexibility in the decision.

338.  What should Judge Nobuku do?

(A)  give the jurors an *Allen* charge urging them to continue deliberations and to listen carefully to the views of other jurors.

(B)   find out the split of tentative juror votes and award the verdict to which ever side had an overwhelming majority of the votes.

(C)   declare a mistrial so the case can be retried and reach a verdict.

(D)   replace all the jurors with alternates and instruct the new jurors to start from scratch in deliberating on the case.

The defendant you are prosecuting became angry at a 90 year-old widow who was walking too slowly on the sidewalk and beat her severely with her cane, causing the loss of sight in one eye and a broken pelvis when she fell from his blows. State law punished aggravated assault by a maximum sentence of 15 years. Another state law increased the penalty by 5 years for any crime of violence involving a victim who was more than 70 years old. You plan on seeking the 20 year sentence but defense counsel has filed a motion to have the 5 year enhancement declared unconstitutional as violating the Double Jeopardy Clause.

339.   How should the court rule on the motion?

(A)   grant the motion since the defendant is essentially being punished twice for the same crime.

(B)   grant the motion because twenty years would be a violation of Double Jeopardy as excessive for a crime such as aggravated assault where no one was killed.

(C)   deny the motion because the Double Jeopardy Clause applies only to sequential trials; it does not apply to a single trial.

(D)   deny the motion because the Double Jeopardy Clause does not prevent multiple punishments in one trial if the legislature intended for the action to be punished under multiple provisions of the criminal law.

340.   Which of the following will NOT routinely result in a potential juror in a child molestation case being excluded for cause from serving on the jury:

(A)   exposure to pretrial publicity.

(B)   awaiting trial on a serious misdemeanor in the same jurisdiction.

(C)   being the defendant's common law husband.

(D)   being the victim's Sunday school teacher.

You are the lawyer for a mobster charged with multiple federal racketeering and extortion counts. Your investigator is frustrated because the F.B.I. agents, victims, and other possible witnesses will not provide any information to help you prepare for trial. Finally, you decide the only way to find out what you need to know in order to plan your trial strategy is to depose the important people who refuse to talk about the case.

341.   Under the Federal Rules of Criminal Procedure, to get a deposition you must obtain the approval of:

(A)   each person to be deposed.

(B)   the prosecuting attorney.

(C)   the court.

(D)  no one; you simply notify the government and the person to be deposed of the time and location of the deposition.

342.  If a hearsay statement is found to be "testimonial" and therefore covered by the Confrontation Clause of the Sixth Amendment, which of the following is NOT necessary in order for the statement to be admissible against the criminal accused at trial:

(A)  the declarant who made the statement must be unavailable.
(B)  the declarant must have been subject to cross examination about the testimonial statement.
(C)  the statement must be hearsay.
(D)  the defendant must have been present when the statement was made.

343.  Which of the following is/are limited in number:

(A)  challenges for cause.
(B)  peremptory challenges.
(C)  trial objections to evidence offered by other side.
(D)  motions *in limine* to admit or exclude evidence.

Beatrice Holzman was arrested after postal authorities discovered a mail bomb had been sent to Judge Ramos, who had presided over Holzman's trial four years ago for auto theft. Holzman had threatened to "get even" many times. Holzman is charged with the following federal crime:

> Section A-46. Sending a Destructive Device. Whoever, with intent to cause physical injury, sends a destructive device through the mail shall be guilty of a felony punishable by a maximum of ten years in prison.

Last year Holzman was convicted in federal court of attempted first degree murder for exactly the same incident involving mailing the bomb to Judge Ramos. The prosecution brought the new case because it believed Holzman's sentence for the attempted murder conviction was too lenient.

Defense counsel in the current destructive device case has filed a Motion to Dismiss Because of Double Jeopardy, arguing that the conviction last year for attempted murder bars prosecution for the destructive device charge.

**344.** You are the federal judge handling the current case. How will you rule on the motion?

ANSWER:

Dexter Livingston was caught red-handed in the middle of the night burglarizing a liquor store. The silent alarm alerted the police who arrested Livingston while still inside the business. When defense counsel thought she had obtained a very good plea offer from the prosecution, she recommended that Livingston accept the deal and he did so.

During the plea hearing, the following colloquy took place:

> Judge: Mr. Livingston, are you ready to enter a plea?

> Defendant: Yes, your honor.

> Judge: I won't waste your time here, today. Have you discussed this with your lawyer?

> Defendant: Yes, your honor.

> Judge: And do you want to plead. I understand the prosecution has offered you two years in prison if you plead guilty.

> Defendant: Yes, that's about it.

> Judge: Do you know that if you plead you waive many issues, constitutional rights that you will not be able to assert in court?

Defendant: Now I do, your honor.

Judge: OK. How do you plead to second degree burglary.

Defendant: I did it, your honor.

Judge: OK. I sentence you to two years in prison. Next case.

Livingston is now in prison and has discovered that his cellmate did essentially the same crime but received probation (later revoked because of a drug arrest) rather than prison. Livingston believes he got a bad deal and now wants to withdraw his plea. He has hired you to review the matter for him.

**345.** How do you assess the validity of his plea and the likelihood of having the plea overturned?

ANSWER:

You are selecting the jury in Melvin's trial for second degree reckless murder allegedly caused by your client's sale of tainted moonshine to the victim. You think that people who have imbibed moonshine would be excellent jurors since they appreciate that buyers of moonshine accept the risk that the substance will be poisonous because they know that the government will not permit it to be made openly and in a totally safe environment. You begin exercising your peremptory challenges to exclude anyone who has not consumed moonshine. The prosecution makes a *Batson* objection on the theory that you are excluding the most educated jurors.

**346.** What ruling should the court make?

ANSWER:

The police arrested Adelphi Fu on a charge of sale of crack cocaine. Fu allegedly sold a quantity of the drug to an undercover agent who promptly arrested Fu. A subsequent lab test showed the substance to be crack cocaine.

You are appointed to represent Fu. Your client told you that he thought the stuff he sold was harmless baking powder, not cocaine. You have reviewed all available evidence and filed a motion to be permitted to test the materials alleged to be cocaine. Today the prosecutor called you to tell you that the drugs were lost and she could not promise they would ever be found.

**347.** What must you establish to have the drug report, showing crack cocaine, suppressed because you are unable to have the alleged cocaine retested by your own laboratory?

ANSWER:

Sharon Davies is charged with intentional homicide for shooting Carl Icon, a local radio personality. Davies and Icon had long been lovers but broke up a month ago when Icon told Davies he had a new girlfriend.

Davies maintains that she did not kill Icon and does not know who did. A police search of Davies' apartment found a .22 caliber pistol that had been recently fired. During trial preparation, Davies' defense lawyer had forensic tests conducted on the .22 caliber bullet that killed Icon. The tests concluded that the bullet was fired from a .22 caliber pistol that did not come from Davies' weapon.

Davies defense lawyer wants to know whether government lab tests concluded the same thing, but does not want to give the government the results of the defense-ordered tests, preferring to surprise the government with them at trial. Your jurisdiction has adopted the Federal Rules of Criminal Procedure.

**348.** You are a law clerk for defense counsel. Advise your boss.

ANSWER:

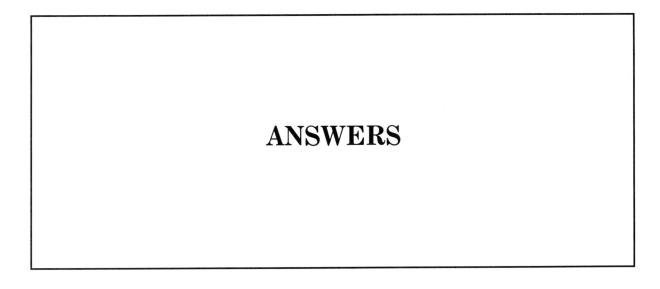

# ANSWERS

1.    **Answer (C) is the correct answer.** In 1884, the Supreme Court said that the due process clause of the Fourteenth Amendment is not a short-hand version of the rights contained in the Bill of Rights (the first eight amendments to the Constitution), and held that a defendant in a state criminal proceeding is not entitled to a grand jury indictment. *Hurtado v. California*, 110 U.S. 516 (1884). Through a process of "absorption" or "incorporation," from 1932 through 1970, most, but not all, of the guarantees contained in the first eight amendments of the Bill of Rights were applied to state criminal proceedings. Simply because a right is one of the enumerated rights in the Bill of Rights does not mean that it was made applicable to the states. Not all of the rights in the Bill of Rights are binding on the states — e.g., the Fifth Amendment right to a grand jury indictment and the Seventh Amendment guarantee of a jury trial in civil cases. The current inquiry is "whether given this kind of system a particular procedure is fundamental . . . to an Anglo-American regime of ordered liberty." *Duncan v. Louisiana*, 391 U.S. 145 (1968). Few observers of the current criminal justice morass believe that devotion to the Fifth Amendment guarantee of a grand jury indictment will provide greater protection to a criminal defendant; rather it is viewed as an institution which causes delay in the criminal justice system without delivering substantial benefits to justify that delay. The grand jury indictment is not likely to be made binding upon the states.

      **Answer (A) is incorrect.** Not quite all of the Bill of Rights have been incorporated into the Fourteenth Amendment and made binding on the states. The Fifth Amendment right to a grand jury indictment is not binding on the states. The Fifth Amendment right to a grand jury indictment remains binding upon federal prosecutions, but does not apply to state criminal prosecutions.

      **Answer (B) is incorrect.** The Fifth Amendment guarantees that a defendant charged with "infamous crimes" has the right to a grand jury indictment. That right is binding upon charges brought in federal courts. It is not binding on the states, and the states are free to adopt or reject the requirement.

      **Answer (D) is incorrect.** If the right to a grand jury indictment were deemed to be a fundamental right, the failure to accord the right could not be harmless error. One would assume that any right contained in the Bill of Rights is a fundamental right. While that applies to most rights contained in the Bill of Rights, the states are not required to commence prosecution with a grand jury indictment.

2.    **Answer (D) is the correct answer.** The Sixth Amendment guarantee applies only to serious offenses carrying a possible jail or prison sentence of more than six months. In *Duncan v. Louisiana*, 391 U.S. 145 (1968), the United States Supreme

Court held that the Sixth amendment right to trial by jury was applicable to the states because "trial by jury in criminal cases is fundamental to the American scheme of justice." The Court further held that the right applies in "all criminal cases which — were they to be tried in a federal court — would come within the Sixth Amendment's guarantee." This was in keeping with the Supreme Court's established practice that the right is enforced against the states according to the same standards that protect those rights against federal encroachment. To determine the full extent of the right carried over to the states, the courts must look to the federal practice. In all federal criminal cases, the right to a jury trial is guaranteed only to those charged with "serious offenses." A serious offense is defined as one carrying a penalty of more than six months. *Baldwin v. New York*, 399 U.S. 66 (1970).

**Answer (A) is incorrect.** Through a process of "absorption" or "incorporation," the Warren Court applied most, but not all, of the guarantees contained in the first eight amendments of the Bill of Rights to state criminal proceedings. Not all of the rights in the Bill of Rights are binding on the states — e.g., the Fifth Amendment right to a grand jury indictment and the Seventh Amendment guarantee of a jury trial in civil cases.

**Answer (B) is incorrect.** The maximum penalty for the misdemeanor in this case was six months; consequently, the charge is classified as a petty offense and does not carry with it the Sixth Amendment right to a jury trial. The states are, however, entitled to extend the right to petty offenses under their own state constitutions.

**Answer (C) is incorrect.** The Supreme Court's holding in *Duncan* applied the Sixth Amendment right to a jury trial to the states. The states are entitled to experiment and extend the rights beyond the minimum set by federal standards of due process. Here, the state could extend the right to trial by jury to an offense not covered by the federal right. The states may not, however, experiment below the minimum standard for due process binding on the states through the Fourteenth Amendment. The federal right guarantees a right to trial by jury for all serious offenses in state courts as well as in federal courts.

3.     The Fourth Amendment standards of reasonableness and probable cause govern in federal and state criminal cases. These governing federal standards provide the minimum acceptable protection consonant with American notions of due process. The states may not violate these minimal standards, and evidence obtained in violation of the Fourth Amendment must be excluded in state as well as federal criminal trials. *Ker v. California*, 374 U.S. 23 (1963). However, although the Fourth Amendment permits police to arrest for a minor traffic offense, *Atwater v. City of Lago Vista*, 532 U.S. 318 (2001), states may choose to prohibit such arrests. Further, the Fourth Amendment, following a custodial arrest, allows for a search of the arrestee and the interior compartment of the vehicle incident to the arrest. *U.S. v. Robinson*, 414 U.S. 218 (1973); *New York v. Belton*, 453 U.S. 454 (1981).

The Fourth Amendment is not the end of the inquiry. Traditionally, the role of the United States Supreme Court in overseeing state criminal procedure is to impose the minimally acceptable standard below which a state may not venture. All that is required is that the states accord their citizens at least as much protection as is provided under the Bill of Rights provision. However, the state has the ultimate responsibility for administering its own system of criminal justice as long as it does not dip below the minimal standards of fairness imposed under the Federal Constitution. The state constitution is a document of independent force. Above and beyond the minimal federal due process standard, the states are free to offer greater protection under their own constitutions by imposing stricter standards upon state criminal justice agencies. The state may do so by interpreting its own law as supplementing or expanding federal constitutional rights. *Michigan v. Long*, 463 U.S. 1032 (1983).

In the problem, the state is free to impose greater protection than the Fourth Amendment, and many states reject *Atwater* and prohibit police from arresting minor traffic offenders. However, state reliance upon the adequate state ground of its own constitution as the basis for greater protection of constitutional rights must be explicit and clear on its face or risk reversal by the United States Supreme Court. By failing to rely solely upon the state constitution, the state Supreme Court risked reversal when it said that the police officer violated the defendant's Fourth Amendment and state constitutional rights. As its reliance on the Fourth Amendment was erroneous, the state court risked reversal by the Supreme Court for failing to rely only on state constitutional grounds.

4.     **Answer (D) is correct.** "Whether an officer is authorized to make an arrest ordinarily depends, in the first instance, on state law." *Michigan v. DeFillippo*, 443 U.S. 31 (1979). However, a warrantless arrest satisfies the Fourth Amendment so

long as the officer has probable cause to believe that the suspect has committed or is committing a crime. The Supreme Court has held "that when states go above the Fourth Amendment minimum, the Constitution's protections concerning search and seizure remain the same." *Virginia v. Moore*, 128 S. Ct. 1598 (2008). The U.S. Supreme Court will not enforce the state's higher standards as part of the Fourth Amendment and will not reverse the conviction.

**Answer (A) is incorrect.** The U.S. Supreme Court will not enforce state standards that exceed Fourth Amendment standards. The state is free to provide greater protections from unreasonable searches and seizures for its citizens under its own Constitution. However, those greater protections do not become part of the Fourth Amendment. The police did not violate the Fourth Amendment when they made an arrest that was based on probable cause but prohibited by state law.

**Answer (B) is incorrect.** The U.S. Supreme Court has held that an arrest based upon probable cause complies with the Fourth Amendment reasonableness command. The state's choice of a more restrictive policy does not render less-restrictive ones unreasonable and unconstitutional.

**Answer (C) is incorrect.** It is not the U.S. Supreme Court's role to enforce a state constitution's greater protection of Fourth Amendment rights than that afforded under the Fourth Amendment itself. Enforcement of the more restrictive policy rests with the state courts. Additional protections are treated "exclusively as matters of state law." *Virginia v. Moore*, 128 S. Ct. 1598 (2008).

5.    **Answer (B) is correct.** The Fourth Amendment protection of privacy that envelopes a home is also applicable to the area surrounding the home and within the curtilage. The Supreme Court applies four factors to determine whether an area close to a home is within the protected curtilage: (1) the proximity to the home of the area claimed to be curtilage to the home; (2) whether the area is included within an enclosure surrounding the home; (3) the nature of the uses to which the area is put; and (4) the steps taken by the resident to protect the area from observation by people passing by. *U.S. v. Dunn*, 480 U.S. 294 (1987). In weighing whether the barn is within the zone of privacy protected by the Fourth Amendment, the court would consider the 50 foot distance from the home and the barn's uses. The proximity of the barn to the house weighs in favor of the homeowner, but the decisive factors in this case will be that the officer never left the driveway to look into the barn and the fact that the owner took no steps to shield the barn from the eyes of persons lawfully on the driveway (such as shutting the barn door).

      **Answer (A) is incorrect.** The barn only satisfies some of the four factors (set out above) to determine whether the barn is within the protected curtilage of the home. Anyone approaching a home or property is entitled to walk on the driveway. The owner took no steps to shield the inside of the barn from view by persons lawfully on the driveway.

      **Answer (C) is incorrect.** Whether a barn is entitled to the same privacy protection as a home depends upon whether it satisfies the standards used to determine the curtilage of the home which is entitled to the same privacy protection as the home.

      **Answer (D) is incorrect.** The barn is not entitled to the same privacy protection as the home because it does not satisfy the four factors set forth by the Supreme Court (set out above). Even though its proximity to the home is a factor in recognizing that it is within the curtilage, an open view of the barn was visible to the officer who was legally on the driveway, and the owner took no steps to shield the inside of the barn from view.

6.    **Answer (C) is correct.** A police officer needs no predicate cause to walk up and talk to any person in a public place. The test for determining whether a person is seized is whether a reasonable person under the circumstances would feel free to walk away and ignore the police officer. *U.S. v. Mendenhall*, 446 U.S. 544 (1980). Under the prevailing test, the officer did not seize the defendant by walking up to him. [Even though it may be unreasonable to conclude that any person would feel free to ignore a police officer under the given circumstances.] A dog sniff is not a search. *U.S. v. Place*, 392 U.S. 1 (1968). Although *Place* involved a dog sniff of

luggage, the ruling has been extended to automobiles, motorists and school children. See, e.g., *Doe v. Renfrow*, 631 F.2d 91 (7th Cir. 1980); compare *United States v. Kelly*, 302 F.3d 291, 293 n.1 (5th Cir. 2002) (although a canine sniff of an object, as opposed to a person, is normally not a search, this circuit has previously held that an up-close canine sniff involving contact with a person's body is a search as defined in the Fourth Amendment."), with *United States v. Reyes*, 349 F.3d 219 (5th Cir. 2003) (non-contact dog sniff of person is not a search). When the dog alerted positively, the officer had probable cause to arrest the defendant, and the drugs were found incident to the lawful arrest.

**Answer (A) is incorrect.** The test for determining whether a person is seized by the police is whether a reasonable person under the circumstances would feel free to walk away and ignore the police officer. *U.S. v. Mendenhall*, 446 U.S. 544 (1980). The Supreme Court has relied on a fiction to conclude that persons approached by an officer feel free to ignore the officer's requests. In similar situations, courts have concluded that an on-the-street inquiry by a police officer is not a seizure and, therefore, requires neither probable cause nor reasonable suspicion.

**Answer (B) is incorrect.** The defendant was not seized prior to the dog alert, nor did the officer have probable cause to justify an arrest or reasonable suspicion to justify a *Terry*-stop. The defendant's change of direction did not even constitute head-long flight. Head-long flight, alone, does not provide reasonable suspicion for a *Terry*-stop but may be considered along with other factors. *Illinois v. Wardlow*, 528 U.S. 119 (2000).

**Answer (D) is incorrect.** Even if the defendant was lawfully seized under *Terry* standards, police could conduct a frisk of outer clothing if there was reasonable grounds to suspect that the defendant was armed. A *Terry*-frisk does not extend beyond a pat-down of outer clothing.

7.    **Answer (A) is the best answer.** In *Kyllo v. United States*, 533 U.S. 27 (2001), the Supreme Court held that a thermal scan of the outside of a home to detect the amount of waste heat escaping from the home is a search. By calling thermal imaging a search, the majority made the technique subject to judicial oversight and the requirements of the warrant clause to meet the Fourth Amendment reasonableness standard. The broad holding of *Kyllo* is that any device which discloses activities within the home is a search; the narrow holding of *Kyllo* is that the rule applies to technology "that is not in general public use." The question here is whether the use of night vision goggles falls under the technology limitation imposed in *Kyllo*. The actual intrusion in *Kyllo* was very slight: measuring the thermal quality of escaping heat. Here the intrusion is much greater. Its use allows police to see into the home and monitor its occupants. Even though night vision goggles might be readily available to the public, it is the very erosion of Fourth Amendment rights that concerned the *Kyllo* majority.

**Answer (B) is not the best answer** because it leaves unprotected to technology the intimate acts in the home. The technology here involves a much greater intrusion upon that intimacy: a visual observation of people within the home. We have to assume that protecting home privacy from technological erosion was the primary concern of the *Kyllo* majority. If that is the case, the commonality of the device used should not be dispositive of the outcome. On the other hand, the use of a flashlight to illuminate a dark space in a structure is not a search if the officer is lawfully present. *Cf. U.S. v. Barajas-Avalos*, 359 F.3d 1204 (9th Cir. 2004), opinion amended and superseded on denial of reh'g, 377 F.3d 1040 (9th Cir. 2004), cert. denied, 125 S. Ct. 1396 (U.S. 2005). There still seems to be a qualitative difference between the use of flashlight and night vision goggles. It could also be argued that Tony could have better protected his privacy within his darkened home by pulling the shades, but that seems to advance an argument that even in our own homes we have no Fourth Amendment protection unless we turn the home into a airtight cocoon.

**Answer (C) is not correct.** The same Fourth Amendment protection applies to the curtilage around a home which is used for the same living activities that take place within the home. *U.S. v. Dunn*, 480 U.S. 294 (1987).

**Answer (D) is not correct**. Obviously, Tony could have better protected his privacy within his darkened home by pulling the shades. When one fails to take the necessary steps to protect one's privacy, it is fair to conclude that the person had no subjective expectation of privacy. However, Tony did operate within his home in total darkness giving him a reasonable expectation of privacy.

8.    **Answer (B) is the correct answer.** This surveillance technique is constitutionally indistinguishable from the use of a pen register to gather phone numbers dialed from or dialing into a particular phone number. E-mail users, like telephone users, are dependant upon third-party providers to engage in communication. The Supreme Court held that telephone users have no expectation of privacy in the numbers they dial because the numbers dialed are shared with the telephone company for billing purposes. *Smith v. Maryland*, 442 U.S. 735 (1979). By analogy, a U.S. Court of Appeals held that an internet user has no expectation of privacy in the email addresses. *U.S. v. Forrester*, 495 F.3d 1041 (9th Cir. 2007).

**Answer (A) is incorrect** because the email addresses are shared with the internet provider. Communication by internet, like telephones, requires the user to voluntarily turn over information to third parties.

**Answer (C) is incorrect.** No warrant is necessary because there is no expectation of privacy in the information. There is an expectation of privacy in the contents of the message, and a search warrant based upon probable cause would be needed to access the content. *Cf. Katz v. United States*, 389 U.S. 347 (1967). Similarly, police may maintain a mail cover, checking the sources of mail sent to a target's home or business address without a warrant, but they would need a warrant to open the mail and access its content.

**Answer (D) is incorrect** because whether the server turned over the information voluntarily or under duress is immaterial as there is no expectation of privacy in the information shared with a third person.

9.    The admissibility of the evidence seized with the search warrant turns on the legitimacy of the information from the informant which provided the probable

cause for the warrant. A warrant is valid if based upon probable cause that, in turn, must be based upon knowledge obtained by the police legally. The issue in this case is whether police could hide behind a visitor to the defendant's home who was working as an agent of the police. The Supreme Court has upheld the police use of a secret agent whom the target voluntarily admits into his or her protected space. What a person voluntarily exposes to others in his or her home is not protected by the Fourth Amendment. *Katz v. United States*, 389 U.S. 347 (1967).

We have the highest expectation of privacy in our homes, but this is a case of "misplaced confidence." We run a risk when we tell anyone a secret that we do not want shared with the world; we accept that risk when we allow people into our homes and share our deepest secrets. We know that the person in whom we have confided may betray that confidence and tell others what was said. When the defendant voluntarily let his classmate into his home, he knew what he was doing. He did not know that the classmate was there on behalf of the police, but he took the risk that the classmate would betray his trust. The classmate's misrepresentation of the reason for his visit does not affect or change the outcome. Police could not have entered without a warrant, but the defendant willingly admitted his classmate into his home and let the classmate into his secrets. *United States v. Hoffa*, 385 U.S. 293 (1966).

The Supreme Court has consistently refused to distinguish between a planted police agent and a confidant who spontaneously betrays a confidence by going to the police. It is a distinction that should be made. The planted police agent gains entrance by misrepresentation and should be treated similarly to a search or a planted listening device.

10.   **Answer (D) is correct.** If a person confides in another, the courts have held that he or she has no expectation of privacy that the confidant will not tell others, including the police, and may in fact be a police agent. *Hoffa v. U.S.*, 385 U.S. 293 (1996). Moreover, a conversation is not protected by the Fourth Amendment even when the confidant is wired and transmitting the conversation directly to law enforcement officers. *U.S. v. White*, 401 U.S. 745 (1971). Police do not need a warrant to listen in to a conversation when one party to the conversation consents to the eavesdropping.

**Answer (A) is incorrect** because police do not need a warrant to eavesdrop on a conversation when one of the parties to the conversation consents to the eavesdropping. "If the conduct and revelations of an agent operating without electronic equipment do not invade the defendant's constitutionally justifiable expectations of privacy, neither does a simultaneous recording of the same conversations made by the agent or by others from transmissions received from the agent to whom the defendant is talking and whose trustworthiness the defendant necessarily risks." *U.S. v. White*, 401 U.S. 745 (1971).

**Answer (B) is incorrect.** Probable cause and the warrant requirements are not alternative requirements. The existence of probable cause does not excuse the failure to obtain a search warrant. The warrant is not valid unless it is supported by probable cause; the two requirements go together. The failure to secure a warrant is excused if the search falls into one of the exceptions to the warrant requirement, as it does here. *Katz v. U.S.*, 389 U.S. 347 (1967).

**Answer (C) is incorrect.** The defendant acted at his risk when he admitted the classmate to his apartment. The fact that the classmate gained admittance through misrepresentation does not change the equation. It is a case of misplaced confidence and the Supreme Court does not distinguish between a confidant who betrays a trust and a government agent who misrepresents his purpose for seeking admission.

11.     **Answer (B) is correct.** This is a very close call. The Fourth Amendment limits official government behavior; it does not regulate private conduct. Courts have regularly declined to exclude evidence when it is obtained by private persons. *Burdeau v. McDowell*, 256 U.S. 465 (1921). For example, no Fourth Amendment issue was raised when Federal Express security officers opened a package they believed might contain drugs and then turned the open package over to Drug Enforcement Administration agents. *U.S. v. Young*, 153 F.3d 1079 (9th Cir. 1998).

The exception applies only to private persons; the Fourth Amendment is applicable to all government officials, not just law enforcement officers. If a private person is acting as an agent of the police, the result is different. Official participation in the planning or implementation of a private person's efforts to secure evidence may taint the operation sufficiently as to require suppression of the evidence. *Coolidge v. New Hampshire*, 403 U.S. 443 (1971).

Although the classmate was an agent of the police when he visited the defendant, his break-in of the defendant's apartment did not involve the police; he was not asked to do so, nor was there any reason for the police officer to anticipate that the classmate might engage in an illegal break-in. Therefore, the search would most likely be considered a private search.

**Answer (A) is incorrect.** The test of government participation is whether under all of the circumstances the private individual must be regarded as an agent or instrument of the state. The classmate was an agent of the state when he visited the defendant. However, that agency ended when the classmate left the defendant's apartment the first time. The police officer had no reason to believe that the classmate would engage in illegal means to obtain the information.

**Answer (C) is incorrect.** Police officers may use information provided by an unnamed, reliable informant to establish probable cause. The identity of such informants need not be disclosed to a judge issuing a warrant or to the court subsequently reviewing probable cause, although a judge who does not believe that the informant exists may refuse to issue the warrant. *McCray v. Illinois*, 386 U.S. 300 (1967). Any time a judge does not believe that the affidavit contains sufficient information, the judge may require an additional presentation by the police affiant or even an appearance by the informant. A search warrant should not be issued if the affiant fails to disclose how the informant knows the information that he provides. In the problem, the specificity of the informant's information, perhaps, should have mandated the police officer to ask him how he knew where the drugs were located.

**Answer (D) is incorrect** because it only presents part of the key to this problem. The evidence is admissible only if the classmate's break-in of the defendant's apartment is not chargeable to the police. If the classmate is found to have acted as a private person, the evidence will not be suppressed.

12.    The court of appeals will reverse the trial judge's ruling and reinstate the criminal case. The Supreme Court has held repeatedly that the manner in which a defendant comes before a court does not affect that court's jurisdiction to try the defendant in a criminal case. *Frisbie v. Collins*, 342 U.S. 519 (1952); *United States v. Alvarez-Machain*, 504 U.S. 655 (1992). If an arrest or search is illegal, the appropriate remedy is suppression of evidence that may have been obtained incident to the search. Any relief to which the defendant may be entitled would come on the motion to suppress. If the drugs and paraphernalia are suppressed, the court or prosecution may eventually dismiss the charges because of lack of proof.

13. **Answer (A) is the best answer.** A search warrant is not just a ticket of admission. The warrant must specify the crimes for which evidence is sought, otherwise the warrant authorizes a fishing expedition. The purpose of the probable cause requirement of the Fourth Amendment is "to keep the state out of constitutionally protected areas until it has a reason to believe that a specific crime has been or is being committed." *Berger v. New York*, 388 U.S. 41 (1967). It was not enough to persuade the judge that the target was a bad person. The warrant needed to specify the crimes so that the warrant was not so open-ended to authorize a search for evidence of any crimes.

    **Answers (B) and (D) are not correct** because the warrant failed to state specific crimes and allowed police to search the entire residence for evidence of any felonies.

    **Answer (C) is not the best answer** because the facts contained in the affidavit may have been sufficient to create probable cause for multiple offenses, but those offenses were neither specified in the affidavit nor the warrant.

14. The warrant was invalid because the judge should have requested information about when the robberies took place. Whether probable cause exists for a search warrant depends upon the time frame for the information creating the probable cause and the nature of the object. The probable cause requirement for a search warrant says that the evidence will be found presently at the place to be searched. Information that evidence existed in the past may or may not help determine whether the evidence is still present at the same location. The more "stale" the evidence becomes, the less likely it is to support probable cause. An affidavit in support of a search warrant must contain some information that would allow the magistrate to independently determine that probable cause presently exists — not merely that it existed at some time in the past. Thus, a supporting affidavit that does not give any time frame for the events it describes fails, as a matter of law, to demonstrate probable cause, and a search warrant issued based solely on that affidavit is invalid.

    There is not a hard and fast rule pertaining to when the information becomes stale. It depends upon the nature of the object sought. For example, one court has held that four weeks is a guideline for staleness in drug cases, absent evidence of long-term continued activity. *People v. Hulland*, 110 Cal. App. 4th 1646 (Cal Ct App 2003). Staleness would rarely be an issue if the police were searching for a stolen piano or an illegal still.

In the problem, the affidavit failed to state when the robberies occurred. The affidavit could have been supplemented by sworn, recorded testimony of the affiant stating the dates of the robberies. Without that information, the issuing magistrate had no basis for concluding that evidence of the robberies was presently located in the hotel room. *U.S. v. Savoca*, 739 F.2d 220 (6th Cir. 1984).

**15.**   **Answer (B) is the correct answer.** The warrant was a valid anticipatory search warrant. Different probable cause issues arise when the evidence to be seized is not yet at the place to be searched. The difficult question is how a magistrate can make a finding of *present* probable cause which anticipates the *future* arrival of evidence at the place to be searched. All search warrants must: (1) be based on facts that establish probable cause; (2) particularly describe the place to be searched; (3) particularly describe the things to be seized; and (4) be issued by a neutral and detached magistrate. An anticipatory search warrant must meet two additional criteria. First, an affidavit seeking an anticipatory search warrant must show that the evidence is on a sure and irreversible course to its destination. Additionally, an anticipatory search warrant must provide adequate judicial control of the warrant's execution. The issuing court should list clear, narrowly drawn conditions in the warrant controlling the discretion of the police executing the warrant. *U.S. v. Grubbs*, 547 U.S. 90 (2006).

**Answer (A) is incorrect.** In *Grubbs*, the Court said the fact that the object sought is not at the house at the time the warrant was issued is irrelevant: "Because the probable cause requirement looks to whether evidence will be found when the search is conducted, all warrants are, in a sense, 'anticipatory.'"

**Answer (C) is not correct.** The police created a "controlled delivery" of the package containing the illegal substance. To comply with the probable cause requirement: (1) there must be a fair probability if the triggering condition (delivery of the package) occurs "that contraband or evidence of a crime will be found in a particular place", and (2) "there is probable cause to believe that the triggering condition will occur. The supporting affidavit must provide the magistrate with sufficient information to evaluate both aspects of the probable-cause determination." The triggering event need not be specified in the warrant provided it is presented to the court in the supporting affidavit.

**Answer (D) is incorrect** simply because it ignores the triggering event. The probable cause requirement for an anticipatory warrant must include that it is probable that the object will be at the place to be searched when the warrant is executed.

**16.**   **Answer (D) is correct.** A cornerstone of the probable cause requirement is that judges, and not police officers, determine the existence of probable cause. For judicial participation in the probable cause determination to be meaningful, the judge must serve as more than a rubber stamp for the police. Therefore, those seeking a warrant, or seeking to justify a warrantless intrusion after the fact must present enough underlying facts and circumstances to allow a judge to draw his or her own inferences about the existence of probable cause. An affidavit couched only in conclusions, *i.e.*, that probable cause exists to believe that evidence of a crime will be found, denies the judge the opportunity to draw those conclusions and robs the Fourth Amendment of its essence. *Johnson v. U.S.*, 333 U.S. 10 (1948). In the problem, Detective Roberts failed to inform the issuing magistrate about any of underlying facts and circumstances which gave rise to the belief that the drugs would be found at Smith's home. In this instance, the magistrate was a rubber stamp, and the warrant was invalid.

**Answer (A) is incorrect.** The answer suggests that even though the warrant may be invalid, it should be saved by the "good faith exception" to the exclusionary rule. However, the exception is not available when the warrant is issued on a "bare bones" affidavit containing no facts allowing the magistrate to make an independent judgment. *U.S. v. Leon*, 468 U.S. 897 (1984).

**Answer (B) is incorrect.** Police may rely upon information supplied by a confidential informant, and they need not disclose the identity of the informant as long as the judge is assured of the reliability of the informant. *McCray v. Illinois*, 386 U.S. 300 (1967). However, maintaining the secrecy of the informant's identity does not extend to failing to provide the magistrate with the underlying facts on which the informant based his conclusion. All Detective Roberts presented to the magistrate was his own conclusion; the result would be the same even if Roberts had said, "I know this to be true because an informant told me so." There are still no underlying facts presented to allow the magistrate to make an independent determination.

**Answer (C) is incorrect.** While Detective Roberts may have had probable cause to believe the drugs would be found at Smith's home, he failed to present the facts and circumstances that would allow the magistrate to judge the correctness of Detective Roberts' conclusions.

17.  **Answer (C) is correct.** The affidavit submitted to the court was insufficient on its face to establish probable cause. The affidavit did not inform the magistrate how Detective Roberts knew that the drugs would be found at Angel Smith's home. An insufficient affidavit may be supplemented by additional information. However, there must be a complete record of the information relied upon by the magistrate who issued the warrant. A witness providing supplemental testimony to fill out the information must be placed under oath, and the testimony must be recorded. A court reviewing the warrant in this case would have no record of the supplemental testimony and would have to determine whether the affidavit standing alone gave rise to probable cause; it clearly did not.

**Answer (A) is incorrect.** The affidavit was insufficient, but the additional information provided by Detective Roberts was enough to bolster the affidavit to create probable cause. However, the additional information cannot become part of the record because Detective Roberts was not under oath, and the additional information was not recorded.

**Answer (B) is incorrect.** An insufficient affidavit may be bolstered by supplemental testimony. That testimony, however, must be given under oath and must be recorded.

**Answer (D) is incorrect.** The affidavit plus the supplemental testimony did create probable cause to issue the warrant. However, the additional information may not be considered in reviewing probable cause because the witness, Detective Roberts, was not sworn and the information was not recorded.

18.     **Answer (D) is the correct answer.** Whether testing the probable cause presented to a magistrate for a warrant or known to a police officer prior to a warrantless arrest or a search, the probable cause test is identical. In the case of a warrantless arrest or search, probable cause must be measured by objective facts known to the police officer prior to a warrantless arrest or search. When determining the sufficiency of probable cause, it is not material that a search revealed the evidence sought. Evidence gathered as the result of a search or arrest may not be used retroactively to establish probable cause. *Smith v. Ohio*, 494 U.S. 541 (1990). In the problem, the state seeks to use the fruits of the illegal search to justify the arrest. If allowed, it would become the arrest incident to a search doctrine; it was not allowed. Antecedent probable cause has been an unquestioned requirement of the Fourth Amendment for 80 years. *Byars v. U.S.*, 273 U.S. 28 (1927).

**Answers (A) and (C) are incorrect.** Even if a court found reasonable suspicion to support a *Terry*-stop in the problem (very unlikely), *Terry v. Ohio*, 392 U.S. 1 (1968), only allows a pat-down search if there are facts and circumstances giving rise to a reasonable belief that the suspect is armed. If there were reasonable suspicion to justify the pat-down frisk, the officer could have patted the paper bag to see if it contained a weapon. There was no need to open the bag. The problem does not present reasonable suspicion for the stop or frisk.

**Answer (B) is incorrect.** The failure of the defendant to heed the officer's "Come here" was not a lawful police order. The officer had not even identified himself as an officer at the time. A reasonable person in the defendant's position would not have believed that he was free to ignore the officer and continue walking away. If the officer was ordering the defendant to stop, there was no reasonable suspicion to support such a stop.

19.     The trial court should grant the defense motion to suppress the drugs found on Hill's person because the officer did not have probable cause to make an arrest. Probable cause is not a scientific term. The hearing court must determine whether, based on the totality of the circumstances, the reasonable police officer could fairly determine that a crime had occurred, is occurring, or is about to occur. Facts and circumstances that seem innocent to the average person might be viewed quite differently by an experienced police officer. While a judge cannot rely solely on an officer's conclusions, a judge evaluating information provided by police should respect an officer's common sense conclusions about human behavior. *U.S. v. Cortez*, 449 U.S. 411 (1981). While a court should respect a police officer's common sense judgments, as well as inferences drawn by an experienced police officer, the hearing court must draw its own conclusion whether at the moment before the arrest the facts and circumstances known to the officer were sufficient to conclude that there is a fair probability that a crime was occurring. *Illinois v. Gates*, 462

U.S. 213 (1983).

Rarely does a police officer actually witness drugs changing hands. Therefore, the police officer, and then the reviewing court, must focus on the variables used by a reasonable police officer to assess whether they rise to the level of probable cause. In the problem, Hill's furtive gesture of hiding his hands, being in the presence of known drug users, and leaving the table as the officer approached were not enough to change the determination, nor was the fact that the bar was notorious for drug sales. Hill's attempt to evade the officer by leaving the bar does not rise to the level of flight and is insignificant. Police officers have no authority to arrest an individual without probable cause to reasonably believe that the suspect committed, is committing, or is about to commit an offense. Those several factors did not rise to the level of probable cause.

The officer should have attempted to engage Hill. It is even questionable whether the facts rose to the level of reasonable suspicion to justify a *Terry* limited seizure, but even if reasonable suspicion is conceded, the officer did not have the authority to conduct a full search of Hill's person.

20.     **Answer (A) is correct.** Probable cause is a factual determination based upon facts and circumstances known to the police officer immediately before the arrest. "In dealing with probable cause, however, as the very name implies, we deal with probabilities. These are not technical; they are the factual and practical considerations of everyday life on which reasonable and prudent men, not legal technicians, act." *U.S. v. Ventresca*, 380 U.S. 102 (1965). Here, the officer observed the men in front of the post officer three minutes before police received a silent alarm; the officer believed the men had turned from the post officer driveway, and few other people were in the vicinity of the reported crime. Location is especially significant because the location in question was the vicinity of an actual crime. It was not a general, amorphous claim that the defendants were in a "high crime" area. Although a close case, the officer had probable cause to arrest the men, and the evidence was found during a search incident to a lawful arrest.

**Answer (B) is incorrect.** Location is significant in this case because there was a crime report and there were few other people in the area. A reasonable police officer would have concluded that Edwards and his companion had committed the break-in.

**Answers (C) and (D) are incorrect.** Certainly the facts and circumstances rise to reasonable suspicion to justify a temporary seizure of the suspects. There was reasonable justification to order the suspects to sit in the police car because the officer was alone. If the order to sit in the police car is reasonable, the officer may conduct no more than a pat-down frisk to ascertain whether the suspects are armed before putting them in the police car. Incident to a *Terry*-stop a police officer may not conduct a full search of the suspects, which is what happened in the problem.

21.     There is a hierarchy of dependability surrounding information from informants. Law enforcement officers who personally observe criminal activity or suspicious

circumstances are obviously good sources of information. A police officer's statements are entitled to be taken at face value and, absent evidence to the contrary, are assumed to be truthful. A magistrate may accept a police officer's sworn accounting of facts and circumstances without inquiring into the officer's veracity. Police officers may also reasonably rely on information provided by other officers when proceeding with a warrantless search or arrest. Similarly, information received over the police radio is considered to be trustworthy for the purposes of establishing probable cause. Next in that hierarchy comes information from disinterested citizen witnesses and crime victims, followed by confidential reliable informants whose veracity and reliability can be vouchsafed. At the very bottom of the hierarchy is the anonymous source, who is unknown to the police officers and whose veracity and reliability cannot be proven.

Information received from an officer over the police radio is considered trustworthy for the purpose of establishing probable cause. However, the broadcast of an anonymous tip over the police radio system is not. Where an officer relies solely upon a dispatch, the state must demonstrate at a suppression hearing that the facts precipitating the dispatch justified probable cause to believe that a crime had occurred. *Whiteley v. Warden, Wyoming State Penitentiary*, 401 U.S. 560 (1971). An anonymous source is inherently unreliable because there is no way to verify the truthfulness of the source or the underlying facts on which the source bases his/her conclusion.

Police may corroborate an anonymous tip. In *Illinois v. Gates*, 462 U.S. 213 (1983), the Court held that police corroboration provided sufficient information to utilize the anonymous tip as the centerpiece of probable cause in that case. Here, however, the police corroboration is of mundane details in no way bolstering the claim that Newton had committed a robbery. All the police corroborated was that Ike was traveling on W. 44th Street within the city, which was not enough information to rise to probable cause for an arrest. The only argument the state could make was that the anonymous tip plus the corroboration rose to the level of reasonable suspicion to justify a *Terry*-stop and temporary seizure. However, under no circumstance would a *Terry*-stop justify a search of the trunk of the vehicle. The state may further argue that the canine sniff provided an independent source for the arrest and retrieval of the drugs in the door of the car. However, it is difficult to separate the canine sniff from the illegal arrest and search.

22. **Answer (C) is the correct answer.** Although the evidence accumulated by the FBI to demonstrate probable cause was from several high tech sources, ordinary Fourth Amendment principles apply. Law enforcement officials may use undercover means to communicate directly with suspects over the Internet. Once police have determined that they are actually "speaking" with the defendant, these chat-room or email exchanges may create probable cause. *U.S. v. Simpson*, 152 F.3d 1241 (10th Cir 2000). When one communicates in person, by telephone or by email or text messaging, one runs the risk that the other party is not the person who the target thinks he is. Here, the information provided more than "a probability or substantial chance" that a search of the defendant's residence would

reveal child pornography contraband or other evidence of child pornography crimes. The application for the warrant and the search occurred within days of his return to the United States with suspected child pornography material. There was adequate probable cause.

**Answer (A) is incorrect.** Engaging would-be child predators on the internet is no different in kind than utilizing an undercover agent to purchase drugs from a suspected drug dealer. The defendant ran the risk that the person he was emailing was not the child with whom he thought he was communicating. Here, the FBI was not fishing in unknown waters. Agents had a basis for suspecting the defendant based upon the report of the child's mother that she was concerned about her son's internet activities. A person has a protected expectation of privacy in the contents of email massages, even though sent and stored through an Internet Service Provider. *Warshak v. U.S.*, 490 F.3d 455 (6th Cir 2007), vacated 532 F.3d 521 (6th Cir 2008). The defendant, however, ran the risk that the person he was communicating with would consent to monitoring of those messages or was an undercover law enforcement officer.

**Answer (B) is incorrect.** A person at a border has a lesser expectation of privacy than a person inside the country. A traveler crossing a border and entering into the U.S. is subject to a search of his person and possessions. U.S. v. Ramsey, 431 U.S. 606 (1977). It is questionable whether customs agents could have screened the films without at least reasonable suspicion to believe that it contained contraband. However, in the problem, the defendant consented to the screening of the films, a fact which helped provide probable cause for the search warrant.

**Answer (D) is incorrect.** There is an expectation of privacy in the content of email messages even though sent through and stored by an Internet Service Provider. *Narchak v. U.S.*, 06-4092 (6th Cir. 2007). However, a person sending an email runs the risk that the person he is messaging is not the person he thought he was emailing.

23.    Jack Turoff's information provided sufficient probable cause for the search warrant. Personal observations of police officers are not required to establish probable cause; reliable information obtained from credible informants will suffice. A report of a crime by an identified victim or a disinterested, identified witness may be taken at face value and acted upon without further checking the veracity of the source of information. *U.S. v. Swihart*, 554 F.2d 264 (6th Cir. 1977). Citizen witnesses are the life-blood of the criminal justice system. Police cannot be everywhere at all times. They are dependant upon information provided by a witness who is not involved in the criminal activity. It is possible that Turoff misread what he observed, but it may be acted on by the police without checking his level of comprehension. A citizen-witness's competency and truthfulness need not be verified. It would be time-consuming, and in most cases not necessary. The ability to inform the issuing magistrate of the source of the information and the source's identity helps to assure the magistrate of the truthfulness of the witness. This contrasts with a confidential informant who may be part of the criminal enterprise; the magistrate has to be certain (1) that she believes that the informant really exists, (2) the credibility of the informant and (3) the reliability of the

informant's information. Rather, the Supreme Court has said that probable cause can be established without evidence of (2) or (3), provided that the totality of the circumstances creates a fair probability that the evidence sought will be found at the place searched. *Illinois v. Gates*, 462 U.S. 213 (1983). Most lower courts continue to require evidence of (2) and (3) when reviewing a probable cause determination provided by an unnamed informant.

24.    **Answer (B) is correct.** Police officers, authorized by a valid warrant to search for specific items, may seize evidence and contraband that they discover during the search for the object specified in the warrant. A new warrant need not be obtained to seize the additional evidence. A judge has already passed on the probable cause that justified the intrusion, and the doctrine of exigency provides justification for not securing a new warrant because the delay might result in the destruction of the evidence. Naturally, however, the admissibility of the additional evidence uncovered during the search is governed by the reasonable scope of the search for the items specified in the warrant. The scope of a search pursuant to a warrant is limited by the nature of the items sought. The specificity required in a search warrant, demanding the particular description of the items to be searched for and the area to be searched based on probable cause determines the limits of the search. The plain view doctrine is not intended to transform a search warrant into a general warrant. Officers may not look for evidence in places where the object specified in the search warrant could not be found. *Horton v. California*, 496 U.S. 128 (1990). Moreover, the incriminating nature of the additional evidence found during the search must have been readily apparent to the officers without picking up and looking through the magazines. *Arizona v. Hicks*, 480 U.S. 321 (1987).

**Answer (A) is incorrect.** Evidence of other crimes found in plain view during execution of a search warrant is admissible if the warrant is valid, the officer is searching in a place where the object sought in the warrant could be located, and it is immediately apparent that the object found is evidence of a crime (probable cause). Even if the item was known to the police before the search and was not included in the warrant, the object may be seized. The discovery of the item not included in the warrant need not be inadvertent. *Horton v. California*, 496 U.S. 128 (1990).

**Answer (C) is incorrect.** A search is circumscribed by the terms of a warrant. If the objects sought have been found, police must terminate the search. When Sanford turned over the marijuana, the police officers could not be certain that there was no more marijuana in the apartment, and they had the right to continue searching. If the warrant had authorized search for a stolen diamond masonic ring and Sanford turned over the ring when the police arrived, the search would have had to terminate. Anything found after seizure of the item sought would not be admissible.

**Answer (D) is incorrect.** The phrase "evidence of any other crimes" in a search warrant is meaningless. It does not expand the authority of police to search for evidence of any crimes other than those for which probable cause was established. Police may only search for evidence of crimes that fits within the context of the crimes and items enumerated in the warrant. *Andresson v. Maryland*, 427 U.S. 463 (1976).

**25.** Ordinarily, it does not matter if an affidavit in support of a search warrant contains factual errors. The critical issue is whether the affidavit provided a substantial basis upon which the magistrate could make an independent determination that probable cause existed for the search. *Illinois v. Gates*, 462 U.S. 213 (1983). Consequently, the defendant is not permitted to pierce the warrant and prove factual inaccuracies.

One narrow exception, however, allows the defendant to focus on misinformation in the affidavit. When misstatements are the result of outright perjury, the integrity of the warrant process is compromised and deviation from ordinary procedures is justified. A defendant is entitled to a hearing on a motion to suppress when there is a "substantial preliminary showing" that a false statement was included by the affiant in the warrant affidavit. This substantial preliminary showing must be more than mere identification of the errors in the affidavit. Instead, the defendant must show by a preponderance of the evidence that the misstatements were made knowingly or with a reckless disregard for the truth. Even then, establishment of the perjury claim does not automatically lead to suppression of the evidence. The affidavit, after the false portion is excised, must be scrutinized to determine whether there are sufficient facts and circumstances remaining to establish probable cause. The prosecution has the opportunity to demonstrate that the false statement was not material to the probable cause finding. If the remaining content is sufficient to establish probable cause, the motion to suppress will be denied, notwithstanding the allegation and proof of perjury. *Franks v. Delaware*, 438 U.S. 154 (1978).

In the problem, the information withheld from the magistrate went to the very claim that the evidence sought was presently at Angel Smith's home. The misinformation, perjury, was material to the probable cause, and the evidence should be suppressed.

**26.** **Answer (C) is correct.** The good faith exception will not save evidence that would be suppressed because of police perjury. The Supreme Court said that the only justifiable purpose for the exclusionary rule is to deter illegal police conduct. The good faith exception provides that when police officers reasonably rely upon a search warrant, the evidence should not be excluded from trial even if the warrant turns out to be invalid. The reasoning behind *Leon* is that police should seek a warrant prior to conducting a search and should be permitted to rely upon the validity of a warrant issued by a judge; the police should not have to be in the business of second guessing the correctness of the warrant judge's decision. However, the *Leon* court said that suppression remains an appropriate remedy where the warrant is invalid because of police perjury. *U.S. v. Leon*, 468 U.S. 897 (1984).

**Answer (A) is incorrect.** Suppression remains an appropriate remedy where the warrant is invalid because of police perjury. *U.S. v. Leon*, 468 U.S. 897 (1984).

**Answers (B) and (D) are incorrect.** If the affiant had informed the magistrate of the information provided by the second informant that Angel Smith reported that he did not currently have the contraband, the magistrate might have decided nonetheless that the first informant's tip provided a sufficient basis for issuance of the search warrant. However, without full disclosure, the magistrate could not make that reasoned judgment. The information provided by the second informant went to the very heart of probable cause: that the evidence sought is presently at the place to be searched.

27.    **Answer (D) is the best answer.** The Fourth Amendment requires that a warrant specify the person and place to be searched or seized A search of Smith at his place of employment was not supported by probable cause. The probable cause was tied to Smith's residence.

**Answers (A) and (B) are incorrect.** The probable cause established that Carl Smith was operating a fencing operation out of his home. The warrant ordered a search of his home and his person. Police had no reason to believe that evidence of the crime would be found on his person away from his home.

**Answer (C) is incorrect** because a warrant ordering that a person be searched ordinarily does not specify where that search should take place. In the problem, however, police did not have probable cause to believe that evidence of the crime would be on Smith's person outside of the home.

28.    The court should grant the motion to suppress. The Fourth Amendment requirement that the warrant describe the things to be seized with particularity is designed to prevent general searches. *Go-Bart Importing Co. v. U.S.*, 282 U.S. 267 U.S. 498 (1925). The purpose of the warrant is to control the discretion of police executing the warrant. By listing the items to be seized, the court is directing and limiting where police may search. For example, if a search warrant orders a search for a stolen 42" television set, police may not search in dresser drawers or in a medicine cabinet because the item sought could not be in the dresser drawers or medicine cabinet. Moreover, once police find the objects listed in the warrant, the search must terminate. *Horton v. California*, 496 U.S. 128 (1990).

Even though police found a 9 mm pistol in Arthur Scott's car prior to executing the search warrant, it was not unreasonable to believe that Arthur Scott, a suspect in multiple violent crimes, may have multiple weapons. The police searched a video tape box and a paper bag knowing that the box and paper bag could not contain automatic pistols. Even though the police claim that the video box and paper bag could have contained gun parts or ammunition, police should have sought a more particularized warrant to search for parts and ammunition. "If police could search for bullets and parts of a gun every time a warrant authorized a search for a firearm, then police searching for a firearm would have no limit to where they could search." *State v. Scott*, 2001 WL 1867806 (Oh. Ct. App 2001). Absent clear guidance from the warrant, police are improperly vested with unlimited discretion. *Marron v. U.S.*, 275 U.S. 192 (1927).

29.    **Answer (A) is correct.** The constitutional requirement that a search warrant specify what items are to be seized poses significant problems when the seizure

involves evidence stored on computers. Some courts have likened the search of a computer to a search of a file cabinet. Police may search other files for evidence of the same crime. In the problem, probable cause existed to believe that Peters was storing child pornography on his computer. The search warrant authorized police to search for additional images of child pornography. *U.S. v. Campos*, 221 F.3d 1143 (10th Cir 2000).

**Answer (B) is incorrect.** Probable cause existed only to search for images containing child pornography. A warrant authorizing police the search all files on a computer for any crime would be a general warrant. Police executing a warrant to search a computer for files related to drug trafficking were held to have exceeded that authority when they searched files with sexually suggestive named and with a jpg suffix indicating that they were image files. The unauthorized search led police to child pornography: the items seized were not authorized by the warrant, nor were the closed files in plain view. *U.S. v. Carey*, 172 F.3d 1268 (10th Cir 1999).

**Answer (C) is incorrect.** Probable cause supported a search of the computer files for child pornography. Police could search any file that might contain the contraband.

**Answer (D) is incorrect.** The warrant ordered police to search the defendant's computer for the two files and for any other files containing child pornography. Probable cause supported such a search, and the search of the other files was specifically covered by the authorizing search warrant.

**30.**     **Answer (C) is correct.** Most state laws require that search warrants be executed during the daytime absent some special showing of need. However, there does not seem to be a federal constitutional requirement that searches be conducted during daytime hours. *Gooding v. U.S.*, 416 U.S. 430 (1974). Moreover, the stricter state requirement does not become part of the Fourth Amendment and will not be enforced by the Supreme Court. *Virginia v. Moore*, 128 S. Ct. 1598 (2008). The Fourth Amendment, however, does require that, absent exigent circumstances, police knock and announce and wait a reasonable time before entering a residence to execute a search warrant. *Wilson v. Arkansas*, 514 U.S. 927 (2002). However, the Supreme Court held that failure to comply with that Fourth Amendment requirement does not render the subsequent search illegal if the search warrant was supported by probable cause. *Hudson v. Michigan*, 547 U.S. 586 (2006).

    **Answer (A) is incorrect.** The Fourth Amendment does not require that searches be executed in daytime hours. *Gooding v. U.S.*, 416 U.S. 430 (1974). However, the Fourth Amendment does require that police knock and announce and wait a reasonable time before entering a residence to execute a search warrant, but the failure to comply with the requirement does not require the evidence found with the valid search warrant be excluded because the evidence would have inevitably been found lawfully. *Hudson v. Michigan*, 547 U.S. 586 (2006).

    **Answer (B) is incorrect.** Absent a showing of need, nighttime searches that take place without compliance with the Fourth Amendment requirement that police knock, announce and wait before entering should shock the conscience of the court. Such searches are evidence of a totalitarian society. However, the Supreme Court is unlikely to use the Due Process "shocks the conscience" standard. Instead, the Court will apply the reasonableness standard of the Fourth Amendment.

    **Answer (D) is incorrect.** Exigent circumstances cannot just rest upon a claim of exigency; it must be supported by facts giving rise to the exigency. Computer files may be deleted, but even deleted files can be recovered. There was no exigency established in the problem.

**31.**     The Supreme Court has upheld police detention of a resident of a home that is to be searched. Although the Court acknowledged that the detention of residents while the premises were searched constituted a significant restraint on their liberty, the majority concluded that the detention: (1) was less intrusive than the search itself; (2) was not likely to be exploited by the officer or unduly prolonged to gain more information; and (3) involved only a minimal increment in the inconvenience or public stigma associated with the search itself. The Court held that where a neutral and detached magistrate had found probable cause to believe that the law was being violated in that house and had authorized a substantial invasion of the privacy of the persons residing there, similar law enforcement interests support the detention of the residents during the search: (1) preventing flight in the event that incriminating evidence is found; and (2) minimizing the risk of harm to the police officers since the search for narcotics may give rise to sudden violence or frantic efforts to conceal or destroy evidence. *Michigan v. Summers*, 452 U.S. 692 (1981).

*Summers* dealt with the detention of a resident, but the Supreme Court in that case talked about occupants. Therefore, the authority is not limited just to residents but may be extended to non-residents who are present at the time of the search, but there must be a relationship and connection between the person detained and the house. Ordinarily, one could argue that mere presence at a house is not sufficient. Lower courts have focused more on presence than on a real connection between the person detained and the contraband that is sought. Where police have a warrant issued upon probable cause that a resident is dealing drugs out of his or her home, courts will be sympathetic to the detention of non-residents who are present when the warrant is executed. The Supreme Court also has found that it was reasonable for police to handcuff non-residents during execution of a search warrant. *Muehler v. Mena*, 544 U.S. 93 (2005). Consequently, the court will conclude that police acted properly when they detained the five non-residents while the search warrant was executed.

32.     **Answer (D) is correct.** The test for custody under the Fourth Amendment is whether a reasonable person under the circumstances would have believed that he was under arrest. *U.S. v. Mendenhall*, 446 U.S. 544 (1980). Following the search and the arrest of the resident, the five non-resident teenagers who had been detained, like the reasonable person, would have believed that they were under arrest. Consequently, police were required to read them their *Miranda* rights before questioning them. Their responses and the subsequently found drugs are inadmissible.

**Answer (A) is incorrect.** The teenagers did not volunteer the information. They were detained (in custody) and expected that the police would search them before allowing them to leave. The admission was the product of custodial interrogation and should have been preceded by *Miranda* warnings.

**Answers (B) and (C) are incorrect.** Absent a direction in the warrant ordering police to search all persons on the premises during execution of a search warrant, police may not conduct a search without a reasonable belief that the person is involved in the criminal activity or is armed and dangerous. Probable cause must exist to conduct a full search of the person; reasonable suspicion that the person is armed will support a pat-down of outer clothing for weapons. *Ybarra v. Illinois*, 444 U.S. 85 (1979). The legitimacy of the search requires a factual predicate and does not flow automatically from the person's presence during the execution of a search warrant.

33. **Answer (B) is the correct answer.** Objects falling in the plain view of an officer who has a lawful right to be in the position to have that view are subject to seizure and may be introduced in evidence. *Harris v. U.S.*, 390 U.S. 234 (1968). However, for the plain view exception to the warrant requirement to apply, a police officer must be lawfully present at the time of both the search and seizure. A police officer may view evidence from a location that she has the right to be. The officer's presence in the bathroom was permissible under the warrant. Her view into Kimberling's room was in plain view. The observation, however, did not justify entry of the room absent a warrant or exigent circumstances. "Incontrovertible testimony of the senses that an incriminating object is on the premises belonging to a criminal suspect may establish the fullest possible measure of probable cause. But even where the object is contraband, . . . the police may not enter and make a warrantless seizure." *Coolidge v. New Hampshire*, 403 U.S. 443 (1990). What the officer observed provided probable cause for issuance of a warrant to search Kimberling's room and seize the contraband. However, there was no need to enter the dorm room because the police could have secured the premises while a search warrant was obtained. *Segura v. U.S.*, 468 U.S. 796 (1984).

   **Answer (A) is incorrect.** Certainly the contents of Kimberling's room were in open view or plain view. The plain view exception does not authorize an officer to enter a residence to seize the evidence that was in open or plain view. Possession of a small quantity of marijuana is not a serious offense and would not justify an immediate entry under exigent circumstances. Police may secure the premises so that the evidence is not destroyed while a search warrant is obtained.

   **Answer (C) is incorrect.** A dorm room is a residence and is entitled to full protection of the Fourth Amendment. Police may not enter a dorm room for purposes of inspection. Just as landlords reserve the right to enter a lessee's apartment for safety or repair purposes, dorm rooms may be subject to periodic inspections by college officials for safety purposes. That fact does not allow either a landlord or college officials to permit police to conduct warrantless searches.

   **Answer (D) is incorrect.** A person who leaves a door open to a house, an apartment or a dorm room runs the risk that someone who is lawfully present outside may see into the house, apartment or dorm room and see evidence of a crime. The officer, however, did not have authority to enter Kimberling's room.

34. **Answer (D) is correct.** The officers were admitted to the apartment with the consent of Frances Todd. He consented to a search for the stolen overcoat. His consent shaped the parameters of the lawful search. In order to seize an item in plain view, it must be "readily apparent" to the officer that the object is evidence of

a crime, meaning that there must be probable cause to believe that the object is evidence of a crime without manipulating the object. Probable cause must exist without moving the object to examine it. *Arizona v. Hicks*, 480 U.S. 321 (1987). Probable cause did not exist until the officer removed the camera case, looked for the serial number, and received confirming information that the camera had been stolen. The motion to suppress should be granted.

**Answer (A) is incorrect.** Police were present in Todd's apartment with his permission. He consented to a search for a stolen overcoat. His consent shapes and limits the scope of the permissible search. The officers are not permitted to manipulate an object to ascertain whether it was stolen. It was not immediately apparent to the officer that the camera was stolen.

**Answer (B) is incorrect.** During a lawful search, police may seize evidence of other crimes if it is immediately apparent that the object is evidence of another crime. It was not immediately apparent to the officer that the camera was stolen property. Therefore, it could not be seized under the plain view exception.

**Answer (C) is incorrect.** The plain view exception requires probable cause to seize an item in plain view, not reasonable suspicion.

35.  The court should grant the motion to suppress. Relying upon the same rationale that underlies the plain view doctrine, the United States Supreme Court held that a "plain feel" corollary to the plain view exception should be recognized. The Court held that the seizure of nonthreatening contraband, detected through the sense of touch during a *Terry* protective pat-down search, is permitted, so long as the search stays within the bounds prescribed by *Terry*. *Minnesota v. Dickerson*, 508 U.S. 366 (1993). The pat-down in *Dickerson* did not stay within those bounds. The frisking officer felt a small lump in the suspect's front pocket and then, upon further tactile examination, concluded that the object was a lump of crack cocaine in a plastic or cellophane bag, which the officer removed from the suspect's pocket. The Court ruled that the seizure of drugs was unlawful because the officer exceeded the bounds of *Terry* by squeezing, sliding, and manipulating the object. The officer's authority was limited to running his hands over the outer clothing of the suspect to determine if he had a weapon. Once he concluded that there was no weapon, the officer had no further authority to run his hands over the suspect's body.

The problem does not involve the same manipulation of the object by the officer. The issue is whether, at the time the officer concluded that the object in the suspect's pocket was not a weapon, the officer had probable cause to believe that the object was evidence of a crime. It requires too great a leap to conclude that the officer had probable cause to conclude that the object in the suspect's pocket was contraband.

**36.**    **Answer (C) is correct.** The Fourth Amendment does not prohibit custodial arrests for minor, trivial offenses even when no valid purpose is served by an arrest rather than a summons. *Atwater v. Lago Vista*, 532 U.S. 318 (2001), involved a custodial arrest for not wearing a seat belt, an offense that carried a $50 fine. Moreover, the arrestee's infant children would have had to accompany their mother to the police station if a neighbor had not rushed out and taken the children from the scene. The Supreme Court held that neither English common law nor United States law at the time of the adoption of the Constitution prohibited arrests for any offenses. The Court rejected the defendant's request to create a "modern arrest rule . . . forbidding custodial arrest, even upon probable cause, when conviction could not ultimately carry any jail time and when the government shows no compelling need for immediate detention." Consequently, the validity of an arrest is determined by state law; in the problem state law authorized either an arrest or issuance of a summons. Incident to a custodial arrest, a police officer may search the arrestee's person. *U.S. v. Robinson*, 414 U.S. 218 (1973).

**Answer (A) is incorrect.** The Fourth Amendment does not prohibit custodial arrests for minor, trivial offenses even when no valid purpose is served by an arrest rather than a summons.

**Answer (B) is incorrect.** Following a custodial arrest, police may search the arrestee's person even though no evidence of the crime for which the person was arrested may exist. Even though there is no evidence of jaywalking, the officer may conduct a full search incident to arrest, not merely a pat-down search for weapons.

**Answer (D) is incorrect.** Police may search an arrestee at the site of the arrest. They need not wait until an inventory search is performed at the police station at the time of booking.

37.   **Answer (D) is correct.** Warrantless arrests, based on probable cause, for felony offenses are always valid when the arrest is made in a public place. *United States v. Watson*, 423 U.S. 411 (1976). The underlying theory for this rule of law was expressed by the Court as precluding endless litigation "with respect to exigent circumstances, whether it was practicable to get a warrant, whether the suspect was about to flee, and the like."

   **Answer (A) is incorrect.** Although the Court obviously is willing to accept litigation on some of these subjects when it comes to invading a home either to arrest or search, it is not willing to do so outside the home. Consequently, even if police had ample opportunity to get an arrest warrant, it is not a contestable issue if the arrest is made in public with probable cause.

   **Answers (B) and (C) are incorrect.** Since the general rule allows for warrantless felony arrests in public, the state need not prove exigent circumstances. If the state needed to prove exigency, the defendant's departure from the jurisdiction would have provided ample justification, but no justification is required.

38.   **Answer (A) is correct.** Certainly there was probable cause to arrest provided by the outstanding warrants and there was probable cause to believe that the fugitive was inside the trailer. However, probable cause is not an alternative to a warrant; it provides the justification for issuance of a warrant. A warrantless entry of a residence, even to make an arrest, violates the Fourth Amendment. *Payton v. New York*, 445 U.S. 573 (1980). Entry of a residence to conduct a search for a non-resident, must be conducted with a search warrant, absent consent or exigent circumstances. *Steagald v. U.S.*, 451 U.S. 204 (1981). The factors to be considered to determine whether there is a real exigency that will permit a warrantless police intrusion into a home to make an arrest are as follows: the offense is a crime of violence; it is reasonably believed that the suspect is armed; there is strong reason to believe that the suspect is on the premises; and it is likely that the suspect will escape if not swiftly apprehended. *Minnesota v. Olson*, 495 U.S. 91 (1990). The facts do not reveal that any of the four elements exist in this problem. Moreover, there was no reason for the officer to reveal himself by walking up to the door of the trailer allowing Moriss to see him. Police, acting without a warrant, may not create an exigency by their own behavior. *Vale v. Louisiana*, 399 U.S. 30 (1970). The weapon was in plain view in the bedroom when the officer arrested Morris, but the officer was not lawfully present in the bedroom.

   **Answer (B) is incorrect.** Police may not create exigent circumstances by their own behavior. The officer unnecessarily put himself in Morris' line of sight. Moreover, the facts do not indicate the nature of the offenses for the outstanding warrants, neither do the facts indicate whether Morris had any alternative exit other than the front door of the trailer. There are no facts indicating anything close to exigent circumstances.

**Answer (C) and (D) are incorrect.** Certainly, a person does not have to be present in her home to have standing to challenge the entry of that home. Standing, however, is not the critical issues here: the question is whether the officer's entry of the trailer without a warrant was justified, and whether he was lawfully in the bedroom when he saw the automatic weapon.

39.     A warrantless entry of a home to arrest a resident violates the Fourth Amendment absent consent or exigent circumstances. *Payton v. New York*, 445 U.S. 573 (1980). The admissibility of the blood alcohol test turns upon whether exigent circumstances justified the warrantless entry of the defendant's home before the evidence of intoxication dissipated. Hot pursuit and imminent destruction of evidence qualify as exigent circumstances in certain instances. In *Welsh v. Wisconsin*, 466 U.S. 740 (1984), the Supreme Court noted that according to the Wisconsin statute the drunk driving violation was a civil offense with a maximum $200 fine. Even though evidence of drunkenness might have disappeared if police had taken the time to obtain a warrant, the Court held that "it is difficult to conceive of a warrantless home arrest that would not be unreasonable under the Fourth Amendment when the underlying offense is extremely minor." The problem involves entry to arrest for a misdemeanor, more serious than a civil offense, but not rising to the level of a crime of violence. Even where police without a warrant entered a home to arrest the getaway driver in a robbery-murder, the Supreme Court did not dispute the state court's determination that there was insufficient justification to enter the home without a warrant where the defendant was staying when the murder weapon had already been recovered, and police had no reason to believe there was any danger in taking the time to secure a warrant. *Minnesota v. Olson*, 495 U.S. 91(1990). Therefore, the warrantless entry violated the Fourth Amendment, and the evidence is inadmissible.

40.     An arrest warrant adequately protects the Fourth Amendment interests of the person to be arrested. An arrest warrant does absolutely nothing to protect the privacy interest of the residents of a home when the warrant is used as the legal authority to enter the residence of a third person to arrest a nonresident who police believe is there. The third person's Fourth Amendment interest involved is the right to be free from an unreasonable invasion and search of his home for the person named in the arrest warrant. Absent exigent circumstances, the only way to protect the third person's privacy interest in his home is to require a search warrant to enter a residence to arrest a nonresident. *Steagald v. U.S.*, 451 U.S. 204 (1981). The Supreme Court saw no reason to depart from the settled doctrine that a search warrant is required to enter a residence when the search of a home is for a person (a nonresident) rather than an object. The Court found it unreasonable that police could enter a third person's home to search for another without a judicial evaluation of the facts that led them to believe that the nonresident would be found at that home. The Court saw too great a potential for abuse if an arrest warrant was deemed sufficient justification for searching a home for a nonresident.

While Tom had no grounds to challenge his arrest with an arrest warrant, a search warrant was needed to enter the home absent exigent circumstances. The court will grant the motion to suppress the magazine.

41.    **Answer (D) is correct.** Jerry was held an entire week before appearing in court. The Fourth Amendment requires a judicial determination of probable cause either prior to arrest or within 48 hours following a warrantless arrest. Here, Jerry was detained by the police so that they could question him about the fraudulent mortgage loans. The confession was the fruit of an illegal detention. The required probable cause determination need not be an adversary hearing; the requirement may be satisfied by a post-arrest warrant. *Gerstein v. Pugh*, 420 U.S. 103 (1975); *County of Riverside v. McLaughlin*, 500 U.S. 44 (1991).

     **Answers (A) and (B) are incorrect.** Compliance with *Miranda* and the due process voluntariness requirements is not the end of the inquiry. Jerry's prolonged detention without a judicial appearance or probable cause determination violated the Fourth Amendment's command that a detention be reasonable.

     **Answer (C) is incorrect.** The facts do not indicate that Jerry asked for an attorney following *Miranda* warnings; therefore the confession was not the product of a *Miranda* right to counsel violation. The Sixth Amendment right to counsel does not attach until the first judicial appearance. However, the prolonged detention violated Jerry's Fourth Amendment rights, and the confession is the fruit of that violation.

**42.** **Answer (D) is correct.** Although the United States Supreme Court has said over and over again that pretext stops and arrests are unconstitutional, the last time it spoke on this issue it virtually eliminated the pretext challenge to stops and arrests. A court may not consider a pretext Fourth Amendment challenge if there is a lawful basis for the stop. *Whren v. United States*, 517 U.S. 806 (1996). Under the facts of this particular case, *United States v. Harvey*, 16 F.3d 109 (6th Cir. 1994), it is quite clear that the officers would not have stopped the vehicle for speeding and the equipment violation but for the race of the defendants. However, since there was probable cause for the traffic and equipment violations, the motive of the police officer may not be considered in determining the legality of the stop under the Fourth Amendment. The Equal Protection clause of the Fourteenth Amendment may serve as a vehicle to challenge the race-based police behavior outside of the context of a criminal prosecution. See *Whren v. United States*, 517 U.S. 806, 813 (1996); *Farm Labor Organizing Comm. v. Ohio State Highway Patrol*, 308 F.3d 523 (6th Cir. 2002).

**Answer (A) is incorrect** because there was a lawful basis for the stop, making the pretext claim irrelevant.

**Answer (B) is incorrect.** In making its broad ruling in *Whren*, the Court also rejected the "reasonable officer test," which had found favor in many state courts.

**Answer (C) is not the best answer.** Although some state courts have held that as little as a single marijuana cigarette found on the driver creates probable cause to believe that more illegal drugs will be found in the vehicle, that is a stretch. Similarly, finding a single rock of crack cocaine on the driver in the question should not create adequate probable cause to dismantle the car and allow for a search of the entire vehicle. A stronger argument would have been that the evidence was found as part of a lawful inventory search following the impoundment of the car.

43. **Answer (C) is correct.** An arrest in a home is dangerous because the officer is on his adversary's home turf. As a precautionary matter, without probable cause or reasonable suspicion, a police officer may, incident to arrest, look in closets and other spaces immediately adjacent to the room where the arrest takes place, from which an attack could be launched. This is not a search for evidence, but solely a way to protect the arresting officers from attack. Evidence that is in plain view in those areas will be admissible at a subsequent trial. This authority naturally extends the scope of a search incident to an arrest. *Maryland v. Buie*, 494 U.S. 325 (1990). The police were entitled to open the closet door and to check the rooms and closets adjacent to the room where the arrest occurred in order to protect their safety. When the officers saw the automatic weapons in plain view they had probable cause to believe that the weapons were used in burglaries and robberies.

**Answer (A) is incorrect.** Even if Break was handcuffed before the officers opened the closet door, they have authority to look into adjacent areas to make sure that there is no hidden threat to their safety.

**Answer (B) is incorrect.** When the police officers opened the closet door they were not searching for evidence. They acted to ensure their safety. Police may look into adjacent areas without reasonable suspicion or probable cause to protect themselves. When they opened the closet door, the weapons were in plain view.

**Answer (D) is incorrect.** Probable cause is not an alternative to a search warrant. Probable cause allows police to obtain a search warrant. A warrantless search of a home is illegal absent probable cause *and* exigent circumstances.

44. Question 43 set forth the proposition that police may look in rooms and closets adjacent to the room where an arrest takes place without either probable cause or reasonable suspicion to believe that someone may be hiding who represents a threat to the safety of the officers. A police officer may conduct a limited protective sweep of the entire dwelling in conjunction with an in-home arrest if there are "articulable facts which, taken together with the rational inferences from those facts, would warrant a reasonably prudent officer in believing that the area to be swept harbors an individual posing a danger to those on the arrest scene." *Maryland v. Buie*, 494 U.S. 325 (1990). The Supreme Court cautioned, though, that it was not sanctioning a "top to bottom search" and stressed that the authority to conduct a protective sweep of the entire house is not automatic, but only available when there is reasonable suspicion to believe that the "house is harboring a person posing a danger." The police had information from an undercover officer that the gang was holed up in Break's home. They had adequate cause to conduct a

protective sweep of the entire house to look for Break's confederates.

However, a sweep is only a cursory inspection of those places where a person may be found. And the authority lasts no longer than it takes to complete the arrest and leave the house. In the problem, the police officer while conducting the sweep opened the small cabinet and found the guns and jewelry. The officer did not have reason to believe that one or more of Break's confederates was hiding in the small cabinet. Consequently, opening the cabinet was not part of the lawful sweep but an illegal warrantless search. The evidence in the cabinet must be suppressed.

**45.**   **Answer (D) is correct.** Incident to a custodial arrest of a motorist, a police officer is empowered to conduct a full search of the motorist's person. The Supreme Court held that the potential for danger following the taking of a suspect into custody and transporting him to the police station is an adequate basis for treating all custodial arrests alike. *U.S. v. Robinson*, 414 U.S. 218 (1973). The evidence is all admissible.

**Answer (A) is incorrect.** Incident to a custodial arrest, a police officer is not limited to searching the arrestee for weapons. Even if the offense is one where there could be no evidence, *e.g.* driving with a suspended license, the officer may conduct a full search of the person at the scene of the arrest.

**Answer (B) is incorrect.** A police officer may, incident to a lawful custodial arrest, search the arrestee at the scene of the arrest.

**Answer (C) is incorrect.** Whether the officer knew or did not know when he felt the pockets that Freeman had contraband on his person, the full search of the arrestee automatically flowed from the custodial arrest. The officer did not need probable cause to conduct the search.

**46.**   **Answer (A) is correct.** Ordinarily, a search incident to arrest may not precede the arrest. Whether the challenged evidence is admissible depends upon whether the officer had probable cause to arrest Freeman immediately before he ordered Freeman to empty his pockets. The facts indicate that the officer had probable cause to arrest Freeman the instant he stepped from his car and was observed to be drunk. A police officer may conduct a search incident to arrest prior to the formal arrest if probable cause to arrest already exists, and the formal arrest follows shortly thereafter. *Cupp v. Murphy*, 412 U.S. 291 (1973).

**Answer (B) is incorrect.** A full search of a motorist's person is permissible following a custodial arrest. *U.S. v. Robinson*, 414 U.S. 218 (1973). The underlying justifications which allow for a warrantless search of a motorist following a custodial arrest do not exist when the motorist is stopped to allow the officer to issue a summons. The same dangers that attach to a custodial arrest are absent, the Supreme Court has said, when the motorist is stopped for a non-custodial traffic offense. *Knowles v. Iowa*, 525 U.S. 113 (1998).

**Answer (C) is incorrect.** A search incident to arrest may precede a formal arrest provided that the probable cause for the arrest already exists and the arrest follows shortly after the arrest. Of course, the evidence found during the incidental search may not provide the probable cause for the arrest. *Smith v. Ohio*, 494 U.S. 541 (1990).

**Answer (D) is incorrect.** The proposition in Answer (D) is generally correct. However, once the intrusion results in probable cause for a custodial arrest, a full search of the person is allowed.

47.    Incident to the arrest of a person, a police officer may use reasonable force to secure evidence on the arrestee's person. The court's ruling will depend upon the reasonableness of the force used. The issue was addressed by the United States Supreme Court half a century ago prior to imposition of the Fourth Amendment exclusionary rule on the states under the Fourteenth Amendment. In *Rochin v. California*, 342 U.S. 165 (1952), the notorious "stomach pumping" case, the Supreme Court found the state's attempts to retrieve evidence swallowed by the arrestee to "shock the conscience" of the Court and violate the Due Process guarantee of the Fourteenth Amendment. In *Rochin*, police officers jumped upon the defendant and unsuccessfully attempted to extract the drug evidence. When that effort failed, the officers handcuffed the defendant, took him to a hospital, where a doctor forced an emetic solution into the defendant's stomach against his will forcing the defendant to vomit two capsules containing morphine. Since *Rochin*, it takes a great deal more to shock the Supreme Court's and other courts' consciences.

Today the court will determine the legality of the officer's behavior according to Fourth Amendment principles. Incident to the arrest of a person, a police officer may use reasonable force to secure the evidence on the arrestee's person. The court's ruling will depend upon the reasonableness of the force used. Reasonableness will turn on whether the method used was life threatening, and whether there were less intrusive means available to obtain the evidence. Here, also, it may be critical that the police officer acted without first giving the suspect the opportunity to open his mouth. It is relevant, as well, that the objects, if swallowed, may have been life threatening to the arrestee. There are alternative means of securing the evidence; all they had to do was wait. However, courts, today, regularly uphold this type of force.

**48.**    **Answer (D) is correct.** Incident to a lawful arrest, police may search the arrestee's person and the area under the arrestee's control. The area within the arrestee's control has been defined as the area from which the arrestee can reach and grab weapons to use to escape or threaten the police officers or to grab evidence that the arrestee might wish to destroy. *Chimel v. California*, 395 U.S. 752 (1969). A warrantless search incident to arrest is not a search for evidence. Such searches incident to arrest are solely for the purposes of protecting the officers and preventing the arrestee from destroying evidence. Determining the proper scope of a search incident to arrest comes down to how one defines and measures control. If control is measured just prior to the arrest or at the moment of arrest, the search incident to arrest would extend to all objects the arrestee could reach at that moment. Although it is not universally agreed, the purpose of the *Chimel* control test was to limit the scope of a search incident to arrest by measuring the control of the arrestee at the moment of the search. Any other measurement of control would allow for a broader search than necessary to protect the arresting officers and prevent the arrestee from access to evidence that she might seek to destroy.

In the facts presented, the Congressman was handcuffed in back and seated prior to the search. He was totally controlled by the police at that moment. A search of his person and of the seat where he was ordered to sit would fit within the parameters of a search incident to arrest; he might be able to retrieve a weapon or evidence on his person or hidden in the seat. Even if the desk was within the grabbing distance of the seat, the search of the desk exceeded the permissible scope of an incidental search. It would have been nearly impossible for the Congressman to get up from the chair, turn around, and reach into the desk drawers. The search was beyond the permissible scope of an incidental search, and the police should have obtained a search warrant before searching the desk. The evidence is inadmissible.

**Answer (A) is incorrect.** The warrant was an arrest warrant, not a search warrant. The warrant authorized police to enter Cranston's home and to seize him. The warrant did not authorize a search of the home, only a limited search incident to arrest of the area within his grabbing or reaching distance. The desk drawer was beyond Cranston's reach once he was handcuffed behind his back and completely under the control of the arresting officer.

**Answer (B) is incorrect.** If the police had probable cause to believe that evidence of bribery would be presently found at Cranston's house, they could have and should have sought a search warrant in addition to the arrest warrant. Probable cause does not justify a warrantless search unless the situation fits into one of the defined and limited exceptions to the warrant requirement.

**Answer (C) is incorrect** as far as it goes. There is nothing in the facts of this problem to indicate that the authorities had probable cause to believe that evidence of bribery would have been presently found at Cranston's home. If such evidence did exist, the police should have obtained a search warrant to go along with the arrest warrant.

49.    Incident to a lawful custodial arrest, with or without a warrant, police may search the area within the control of the arrestee, meaning the "reaching or grabbing" distance. *Chimel v. California*, 395 U.S. 752 (1969). The *Chimel* test brilliantly draws a line between (1) warrantless searches that serve the underlying justification for warrantless searches incident to arrest, to protect the police officers from weapons the arrestee may grab and to prevent the arrestee from destroying evidence of any crime, (2) and warrantless searches that are merely searches for evidence not supported by the underlying justifications.

In the problem, once police had handcuffed Cranston and moved him away from the desk and the cash, they had no authority to extend the scope of the warrantless search. Of course, they had authority to seize the evidence sitting on top of the desk and protruding from the drawers. That evidence was in plain view. However, they had no additional authority to search the desk or the library. They could have secured the room from entry by Cranston's wife or others while they sought a search warrant. Although barring Mrs. Cranston from a room in her home is a substantial intrusion on her privacy, the Supreme Court has adopted a balancing test to determine when such an intrusion is permissible and concluded: "We have found no case in which this Court has held unlawful a temporary seizure that was supported by probable cause and was designed to prevent the loss of evidence while the police diligently obtained a warrant in a reasonable period of time." *Illinois v. McArthur*, 531 U.S. 326 (2001).

50.    **Answer (A) is correct.** Clearly police may not arrest outside a home and then move the arrestee into the house for the purpose of conducting a search. The same principle should be applicable to movements within a house. *Chimel* dictates that law enforcement officers cannot create a fiction of control. For example, police may not move an arrestee from room to room or even within a room, such as to place him within reach of a desk or dresser, to create the fiction of control for the purpose of conducting a warrantless search. The natural order of events, however, may result in an extension of control, thus permitting a broader search incident to arrest. If it is necessary for the arrestee to dress prior to being transported to the station house, police may search the closet or dresser from which the arrestee intends to secure clothing, and that search may take place even if the closet or dresser is in a different room from the one where the arrest takes place. The search is consistent with the *Chimel* test because the arrestee's control has extended to areas beyond his reaching or grabbing distance at the time of the arrest. Police may remain at the elbow of an arrestee at all times. *Washington v. Chrisman*, 455 U.S. 1 (1982). Recognition that control may be extended for legitimate reasons permitting a wider incidental search should not be misconstrued as a license to defeat the intent of the Supreme Court in adopting the *Chimel* test.

**Answer (B) is incorrect.** Allowing Cranston to dress does not rise to the level of exigent circumstances. Exigency should be reserved for situations where real necessity exists. The search was lawful incident to the arrest of Cranston. A police officer may remain at the elbow of an arrestee at all times. Allowing Cranston to change clothing meant that police could follow him into the bedroom and search where Cranston reached.

**Answer (C) is incorrect.** The fact that there was an alternative, perhaps less intrusive, method to the one the police officers chose does not make the method used unreasonable under the Fourth Amendment.

**Answer (D) is incorrect.** This is one of the few instances where without exigent circumstances, requiring a search warrant would be unreasonably time-consuming and burdensome. Police acted humanely by allowing Cranston to change his clothing rather than face embarrassment from arriving at the police station in pajamas. Following an arrest, police seek to move the arrestee expeditiously to the police station. Delaying their departure until a search warrant was obtained would have been unreasonable.

**51.**    **Answer (C) is correct.** Society expects police to respond to emergency situations. Securing judicial authorization to search for persons in need of help would limit the ability of police to respond to an emergency situation. Conflicts arise when police seize evidence "in plain view" while responding to the emergency, leading to a claim that the emergency was contrived. Unquestionably, police officers may enter and investigate in an emergency without the accompanying intent to either search or arrest. *U.S. v. Barone*, 330 F.2d 543 (2d Cir. 1964). The officers' entry was reasonable under the Fourth Amendment as they were discharging their statutory duty to prevent crime, preserve the peace, and protect persons and property. The officers had reasonable ground to believe that there was an emergency in the house and it was their duty to enter and investigate to determine if anyone needed assistance. They could enter without the defendant's consent. While looking to see if anyone needed assistance, the officer observed the marijuana in plain view. They were entitled to seize that evidence. *State v. Frankel*, 847 A.2d 561 (NJ 2004), cert. denied, 125 S. Ct. 108, 160 L. Ed. 2d 128 (U.S. 2004).

**Answer (A) is incorrect.** Where exigent circumstances arise, police do not have to accept the home owner's claim that no one needs help. The officers had reasonable cause to believe that someone inside the house could have been in need of assistance. They were entitled to enter even over the owner's objection.

**Answer (B) is incorrect.** Perhaps the police should have asked the defendant if anyone else was present in the house. Even if he had answered in the negative, they were entitled to investigate to determine if anyone else was present and in need of assistance.

**Answer (D) is incorrect.** The defendant's refusal to grant consent does not create probable cause to conduct a search. Moreover, probable cause, alone, does not justify a warrantless search of a home or business. The warrantless entry was justified by exigent circumstances: the need to determine whether anyone was in need of assistance.

**52.**    **Answer (B) is correct.** It has not been unusual for an exception to the warrant requirement (*e.g.* the automobile exception) originally justified by exigent circumstances to lose its emergency characteristic as the exception develops. That same expansive growth has not marked the development of searches justified by emergency situations. The scope of warrantless searches justified by emergency or exigent circumstances has remained linked to the nature and scope of the emergency; the search has not been allowed to become a fishing expedition for evidence. Once the actual emergency is alleviated, and the danger associated with it has been relieved, the authority to search without a warrant terminates. The

Supreme Court has insisted on maintaining reasonable controls on warrantless searches justified by exigent circumstances. In these cases, the Court has required law enforcement authorities to comply with the warrant requirement once the exigency that justified the initial intrusion has passed. *See e.g. Michigan v. Tyler*, 436 U.S. 499 (1978). In the problem, the police were looking for someone in the house who needed assistance. They had no authority to look into the dresser drawer.

**Answer (A) is incorrect.** The police had reason to look through the entire house to determine if anyone was present who needed their help. They were entitled to enter the bedroom and to look in the closet and under the bed for such a person. They had no authority to extend the search to the dresser drawer. A search justified by exigent circumstances may not be transformed into a fishing expedition for evidence of a crime.

**Answer (C) is incorrect.** Whether the discovery of marijuana provided probable cause to search for other contraband, it would not justify a warrantless search of the house for evidence. Under the circumstances, the police were entitled to seize the marijuana in plain view and to secure the house while they attempted to obtain a search warrant. The Supreme Court has said that securing a house while a warrant is sought imposes a significantly lessor intrusion on privacy than the intrusion that occurs when police search a home without a warrant. *Illinois v. McArthur*, 531 U.S. 326 (2001).

**Answer (D) is incorrect.** On the basis of the 911 call, police had authority to enter the house and search for anyone who needed assistance. They could not legally search the dresser without a warrant.

53.    If the officers had arrived on the scene and found a party that was not unruly but saw juveniles inside illegally drinking beer, they would not have had the authority to enter the house without permission or a warrant. *See State v. Andrews*, 2008-OHIO-3993 (Oh. Ct. App. 2008). However, in the problem, the officers did see a fight taking place. The issue is whether police were permitted to enter the premises under the emergency aid doctrine which requires an objectively reasonable belief that a warrantless entry was necessary to prevent physical harm. The Supreme Court evaluated the facts in this problem and concluded that "[i]n these circumstances, the officers had an objectively reasonable basis for believing both that the injured adult might need help and that the violence in the kitchen was just beginning. Nothing in the Fourth Amendment required them to wait until another blow rendered someone unconscious or semi-conscious or worse before entering." *Brigham City v. Utah*, 547 U.S. 398 (2006).

Ordinarily, entry of a home under the emergency or exigent circumstances doctrine requires that the police officer must not be motivated by traditional law enforcement purposes. The point is to prevent the exigency and emergency doctrines from serving as a pretext to enter to search of arrest. The *Brigham* Court rejected such a limitation. The Court said that it did not matter whether the officers entered the kitchen to arrest respondents and gather evidence against them or to assist the injured and prevent further violence. This aspect of the decision has been interpreted to eliminate inquiry into whether police officers were motivated to enter by an investigatory intent. *U.S. v. Najar*, 451 F.3d 710 (10th Cir 2007).

54. **Answer (C) is correct.** The presence of evidence in a dwelling does not create an emergency. Probable cause, no matter how well founded, that an article sought is concealed in a dwelling does not constitute exigent circumstances and does not furnish justification for a warrantless search. *Agnello v. United States*, 269 U.S. 20 (1925). A warrantless entry of a home by law enforcement authorities, even upon probable cause, cannot be justified by exigent circumstances of their own making. The exigent circumstances were the direct result of the police officers' actions. Despite their belief that Sheppard was inside, the officers went to the apartment without a warrant. When they could not gain entry at the door, they used the fire escape to look through the window. The officers' presence on the fire escape caused Sheppard to run and the officers to fear that he might be obtaining a gun or destroying evidence. Because the exigent circumstances were of the officers' own making, those circumstances did not justify the warrantless entry into the residence.

**Answer (A) is incorrect.** The most common example of exigent circumstances justifying a warrantless intrusion occurs when police are chasing a suspect and that pursuit leads them into a building. Police may seize weapons as well as evidence that they discover while in hot pursuit of a suspected criminal. *Warden v. Hayden*, 387 U.S. 294 (1967). Hot pursuit commonly involves a chase but it need not be an extended hue and cry in and about public streets. It involves immediate and continuous pursuit from the moment probable cause arose to arrest. A suspect may not thwart police attempts to arrest him in public by ducking into his house. *U.S. v. Santana*, 427 U.S. 38 (1976). However, any time the pursuit is discontinued, even for a few minutes while a pursuing officer awaits back-up assistance, the authority to enter in hot pursuit is terminated. Here, police went to Sheppard's home the day after he eluded arrest. The officers did not enter his apartment in hot pursuit.

**Answer (B) is incorrect.** Police may not rely upon an exigency created by their own conduct. Police went to Sheppard's home expecting to find him there. They needed a warrant to enter and arrest him.

**Answer (D) is incorrect.** Police may enter a home without a warrant to arrest a resident with consent or exigent circumstances. The exigent circumstances may not be of the police own making which is what happened in the problem. To enter the home to search for a weapon or evidence necessitated a search warrant.

**55.**    **Answer (D) is correct.** In performance of their caretaking function, police may stop vehicles or inquire of people in parked cars. Police are also under a duty to render assistance to stranded motorists or disabled vehicles. The key to such permissible police activity is the reasonableness required by the Fourth Amendment. When approaching a vehicle for safety reasons, the police officer must be able to point to reasonable, articulable facts upon which to base his safety concerns. Such a requirement allows a reviewing court to evaluate the officer's conduct. Do the facts available warrant a police officer of reasonable caution believing that the action was appropriate? Here, the officer saw a man slumped over the wheel. He also called for an ambulance. The officer clearly acted reasonably when he tried to rouse the driver and called for assistance. Moreover, a police officer when interacting with a motorist may order the motorist out of the car or to remain in the car without justification. *Pennsylvania v. Mimms*, 434 U.S. 106 (1977). However, the means used by the officer must be narrowly tailored to satisfy the limited purpose for the interaction. Once the officer ascertained that the driver was awake and not drunk, he should have terminated the intrusion. There was no factual predicate for the officer to search anywhere in the car.

**Answer (A) is incorrect.** Courts rarely question a police officer's claim to conduct a search for weapons. However, even a limited pat-down of a person or of the automobile which the person will re-enter must be supported by facts and circumstances giving rise to a reasonable concern for safety. No facts were offered in this case. *Michigan v. Long*, 463 U.S. 1032 (1983). The officer had no authority to look under the seat.

**Answer (B) is incorrect.** Of course the officer had authority to inquire and make sure that the person slumped over the wheel of the car did not need assistance. Once the officer ascertained that the person did not need assistance, the officer's authority to intrude ended and he should have terminated the encounter.

**Answer (C) is incorrect.** The officer did properly invoke the caretaking function to make sure that the person slumped over the wheel did not need assistance. Once the officer learned that the person was neither ill nor drunk, there was no need to continue the encounter. To search the person or the vehicle for a weapon, the officer must have facts and circumstances rising to a reasonable belief that the person was armed or represented a threat to the officer's safety. There were no facts justifying either a frisk of the driver or the vehicle.

56. **Answer (D) is the best answer.** Incident to the custodial arrest of a motorist, a police officer may search the interior compartment of the vehicle. The search incident to arrest flows directly from the arrest and needs no additional justification. A search incident to arrest does not extend to the trunk of the vehicle. *New York v. Belton*, 453 U.S. 454 (1981). The prosecution should have argued that the search was an inventory of the vehicle, assuming that the police department had policies for inventory searches in this situation.

   **Answer (A) is incorrect.** Once the motorist is out of the car and unable to reach into the inteior compartment, police may not search the interior compartment. *Arizona v. Gant*, 129 S. Ct. 1710 (2009). A search incident to arrest does not extend to the trunk of a vehicle even if the arrest itself was lawful.

   **Answer (B) is incorrect.** A search of the trunk would have been lawful under the automobile exception if the officer had probable cause to believe that evidence of a specific crime would be found in the car. *California v. Carney*, 471 U.S. 386 (1985). Probable cause could have developed from something found during a search of the motorist or the interior compartment of the vehicle, giving rise to a belief that evidence of a crime might be in the car, but it did not. There was no probable cause to search the rest of the vehicle.

   **Answer (C) is incorrect.** A custodial arrest for a traffic offense does not violate the Fourth Amendment; its legality depends upon state law. Here, state law allowed the officer to issue a traffic ticket or arrest the motorist. *Atwater v. City of Lago Vista*, 532 U.S. 318 (2001). The officer's discretion was not exercised arbitrarily in this case because the officer sought to ensure that an unlicensed motorist did not get back behind the wheel.

57. **Answer (C) is the best answer.** The evidence is inadmissible. The search of the interior compartment of the vehicle was not a lawful search incident to arrest. Police may search the interior compartment of a vehicle and all containers found in that compartment incident to the arrest of an occupant of the vehicle. However, the incidental search of the vehicle is not lawful after the arrestee is out of the car, handcuffed, and in the back of the police car where he or she certainly is no longer in control of the contents of the vehicle. *Arizona v. Gant*, 129 S. Ct. 1710 (2009). The *Belton* bright-line rule was premised upon the hypothetical "control" of a recent occupant of the vehicle even when that occupant is out of the car and unable to reach or grab into the vehicle. Even under *Belton* once an arrestee was removed from the scene of the arrest, here transported to the police station, the legal fiction of "control" upon which *Belton* rested no longer provided authority for a warrantless search.

**Answer (A) is incorrect.** Once an arrestee is removed from the scene of the arrest and taken to the police station, the *Belton* authority to search the interior of the vehicle is terminated.

**Answer (B) is incorrect.** An alternative theory that might allow for a search of a vehicle is under the inventory exception to the warrant requirement. An inventory search is not a search for evidence; it is an administrative procedure, comparable to booking at the police station, which permits police to inventory the contents of a vehicle in order to protect the owner's property and to insulate police from false claims of loss. *South Dakota v. Opperman*, 428 U.S. 364 (1976); Colorado v. Bertine, 479 U.S. 367 (1987). Authorization to conduct an inventory, however, rests upon a lawful impoundment. If the car is impounded, police may conduct an inventory of its contents and the contents of closed containers provided it is part of a standardized procedure. *Florida v. Wells*, 495 U.S. 1 (1990). There was no valid reason to impound the vehicle. It was not damaged, and the arrestee's wife, presumably a co-owner of the vehicle, was prepared to take possession of the car. The officer indicated, prior to the search, his intent to permit the wife to take the car. If there is no lawful impoundment, there is no lawful inventory.

**Answer (D) is not the best answer.** From the outset, there was no factual justification for an inventory search. An inventory search of a vehicle is dependent upon a lawful impoundment of the vehicle. There was no valid reason to impound the vehicle. The officer agreed to allow the arrestee's wife to take the car.

58.  The motion to suppress will be granted. The Belton rule was extended to allow a search of the interior compartment of an automobile even though the occupant of the vehicle was outside the car when police made first contact with him. Thornton v. U.S., 541 U.S. 615 (2004). However, in 2009, the Supreme Court reasserted the Chimel control test to searches of the interior compartment of a vehicle incident to arrest when the interior compartment is within reach of the motorist. The court said, "Police may search a vehicle only if the arrestee is within reaching distance of the passenger compartment at the time of the search or if it is reasonable to believe the vehicle contains evidence of the offense of arrest." Frances was arrested on a bench warrant after she had legally parked and locked her car. Following the arrest, Frances could not reach into the locked vehicle, nor did the officer have any reason to believe that the vehicle contained evidence associated with the offense.

59. **Answer (B) is the best answer.** Police may search a vehicle without a warrant under the automobile exception when the vehicle is lawfully stopped and the officer has probable cause to believe that evidence of a specific crime will be found somewhere in the vehicle. Once probable cause exists, the officer may search the entire vehicle. This exemption from the warrant requirement originally rested on exigent circumstances because it was likely that the evidence would be gone before police could obtain a search warrant. *Carroll v. U.S.*, 267 U.S. 132 (1925). Ultimately, the "general mobility of a vehicle" and the "diminished expectation of privacy that one has in an automobile" became the bases for the exception, and police no longer need prove exigent circumstances. *Maryland v. Dyson*, 527 U.S. 465 (1999). The critical issue here is whether the smell of burnt marijuana and the discovery of a small remnant of a roach in the ashtray provided probable cause to search the entire vehicle including the trunk. Courts are divided on this issue. Several state courts have taken the position that different standards of probable cause apply to the trunk and interior compartment: "The odor of burnt marijuana in a passenger compartment of a vehicle does not, standing alone, establish probable cause for a warrantless search of the trunk." *See e.g. State v. Farris*, 849 N.E.2d 985 (Ohio 2006).

     **Answer (A) is not the best answer.** Although courts differ on this conclusion, the smell of burnt marijuana and a roach in the ashtray do not establish probable cause to believe that additional amounts of marijuana will be found outside the interior compartment of the vehicle.

     **Answers (C) and (D) are incorrect.** The state would not have argued that the marijuana was discovered during a search incident to arrest. Police may search the interior compartment of a vehicle following the arrest of a recent occupant of the vehicle. Officer Trapper had no authority to arrest the defendant for the traffic offense or possession of a small quantity of marijuana. There was no custodial arrest until the evidence was found in the trunk. A search incident to arrest extends only to the interior compartment of the vehicle. Police may not search the trunk of a vehicle incident to the custodial arrest of the driver. *New York v. Belton*, 453 U.S. 454 (1981). Officer Trapper needed probable cause to search the trunk.

60. **Answer (B) is correct.** The automobile exception authorizes a warrantless search of the vehicle when there is probable cause to believe that contraband or evidence of a specific crime will be found in the vehicle. Although originally premised on exigent circumstances, the requirement of exigency no longer exists. Under the automobile exception, police may search the vehicle and its contents at the location where the vehicle was stopped or later at the police station. There need be no

justification for the delayed warrantless search. *Maryland v. Dyson*, 527 U.S. 465 (1999). A substantial delay between the seizure of the vehicle and the search does not affect the authority granted under the automobile exception; the delayed search of the contents is permissible even if the contents are stored separately from the vehicle by the police. *U.S. v. Johns*, 469 U.S. 478 (1985).

**Answer (A) is incorrect.** Police may search the interior compartment of a vehicle incident to the driver's arrest. The search must take place at the site of the arrest while the driver is within reach of the interior. A search incident to the arrest of the driver does not extend to the trunk of the vehicle. *New York v. Belton*, 453 U.S. 454 (1981). Although items associated with the person of the arrestee may be searched at the scene of an arrest or later at the police station, *U.S. v. Edwards*, 415 U.S. 800 (1974), that authority does not extend to a search of the vehicle at the police station.

**Answer (C) is incorrect.** The proposition stated in Answer (C) does not state the current law. The automobile exception was originally based upon exigent circumstances, allowing police to search a vehicle at the scene because delay to obtain a warrant risked the loss of the evidence. The requirement of exigent circumstances no longer exists, and police may delay searching the vehicle until it is removed to the police station, even though at that point there remains no justification for not getting a search warrant. However, police having probable cause to search a vehicle do not need a search warrant whether the search takes place at the scene or later at the police station. *Chambers v. Maroney*, 399 U.S. 42 (1970).

**Answer (D) is incorrect.** A search, supported by probable cause, under the automobile exception extends to the entire vehicle and containers within the vehicle that could house the object sought. *U.S. v. Ross*, 45 U.S. 798 (1982).

61. A police officer may act upon reports received from the police dispatcher. If probable cause is later challenged, the state will have to establish that the source of the information had probable cause. *Whiteley v. Warden*, 401 U.S. 560 (1971). In the problem the officer had cause to stop the vehicle matching the police report. At the very least, the facts gave rise to reasonable suspicion to stop the vehicle and make inquiry. Probably, however, the uniqueness of the vehicle rose to the level of probable cause to arrest and search.

A police officer with probable cause to believe that evidence of a specific crime will be found in a vehicle may conduct a warrantless search of the entire vehicle including containers in the vehicle. The scope of a search under the automobile exception is as broad and extensive as a search with a warrant. *U.S. v. Ross*, 456 U.S. 798 (1982). However, like a search with a warrant, the scope of the search under the automobile exception is limited by the probable cause supporting the search. Under the facts of this problem, the officer had probable cause to search the van for a 42″ inch television. The officer was authorized to look anywhere in the van and in any containers where the television set could be hidden. *California v.*

*Acevedo*, 500 U.S. 565 (1991). A 42″ television set could not be in the briefcase. The officer had no authority to open the briefcase or the canisters within the briefcase because they could not contain the television set. The items found in the canisters are inadmissible.

62. **Answer (B) is correct.** Under the automobile exception police with probable cause may search all containers within a vehicle that could contain the objects sought. Consequently, the automobile exception extends to a passenger's belongings. *Wyoming v. Houghton*, 526 U.S. 295 (1999). The Supreme Court upheld the search of a passenger's belongings provided that probable cause focuses upon the entire vehicle, even though the probable cause arose only from information pertaining to the driver. The Court distinguished the search of a passenger's belongings from the search of the passenger, himself, which the Court had previously disallowed under the automobile exception. *U.S. v. DiRe*, 332 U.S. 581 (1948). The Court utilized a balancing test to conclude that the government's interest in searching "a passenger's personal belongings when there is reason to believe contraband or evidence of criminal wrongdoing is hidden in the car" outweighs the "[p]assenger's, no less than the driver's, . . . reduced expectation of privacy with regard to the property that they transport in cars." The police officer is not required to first ascertain if the passenger is involved in the driver's illegal enterprise. Moreover, it is possible that a driver might place, unknown to the passenger, contraband in the passenger's belongings.

**Answer (A) is incorrect.** A police officer does not need probable cause to link a passenger to the driver's illegal enterprise in order to search a passenger's belongings. The automobile exception allows an officer to search the entire vehicle and all containers within the vehicle when probable cause focuses on the vehicle. The only limitation is that the officer may not search containers which could not hold the object which is sought. Here, cash could have been in any of the suitcases. The marijuana was in plain view during the lawful search of Frankel's suitcase.

**Answer (C) is incorrect.** When probable cause focuses generally on a vehicle, police may search any container within the vehicle where the object sought could be hidden. Police lawfully detained the Frankels while they sorted out the situation. There was no probable cause to implicate the Frankels in VanBuren's illegal operation, but the police could lawfully detain them for a short period of time until they searched their belonging.

**Answer (D) is incorrect.** Probable cause did not exist to implicate the Frankels in Van Buren's criminal enterprise. Therefore, they could not be arrested until probable cause arose from the search. Their suitcases, however, were subject to search under the automobile exception because probable cause focused generally on the vehicle. Police may lawfully search any container in the vehicle which contains the object sought. *U.S. v. Ross*, 456 U.S. 798 (1982).

63. **Answer (C) is correct.** Incident to arrest, police may search the arrestee and objects within the "control" of the arrestee. A search incident to arrest without a warrant is permitted to prevent the arrestee from gaining access to weapons that might threaten the safety of the arresting officers or to evidence which the arrestee might seek to destroy. *United States v. Robinson*, 414 U.S. 218 (1973). In this case, the arrestee was in custody of the police. He was handcuffed and placed in the back of the police car. The officers had found the key to the footlocker in Van Buren's pocket, and there was no way he could have gained access to the contents of the footlocker. *Chimel v. California*, 395 U.S. 752 (1969). Therefore, it was no longer within his control, and the fiction that allows police to search the interior compartment of a vehicle incident to the arrest of an occupant applies only to an arrestee seized while in a vehicle. *New York v. Belton*, 453 U.S. 454 (1981). It does not apply on the street.

    **Answer (A) is incorrect** because the footlocker was no longer in Van Buren's control and the search was unlawful.

    **Answer (B) is incorrect.** Probable cause and a warrant are not alternative prerequisites to a valid search. Ordinarily, a warrant based upon probable cause is required to allow a search unless the facts fall within one of the exceptions to the warrant requirement. Exigent circumstances would provide a legitimate reason not to get a search warrant, but there is no exigency here. Once Van Buren was arrested and placed in the police car, and the officers had total control of the locked footlocker and the key, there was no exigency. They were entitled to seize the footlocker on probable cause and hold it while they obtained a warrant. There was no need to conduct a warrantless search. Police might have waited and searched the footlocker as part of an inventory search at the police station. An inventory is an administrative procedure to safeguard the owner's property and protect the police from false claims of loss. The inventory would have to be done at the police station. Otherwise it would be a thinly disguised search for evidence; an inventory is not a search for evidence. *Illinois v. Lafayette*, 462 U.S. 640 (1983).

    **Answer (D) is incorrect.** There was ample probable cause to arrest Van Buren and to secure a warrant to search the footlocker. The confidential informant's tip provided the police with probable cause to believe contraband was in the footlocker.

64. The cash and the drugs are admissible. Under the automobile exception to the warrant requirement, police may search the entire vehicle and any container found in the vehicle that might hold the object of the search. All that is necessary for a valid search under the automobile exception is independent probable cause to

believe that evidence of a specific crime will be found in the automobile. To prevent police from exploiting the automobile exception, earlier Supreme Court cases held that if probable cause focused upon a container before it was placed in an automobile but the police delayed the search until after the item was in the vehicle, the container could not be searched legally without a warrant under the automobile exception. *United States v. Ross*, 456 U.S. 798 (1982); *Arkansas v. Sanders*, 442 U.S. 753 (1979). However, the Supreme Court eliminated that limitation upon the automobile exception. Now police may search a container seized from an automobile even though they had probable cause to search the container before it was placed in the automobile. California v. Acevedo, 500 U.S. 565 (1991).

**Authors' Note:** The purpose of this question and the previous question is to focus on the different rules that apply when the footlocker is seized in public and when it is seized from an automobile. If the footlocker is being carried in a public place, police may seize it on probable cause and hold it while a warrant is obtained. If the footlocker is seized from an automobile, police acting on probable cause may search it without a warrant solely because it was in an automobile. No explanation for this difference can be based upon exigency.

If Van Buren had placed the suitcase in the backseat of the automobile, it could be searched after the car was stopped and Van Buren arrested either under the automobile exception because there was probable cause or as a *Belton* search incident to the arrest of an occupant of a vehicle before the suspect is placed in the police car. None of the underlying justifications for either exception to the warrant requirement explains the different result if Van Buren had been arrested on the sidewalk and the footlocker seized. Some members of the Supreme Court have always argued that incident to arrest, police may search all packages and containers being carried by the arrestee, but that position has never found itself into a Supreme Court majority opinion. *Compare United States v. Chadwick*, 433 U.S. 1, at 23 (Blackmun, J., dissenting) ("It is well established that an immediate search of packages or luggage carried by an arrested person is proper."), with *id.* at 16–17 (Brennan, J., concurring) ("[I]t is not at all obvious that the agents could legally have searched the footlocker at the time and place of the arrests.").

The police could search the footlocker at the police station as part of an inventory of an arrestee's effects. The inventory would have to be done at the police station. Otherwise it would be a thinly disguised search for evidence; an inventory is not a search for evidence. *Illinois v. Lafayette*, 462 U.S. 640 (1983).

**65.** **Answer (A) is correct.** An inventory search that satisfies the Fourth Amendment is not a search for evidence; it is a search intended to protect the owner's property and the police from false claims of loss. The legality of the inventory search depends upon a lawful impoundment. Generally, police may impound a vehicle when it is evidence of a crime, if it is abandoned, or if the driver has been arrested and there would be a traffic hazard if the car were left where the arrest occurred. A legally parked vehicle may not be impounded merely because the owner has been arrested while away from the car. The car was lawfully parked, and the defendant, charged with shoplifting, could have arranged for a family member to retrieve the car. There was no justification for the police to tow the vehicle. *South Dakota v. Opperman*, 428 U.S. 364 (1976).

**Answer (B) is incorrect.** State law that allows police to arrest for minor offenses does not violate the Fourth Amendment. *Atwater v. City of Lago Vista*, 532 U.S. 318 (2001). The arrest here is not at issue. The car was legally parked and not subject to impoundment.

**Answer (C) is incorrect.** The validity of the inventory search hinges here on the legitimacy of the impoundment. The car was legally parked. The defendant was arrested away from the vehicle. There was no justification for impounding the vehicle; consequently, the inventory was not lawful.

**Answer (D) is incorrect.** Incident to the arrest of an occupant of a vehicle, police may search the interior compartment of the vehicle and all containers located within the compartment. *New York v. Belton*, 453 U.S. 454 (1981). A *Belton* search is not applicable to the facts here where the offense occurred more than a couple of minutes after the arrestee left the vehicle. Moreover, a search incident to arrest is different from an inventory search. Different underlying justifications buttress the two exceptions to the warrant requirement. They should not be confused. Here, the car was lawfully parked and could not be impounded. There was no justification for an inventory of the car's contents.

**66.** **Answer (B) is correct.** During a lawful inventory, police may open closed compartments of the vehicle. *South Dakota v. Opperman*, 428 U.S. 364 (1976). However, inventory searches must be governed by standardized departmental procedures restricting the discretion of police officers. The Fourth Amendment does not prohibit inventory searches of vehicles that extend to closed containers if there is a written standard policy governing such inspections. *Florida v. Wells*, 495 U.S. 1 (1990). The key in this question is that there was such a standardized policy authorizing police officers to open and inventory the contents of closed containers found in unlocked compartments of the vehicle. The inventory of the interior of the vehicle and the glove compartment where the officer found the watch was lawful. The policy did not extend to locked compartments; therefore, the search of the trunk was illegal. The watch is admissible, but the marijuana is inadmissible.

**Answer (A) is incorrect.** Police may impound cars that are blocking traffic and inventory the car's contents. However, the scope of the inventory must be governed by standardized procedures. The departmental procedure did not authorize an inventory of locked compartments. The officer was not authorized to open the trunk and inventory its contents.

**Answer (C) is incorrect.** A lawful inventory is not restricted to objects that are visible within the interior compartment of a vehicle. Police may inventory the contents of all compartments within the vehicle and may open closed containers found anywhere in the vehicle. The authority to inventory, however, must be determined by departmental procedures. Metropolis police regulations would not have violated Tina's Fourth Amendment rights even if the regulations authorized an inventory of all compartments and closed containers within the compartment. The regulations did not grant the officer permission to inventory the contents of locked compartments. The officer violated Tina's Fourth Amendment rights by opening the locked trunk because it was not authorized by departmental regulations.

**Answer (D) is incorrect.** The issuance of a traffic citation is not a custodial arrest. Police may not conduct a *Belton* search of a vehicle incident to the issuance of a traffic citation. *Knowles v. Iowa*, 525 U.S. 113 (1998). Even if failure to yield was an arrestable offense in Metropolis, the *Belton* search incident to arrest would not extend to the trunk of the car and would not extend to the interior once the defendant was unable to gain access to the interior compartment. *Arizona v. Gant*, 129 S. Ct. 1710 (2009)..

**67.**    This Question tests whether there are any limits on the ability of police to search a vehicle without a search warrant. In the present situation, we have to consider the facts under the following exceptions: inventory, automobile, and search incident to arrest. The impound of the vehicle following the arrest of the driver was lawful and, accordingly, the car may be inventoried pursuant to department regulations. The driver was arrested, and there were no other occupants to take custody of the vehicle. If the car had been left where it was stopped, it would have posed a hazard to other vehicles on the highway or may have been stolen or vandalized. The purpose of an inventory is to protect the owner's property and to protect the police from false claims of loss. The vehicle inventory must be done according to standardized procedures. *South Dakota v. Opperman*, 428 U.S. 364 (1975); *Florida v. Wells*, 495 U.S. 1 (1990). The Ionscan test served neither of the purposes that justify inventory searches of vehicles. Because it was only a search for evidence, it cannot be upheld as an inventory search.

There is no basis for upholding the Ionscan test as a search incident to arrest. Although *Belton* settled the question that the interior compartment (and all compartments therein) and all containers found in the interior may be searched incident to arrest, there needs to be a nexus between the search and the underlying justifications for warrantless searches incident to arrest: prevent the arrestee from access to weapons or evidence. *New York v. Belton*, 453 U.S. 454 (1981). That nexus ends when the arrestee is removed from the car and is unable to reach back into the car. In this case, a search 60 days after the arrest would not be to protect the officers or prevent the arrestee from destroying evidence.

The state's strongest argument arises under the automobile exception to the warrant requirement, but there, too, the argument will fall short. A search under the automobile exception extends to the entire vehicle. The delay between the seizure of the vehicle and its search does not negate the authority under the automobile exception. *Chambers v. Maroney*, 399 U.S. 42 (1970); *United States v. Johns*, 469 U.S. 478 (1985). However, the authority under the automobile exception rests upon the existence of probable cause to believe that evidence of a specific crime will be found somewhere in the vehicle. The officer searched the compartment at the time of the arrest, but it was empty. It is irrelevant whether the Ionscan test was conducted months after seizure of the vehicle. The only evidence was the existence of the compartment. Without anything more, the existence of the compartment did not rise to the level of probable cause. *United States v. Lake*, 233 F. Supp. 2d 465 (E.D. N.Y. 2002). The evidence must be suppressed.

**68.**   **Answer (D) is the best answer.** Police may talk to a person without probable cause to make an arrest. The Fourth Amendment does not prohibit police from engaging people in conversation on the street. Police need no factual basis for conversing with a person on the street, provided that a reasonable person (not necessarily the suspect) would know that he or she is free to refuse to cooperate or walk away from the officers. This type of encounter is called a "consensual encounter" and is not considered a "seizure" regulated by the Fourth Amendment. *United States v. Mendenhall*, 446 U.S. 544 (1980). The difference between a consensual encounter and a *Terry* stop is not always easy to discern. Police persistence does not necessarily transform a consensual encounter into a *Terry* stop. The Fourth Amendment test is whether a reasonable person, under the circumstances, would feel free to walk away and refuse the police request to cooperate. A *Terry*-stop involves an interaction where a reasonable person would not feel free to leave. Here the balance was tipped in favor of a *Terry*-stop when the officers retained Glick's driver's license. A reasonable person would not feel in that situation free to walk away and forfeit the I.D. Incident to a lawful *Terry* stop based on reasonable suspicion, police may conduct a limited frisk for weapons if facts and circumstances give rise to a reasonable belief that the suspect is armed or represents a threat to them. A legitimate frisk is only a search for weapons, not for evidence. A frisk consists of a pat-down of the outer clothing of a suspect. *Terry v. Ohio*, 392 U.S. 1 (1968). In this case, a frisk could have extended to feeling the soft backpack for a weapon. That is not what the police officer did. He opened the backpack obviously looking for drugs. The drugs are not admissible at Glick's trial.

**Answer (A) is incorrect.** Glick did not voluntarily consent to a search of his backpack. His consent was the product of police coercion: they told him he could leave only if he consented to a search; they had his driver's license. The consent to search was not voluntary.

**Answer (B) is incorrect.** The prosecution could make a reasonable argument that Glick was lawfully detained. He was in a hallway where police were investigating reports of illegal drug sales, and he lied to the police about why he was there and where he lived. A *Terry* stop is a seizure of a person based upon facts and circumstances giving rise to reasonable suspicion that criminal activity is occurring. The seizure allows police to freeze the situation while they confirm or dispel the suspicion about criminal activity.

**Answer (C) is incorrect.** The search of Glick's backpack was not a limited search for weapons. A limited search would not have involved opening the bag. The officers opened the bag looking for evidence of drug dealing.

69.     **Answer (B) is correct.** An anonymous tip by itself cannot form the basis for reasonable suspicion. However, an anonymous tip which provides police with specific information that is corroborated by the police can rise to the level of reasonable suspicion required for a *Terry* stop. When police arrived in the middle of the night at the deserted parking lot behind the closed drug store, in an area known for drug transactions, they had sufficient facts and circumstances to justify a seizure to confirm or dispel that a crime was about to occur. *Alabama v. White*, 496 U.S. 325 (1990). The fact that Cole was alone in the parking lot did not automatically dispel the claim that a drug deal was about to take place. Conduct that gives rise to reasonable suspicion may be susceptible to an innocent explanation. Cole could have been there awaiting a drug dealer. Police interrupting a possible drug deal in the middle of the night in a dark parking lot may be in danger. The facts gave rise to a reasonable suspicion that Cole might be armed or dangerous, thus, justifying a frisk for weapons. When Cole reached into his jacket, the officer could dispense with the pat-down and reach for any weapon that Cole might have in the jacket. The limited search for weapons was reasonable.

   **Answer (A) is incorrect.** An anonymous tip is not sufficient by itself to justify a *Terry* stop. The Supreme Court has indicated that an anonymous tip alerting police to a major emergency, *i.e.* a weapon in a school, would be sufficient to warrant police action. However, an anonymous tip that a man in a plain shirt on a street corner had a gun, did not justify a *Terry* stop and frisk even though the defendant matched the description. *Florida v. J.L.*, 529 U.S. 266 (2000), *but see U.S. v. Holloway*, 290 F.3d 1331 (11th Cir 2002) (anonymous report of an emergency situation justified a *Terry* intrusion).

   **Answer (C) is incorrect.** The anonymous tip that the defendant would be in a deserted parking lot in the middle of the night is sufficiently specific to allow the police to conduct a *Terry* stop when they corroborated some of the facts in the tip.

   **Answer (D) is incorrect.** A *Terry* frisk is a pat down of a suspect's outer clothing to determine if he has a weapon. If, during the pat down, the officer feels what is reasonably likely a weapon, the officer may reach into the pocket to remove the weapon. It would be overly formalistic to require a pat down when it is reasonable to believe that the suspect is reaching for a weapon. The only justification for the *Terry* frisk is to protect the officer. In the facts it was reasonable for the officer to reach inside Cole's jacket when he thought Cole was reaching for a gun.

70.     **Answers (A) and (B) are best answers.** In determining whether the facts and circumstances known to a police officer prior to the *Terry* seizure rose to the level of reasonable suspicion, a court must make the determination based on the totality of the circumstances. That totality must be evaluated "through the eyes of a reasonable and cautious police officer on the scene, guided by his experience and training." *U.S. v. Cortez*, 449 U.S. 411 (1981). However, the reviewing court must not be a rubber stamp. *Terry* requires the court to distinguish between inarticulable hunches on one hand, and facts and circumstances giving rise to reasonable suspicion. In the particular case, the state Supreme Court found reasonable suspicion based primarily upon the place where the stop occurred: "'The reputation of an area for criminal activity is an articulable fact upon which a

police officer may legitimately rely' in determining whether an investigative stop is warranted." In fact, the other factors, such a furtive movement, were window dressing. *State v. Bobo*, 524 N.E.2d 489 (Ohio 1989). An evaluation of the court's analysis might be helped along by knowing that the occupants of the vehicle were a man and a woman, and while that does not rule out a drug transaction, it opens the door to consideration of other, innocent behavior (in fact, the officer "testified that when he looked into the car, 'she [the female occupant] was fastening her clothing.'") Even though an area is known for high drug activity, residents engage in all of the activities other people engage in their home neighborhoods. In fact, one could question whether the activity within the car fit the profile of a drug transaction. Ordinarily, a drug transaction in a vehicle is hurried; the parties do not linger in the car as if to socialize. The search of area around the front seat of the vehicle for a weapon has been upheld under the rubric of a *Terry* frisk. *Michigan v. Long*, 463 U.S. 1032 (1983).

**Answer (C) is incorrect.** Incident to a *Terry* stop of a vehicle, police may search the area around the driver's seat for a weapon if facts and circumstances give rise to a reasonable suspicion that the driver may be armed, and the driver will be allowed to return to the vehicle after the stop concludes. *Michigan v. Long*, 463 U.S. 1032 (1983).

**Answer (D) is incorrect.** The facts marginally allow for a finding of reasonable suspicion to justify a *Terry* seizure; they do not rise to the level of probable cause to justify an arrest or a search of the vehicle under the automobile exception.

71. Police must have reasonable suspicion that a crime is occurring, has occurred or is about to occur to make a *Terry* stop. Prior to a *Terry* stop, a police officer needs no justifiable predicate to engage a citizen on the street. An officer may talk to anyone and request information; such an encounter rises to the level of a *Terry* stop when a reasonable person would not feel free to walk away. However, a police officer's conduct and a reasonable person's perception of that conduct are not the only measurements of whether a seizure has occurred. Rather, the suspect's response to the police conduct is highly relevant. Until the police officer's attempt to affect an investigatory stop succeeds, no seizure takes place and, therefore, no Fourth Amendment review of the reasonableness of the officer's decision to intrude on the suspect's privacy may occur. *California v. Hodari*, 499 U.S. 621 (1991).

Therefore, Warble was not seized until he was caught by the other police officer, and police do not have to justify the chase. Reasonable suspicion will not be evaluated until the moment Warble was caught and forced to stop. Moreover, Warble's flight when he saw Officer Carbonari is a fact that may be considered by a court reviewing whether reasonable suspicion justified the seizure: "Headlong flight — wherever it occurs — is the consummate act of evasion: it is not necessarily indicative of wrongdoing, but it is certainly suggestive of such." While flight alone does not provide sufficient reasonable suspicion for a *Terry* stop, it is a factor that may be considered along with other facts. *Illinois v. Wardlow*, 528 U.S. 119 (2000). Warble's conduct during the chase was not the result of an illegal seizure. Police may collect what he threw away during the flight and use it at trial.

72.     **Answer (B) is the correct answer.** Evan was not properly seized under the Fourth Amendment when he was required to identify himself. The ordinance requires a person lawfully stopped to identify himself or herself. The prerequisite to the duty imposed by the ordinance is a legitimate *Terry* stop based on facts and circumstances giving rise to a reasonable suspicion that a crime is occurring, has occurred or is about to occur. The race of a suspect rarely, if ever, is a relevant characteristic in determining reasonable suspicion. Police may have wanted to talk to Evan, but they did not have the factual predicate to require that he stop and cooperate.

     **Answer (A) is incorrect.** One of the articles of faith of the *Terry* Court was that a person seized under *Terry* need not answer any questions, including those pertaining to his identity. *Terry v. Ohio*, 392 U.S. 1 (1968). Even though a suspect need not identify himself or answer an officer's questions about his suspicious behavior, those facts are relevant in a determination of the legitimacy of a subsequent frisk of the suspect, and likely will justify a longer detention while the suspicious circumstances are checked out. The Supreme Court has held that a statute which made it an offense for a person lawfully stopped to refuse to identify himself did not violate either the Fourth or Fifth Amendment. The Court said that "[t]he request for identity has an immediate relation to the purpose, rationale, and practical demands of a *Terry* stop." And further, that "[t]he officer's request was a common sense inquiry, not an effort to obtain an arrest for failure to identify after a *Terry* stop yielded insufficient evidence." *Hibel v. Sixth Judicial District of Nevada*, 542 U.S. 177 (2004). Even though the Metropolis ordinance did not violate the Fourth or Fifth Amendments, Evan was not seized legally and could not be subject to prosecution for his failure to identify himself.

     **Answer (C) is incorrect.** Evan was not lawfully arrested for failing to identify himself. The ordinance imposes that duty only on persons subject to a lawful *Terry* stop. Evan was not lawfully seized under *Terry*.

     **Answer (D) is incorrect.** The ordinance does not, nor could it, impose an obligation upon everyone to identify himself or herself when asked by a police officer. The obligation under the ordinance is imposed only when police have reasonable suspicion to justify a *Terry* stop. A lawful *Terry* stop may not be based solely on race.

73.     **Answer (D) is correct.** A traffic stop for a non-arrestable offense is measured and governed by the *Terry* standards. Ordinarily one difference between a forcible *Terry* stop and an arrest is the amount of force used. Most *Terry* stops and traffic stops do not necessitate the use of force to accomplish the purpose of conducting an inquiry. Comparisons often have been drawn between an arrest situation, where the use of force is expected and automatic, and a *Terry* stop, where there is rarely a threat of violence and the intrusion is conducted in a polite manner generally devoid of force and humiliation. The amount of force that may accompany a *Terry* stop or a traffic stop is subject to a reasonableness inquiry. The force must be reasonably limited in scope and intensity which will vary depending on the crime investigated and the reasonable risk perceived by the investigating officers. When police use force during an investigative detention they should be able to point to

specific facts or circumstances that justify the degree of force used. In this problem, no facts are presented to justify the use of force or the frisk. Following a traffic stop, a police officer may order the occupants of a vehicle out of the car; no factual justification need be presented for that order. *Pennsylvania v. Mimms*, 434 U.S. 106 (1977). Any intrusion beyond ordering the occupants out of the vehicle must meet the reasonableness standard. There was no reason offered for the use of force or the frisk for a weapon. The evidence found during the unlawful frisk must be suppressed.

**Answer (A) is incorrect.** Police may not frisk a motorist stopped for a traffic violation unless facts and circumstances exist to believe that the motorist may be armed or a danger to the officer's safety. Here, the police came on like gangbusters, but there were no facts to justify the use of excessive force or the frisk.

**Answer (B) is incorrect.** As a general proposition the statement is true. Police may take reasonable steps to protect their safety during a stop for a traffic violation. They may order a motorist and other occupants out of the vehicle. However, any other steps, such as a frisk of the motorist or of the vehicle for weapons, must be supported by facts and circumstances rising to a reasonable belief that the motorist is armed or a threat to the officer's safety. No such facts exist in the problem; the police used unreasonable force and the frisk was illegal. The same standards governing the frisk of a motorist apply to passengers in a lawfully stopped vehicle. If there is reasonable suspicion to believe a passenger is armed, police may frisk the passenger. *Arizona v. Johnson*

**Answer (C) is incorrect.** The force used by the police would be permissible in the context of a custodial arrest. However, there was no probable cause until the officer found the weapon. The use of force and the frisk were unreasonable in the context of a traffic stop absent actual facts to justify such behavior.

74.     **Answer (A) is the correct answer.** Following a lawful stop of a vehicle to issue a traffic citation, police may walk a drug dog around the vehicle to check for drugs. There need be no factual justification for using the drug dog beyond the lawful stop for a traffic violation. The use of the drug dog does not constitute a search, and the positive alert provided probable cause to search the trunk of the car under the automobile exception to the warrant requirement. The only limit on the police behavior is the time required for the drug dog to reach the scene of the traffic stop may not unreasonably extend the time required to issue a traffic citation. *Illinois v. Caballes*, 543 U.S. 405 (2005). The dog sniff of the vehicle occurred simultaneously with the use of excessive force by the police, five minutes after the defendant's car was stopped. That would fit within the time required for issuance of a traffic summons. The use of excessive force would not affect the legality of the use of the drug dog.

**Answer (B) is incorrect.** A search of an automobile incident to the lawful, custodial arrest of an occupant of the vehicle would not extend to the trunk of the vehicle.

**Answer (C) is incorrect.** The use of excessive force does not taint the probable cause provided by the drug dog. There is no causal connection between the excessive force and the probable cause to search the trunk.

**Answer (D) is incorrect.** Police need neither probable cause nor reasonable suspicion to use a drug dog to check out an automobile following a lawful traffic stop. The only issue is whether the time police need to get the drug dog to the scene unreasonably extends the time to write the traffic citation. Here the officer observed the defendant run a read light. Police may use a drug dog to check any vehicle lawfully stopped.

**75.** The motion to suppress should be denied. The answer turns on the legality of the checkpoint stop for information pertaining to a past crime. A police order to a motorist to stop is a Fourth Amendment seizure of the vehicle and all of its occupants. The stop must meet the reasonableness standard of the Fourth Amendment. The Supreme Court has upheld checkpoint stops to ensure that the motorist is properly licensed and the vehicle properly registered. Checkpoint stops may include testing the safety of the vehicle. These checkpoints are related to ensuring safety on the highway. Checkpoint stops are lawful provided that police discretion is limited, and who is stopped is not left to the arbitrary exercise of discretion by the officers manning the checkpoint. *Delaware v. Prouse*, 440 U.S. 648 (1979). The same reasoning that led to license and safety checks now permits roadblocks to check for drunk drivers. *Michigan Dept of State Police v. Sitz*, 496 U.S. 444 (1990). Although safety concerns are paramount here as they are in safety checks, the immediate result of a violation is a criminal charge. The Supreme Court disallowed a checkpoint stop for illegal drugs: "We have never approved a checkpoint program whose primary purpose was to detect evidence of wrongdoing." *City of Indianapolis v. Edmond*, 531 U.S. 32 (2000). The Court, however, did uphold a roadblock stop designed to obtain from motorists information about a fatal hit-and-run accident that occurred at the same location exactly one week earlier, very similar to the stop in the problem. The Court used a balancing test to uphold the stop, finding that the importance of soliciting citizen information outweighed the defendant's Fourth Amendment right not to be seized without individualized suspicion. *Illinois v. Lidster*, 540 U.S. 419 (2004).

Once a checkpoint passes Fourth Amendment muster, the issue then focuses on the facts and circumstances which support singling out a particular motorist for further inquiry. Once a motorist is diverted from the regular flow of traffic past the checkpoint, the routine standardized stop of all vehicles becomes an investigative stop of a single vehicle for which particularized suspicion is required. Field sobriety tests may be administered only if reasonable suspicion to believe that the motorist is impaired develops from the initial minimal encounter. Obviously, then, these minor intrusions may escalate into probable cause to arrest. The police officer noticed Evans' impaired condition during the minimal intrusion involved in handing each driver a handbill. Those facts and circumstances rose to the level of reasonable suspicion to allow for further inquiry. When Evans failed field sobriety tests, probable cause arose for an arrest. Police may administer a Breathalyzer test once there is probable cause to arrest. The incremental escalation of the Fourth Amendment intrusion grows as individualized cause, as in the problem, develops. The evidence pertaining to the field sobriety tests is admissible because the officer had reasonable suspicion to believe that Evans was driving while impaired. The Breathalyzer result is admissible because the field sobriety tests gave rise to probable cause.

76.   **Answer (C) is the correct answer.** This question explores whether police may extend a traffic stop to ask questions unrelated to the stop or safety and whether police may ask for permission to search a stopped car for contraband. The Supreme Court took a very expansive view of these issues when it said the only question was whether the defendant's consent to search the vehicle was voluntary. Whether the consent is voluntary is to be determined by the totality of the circumstances. Whether the motorist is advised that he or she need not consent is only one issue to be considered and does not weight the equation against a finding of voluntariness. *Ohio v. Robinette*, 519 U.S. 33 (1996); *Schneckloth v. Bustamonte*, 412 U.S. 218 (1973). In the case arising out of these facts, the Supreme Court concluded that the defendant's consent was voluntary and not the product of police coercion.

**Answer (A) is incorrect.** The immediate question and search in the *Robinette* case were incident to a valid traffic stop. However, the duration of such a stop may not be unreasonably extended beyond the time it takes to process the traffic violation. For example, police may bring a drug dog to the locale of a valid traffic stop and subject the stopped car to a dog sniff, provided that the delay involved in bringing the dog to the scene does not unreasonably extend the time required to write a traffic ticket. *Illinois v. Caballes*, 543 U.S. 405 (2005). In *Robinette*, even though the Deputy had already issued the warning to Robinette, the Supreme Court was not concerned that the questioning and search extended the seizure.

**Answers (B) and (D) are incorrect.** Both the *Robinette* and *Caballes* cases indicate that short extension of a traffic stop to ask about other offenses or to bring a drug dog to the scene of the stop does not violate the Fourth Amendment. *Arizona v. Johnson*, 129 S. Ct. 781 (2009). Some courts, however, focus on whether the traffic ticket or warning was already issued before police ask to search the car. Most federal courts have held that asking a motorist about the presence of guns or drugs in the vehicle during or immediately at the conclusion of the traffic stop does not unreasonably extend the stop. *See, e.g., U.S. v. Stewart*, 473 F.3d 1265 (10th Cir 2007); *U.S. v. Childs*, 277 F.3d 947 (7th Cir 2002). One federal court held that delaying the motorist after issuance of the traffic ticket to await arrival of drug sniffing dog was an illegal detention. *See United States v. Salzano*, 149 F.3d 1238 (10th Cir. 1998).

Many state courts impose stricter rules on the police. Some limit questions about other offenses or requests to search the automobile to cases where reasonable suspicion about the other offense exists. *See, e.g., State v. Carty*, 790 A.2d 903 (N.J. 2002) (as a matter of state constitutional law, police making a traffic stop may not request permission to search the car absent reasonable suspicion). Other courts focus on the length of the traffic stop. *People v. Cox*, 782 N.E.2d 462 (Ill. 2002) (fifteen minutes was too long to write traffic ticket). And still others focus on whether the purpose of the original stop — issuance of a traffic citation — was completed. Some courts take the position that if the traffic citation or warning was issued, then the continued detention is illegal and the traffic officer may not ask questions about other offenses or ask for consent to search the vehicle without explaining to the motorist that he or she is free to leave. *See, e.g., State v. Robinette*, 685 N.E.2d 762 (Ohio 1997) (upholding limited questions about drugs and weapons after issuance of the warning as in the public interest, but holding that a request for consent to search after issuance of ticket or warning is the product of an illegal detention). The Supreme Court said, "An officer's inquiries into matters unrelated to the justification for the traffic stop . . . do not convert the encounter into something other than a lawful seizure. . . ." *Arizona v. Johnson*, 129 S. Ct. 781 (2009).

**77.**   **Answer (C) is correct.** The tavern owner consented to the police officer's presence in the private area behind the tavern. No warrant was necessary to inspect the tavern open to the general public because there is no Fourth Amendment protected privacy interest in areas open to the public. The same rule would apply to police officers entering such areas open to the public. The back room, however, is a private area not open to the public. The tavern owner took the officer into the back private area to check the occupancy permit which should have been posted up front. Once the officer was legally present in the office, he saw in plain view the blocked exit and the pipe and marijuana. If the owner had refused to allow the officer into the backroom, a search warrant would have been required to enter the private areas behind the tavern. An administrative search warrant is issued based upon a watered-down probable cause standard. However, an administrative search warrant is not necessary unless the owner or lessee of the place to be inspected refuses admittance. *Camera v. Municipal Court*, 387 U.S. 523 (1967). The owner's permission, however, negates the necessity for a search warrant.

**Answer (A) is incorrect.** A safety inspection may be conducted by a government official or a police officer under a valid state or municipal safety code. The Fourth Amendment warrant requirement is applicable to administrative searches of businesses. However, an administrative warrant is only necessary when the owner of the business to be searched refuses entry. *See v. City of Seattle*, 387 U.S. 541 (1967).

**Answer (B) is incorrect.** A business owner who consents to the safety inspection of private areas of the business, can limit what the inspector sees by limiting where the inspector may go. However, any time a police officer is legally present, even to conduct a safety inspection, the officer may seize evidence of a crime that is in plain view when probable cause develops.

**Answer (D) is incorrect.** The Fourth Amendment's reasonableness command applies to all government searches, not just traditional police searches for evidence of a crime. Moreover, the Fourth Amendment also protects business establishments. *See v. City of Seattle*, 387 U.S. 541 (1967). Any distinction between constitutional protections based upon whether the intrusion is a traditional search or an administrative search would make little sense. Inspections often are carried out by police officers and violations of administrative codes often are prosecuted as minor criminal offenses.

78.     **Answer (C) is correct.** A dog sniffing backpacks and gear bags, like a dog sniffing luggage at an airport, is not a search and does not implicate Fourth Amendment interests. *United States v. Place*, 462 U.S. 696 (1983). Therefore, school authorities do not need reasonable suspicion or probable cause before the dog is brought into the school. A drug dog's positive alert creates probable cause, which is more than the required reasonable suspicion, necessary to conduct a search in a school. However, there is a significant difference between a dog sniffing a student's property (backpacks and gear bags), and a dog sniffing a person. A child, especially one who is afraid of dogs, may be terrorized by such an experience. A dog sniffing a person is a very personal intrusion upon the child's space, unlike a dog sniffing gear bags, lockers, or cars. Two United States Courts of Appeals have held that dog sniffing of school children is a search. *B.C. v. Plumas Unified School District*, 192 F.3d 1260 (9th Cir. 1999); *Horton v. Goose Creek Independent School District*, 690 F.2d 470 (5th Cir. 1982), cert. denied, 463 U.S. 1207 (1983). One earlier Court of Appeals held it is not a search. *Doe v. Renfrow*, 631 F.2d 91 (7th Cir. 1981).

If it is a search, the search of each student must be supported by reasonable suspicion. The Supreme Court held that the "special needs" in schools make the warrant and probable cause requirements inapplicable to school searches. The key is the Fourth Amendment's reasonableness standard. Courts use a balancing test to determine the legitimacy of the search in schools: balance the societal needs against the nature of the intrusion. The existence of a drug problem in the school would be a significant factor in allowing the searches. In place of probable cause, reasonable suspicion is required to conduct an individualized search. Once reasonable suspicion is established a full search of the student and his or her effects is permitted, unlike under a stop and frisk situation where reasonable suspicion only allows for a pat down search of outer clothing. *New Jersey v. T.L.O.*, 469 U.S. 325 (1985).

**Answer (A) is incorrect.** Although the search in T.L.O. was conducted by school authorities, later courts have not drawn distinctions between searches at schools conducted by police or school authorities.

**Answer (B) is incorrect.** Searches at public schools are considered to be "special circumstances" searches, an expanding offshoot of administrative searches. Society has an important interest in keeping the schools safe and in maintaining an atmosphere conducive to learning, which among other things includes maintaining a drug-free environment. Nonetheless, children in public schools do have some Fourth Amendment rights. *New Jersey v. T.L.O.*, 469 U.S. 325 (1985).

**Answer (D) is incorrect.** A dog sniff of a back pack or gear bag is not a search. Once the dog indicated the presence of narcotics in the bag, authorities had probable cause to search the bags. A dog sniff of a student's person, on the other hand, likely would be held to be a search. Such searches in a school context must be supported only by reasonable suspicion. The dog sniff of the student's person was not, in this Question, and the results of the illegal intrusion cannot provide the basis for a lawful full search of a student where marijuana was not found in the earlier search of that student's backpack.

79.    The school board's drug testing policy for these two groups of students is valid. Compulsory urinalysis is a search and is subject to Fourth Amendment standards. Drug testing must meet the overall standard of reasonableness contained in the Fourth Amendment, but individualized suspicion is not always an essential requirement. *Vernonia School District 47J v. Acton*, 515 U.S. 646 (1995). Urine testing in the presence of a government official is as intrusive as a strip search.

The application of drug testing to all students participating in extra-curricular activities and to students seeking permission to drive to school and park on school property, fits the category approved by the Supreme Court's allowance for random, suspicionless drug testing. The Supreme Court initially upheld random drug testing of junior high school athletes on the basis of: (1) the diminished expectation of privacy of school children and the doctrine of loco parentis; (2) the special situations of athletes: "students who voluntarily participate in school athletics have reason to expect intrusions upon normal rights and privileges, including privacy," because they are subject to physical exams in schools and are often undressed in locker room settings; (3) drug testing is necessary to prevent injury among the athlete group as well as to deter drug use in the school by curtailing its use by athletes who serve as role models; and (4) the search is noncriminal and the results of the tests are subject to very limited disclosure. *Vernonia School District 47J v. Acton*, 515 U.S. 646 (1995). Then the Supreme Court upheld a plan that required drug testing of all children taking part in extracurricular activities. The majority affirmed the legitimate interest of a school district in protecting its students' safety and health: "the nationwide drug epidemic makes the war against drugs a pressing concern in every school." The Court asserted that a school district need not demonstrate that there is a drug abuse problem among a sufficient number of students who would be subject to testing in order to validate a testing program. However, there was no clear majority that would allow a school to test an entire student body. In fact, Justice Breyer's fifth vote seemed premised upon the absence of consequences, other than being unable to participate in extra-curricular activities, for a student who refused testing. *Board of Education of Pottawatomie v. Earls*, 536 U.S. 735 (2002). In the present case, the argument for extending the testing to all students seeking permission to drive to school rests totally on the need to protect the safety of all students. Students who drive in an impaired condition threaten not only their own safety, but the safety of other students who may ride with them as well as the safety of others on the road.

80. **Answer (A) is correct.** The validity of the teacher-testing program is linked entirely to those teachers' proximity to the groups of students (athletes and students participating in extra-curricular activities) where a drug problem has been proven. Drug testing is an invasion of Fourth Amendment privacy. Ordinarily, particularized suspicion is required for such an extensive intrusion. The Supreme Court did uphold the testing of customs agents where the testing was: (1) limited to specific positions of persons involved in the interdiction of illegal drugs at the borders; (2) prospective employees were notified of the drug-testing requirement; and (3) test results were used for very limited purposes. *National Treasury Employees Union v. VonRaab*, 489 U.S. 656 (1989). In the case at hand, the testing is limited to teachers in close contact with students where the problem existed, but there is no reason to believe that the problem extended to coaches and teachers. Moreover, the teachers were not aware of the requirement before accepting employment, but that is not likely to be a decisive factor. This testing violates the Fourth Amendment because the testing is not aimed at discovering and curing a problem. The program does not indicate that treatment would be available to teachers and coaches who test positively. Rather, a positive drug test likely will result in a professional "death penalty" — loss of employment rather than treatment. The testing program is punitive rather than remedial and violates the Fourth Amendment.

    **Answer (B) is incorrect.** The suspicionless testing of coaches and teachers is unreasonable absent the existence of a proven problem with that group. Mere proximity to the groups of students where a drug problem was found to exist does not justify extending testing to coaches and teachers. Moreover, the penalty for a teacher who tests positively is dismissal. The Board cannot claim that its policy is remedial.

    **Answer (C) is incorrect.** Although the Supreme Court has upheld drug testing of student athletes and students involved in extra-curricular activities, the legality of such testing is not dependant upon its extension to other groups.

    **Answer (D) is incorrect.** The Equal Protection Clause does not demand similar treatment for persons in different groups. Here, the testing is limited to persons who were in proximity to the groups of students where the problem was found to exist. Not extending the testing to teachers and coaches who were not traveling with the students when drugs were found does not violate the Equal Protection Clause of the Fourteenth Amendment because the classification is rational (presuming the testing of any teacher is rational).

81.    **Answer (B) is correct.** Bailey did not voluntarily consent to a search of his person. A court reviewing a state claim of consent must determine, on the totality of the circumstances, whether the defendant's abandonment of Fourth Amendment rights and the consent to search was an act of free will, voluntarily given, and not the result of duress or coercion, express or implied. Police need not advise a person that he has the right to refuse, but that fact is pertinent in determining voluntariness. *Schnekloth v. Bustamonte*, 412 U.S. 218 (1973). Bailey was surrounded by three officers as soon as he left the hotel room. The request to empty his pockets simultaneously occurred with police surrounding him. He was not in the process of cooperating with the officers. Based on the totality of the circumstances, Bailey emptied his pockets involuntarily; he acquiesced to the police demand.

    **Answer (A) is incorrect.** The police pressured Bailey by surrounding him and asking him to empty his pockets. That was not a polite request but a demand emphasized by the number of police and his inability to ignore them and walk away. Therefore, he did not consent voluntarily to the search.

    **Answer (C) is incorrect.** Whether or not police had reasonable suspicion to stop Bailey coming out of the hotel room, there was no legal authority to conduct a search.

    **Answer (D) is incorrect.** The state could mount an argument that there was reasonable suspicion to detain Bailey to confirm or dispel the suspicion that he went to the hotel room to purchase drugs. Nonetheless, absent probable cause to arrest him, a search of his pockets was illegal.

82.    **Answer (C) is correct.** Consent is not voluntarily given when it follows on a police officer's assertion that she has lawful authority, such as a warrant, to conduct a search. A consent following a claim of authority is not voluntarily given but merely an acquiescence and an acknowledgment of authority. Similarly, when an officer claims that absent consent she can get a search warrant and search the house, consent which follows upon such a statement is not voluntarily given. The consent is merely capitulation to the claim of authority. *Bumper v. North Carolina*, 391 U.S. 543 (1968). A police officer who never mentions a warrant but announces, instead, upon arrival that "we have come to search" cannot claim that the home owner who steps aside voluntarily consented to the search. The owner is conceding to the claim of authority.

    **Answer (A) is incorrect.** Police need not have a warrant to search a home when an occupant voluntarily consents to the search.

**Answer (B) is incorrect.** The facts do not support a claim of exigent circumstances, nor would a claim of exigency stand up when the police officers by their own conduct create the exigency. Mrs. Bailey would not have known that the police officers suspected her husband of any offense other than possession of cocaine until they showed up at her door and sought permission to search.

**Answer (D) is incorrect.** Based on the totality of the circumstances, the state cannot meet its burden of showing that Mrs. Bailey's consent was voluntarily given. She let the police in to search when an officer told her that refusal was not an option because they could always get a search warrant. That claim was not true. The officer did not have probable cause to secure a search warrant.

83.   The evidence found in the basement, regardless of when it was found, is inadmissible. The evidence found in the closet is admissible. The evidence found after Mrs. Bailey ordered the police to stop the search and leave the house is inadmissible. A search that rests on consent is limited by the parameters of the consent. When police rely on a consent to search, they are limited by any conditions, express or implied, attached to the consent. *Florida v. Jimeno*, 500 U.S. 518 (1991). A person consenting may set limits on the time, duration, area and intensity of the search, as well as set conditions governing the search. An intrusion beyond those limitations would not be based on an intentional relinquishment of a right, and the voluntariness standard would not be met. The actual terms of the consent, including explicit and implicit limits, will govern the scope of the search. *U.S. v. Carey*, 172 F.3d 1268 (10th Cir 1999).

The Supreme Court has never determined whether a valid consent may be withdrawn once police begin to find evidence of a crime. However, a search that rests on consent is limited to the extent of that consent. While lower courts have split on this issue, the prevailing opinion favors an individual's right to countermand the original consent and withdraw that consent. The police were not without remedy in the problem case. Once they found incriminating evidence, they could have secured the house, limiting Mrs. Bailey's unfettered access, while they sought a search warrant to continue the search. *Segura v. U.S.*, 468 U.S. 796 (1984).

84.   **Answer (B) is correct.** The police asked Mrs. Stewart for permission to enter her apartment and talk with her. Her consent to enter was valid whether or not she knew she could refuse. However, she was not asked to consent to a search, nor did she consent to a search of any part of her apartment. If the police while lawfully present in Mrs. Stewart's apartment pursuant to her consent had seen the drugs in plain view, they could have seized the drugs. They could not, however, expand her permission to enter into permission to search.

**Answers (A) and (C) are incorrect.** In this question, the state relies upon the defendant's consent to support the warrantless search. Whether a defendant knows that he or she may refuse a police request to conduct a search is one factor to be considered when determining the validity of a consent to search. The validity of a consent to search should be determined on the totality of the circumstances, and a defendant's ignorance of his or her rights will not cause an otherwise valid consent to fail. *Schneckloth v. Bustamonte*, 412 U.S. 218 (1973); *Ohio v. Robinette*, 519 U.S. 33 (1996). Thus, Answers (A) and (C) are both incorrect. Knowledge of the right to refuse is not irrelevant, but it is only one fact to consider in the analysis.

**Answer (D) is incorrect.** Ordinarily, police need both probable cause and a search warrant to enter a home to conduct a search, absent a valid consent or exigent circumstances. Probable cause and the warrant requirement are not alternative requirements; a warrant should not issue but upon probable cause. Therefore, the existence of probable cause, without some exigency, would not support a warrantless search.

85.    **Answer (A) is correct.** The question turns upon the third person, Len's, privacy rights in the area or room that he consented to have searched, here the roommate's bedroom that he did not share. Persons may maintain a zone of exclusive privacy even in a shared residency. The question becomes whether a roommate's right to common access extends to the entire house including his roommate's bedroom. The rules governing apparent authority will prevail. The rules pertaining to apparent authority provide that police may not rely upon the consent of a third person when facts and circumstances would alert the reasonable person to question the third-person's authority. *Illinois v. Rodriguez*, 497 U.S. 177 (1990). Here, the facts should have put the police on notice that the roommate did not have unlimited access to Dennis' bedroom. In our society where unmarried people share living spaces, each has an expectation of privacy in a private room or space. The police were on notice that the roommates did not share a single bedroom and, therefore, could not consent to a search of the other's bedroom.

**Answer (B) is incorrect.** Police may seek third-party consent. They do not first have to seek the consent of the target of the search. *Cf. United States v. Matlock*, 415 U.S. 164 (1974).

**Answer (C) is incorrect.** Although such consent could sometimes be acceptable, under the circumstances the police were put on notice that the roommates had separate bedrooms and Len may not have had free access to Dennis' bedroom and, therefore, could not consent to a search of Dennis' bedroom. Not all courts subscribe to this conclusion. *See U.S. v. Reeves*, 594 F.2d 536 (6th Cir 1979), where a defendant did not impair his roommate's access to his room by locking the door, the roommate's consent to search was upheld.

**Answer (D) is incorrect.** The issue surrounding consent by a third person — whether a parent, spouse, roommate, etc. — is to be resolved by determining the authority of the consenting person. The question should not be resolved under an agency theory. A third person may not waive another person's Fourth Amendment rights. The question comes down to whether Len had sufficient access to his roommate's room to waive his own Fourth Amendment right.

86.    **Answer (D) is correct.** The inquiry must focus on whether the consenting party has authority to admit police and consent to a search and the rational limits of that authority. Even in a common abode, individuals sharing the premises may hold an expectation of privacy against the other persons in the home, which may not be

invaded. Attention, then, must focus on the extent to which parties share common authority over premises, as well as over parts of premises. *U.S. v. Matlock*, 415 U.S. 164 (1974). Generally, each spouse may consent to a search of their shared home. However, persons may maintain a zone of privacy within a shared home even from a spouse. The scope of spousal consent should be limited to a search of areas of the abode under common control, as distinguished from a search directed toward the personal effects of the absent spouse. Here, even within the shared family room, the husband maintained sole authority over the filing cabinet. Mrs. Masten did not have a key, and police could not reasonably rely upon her authority to break the lock and search the filing cabinet. The pictures should have been suppressed.

**Answer (A) is incorrect.** The appellate court should not defer to the trial court on questions of law. A trial court, in reviewing a motion to suppress, is the sole trier of fact and is in the best position to resolve questions of fact and evaluate the credibility of witnesses. If the factual findings of the trial court are supported by competent, credible evidence, a reviewing court must give deference to those findings. Questions of law, are subject to a de novo determination by the appellate court without deference to the trial court's decision. *Ornelas v. U.S.*, 517 U.S. 690 (1996). The validity of the consent is a question of law.

**Answer (B) is incorrect.** Ownership is an element in a determination of a third person's authority to consent to a search. It is not, however, the only factor. The ultimate issue turns on whether the third person's privacy interest extended to the cabinet. Mrs. Masten did not have a privacy interest in the filing cabinet even though she owned the house and shared the room where the cabinet was located. Even within the shared family room, Mr. Masten maintained sole authority over the filing cabinet. Mrs. Masten did not have a key, and police could not reasonably rely upon her authority to break the lock and search the filing cabinet. The pictures should have been suppressed.

**Answer (C) is incorrect.** Police do not need a target's consent to search a home or an object within the home. They may rely upon the authority of a wife to search her shared home because her privacy interest extends to the entire home. However, her privacy interest and shared authority did not extend to the locked filing cabinet. Mr. Masten had the only key, and police could not rely upon Mrs. Masten's authority to break the lock and search the cabinet.

87. **Answer (B) is correct.** The Supreme Court has taken the position that police may not enter and conduct a search where the target of the search is present and objected to the officers' entry, even though the target's spouse consented. *Georgia v. Randolph*, 547 U.S. 103 (2006). One member of the majority advocated a holding that "neither [spouse] is a master possessing the power to override the other's constitutional right to deny entry to their castle." That broader holding is not likely to be accepted by a majority. Two U.S. courts of appeals have delved into the unanswered, remaining issues not decided in *Randolph*. One court held that *Randolph* applies even though the non-consenting spouse is not physically present at the house, regardless of whether he is outside in a police car or at his place of employment. *U.S. v. Hudspeth*, 459 F.3d 922 (8th Cir 2007). Another court of appeals said that there are two elements that must be met to fall under the

*Randolph* holding: that the objecting spouse must be present and objecting. Therefore, when the target was arrested and placed in a police car without first objecting to the search, his wife could validly consent to a search of the shared residence. *U.S. v. DiModica*, 468 F.3d 495 (7th Cir. 2006). That court carried it even further, holding that if the objecting spouse is arrested and removed from the home, he is no longer present and objecting, and can no longer effectively bar the voluntary consent of his wife. *U.S. v. Henderson*, 536 F.3d 776 (7th Cir. 2008). However, the Seventh Circuit decisions undermine *Randolph* and negate its holding. Therefore, it is likely that the husband's objection, even though he was removed from the home following arrest, will prevail.

**Answer (A) is incorrect** unless the Supreme Court severely limits *Randolph* to allow a spouse to grant consent once the objecting spouse is arrested and removed to a police car. *See U.S. v. Henderson*, 536 F.3d 776 (7th Cir. 2008).

**Answer (C) is incorrect.** Incident to the lawful arrest of a defendant in his residence, police may search only the area of the arrestee's control — that area within his reaching and grabbing distance. *Chimel v. California*, 395 U.S. 752 (1969). The police did not have authority to search the entire house incident to Masten's arrest.

**Answer (D) is incorrect.** Police must have an arrest warrant to enter a home to arrest a resident absent consent or exigent circumstances. *Payton v. New York*, 445 U.S. 573 (1980). Mrs. Masten consented to the police entry to arrest her husband.

**88.** The eavesdropping warrant was too broad. Evidence about the calls recorded on Margaret's cell phone are admissible; all of the other evidence is inadmissible. Wiretapping and electronic eavesdropping intrude upon justified expectations of privacy. The practice is constitutionally permissible if authorized by a valid warrant. *Katz v. United States*, 389 U.S. 347 (1967). Applications for such warrants are governed by Title III of the Omnibus Crime Bill, 18 U.S.C. § 2510 et seq. Wiretaps involve extreme intrusions on privacy. Unlike a search of a residence with a warrant, a wiretap involves an ongoing search. Because wiretaps involve such an extensive intrusion on privacy, warrants for such authorization are subject to greater scrutiny than ordinary search warrants. An application for an eavesdropping warrant must state why this type of intrusion is necessary and why the evidence is not likely to be secured through other investigatory means. *Berger v. New York*, 388 U.S. 41 (1967). Here, the police did not include, and the court did not require, a statement justifying this type of extraordinary search beyond the statement setting out probable cause. The facts presented to the magistrate presented adequate probable cause to justify a wiretap of Margaret's cell phone, which she indicated her father used in his illegal business, and the two leased land lines since Postum operated the illegal business out of his home. There was no probable cause to justify eavesdropping on her mother's or siblings' phone lines.

Additionally, an eavesdropping order must contain limits on the authority of the police to eavesdrop to ensure that it is not a fishing expedition extending to all conversations whether or not related to the criminal enterprise. Since the tap was of telephones at the defendant's home and cell phones used by all members of the family, there would be personal conversations separate and apart from those involving the drug business. Such limits are accomplished by requiring the filing of a minimization plan indicating how the investigating officers will avoid listening to conversations unrelated to the crimes being investigated. The facts of the question do not indicate that there was a minimization order. The Supreme Court has weakened the minimization requirement by failing to strictly enforce minimization orders, *Scott v. United States*, 436 U.S. 128 (1978), but it has never abandoned the requirement that such warrants must contain minimization plans.

The inclusion of all telephones leased to the family is indicative of a general search. Any evidence secured on cell phones other than Margaret's is inadmissible. The conversations recorded from Margaret's cell phone are admissible. She consented to have her telephone conversations recorded. Where one party to a conversation consents to the recording of the conversation, the eavesdropping and recording do not violate any expectation of privacy and are outside the Fourth Amendment protections. The party who has not consented runs the risk that the person with whom he or she is talking will disclose information exchanged during the conversation, depriving the non-consenting party of a protected expectation of privacy.

**89.** **Answer (C) is correct.** The trial judge did not commit error by failing to exclude the evidence found in Carr's home. The Supreme Court has held: "A State's operation of a probation [and parole] system, like its operation of a school, government office or prison, or its supervision of a regulated industry, likewise presents 'special needs' beyond normal law enforcement that may justify departure from the usual warrant and probable cause requirements." *Griffin v. Wisconsin*, 483 U.S. 868 (1987). The Court has gone on to hold that parolees, like prisoners, have no reasonable expectation of privacy, and therefore a state's blanket policy subjecting parolees to suspicionless searches at any time does not violate the Fourth Amendment. *Samson v. California*, 547 U.S. 843 (2006). Moreover, the Court also held that the exclusionary rule does not bar the use at parole revocation hearings of evidence seized in violation of the Fourth Amendment. *Pennsylvania Board of Probation* and *Parole v. Scott*, 524 U.S. 357 (1998).

**Answers (A) and (B) are incorrect.** Parolees, like prisoners, have no reasonable expectation of privacy, and therefore a state's blanket policy subjecting parolees to suspicionless searches at any time does not violate the Fourth Amendment. A parole officer does not need to establish either probable cause or reasonable suspicion for the search.

**Answer (D) is incorrect.** The elimination of Fourth Amendment protection does not apply to all convicted felons. It applies only where submission to warrantless searches is a condition of probation or parole.

**90.** The U.S. Supreme Court will deny the defendant's appeal. The Fourth Amendment requirements are limited to requiring warrants (when applicable) and the probable cause or reasonable suspicion standards. The police officer did not violate the Fourth Amendment when she arrested the defendant on probable cause even though the arrest was prohibited by state law. The legality of an arrest based on probable cause is a matter for state law. When a state law chooses to protect its citizens privacy beyond the level required by the Fourth Amendment, those additional requirements to do not attach to the Fourth Amendment. *Virginia v. Moore*, 128 S. Ct. 1598 (2008).

The United States Supreme Court has held that the federal Constitution requires the exclusion of evidence only when a particular arrest, search, or seizure violates the Fourth Amendment. States remain free to fashion their own remedies when a particular procedure violates only state law. They may choose to exclude evidence in such cases, but exclusion flows from the state law and is not mandated under the

United States Constitution.

"While a State is free as a matter of its own law to impose greater restrictions on police activity than those this Court holds to be necessary upon federal constitutional standards, it may not impose such greater restrictions as a matter of federal constitutional law when this Court specifically refrains from imposing them." *Arkansas v. Sullivan*, 532 U.S. 769 (2001). The trial judge erred when deciding that the arrest violated the defendant's Fourth Amendment rights. The officer violated the higher standard imposed by state law. The state courts are free to decide, but are not compelled, to exclude the evidence.

**91.**     **Answer (D) is correct.** The exclusionary rule is viewed by the Supreme Court as an extreme and unfavorable remedy. The Court limited the reach of the exclusionary rule by adopting a good faith exception. Under the exception, evidence may not be excluded from a criminal trial if exclusion would not have deterred the illegal police practice. The exception rewards police for obtaining a search warrant. When police seek a search warrant they pursue the constitutionally favored procedure by allowing a magistrate to determine whether they may conduct the search. The pursuit of a warrant ordinarily will be rewarded so that even if it is later determined that the warrant was invalid, the evidence will be admissible if "the officer's reliance on the magistrate's determination of probable cause was objectively reasonable." *U.S. v. Leon*, 468 U.S. 897 (1984). The good faith exception will also save police negligence in record keeping that is not recurring. *Herring v. U.S.*, 129 S. Ct. 695 (2009). Nonetheless, the evidence is inadmissible. The officer's characterization of the place to be searched as a "drug house" on the basis of a single baggy of marijuana was preposterous. Officer Merit should have known that he could not expect to find all the items listed in the warrant. Consequently, he could not reasonably rely upon the warrant based upon such an insufficient and misleading affidavit.

    **Answer (A) is incorrect.** Officer Merit's observation of a single bag of marijuana did not provide probable cause to believe that the place to be searched was a "drug house" and that he would find all of the controlled substances listed in the warrant.

    **Answer (B) is incorrect.** The warrant was not supported by adequate probable cause. However, that is not the final answer. The key question is whether, despite the inadequacy of the probable cause, a reasonable officer could rely upon the warrant. If Officer Merit possessed additional information which would have bolstered the probable cause, he elected not to share that information with the magistrate and did not allow the magistrate to make an informed judgment.

    **Answer (C) is incorrect.** The warrant was so deficient in probable cause that a reasonable officer could not reasonably rely upon the search warrant.

**92.**     The evidence is inadmissible. The affidavit was so lacking in probable cause that a well-trained officer could not rely upon the warrant. The first issue is whether the search warrant was supported by adequate probable cause. In reviewing a lower court's conclusion of probable cause, the duty of the appellate court is to ensure that the issuer of the warrant had a "substantial basis" to determine that probable cause existed. "The task of the issuing magistrate is simply to make a practical, common-sense decision whether, given all the circumstances set forth in the affidavit before him, including the 'veracity' and 'basis of knowledge' of persons supplying hearsay information, there is a fair probability that contraband or evidence of a crime will be found in a particular place. And the duty of a reviewing court is simply to ensure that the magistrate had a 'substantial basis for conclud[ing]' that probable cause existed." Illinois v. Gates, 462 U.S. 213 (1983). Similarly, reviewing courts may not substitute their own judgment for that of the issuing magistrate by conducting a *de novo* determination as to whether the affidavit contains sufficient probable cause upon which the reviewing court would issue the search warrant. The officer's affidavit sets out information supplied by informants. Other than drug activity, the information is the identification of the defendant and his address. Both of these facts were verified by observation of the officer. Further, the informants' information regarding a vehicle driven by appellant was likewise confirmed by observation of the officer. These two facts do not provide verification of drug activity. The fact that evidence was seized at the same location two years before is not verification that current drug activity was afoot. The officer stated in his affidavit that his investigation confirmed drug activity by the defendant and that the sources have been proven reliable.

The affidavit contained no statements providing indicia of either the veracity of the informants or the basis of their knowledge. The affidavit contains no information about how the officer confirmed the drug activity or why the sources have been proven reliable. Filtering the hearsay statement of an informant through a law enforcement agency establishes neither the truth of the statement nor the reliability of the informant. The affidavit was so deficient that the magistrate did not have a substantial basis for finding probable cause.

The Fourth Amendment exclusionary rule will not be applied to bar the use in the prosecution's case-in-chief of evidence obtained by officers acting in objectively reasonable reliance on a search warrant issued by a detached and neutral magistrate but ultimately found to be unsupported by probable cause. A police officer may not rely on "a warrant based on an affidavit 'so lacking in indicia of probable cause as to render official belief in its existence entirely unreasonable." Moreover, "a warrant may be so facially deficient — *i.e.* in failing to particularize the place to be searched or the things to be seized — that the executing officers cannot reasonably presume it to be valid." *U.S. v. Leon*, 468 U.S. 897 (1984). The test for the good-faith exception is "whether a reasonably well trained officer would have known that the search was illegal despite the magistrate's authorization." Officer Constable would have known, and should have known, that this affidavit was not sufficient. Therefore, the "good-faith" exception does not apply.

93.     **Answer (C) is correct.** A police officer must have reasonable suspicion to believe that a crime has been or is about to be committed to forcibly stop and detain a suspect. The purpose of the stop is to confirm or dispel the officer's suspicion. In order to conduct a frisk, the officer must have reasonable suspicion to justify the stop and reasonable suspicion to believe that the person lawfully stopped is armed. *Terry v. Ohio*, 392 U.S. 1 (1968).

**Answer (A) is incorrect.** If a stop or search is illegal, the evidence should be suppressed. The good faith exception to the exclusionary rule, which allows for admission of evidence seized pursuant to an invalid search warrant if the officer reasonably relied upon the validity of the warrant, does not apply to warrantless searches.

**Answer (B) is incorrect.** Police may not seize a person in a public park without reasonable suspicion or probable cause. A person in a public park has the same expectation of privacy as anyone on a street or in any other public place.

**Answer (D) is incorrect.** Even if the officer's belief as to the law was reasonable, it is incorrect and cannot be the basis for application of the good faith exception to the warrant requirement. The exception is not applicable to warrantless searches.

**94.** *Miranda* requires that a suspect be given warnings prior to custodial interrogation: that he has a right to remain silent; that anything he says can and will be used against him; that he has a right to consult with a lawyer prior to and during questioning, and that if he cannot afford a lawyer one will be provided for him. The purpose of the warnings is to alleviate the inherent coerciveness of custodial interrogation. If a suspect is not in custody or is not interrogated, the warnings need not be given. In this case, several factors point in opposite directions. Donald was not arrested, and was told so, as well as informed he was free to go. He and his family went to the social worker's office; his wife was present in the room during the interrogation, and he was permitted to leave and return home at the conclusion of the interview. The last fact is often considered critical. However, they did not wish to go to the office in the first place: they were compelled to show up upon threat that Sandra might be removed from their home if they did not attend the interview. The atmosphere during the interview was physically intimidating.

The relevant inquiry is whether a reasonable person would have believed during the interrogation that he was in custody. Neither the subjective intent of the suspect nor the interrogator is relevant in this analysis. While the fact that Donald was not arrested and was permitted to return home at the conclusion of the interview might be dispositive in a close case, this is not a close case. Unlike an ordinary probation interview, "arranged by appointment at a mutually convenient time," everything about this interview conveyed to Donald "a message that he had no choice but to submit to the officer's will and to confess." The atmosphere prior to the interview and the facts of the interrogation were extremely coercive. During the interrogation, a reasonable person in Donald's position would not have believed that he could terminate the interview and leave. *Miranda* warnings should have been given. Donald's statements are inadmissible. *Miranda v. Arizona,* 384 U.S. 436 (1966); *Berkemer v. McCarty,* 468 U.S. 420 (1984); *Minnesota v. Murphy,* 465 U.S. 433 (1984).

**95.** **Answer (D) is correct.** The *Miranda* warnings are intended to alleviate the coercive atmosphere that arises when a person in custody is subject to police interrogation. Although Carrie undoubtedly felt coerced when she was detained and questioned by the store detective, the *Miranda* rights are not applicable. The store detective is not a government employee and is not subject to the *Miranda* requirements. **Answer (C) is also correct** because the Fourth Amendment only limits government behavior. Carrie was detained by a security guard working for a private business. *Burdeau v. McDowell,* 256 U.S. 465 (1921); *U.S. v. Jacobsen,* 466 U.S. 109 (1984).

**Answer (A) is incorrect** because the store detective was not a government agent and is not limited by the *Miranda* requirements.

**Answer (B) is incorrect** also because there was no government or police behavior. The store detective was a private employee not subject to the same restrictions that would apply to a police officer. This result does not seem fair when often private security guards are licensed by the state. *Cf. Colorado v. Connelly*, 479 U.S. 157 (1986). Perhaps egregious situations involving private interrogation could lead to a Due Process violation, but the instant case does not seem to rise to the level of coercion and abuse.

**96.**     **Answer (B) is the correct answer.** Following an arrest police may question an arrestee without first giving *Miranda* warnings to defuse a potentially dangerous situation. The public safety exception to *Miranda* applies when a reasonable police officer would believe that danger to members of the public or to the police warrants immediate action. Whether the officer is motivated by public safety concerns or simply is looking for evidence is irrelevant; the court must apply an "objective reasonable police officer" test. *New York v. Quarles*, 467 U.S. 649 (1984).

**Answer (C) is incorrect** because the officer was operating under the public safety exception to *Miranda*.

**Answer (A) is incorrect.** Although the arresting officer could have searched the passenger compartment of the vehicle incident to the arrest of the driver, the authority to conduct the search no longer existed once the driver was removed from the scene of the arrest. Moreover, a search of the vehicle incident to the arrest of the driver or passenger does not extend to the trunk of the vehicle. *New York v. Belton*, 453 U.S. 454 (1981).

**Answer (D) is incorrect** because the search of the trunk of the vehicle was lawful. Officer Charles' admission that the gun was in the trunk of the car provided probable cause for police to search the trunk, under the automobile exception, to find and remove the gun. Once they had legal authority to search the trunk, evidence found in the trunk in plain view became admissible at trial. This was not an inventory search under standardized procedures: the car had already been towed, and this was a search for specific evidence.

**97.**    **Answer (D) is correct.** Police must give *Miranda* warnings prior to interrogating a person who is in custody. However, answers to questions that are asked as part of a standardized booking process are admissible without prior administration of *Miranda* warnings. Videotaped answers to so-called pedigree questions — names, address, height, weight, etc — are not rendered inadmissible simply because the slurred nature of the defendant's speech is incriminating. The line, which is not altogether clear, is crossed when a defendant's response is incriminating not just because of delivery but because the content of the answer demonstrates the defendant's cognitive impairment, an element of the offense. The Supreme Court held that the line was crossed when a defendant, arrested for drunk driving, could not provide police with the correct date of his sixth birthday, and the content of his answer supported an answer that his mental state was confused. *Pennsylvania v. Muniz*, 496 U.S. 582 (1990).

**Answer (A) is incorrect.** Standardized booking questions are exempted from the *Miranda* warning requirement. It is only when a question is asked that is not a standardized booking question that *Miranda* comes into play. Here, when the officer asked Brewster to state the alphabet, he was not seeking booking information. He was attempting to demonstrate the confused nature of Brewster's mind. That question would not be exempted from the *Miranda* requirement.

**Answer (B) is incorrect.** The question about the alphabet was not a pedigree question exempted from the *Miranda* requirement. The question was intended to demonstrate that Brewster was impaired. It would not fall under the exception to the *Miranda* rules.

**Answer (C) is incorrect.** Police are not required to issue *Miranda* warnings immediately following an arrest. Warnings must be issued following an arrest and prior to police interrogation. If police never interrogate an arrested person, they need not give *Miranda* warnings.

**98.**    **Answer (A) is correct.** The *Miranda* warnings were intended to alleviate the inherent coerciveness of custodial interrogation. "The fundamental import of the privilege while an individual is in custody is not whether he is allowed to talk to the police without the benefit of warnings and counsel, but whether he can be interrogated. . . . Volunteered statements of any kind are not barred by the Fifth Amendment and their admissibility is not affected by our holding today." *Miranda v. Arizona*, 384 U.S. 436, at 478 (1966). Police are not obligated to stop a suspect who volunteers an incriminating statement while they advise him of his rights.

**Answer (B) is incorrect.** If Danny's statement had been in response to a police officer's question, the statement would be inadmissible even if prosecutors could prove that Danny had prior knowledge of the *Miranda* warnings. The Supreme Court believed that the inherent coerciveness of custody must be mitigated by the warnings prior to any interrogation. Here, of course, there was no interrogation.

**Answers (C) and (D) are incorrect.** *Miranda* required that a suspect be warned prior to interrogation. Unlike on television, police are not obligated to issue the warnings at the time of arrest or while transporting an arrestee to the jail. Warnings must be given prior to interrogation. If the arrestee is never interrogated, police need not administer the *Miranda* warnings.

99. The confession is inadmissible. *Miranda* warnings must be given prior to any custodial interrogation. *Miranda v. Arizona*, 384 U.S. 436 (1966). The defendant was not advised of his right until after he had confessed to the crime.

Interrogation is defined as "express questioning or its functional equivalent." Functional equivalent was further defined as "any words or actions on the part of police (other than those normally attendant to arrest and custody) that the police should know are *reasonably likely to elicit an incriminating response* from the suspect. In determining whether police conduct constitutes interrogation, the courts are to apply this objective standard In the problem, there was no reason to subject the defendant to the victim's family's abuse other than to provoke an emotional response from the defendant. The defendant was forced to sit close to the family for a period of 20 minutes. It would have been different if there was an accidental and momentary contact between the defendant and the anguished family. Here, however, the detective knew what was happening; there was no reason to allow the prolonged contact other than to provoke the defendant into an admission. Unlike *Rhode Island v. Innis*, 446 U.S. 291 (1980), where the Court held that a reasonable officer would not have anticipated that the defendant would respond to a worried general statement about handicapped children finding the missing gun, here the officers were aware of the situation that they allowed to unfold. The police behavior was the functional equivalent of interrogation.

100. **Answer (A) is correct.** *Miranda* is intended to alleviate the inherent coercion attendant upon custodial interrogation. Hothead was in custody and was being interrogated by the police, but he did not know it. The Supreme Court has said that when a person does not know he is being interrogated by a police officer, even while in custody, there is absent the inherent coercion attendant upon interrogation by a person known to the defendant to be a police officer. Therefore, the questioning lacks the pressure that attaches when a suspect is facing a police officer who demands answers. Even though Hothead was questioned by a police officer while in a jail cell, he thought he was dealing with someone in the same situation as he. He could have resisted more easily the pressure by the cellmate to confess to the crime. Consequently, there was no police interrogation that would have required *Miranda* warnings. *Illinois v. Perkins*, 496 U.S. 292 (1990). There are two different rules for jail house snitches. See Question 111 for the legal rules pertaining to jail house snitches under the Sixth Amendment.

**Answer (B) is incorrect.** Because Hothead did not volunteer his confession. He made the confession in response to questioning by his cellmate.

**Answer (C) is incorrect.** Because the defendant did not know he was being questioned by the police, there was no need to inform him of his *Miranda* rights before the questioning.

**Answer (D) is incorrect.** The Supreme Court that decided *Miranda* found trickery to be an unacceptable technique for securing a confession. The successor Courts do not share the same disdain for trickery. *Moran v. Burbine*, 475 U.S. 412 (1986).

**101.** The Supreme Court said that "when an individual is taken into custody or otherwise deprived of his freedom by the authorities in any significant way and is subjected to questioning, the privilege against self-incrimination is jeopardized. Procedural safeguards must be employed to protect the privilege." Those safeguards which require that the suspect be advised prior to any questioning are as follows:

(1)   The suspect has the right to remain silent;

(2)   Anything the suspect says can be used against the suspect in a court of law;

(3)   The suspect has the right to the presence of an attorney; and

(4)   If the suspect cannot afford an attorney, one will be appointed prior to any questioning if the suspect so desires. Miranda v. Arizona, 384 U.S. 486 (1966).

The warnings given to the defendant in the question are unclear. While the detective informed the defendant that he had the right to seek a lawyer's advice prior to answering any questions, the language also suggests that he was not entitled to appointed counsel until charges are filed against him and he appeared in court. However, the Supreme Court rejected that argument and noted that it had "never insisted that *Miranda* warnings be given in the exact form described in that decision." The Court concluded that the warnings, as a whole, conveyed the information required by *Miranda*. *Duckworth v. Eagan*, 492 U.S. 195 (1989). Although the *Miranda* warnings are easy enough to read precisely as they were written, the Supreme Court said, "This Court has never indicated that the 'rigidity' of *Miranda* extends to the precise formulation of the warnings given a criminal defendant." Rather, the Supreme Court has been satisfied if the police officer giving the warnings touches all the bases. *California v. Prysock*, 453 U.S. 355 (1981).

**102.**   **Answer (C) is correct.** The relinquishment of the right must be voluntary, not the result of intimidation, coercion, or deception. The waiver must be made with a full awareness of both the nature of the right being abandoned and the consequences of that decision. The defendant was aware that he could remain silent and that anything he said could be used against him. The knowingly requirement is limited to knowledge of constitutional rights, not every possible consequence of a waiver of the privilege. Police need not inform a suspect of all of the crimes they will question him about. *Colorado v. Spring*, 479 U.S. 564 (1987).

**Answer (A) is incorrect** because a waiver of *Miranda* rights is not offense specific.

**Answer (B) is incorrect** because this kind of trickery and deceit is clearly permissible. The legitimacy of a *Miranda* waiver is not affected by police trickery in luring a suspect into believing that the interrogation is about one crime when, in reality, they are most interested in a different crime.

**Answer (D) is incorrect** because the statement is too broad. Deceit and trickery about the subject matter of the interrogation are permissible, but deceit and trickery would not be permissible in advising a suspect about his *Miranda* rights.

**103.** **Answer (D) is correct and the best answer.** Stone's half-hearted "I guess so" may not have satisfied the *Miranda* Court's understanding of a knowing, intelligent and voluntary waiver, but the waiver standard has changed. While the *Miranda* Court never said that an explicit waiver only would suffice, that meaning was fairly clear from the decision. The Court has since backtracked and said that "waiver can be clearly inferred from the actions and words of the person interrogated." Here, the defendant's words would satisfy the waiver requirement. *North Carolina v. Butler*, 441 U.S. 371 (1979).

**Answer (A) is incorrect.** The *Miranda* rights are personal to the suspect and must be exercised by the suspect. Although the information given to Stone was incomplete when the police failed to inform him that a lawyer was there to see him, police are not obliged to inform a suspect of that fact. *Moran v. Burbine*, 475 U.S. 412 (1986).

**Answer (B) is correct but not the best answer. Answer (C) is incorrect.** There has been a shift in the Supreme Court since the *Miranda* decision. At the time of *Miranda* the Court seemed concerned to find out whether a suspect wanted to speak to the police. In recent times, the Court appeared concerned only with whether the suspect invoked her right to silence or her right to counsel. Silence on the part of the suspect, especially when followed shortly thereafter with a statement (even a hesitating statement) indicating a willingness to talk with the police, will not be construed as an invocation of either the right to remain silent or the right to counsel.

**104.** The motion to suppress will be granted. Dealer clearly invoked his *Miranda* right to counsel. Once an accused makes a clear indication that he wishes to consult with an attorney, police must accept that assertion at face value and may not undermine its clarity by asking follow-up questions or by talking the suspect into changing his mind. An accused's post-request responses to further interrogation may not be used to cast doubt on the clarity of the initial request for counsel. *Smith v. Illinois*, 469 U.S. 91 (1984).

When a suspect invokes the right to counsel, police must stop the interrogation until the suspect has an opportunity to consult with an attorney. Statements from an accused who has asked to see an attorney, following a valid waiver of the right, also may be admissible even if he has not consulted with counsel, if a strict, two-step waiver test is met. First, an accused who has asked to see an attorney "is not subject to interrogation by the authorities until counsel has been made available to him, unless the accused himself initiates further communication, exchanges, or conversations with the police." Second, if the accused has initiated discussion about the case, the inquiry shifts to whether there was a valid waiver made of *Miranda* rights. *Edwards v. Arizona*, 451 U.S. (1981). Here, the detective improperly initiated the discussion about the crime leading Dealer to agree to further interrogation. Dealer's right to counsel was violated.

105.    **Answer (C) is correct.** The first confession is inadmissible because the officer failed to comply with the *Miranda* requirements. The second confession is admissible because it was taken at the police station by a different officer following *Miranda* warnings and Freddy's waiver. The Supreme Court has said "that a suspect who has once responded to unwarned uncoercive questioning is not thereby disabled from waiving his rights and confessing after he has been given the requisite *Miranda* warnings." *Oregon v. Elstad*, 470 U.S. 298 (1985). That decision is subject to fair criticism because Freddy did not know that the first statement was inadmissible and the "cat was already out of the bag" when he confessed at the police station.

**Answer (A) is incorrect.** The first confession is inadmissible, but the second confession is likely admissible because the detective administered *Miranda* warnings and there was a complete break between the first statement and the second.

**Answer (B) is incorrect.** The first statement was given by Freddy in response to the arresting officer's provocative and false comment. Even though the officer did not ask Freddy a question, his comment was the functional equivalent of interrogation because a reasonable officer should have known that his comment would provoke a response. *Rhode Island v. Innis*, 446 U.S. 291 (1980).

**Answer (D) is incorrect.** An incriminating statement secured in violation of *Miranda* requirements is rarely harmless error. The only time harmless error may become an issue is if there is other overwhelming evidence of guilt, and the reviewing court is convinced beyond a reasonable doubt that the confession did not play a role in the jury's determination of guilt.

106.    **Answer (C) is the correct answer.** Ordinarily, when a person responds to police questioning in his home, he is not in custody and is in familiar surroundings. However, the test for custody is not what the defendant believed, but whether a reasonable person under the circumstances would believe he has been arrested. *Berkemer v. McCarty*, 468 U.S. 420 (1984). A reasonable person would have believed that he was under arrest when the detective told Ramirez that he knew what had transpired in the telephone conversation between Ramirez and his accomplice. All that took place up to the time that Ramirez was *Mirandized* was, in fact, custodial interrogation, and must be suppressed because of the absence of *Miranda* warnings. Moreover, the officers exploited the pre-warning statement in obtaining a waiver of *Miranda* rights, and the statements given after the warnings also are inadmissible. *Missouri v. Seibert*, 542 U.S. 600 (2004).

**Answer (A) is incorrect.** Even though the officers continued to tell Ramirez that he was not under arrest, a reasonable person under the circumstances would believe that he was. Police statements to the contrary, especially when they are intended to put the defendant off guard, do not govern the situation.

**Answer (B) is incorrect.** Agreed that the statements made before *Miranda* warnings were given were the product of custodial interrogation and, thus, are inadmissible. Moreover, a statement following proper *Miranda* warnings is not inadmissible because of an earlier inadmissible, but voluntary, statement. *Oregon v. Elstad*, 470 U.S. 298 (1985). However, when police deliberately exploit the first inadmissible statement in order to obtain the second statement obtained following *Miranda* warnings, the second statement is also inadmissible. *Missouri v. Seibert*, 542 U.S. 600 (2004).

**Answer (D) is incorrect.** Agreed that the statements at the police station before and after *Miranda* warnings are inadmissible. The first statement at the police station was the product of custodial interrogation without *Miranda* warnings, and the second statement, following *Miranda* warnings, was the product of "the two-step interrogation technique" "used in a calculated way to undermine the *Miranda* warning without any "curative measures." *Missouri v. Seibert*, 542 U.S. 600, 622 (2004)(Kennedy, J., concurring). But even the statements made by Ramirez at his home were the product of custodial interrogation because a reasonable person would have believed that he was in custody, even though he was still at home when he made the statements.

**107.**   **Answer (C) is correct.** A suspect who invokes the right to consult with a lawyer before interrogation must do so unequivocally. The clarity of a suspect's invocation of the right to counsel is critical. In a step that fundamentally weakened the position of the suspect who is fumbling and unsure of himself prior to interrogation, the Supreme Court said that if a suspect's reference to an attorney is ambiguous or equivocal, police need not cease questioning. Instead, police may continue as though the reference was never made. Only a clear invocation of the right imposes a duty upon the police to cease any attempt at questioning. Police are not required to ask any clarifying questions. *Davis v. U.S.*, 512 U.S. 452 (1994). Here, the suspect failed to effectively indicate that she wanted to see an attorney. The detective was not obligated to answer the suspect's question or pursue whether the suspect wanted an attorney

**Answer (A) is incorrect.** The suspect's nod of the head may not have satisfied the *Miranda* Court's understanding of a knowing, intelligent and voluntary waiver, but the waiver standard has changed. While the *Miranda* Court never said that an explicit waiver only would suffice, that meaning was fairly clear from the decision. The Court has since backtracked and said that "waiver can be clearly inferred from the actions and words of the person interrogated." Here, the suspect's nod of the head in response to the detective's question would satisfy the waiver requirement. North Carolina v. Butler, 441 U.S. 371 (1979).

**Answer (B) is incorrect** because a reviewing court would not interpret the suspect's statement and question as a clear invocation of the right to counsel.

**Answer (D) is incorrect** because the suspect never invoked her right to counsel. The suspect's comment that "Maybe I should talk with a lawyer?" followed by her question to the officer may have meant that she wanted to see a lawyer, but it would not satisfy the requirement of an unequivocal assertion of the right. If the reviewing court interpreted the suspect's statement as an assertion of the right to counsel, that assertion would not be revoked by her nod of the head in response to the detective's question whether she was ready to proceed with the interrogation. If a suspect asserts the right to counsel, all questioning must stop until the suspect has the opportunity to consult with a lawyer *or* the suspect initiates discussion about the crime. *Edwards v. Arizona*, 451 U.S. 477 (1981).

**108.**    **Answer (B) is correct.** The Supreme Court said that a suspect who has waived *Miranda* rights and agreed to questioning may stop the interrogation at any time. "Once warnings have been given, the subsequent procedure is clear. If the individual indicates in any manner, at any time prior to or during questioning, that he wishes to remain silent, the interrogation must cease. At this point he has shown that he intends to exercise his Fifth Amendment privilege; any statement taken after the person invokes his privilege cannot be other than the product of compulsion, subtle or otherwise. Without the right to cut off questioning, the setting of in-custody interrogation operates on the individual to overcome free choice in producing a statement after the privilege has been once invoked." *Miranda v. Arizona*, 384 U.S. 436, 473–474 (1966). Allison unequivocally invoked her right to cut off questioning by her comment. Some state courts have found it very difficult to recognize such comments as an invocation of the right to silence. *See, e.g., State v. Anspaugh*, 547 P.2d 1124 (Idaho 1976); *State v. Nichols*, 512 P.2d 329 (Kansas 1973); *State v. Murphy*, 747 N.E.2d 765 (Ohio 2001).

**Answer (A) is incorrect** because Allison retained the right, following her waiver, to cut off questioning and invoke the right to remain silent or the right to counsel.

**Answer (C) is incorrect.** Allison answered later questions because, notwithstanding her attempt to cut off interrogation, the questions kept coming. She may have felt that the officer could continue to ask her questions even though she had tried to stop the questioning. Her submission to authority is not an indication that she did not wish to cut off further interrogation.

**Answer (D) is incorrect** because exercising the right to remain silent does not also invoke the right to counsel. The exact words expressed by the suspect will control whether the suspect has invoked the right to remain silent or the right to counsel. Although the *Miranda* Court intended to protect suspects who did not understand their rights before and during interrogation, whether the suspect utters magic words about counsel or not answering questions will dictate how the police may continue following the suspect's claim of right.

**109.** Lewing's confession is admissible. The defendant signed a waiver of *Miranda* rights but then indicated that he did not want to talk the police any more. The detective cut off questioning at that point. A defendant who says he or she does not want to talk does not receive the same level of protection as a defendant who asks for an attorney. The defendant who exercises the right to remain silent is exposed to further interrogation.

In *Michigan v. Mosley*, 423 U.S. 96 (1975), the Supreme Court said that *Miranda* requires police to stop questioning a suspect when he or she exercises the right to remain silent, but the exercise of the right does not insulate the suspect from later questioning. The defendant in *Mosley* was taken several hours after the first interrogation for questioning in a different location, by a different detective, and questioned about a different, though related, crime. At the second interrogation the defendant waived his rights after being given *Miranda* warnings again. The Court found the resumption of interrogation valid under these circumstances. However, *Mosley* now stands for little more than the police may not ignore a defendant's exercise to remain silent and simply repeat the warnings as though the defendant said nothing.

In this problem the facts are very different: Lewing was kept in the same place, and then interrogated by the same detective about the same crime. Moreover, he was not given the warnings again prior to the second interrogation, but the short span of time between the interrogation session likely will result in the omission being forgiven. The distinctions in *Mosley* have largely been ignored by lower courts, and the factual differences between the facts here and *Mosley* are unlikely to cause a different result. The rule has come to mean that the officers must stop the questioning but may resume later.

**110.** Scott's statements are inadmissible. Once a suspect unambiguously asserts the *Miranda* right to counsel, police may not resume interrogating the suspect until the suspect sees an attorney or initiates discussion about the crime. After the suspect has initiated further conversation about the crime, statements which are the product of interrogation are admissible only if there is a finding that the defendant knowingly and intelligently waived the right to counsel. *Edwards v. Arizona*, 451 U.S. 477 (1981).

The Supreme Court weakened the *Edwards* two-part test when it held that a suspect who had requested counsel, initiated discussion about the crime as he was being moved from the police station to the jail, when he asked, "Well, what is going to happen to me now?" The Supreme Court said that a reviewing court must look to see whether the suspect's statement evidenced a willingness and a desire for a general discussion about the investigation — as opposed to "a request for a drink of water or a request to use a telephone that are so routine that they cannot be fairly said to represent a desire on the part of an accused to open up a more generalized discussion relating directly or indirectly to the investigation." The Supreme Court concluded that the defendant's inquiry as to what would happen to him, although ambiguous, "evidenced a willingness and a desire for a generalized discussion about the investigation." *Oregon v. Bradshaw*, 462 U.S. 1039 (1983). In the problem, Scott's expletive was a reaction to his predicament and cannot be construed as a willingness and desire for a generalized discussion about the investigation.

111.  **Answer (C) is correct.** Following invocation of the Miranda right to counsel, police may not reinitiate interrogation without counsel present even though the accused has consulted with the requested attorney. *Minnick v. Mississippi*, 498 U.S. 146 (1990), clarified the *Edwards* requirement that counsel be made available to the accused by holding that this requirement refers not only to the opportunity to consult with an attorney outside of the interrogation room, but also to the right to have counsel present in the interrogation room during custodial interrogation. *Minnick* was based on an understanding of *Miranda* that when an accused requests counsel, he is expressing the thought that he is unable personally to deal with the police interrogation and wishes to do so only through an attorney.

**Answer (A) is incorrect** because a suspect's right includes having the attorney present during interrogation.

**Answer (B) is incorrect** because the defendant's waiver was not knowingly, intelligently and voluntarily made. He acceded to the authority of the officer who did not reread defendant the *Miranda* warnings and did not tell the defendant that he had the right to have his lawyer present during interrogation.

**Answer (D) is incorrect.** The officer should have read defendant the *Miranda* warnings prior to the second interrogation, but that would not have cured the error. The defendant did not initiate the discussion, and the defendant had the right to have his attorney present during any interrogation.

**112.** **Answer (D) is correct.** Unlike the Sixth Amendment right, *Miranda* rights only attach to custodial interrogation when a suspect knows that he is being questioned by a police officer or police agent. The *Miranda* rights are intended to alleviate the inherent coerciveness that attaches to official interrogation in a custodial setting, when a suspect presumably feels pressured by the questioner to respond to the questions. In the jail cell setting, Arthur did not know that the person questioning him was an undercover agent, therefore he was not subject to those pressures. The agent was not required to administer the *Miranda* warnings prior to questioning. *Illinois v. Perkins*, 496 U.S. 292 (1990).

**Answer (A) is incorrect.** *Miranda* warnings are intended to alleviate the inherent coerciveness of custodial interrogation. Arthur was in custody, but he did not know that he was being interrogated by a police officer in his cell. Therefore, the conversation between two cellmates lacked the coercion that would attach when a suspect is questioned by police. The premise of *Miranda* is that danger of coercion results from the interaction of custody and official interrogation by a police officer who appears to control the suspect's fate. The Supreme Court has concluded that those pressures do not exist when the suspect is unaware that the person questioning him is not a police officer.

**Answer (B) in incorrect.** The defendant's Sixth Amendment right to counsel had attached when he appeared in court on the drunk driving charge. Under the Sixth Amendment, the definition of interrogation differs from *Miranda*. Police may not engage in behavior that is likely to elicit incriminating comments from a defendant whose Sixth Amendment rights have attached without the presence of counsel unless the defendant has waived counsel. However, the Sixth Amendment right is *offense specific*. Arthur's right to counsel had attached to the drunk driving charge at the time of the preliminary arraignment which marked the commencement of formal adversary proceedings. Police could not have questioned him about the drunk driving charge. The Sixth Amendment right is offense specific and does not apply to other charges that are not considered the same offense (*i.e.* lesser included offenses). The Sixth Amendment right did not apply to the robbery and murder charges. *McNeil v. Wisconsin*, 501 U.S. 171 (1991); *Texas v. Cobb*, 532 U.S. 162 (2001).

**Answer (C) is incorrect.** There is no question that the defendant voluntarily confessed to the undercover agent. However, that is not the test under the Sixth Amendment. The Sixth Amendment prohibits the government from deliberately eliciting incriminating information from a defendant whose Sixth Amendment right has attached. It does not matter whether the defendant is directly questioned or indirectly questioned by someone who he does not know is a police officer or government agent. Here, the questioning would have met the Sixth Amendment test for interrogation, but the Sixth Amendment right is offense specific, and it had attached only to the drunk driving offense. *Brewer v. Williams*, 430 U.S. 387 (1977); *Kuhlmann v. Wilson*, 477 U.S. 436 (1986); *McNeil v. Wisconsin*, 501 U.S. 171 (1991).

**113.** Even though the undercover agent did not ask any questions about the pending drunk driving charge, Arthur's incriminating statement about the drunk driving charge will not admitted at trial. Arthur's Sixth Amendment right to counsel on the drunk driving charge attached at the first court appearance which marked the commencement of formal judicial proceedings. The Sixth Amendment right is a trial right and following its attachment the state is not permitted to question the defendant without the defendant's attorney being present unless the defendant knowingly, intelligently, and voluntarily waives the right to counsel. *Massiah v. U.S.* (1964). However, in *Montejo v. Louisiana*, 129 S. Ct. 2079 (2009), the Supreme Court said the formal attachment of the Sixth Amendment right, absent a defendant's request for counsel, does not preclude police frm attemptin to question the defendant following *Miranda* warnings.

The Sixth Amendment right is offense specific, so the police could question the defendant about other crimes. This contrasts with *Miranda* rights where when a defendant asserts a *Miranda* right to counsel, police may not question the suspect about any crimes. Even though the undercover agent did not question Arthur about the drunk driving charge, his incriminating statement about the pending drunk driving charge is inadmissible. While police may question a formally charged suspect about uncharged crimes, the evidence secured may not be used on the pending charge. *Maine v. Moulton*, 474 U.S. 159 (1985).

**Author's Note.** The purpose of this and the previous question is to focus on the different rules applicable under *Miranda* and the Sixth Amendment right to counsel. It is important to note that the purposes, coverage and scope of the rules differ. You should be able to understand them and be able to apply them separately rather than jumble them together.

114.    **Answer (D) is correct.** The voluntariness of a suspect's statement has always been the constitutional test for admissibility under the Fifth Amendment Due Process test. It became submerged, however, within the framework of the *Miranda* rules, which were deemed the best way to ensure that the statements were given voluntarily. But even the *Miranda* Court recognized that compliance with the warning requirements was not totally dispositive of the admissibility of a statement. The Court indicated that a statement, which was forthcoming shortly after a suspect was informed of his rights and indicated his willingness to talk with the police, would satisfy the constitutional requirements. On the other hand, the Court also noted that a statement coming after prolonged interrogation, even if *Miranda* warnings had been given at the outset, might indicate that the suspect's will had been overborne by the interrogation. *Miranda v. Arizona*, 384 U.S. 486 (1966). However, even the Supreme Court has acknowledged that it is difficult to prove that a confession is involuntary once there is a *Miranda* waiver. *Dickerson v. U.S.*, 530 U.S. 428 (2000). Whether a confession is voluntary is determined on the totality of the circumstances determining whether a defendant's will was overborne and his capacity for self-determination critically impaired because of coercive police conduct. In the problem, the defendant's will to resist the police was overcome by the prolonged, relentless interrogation.

   **Answer (A) is incorrect** because waiver of *Miranda* rights is not totally dispositive. The voluntariness of the confession is the ultimate constitutional test for admissibility. While a waiver of *Miranda* right is persuasive, it is not dispositive.

   **Answer (B) is incorrect** because even though the defendant waived *Miranda* rights, his will was overborne by the prolonged, relentless interrogation.

   **Answer (C) is incorrect** because the officer properly read the *Miranda* warnings and then re-read them, and the defendant waived *Miranda* rights. However, waiver of *Miranda* rights, while persuasive, is not the end of the inquiry. The voluntariness of the confession is the ultimate constitutional test for admissibility under the Fifth Amendment.

115.    **Answer (C) is correct.** The due process test for voluntariness is the constitutional standard for admissibility of a confession. A confession is voluntary if it is the product of a defendant's free choice rather than the result of police coercion. Whether a confession is voluntary is determined by assessing the totality of the circumstances. In this question, the investigating officer adhered to the *Miranda* rules and engaged in no third-degree methods. However, the police conduct will result in the confession being excluded from evidence because it was involuntary.

The police promise that if the defendant cooperated and confessed she would be charged in juvenile court rather than adult court is a misstatement of law. She cannot be prosecuted in juvenile court. The misstatement of law likely had an enormous impact upon the defendant's willingness to cooperate and upon her admission, rendering the confession involuntary and inadmissible. Even though the Supreme Court's broad prohibition on promises "does not state [the current] standard for determining the voluntariness of a confession," the misstatement of law contained within the promise will control the outcome in this case. *Arizona v. Fulminante*, 499 U.S. 279 (1991).

**Answers (A) and (B) are incorrect.** Although the police officer complied with the *Miranda* rules and the interrogation was not long or abusive, the voluntariness standard will be controlling in this problem because the confession is likely a result of a misstatement of law.

**Answer (D) is incorrect.** The defendant validly waived her *Miranda* rights and did not ask to consult with an attorney. The right to counsel under *Miranda* is not self-executing.

116. The evidence about the lineup identification is not admissible. Once adversary proceedings have begun, a defendant has the right to have an attorney present during a lineup. The defendant's right to counsel attached after she was indicted and arraigned on the indictment. If the defendant were arraigned on the preliminary charges (often called a preliminary appearance) prior to the indictment by a grand jury, her right to counsel would have attached at the earlier arraignment. *Kirby v. Illinois*, 406 U.S. 682 (1972). *Brewer v. Williams*, 430 U.S. 387 (1977).

The Supreme Court labeled a lineup as a critical stage for purposes of the right to counsel because it is "peculiarly riddled with innumerable dangers and variable factors which might seriously, even crucially, derogate from a fair trial." The Court said that eyewitness identification is "untrustworthy" and a major factor contributing to miscarriages of justice because of "the degree of suggestion inherent in the manner in which the prosecution presents the suspect to witnesses for pretrial identification."

The defendant's right to counsel attached in this case, and there is no claim that the defendant waived counsel. The prosecutor was obligated to notify defendant's counsel of the lineup. Consequently, the witnesses may not testify regarding the pretrial identification. *U.S. v. Wade*, 388 U.S. 218 (1967); *Gilbert v. California*, 388 U.S. 263 (1967).

117. The rule also bars in-court identifications that are the product of pretrial identifications in violation of the defendant's Sixth Amendment right to counsel. However, the rule does not mandate exclusion of in-court identification testimony when an in-court identification does not amount to exploitation of the tainted lineup. The identification may be premised on observations of the accused at the time of the alleged criminal act, which would be an adequate independent source to overcome the constitutional failure to have counsel present at the lineup. The prosecution must demonstrate by clear and convincing evidence that the in-court identification is derived from an independent source and not the product of the tainted confrontation. *U.S. v. Wade*, 388 U.S. 218 (1967). Whether the witnesses who identified the defendant at the tainted lineup may be able to identify her in court will turn on the strength of their testimony about their prior encounters with the accused.

118. **Answer (A) is the correct answer.** Even though the defendant's Sixth Amendment right to counsel had attached, the right to counsel is not applicable to photographic displays conducted by police for the purpose of allowing a witness to

attempt an identification of an offender. The Supreme Court said that a photographic identification differs from a lineup because there are substantially fewer possibilities of suggestion and any unfairness in the composition of the array can be readily reconstructed at trial. *U.S. v. Ash*, 413 U.S. 300 (1973).

**Answer (B) is incorrect** because the witness may testify about his or her pretrial identification from the photo array. Consequently, the prosecution need not base the witness' identification on prior contacts.

**Answer (C) is incorrect** because the Sixth Amendment right to counsel does not attach to photographic displays even after the defendant has counsel.

**Answer (D) is incorrect** because there is nothing in the facts to indicate that the photo array was unnecessarily suggestive to require exclusion of the testimony. The defense may undermine the witnesses' credibility, and the jury will decide whether or not to believe the witnesses.

119.    **Answer (D) is the correct answer.** Even where the Sixth Amendment right to counsel has not attached, a defendant may allege and prove that the photo identification procedure resulted in such unfairness that it violated the defendant's right to due process of law. The due process claim will be based upon the totality of the circumstances: whether the identification procedure was so "unnecessarily suggestive and conducive to irreparable mistaken identification." *Stovall v. Denno*, 388 U.S. 293 (1967). The Supreme Court has said,

> It must be recognized that improper employment of photographs by police may sometimes cause witnesses to err in identifying criminals. A witness may have obtained only a brief glimpse of a criminal, or may have seen him under poor conditions. Even if the police subsequently follow the most correct photographic identification procedures and show him the pictures of a number of individuals without indicating whom they suspect, there is some danger that the witness may make an incorrect identification. This danger will be increased if the police display to the witness only the picture of a single individual who generally resembles the person he saw, or if they show him the pictures of several persons among which the photograph of a single such individual recurs or is in some way emphasized. The chance of misidentification is also heightened if the police indicate to the witness that they have other evidence that one of the persons pictured committed the crime. Regardless of how the initial misidentification comes about, the witness thereafter is apt to retain in his memory the image of the photograph rather than of the person actually seen, reducing the trustworthiness of subsequent lineup or courtroom identification." *Simmon v. U.S.*, 390 U.S. 377 (1968).

In the problem case, Tina had only a brief view of the thief. Her view lasted less than a minute, it was dusk, and she only had a three-quarter view of the thief. Moreover, the photo array was unduly suggestive because only the defendant matched her description, and the police had allowed her to reread her description before she was shown the photos.

**Answer (A) is incorrect.** The defendant was in custody based upon the raid of the chop shop. He was not charged in connection with the theft of the vehicle. His Sixth Amendment right to counsel had not attached to the auto theft charge. However, a due process challenge exists separate and apart from the right to counsel. "[R]eliability is the linchpin in determining the admissibility of identification testimony."

**Answer (B) is incorrect.** Tina had no reason to lie. However, she picked the defendant from a photo array that was unnecessarily suggestive and conducive to irreparable mistaken identification. Her view of the defendant was limited and brief, at dusk, and from a considerable distance. There was no evidence to conclude that her trial identification was not affected by the tainted photo array.

**Answer (C) is incorrect.** Police are free to investigate other crimes following the arrest of a defendant. In pursuing other crimes, police need not contact the attorney representing the accused on pending charges, before showing photos to a witness. Defendant's Sixth Amendment right to counsel on the auto theft charge had not attached when police interviewed Tina and showed her the photo array.

120. **Answer (B) is the correct answer.** A show-up is the most suggestive identification procedure. The danger involved in showing suspects singly to persons for the purpose of identification, rather than as part of a lineup, is that it sends the message to the witness that the police believe they have caught the right person. To establish a due process violation, a defendant must prove that the out-of-court confrontation was "unnecessarily suggestive and conducive to irreparable mistaken identification." The test does not create a *per se* exclusionary rule based on the procedures used but, instead, focuses on the reliability of the resulting identification. To make that determination, the court should consider several factors: "includ[ing] the opportunity of the witness to view the criminal at the time of the crime, the witness' degree of attention, the accuracy of the witness' prior description of the criminal, the level of certainty demonstrated by the witness at the confrontation, and the length of time between the crime and the confrontation." *Neil v. Biggers*, 409 U.S. 188 (1972). In the problem both victim and mother had ample time to view the assailant during the crime, and their attention had been completely focused as the mother tried to rescue her daughter. Descriptions given to police prior to confrontation matched the defendant; the identification was positive, and the identification occurred very shortly after the crime. Even though the show-up in the hospital was unnecessary, the motion to suppress will fail.

**Answer (A) is incorrect.** Regardless of how the police described the defendant's status at the time they took him to the police station, a reasonable person in the defendant's position would not have felt free to refuse to accompany the police. He was in custody when he and the police left his father's house for the hospital. There was probable cause to arrest the defendant. Nevertheless, the hospital identification was permissible.

**Answer (C) is incorrect.** The show-up was unnecessarily suggestive. A proper lineup could have been arranged as soon as Melinda and her mother left the hospital. However, suggestiveness is only one part of the test; the second part focuses on the reliability of the resulting identification, which, here, was quite strong.

**Answer (D) is incorrect.** The defendant was in custody, but his Sixth Amendment right to counsel would not attach until the commencement of adversary proceedings, which would occur when a complaint is filed and the defendant appears in court. *Brewer v. Williams*, 430 U.S. 387 (1977).

121. The trial court ruled correctly. Entrapment is well-established as an affirmative defense. It is usually not a constitutional issue, but a question of fact for the jury. "Entrapment is the conception and planning of an offense by an officer and his procurement of its commission by one who would not have perpetrated it except for the trickery, persuasion or fraud of the officer." *Sorrells v. U.S.*, 287 U.S. 435 (1932). The Supreme Court and a majority of the states apply a subjective test which has two related elements: [1] government inducement of the crime, and [2] a lack of predisposition on the part of the defendant to engage in the criminal conduct." If the accused was induced and was not predisposed, entrapment is established. *Matthews v. U.S.*, 485 U.S. 58 (1988). The entrapment defense seeks to distinguish between the innocent person who is unwilling to commit a crime but who is induced to do so by a government agent and the unwary criminal who accepts the bait and is caught. Because the entrapment defense focuses on predisposition, a defendant's prior acts and convictions are relevant to the determination.

Like all questions of fact, the issue is submitted to the jury. Unless entrapment can be decided as a matter of law because a reasonable jury could not find otherwise, "the issue of whether a defendant has been entrapped is for the jury as part of its function of determining the guilt or innocence of the accused." *Sherman v. United States*, 356 U.S. 369, 377, 78 S. Ct. 819, 823, 2 L. Ed. 2d 848 (1958). To justify an acquittal as a matter of law, the defendants "must point to *'undisputed evidence making it patently clear that an otherwise innocent person was induced to commit the illegal act'* by government agents." The facts were in dispute in this case. *U.S. v. Mkhsian*, 5 F.3d 1306 (9th Cir. 1993).

122. **Answer (C) is the correct answer.** The Supreme Court said that "the prosecution must prove beyond a reasonable doubt that the defendant was disposed to commit the criminal act prior to first being approached by government agents." *Jacobson v. United States*, 503 U.S. 540 (1992). This has been interpreted by some United States Courts of Appeals to require proof that the defendant was predisposed to commit the crime before the government agent arrived on the scene. Here, although Blue bought and used marijuana, there was no reason for Sally to believe that Blue was predisposed before Sally made the offer to sell illegal drugs.

**Answer (A) is incorrect.** There is a world of difference between buying and selling marijuana. Buying small quantities of marijuana does not indicate a predisposition to commit the more serious crime of selling.

**Answer (B) is incorrect** because Sally did much more than provide the means for Blue to commit the crime. She offered Sally the opportunity many times to commit the crime, and Blue did not take her up on the offer until she was desperate. A government agent should not be permitted to cajole a desperate person to commit a crime.

**Answer (D) is incorrect.** The defense of entrapment is not proven because a defendant refuses the first opportunity to commit a crime.

**123.** **Answer (C) is the correct answer.** Incident to a non-custodial traffic stop, a police officer may order the occupants of the vehicle out of the car, but may not search the vehicle without probable cause to believe that evidence of a crime will be found inside the car. *Pennsylvania v. Mimms*, 434 U.S. 106 (1977); *Knowles v. Iowa*, 525 U.S. 113 (1998). Even though the search of the car was illegal, a passenger in a vehicle does not have standing to challenge the search of the vehicle. *Rakas v. Illinois*, 439 U.S. 128 (1978). In order to prove standing, a defendant must prove that his or her right to privacy was violated. The driver of the vehicle has standing to challenge the illegal search, but a passenger does not.

**Answer (A) is incorrect.** The officer illegally searched the vehicle. However, a passenger in a vehicle does not have standing to raise the illegality of the search.

**Answer (B) is incorrect.** If the officer had probable cause to search the vehicle, the search under the automobile exception to the warrant requirement extends to the entire vehicle and all of its contents where the evidence sought could be found. An officer does not need separate probable cause to search a passenger's belongings provided that the officer has probable cause to search the car. *Wyoming v. Houghton*, 526 U.S. 295 (1999).

**Answer (D) is incorrect.** A police officer may not conduct a search of a vehicle incident to a traffic stop for the purpose of issuing a citation. The answer changes if state law allows a custodial arrest for a minor traffic offense. In that case, the officer may arrest the motorist for the offense and search the interior compartment of the vehicle. *New York v. Belton*, 453 U.S. 454 (1981). However, the passenger still lacks standing to contest the search.

**124.** **Answer (B) is the correct answer.** A passenger has standing to challenge the illegal stop of the vehicle in which he is riding. A police stop of a vehicle constitutes a Fourth Amendment seizure of both the driver and passengers of the vehicle. A passenger in a car that is illegally stopped has standing to challenge the stop. "A traffic stop necessarily curtails the travel a passenger has chosen just as much as it halts the driver, diverting both from the stream of traffic to the side of the road, and the police activity that normally amounts to intrusion on 'privacy and personal security' does not normally (and did not here) distinguish between passenger and driver." The Court pointed out that it made no sense for the passenger not to feel the suspicion of the stop, even if the focus is on the driver. *Brendlin v. California*, 127 S. Ct. 2400 (2007).

**Answer (A) is incorrect.** The search was illegal, but a passenger in a vehicle does not have standing to raise the illegality of the search of the car. Here, however, the stop was also illegal, and a passenger has standing to challenge the illegal stop.

**Answer (C) is incorrect.** The passenger has standing to challenge the stop of the vehicle. If the stop had been legal, the passenger would not have had standing to challenge the search.

**Answer (D) is incorrect.** A passenger in a vehicle does have standing to challenge the illegal stop of the vehicle because a stop of a vehicle is a seizure of all occupants of the car.

125. The motion should be granted, but it is not a certainty. The search was illegal. Police may not search every person present even during execution of a valid search warrant without probable cause to believe that the person is linked to the criminal enterprise. *Ybarra v. Illinois*, 444 U.S. 85 (1979). The appellate court will consider the substantive Fourth Amendment issue concerning the legality of the search only if the court finds that the defendant has standing to raise the issue.

The question turns on whether a guest at a party has standing to challenge the illegal search of his date's purse. To establish standing, a defendant must demonstrate a privacy interest in the place searched and the objects seized. Standing rules were liberalized by the Warren Court to provide automatic standing for any person charged with a possessory offense. Later Supreme Court rulings eliminated automatic standing, requiring a defendant in every case to establish that his or her personal, constitutional rights were violated.

In a case with similar facts, the Supreme Court held that a defendant did not have a protected privacy interest in his girlfriend's purse because their relationship was casual (even though they had spent the previous 48 hours together), and because the defendant did not have authority to prevent others from access to the girlfriend's purse (the girlfriend had permitted her girlfriend to store her hairbrush in the purse along with the defendant's marijuana). *Rawlings v. Kentucky*, 448 U.S. 98 (1980). In dictum, five justices of Supreme Court have argued that all social guests should have standing to challenge a search of the premises. *Minnesota v. Carter*, 525 U.S. 83 (1991)

126. **Answer (D) is the best answer.** The Supreme Court has said that an overnight guest at a home has standing to challenge an illegal search of the home. *Minnesota v. Olson*, 495 U.S. 91 (1990). The Court made it clear that a place need not be a defendant's home in order for there to be a legitimate expectation of privacy. However, there is no mention in the facts whether Carter was an overnight guest. Later, in *Minnesota v. Carter*, 525 U.S. 83 (1991), the Court held that a defendant did not have a legitimate expectation of privacy in an apartment used for a short time for a purely illegal commercial purpose and, thus, did not have standing to challenge the search. However, five members of the *Carter* Court, both concurring and dissenting judges, agreed in dictum that a social guest should have standing to challenge an illegal search. In the problem, the defendant was a social guest in the home *and* used the home for an illegal commercial purpose. The combination of the two purposes would be sufficient to distinguish the case from the holding in *Minnesota v. Carter* and provide standing to challenge the illegal entry and search

of the apartment. However, Justice O'Connor, one of the five justices who said that a social guest need not spend the night to have standing, has retired so it is not altogether clear whether the new Court would affirm the standing of a social guest, who is not staying overnight, to challenge a search of the home. The answer to this question will not be known until the Court elaborates on the themes in the *Carter* case.

**Answer (A) is incorrect.** Before the court rules on the legality of the entry and search, the court first would have to determine whether the defendant has standing to raise the Fourth Amendment issue.

**Answer (B) is incorrect.** It is difficult to justify the police decision not to seek a warrant when there is no evidence leading them to believe that the defendant knew that they were on to him. Moreover, the trial court would not have to reach this decision if they rule that the defendant does not have standing.

**Answer (C) is incorrect.** In *Minnesota v. Carter*, 525 U.S. 83 (1991), the Supreme Court found no standing where the defendant used the apartment solely for an illegal commercial purpose. The defendant here was a social and sexual guest. He was not there solely for the illegal purpose.

127.    **Answer (C) is correct.** A trial court's finding of fact is entitled to great deference
        on appeal. The hearing judge saw the witnesses and heard their testimony. The
        appellate court may not substitute its own judgment for that of the trial judge on a
        question of fact as long as there is any evidence in the record to support the
        finding.

        **Answer (A) is incorrect.** Issues of credibility are questions of fact to be decided by
        the trier of fact. Credibility is not merely how many witnesses appeared on each
        side.

        **Answer (B) is incorrect.** The appellate court may not substitute its judgment for
        that of the trial court's on a question of fact, even if the appellate court would have
        decided the matter differently.

        **Answer (D) is incorrect.** Answer (D) is partially correct. A trial court's finding of
        fact will generally stand on appeal provided that there is some evidence in the
        record to support the trial court's finding. The answer is incorrect because the trial
        judge's findings of fact are subject to review on appeal. The appellate court,
        however, may not substitute its own conclusion for that of the trial judge.

128.    **Answer (B) is correct.** Unlike decisions based upon questions of fact, the trial
        judge's conclusions of law are not entitled to any deference. The court of appeals is
        entitled to substitute its own judgment on matters of law. A search conducted with
        a warrant is presumptively legal because the police have followed the preferred
        constitutional procedure by seeking prior judicial authority to conduct the search.
        Consequently, a defendant challenging a search conducted with a warrant has the
        burden of proof on a motion to suppress. A search conducted without a warrant
        carries no presumption of regularity and correctness. The burden falls upon the
        prosecution to prove the legality of such a search. Therefore, in this case, the
        prosecution had the burden to prove that the search was voluntary. The trial court
        erred in its assignment of the burden of proof to the defendant.

        **Answer (A) is incorrect.** The finding of fact will stand, but the error is based upon
        the court's erroneous assignment of the burden of proof, a matter of law.

        **Answer (C) is incorrect.** The trial court's decisions on a legal issue are entitled to
        no deference. The court of appeals may substitute its own conclusion of law for that
        of the trial judge's.

        **Answer (D) is incorrect.** The trial court erroneously assigned the burden of proof
        to the defendant on the issue of law. The burden rests upon the state to prove that

the consent to search was voluntary.

**Authors Note:** The prosecution has the burden of proving that a confession is voluntary, *Lego v. Twomey*, 404 U.S. 477 (1972), or was secured in compliance with *Miranda* requirements. *Fare v. Michael C.*, 442 U.S. 707 (1979). When identification evidence is challenged, the defendant has the burden of proving that the identification violated the right to counsel, but the prosecution has the burden of proving an independent source for that identification. *United States v. Wade*, 388 U.S. 218 (1967). The defendant has the burden of showing that an identification procedure violates due process because it was so suggestive as to create a likelihood of misidentification. *Stovall v. Denno*, 388 U.S. 293 (1967).

129.  A trial judge's determination that probable cause or reasonable suspicion exists, even though based on factual conclusions, is a matter of law. A trial court's conclusions of law on constitutional issues are entitled to no deference. Those issues of law are subject to a *de novo* review in an appellate court. *Ornelas v. United States*, 517 U.S. 690 (1996).

Here, the trial court's decision that probable cause existed to arrest the young man was erroneous. At most the police officer had reasonable suspicion to stop and question the suspect to confirm or dispel his suspicion that the defendant was on the corner dealing drugs. Standing on a street corner, without more, does not rise to the level of reasonable suspicion allowing for a *Terry*-stop. The fact that a suspect runs when police come on the scene is only one of many factors to be considered when determining whether the officer was justified in making a Terry-stop. *Illinois v. Wardlow*, 528 U.S. 119 (2000).

In this case, the defendant walked away from the corner when he saw the police officer heading in his direction; he did not run. Moreover, he stopped immediately when the officer ordered him to stop. Even if the court had found that reasonable suspicion existed to stop the defendant, the police officer only could do a pat down of the defendant's clothing to determine whether the defendant had a weapon. The defendant's dress, however, might not even allow for a pat down for weapons if the officer could have seen a weapon without a pat down. But the officer did not frisk for weapons; he reached into the defendant's shorts and removed the evidence. A full search incident to arrest is permitted only following a lawful arrest. Since the officer did not have probable cause to arrest, this was not a lawful arrest, and the search was illegal. The evidence should have been suppressed.

130.  In most state and federal jurisdictions, the appellate court will consider the state's appeal from the ruling to suppress the evidence. Ordinarily a party to a law suit (including a criminal case) may not appeal a trial judge's preliminary or trial ruling. For example, in a criminal case a defendant may not appeal from an adverse ruling on her motion to suppress evidence. The principal reason for that rule is that the defendant may yet prevail at trial and will no longer need to appeal from the adverse ruling. However, to conserve time and resources, federal courts and many state jurisdictions do not require the defendant to go trial to preserve a right to appeal an adverse ruling on a motion to suppress. The defendant may preserve the right to appeal from the pretrial ruling denying her motion to suppress by entering

a conditional plea.

However, if the trial court grants the motion to suppress evidence, the prosecution may not have any additional evidence to proceed to trial. Consequently, many jurisdictions, including federal courts, allow the prosecution a limited interlocutory appeal from an adverse ruling by the trial court on a motion to suppress. *See, e.g.*, 18 U.S.C. § 3731. The justification for allowing the prosecution to appeal, while not allowing the defense the same appeal, is that the prosecution may lose its right to prosecute the case altogether based upon an erroneous decision suppressing evidence. If the state proceeds to trial without the evidence and the defendant is acquitted, the double jeopardy prohibition precludes the state from appealing from an acquittal. Some jurisdictions require the state to seek leave to appeal from the appellate court, and some jurisdictions also require the prosecutor to claim that the state will be unable to proceed to trial if the pretrial decision to suppress evidence is not overturned.

**131.** The exclusionary rule reaches not only primary evidence obtained as a direct result of an illegal search or seizure, but also evidence later discovered and found to be derivative of an illegality, or "fruit of the poisonous tree." The reason is if derivative evidence were not suppressed, police would have an incentive to violate constitutional rights in order to secure admissible derivative evidence even though the primary evidence secured as a result of the constitutional violation would be inadmissible. "To forbid the direct use of methods thus characterized but to put no curb on their full indirect use would only invite the very methods deemed 'inconsistent with ethical standards and destructive of personal liberty.' " *Nardone v. United States*, 308 U.S. 338 (1939).

At the very most, the police officer was permitted to conduct a *Terry*-stop of the vehicle to confirm or dispel his suspicion of illegal activity. The police, however, treated the stop as an arrest; the use of drawn weapons is indicative of an arrest, and the officer did not have probable cause to arrest the suspect or to search the vehicle. It was not a valid search incident to arrest, nor a valid warrantless search under the automobile exception to the warrant requirement. The evidence found in the car as a result of the illegal search provided the evidence for probable cause to secure a search warrant. While the search warrant was, itself, valid based upon probable cause, the probable cause obtained during the illegal search was the fruit of the illegal search and, therefore, tainted. The evidence found during the execution of the search warrant is the fruit of the "poisonous tree" because of the original illegal search.

In order to undo the taint of the original illegality, the state would have to demonstrate that the evidence obtained with the search warrant was not the result of the search of the Bronco. Had the judge who issued the search warrant not been provided with the evidence of the cocaine found in the Bronco as a result of a violation of the Fourth Amendment, the search warrant would not have been issued. Therefore, evidence obtained in the execution of the search warrant must likewise be suppressed. Moreover, the good faith exception to the exclusionary rule does not apply where a search warrant is issued on the basis of evidence obtained as a result of an illegal search. *United States v. Vasey*, 834 F.2d 782 (9th Cir. 1987); *United States v. Scales*, 903 F.2d 765 (10th Cir 1990).

**132.**   **Answer (C) is correct.** The statement of the defendant was the product of custodial interrogation. The police should have given *Miranda* warnings to the defendant; the failure to *Mirandize* the defendant renders the statement inadmissible. However, *Miranda* violations do not taint physical evidence obtained as a result of the violation. The failure to give *Miranda* warnings, by itself, does not violate a defendant's constitutional rights. A statement taken without *Miranda* warnings will not serve as a poisonous tree and will not taint the evidence that is discovered as a result of that statement, provided that the statement is voluntary. An involuntary statement violates the defendant's Fifth Amendment rights, and the evidence secured as a result of that violation would be inadmissible. *U.S. v. Patane*, 542 U.S. 630 (2004).

  **Answer (A) is incorrect.** There was a *Miranda* violation, and the jewelry is derivative of that violation. However, a statement taken without *Miranda* warnings will not serve as a poisonous tree and will not taint the evidence that is discovered as a result of that statement, provided that the statement is voluntary.

  **Answer (B) is incorrect.** There was no public safety emergency once the defendant was disarmed. A reasonable police officer would not have believed that finding the jewelry was part of such an emergency. Therefore, that exception to the *Miranda* rules does not apply.

  **Answer (D) is incorrect.** A violation of the *Miranda* rules does not automatically render the statement involuntary. The Supreme Court treats *Miranda* violations differently than other Fifth Amendment violations. Sometimes it is difficult to rationalize the difference, since *Miranda* warnings are constitutionally required. *Dickerson v. U.S.*, 530 U.S. 428 (2000). Evidence which is derivative of a Fifth Amendment violation is fruit of the poisonous tree; evidence which is derivative of a *Miranda* violation is not the fruit of the poisonous tree, provided that the statement was voluntary.

133.  **Answer (D) is the correct answer.** The warrantless entry of the defendant's apartment to make the arrest violated the defendant's Fourth Amendment rights. An arrest warrant is needed to enter a home to arrest a resident absent consent or exigent circumstances. *Payton v. New York*, 445 U.S. 573 (1980). However, the Supreme Court has held that such an illegal arrest, provided there is probable cause, is not a poisonous tree once the arrestee is removed from the residence. Provided there is probable cause to justify the arrest, the detention is lawful once the defendant is taken from the house. *New York v. Harris*, 495 U.S. 14 (1990).

**Answer (A) is incorrect.** There were no exigent circumstances to justify the warrantless entry to arrest. The police had probable cause to arrest and could have made the arrest in a public place without a warrant, and then sought a search warrant for the apartment.

**Answer (B) is incorrect.** The entry of the apartment was illegal. However, *New York v. Harris*, 495 U.S. 14 (1990), stands for the proposition that even though a constitutional violation is established, evidence will not be excluded unless it is obtained as a direct consequence of the illegal act. The rule separates the confession from the constitutional violation, once the violation ends.

**Answer (C) is incorrect.** Police had probable cause to arrest the defendant. Based on the totality of the circumstances, probable cause existed to believe that the defendant who was the sole employee was responsible for the evidence disappearing over a period of days.

**134.**   **Answer (A) is correct.** The facts are clear that the defendant's in-court presence and identification followed an illegal arrest and a lineup identification derivative of the illegal arrest. However, the power of the court to try a person for a crime is not impaired by the fact of an illegal arrest. *Frisbie v. Collins*, 342 U.S. 519 (1952). Even if the defendant is in court as a result of an illegal arrest, he cannot have his face suppressed as the fruit of an illegal arrest to prevent an in-court identification. *U.S. v. Crews*, 445 U.S. 463 (1980).

**Answer (B) is incorrect.** The arrest following the lineup was derivative of the illegal arrest and the lineup identification. However, the illegal arrest and subsequent lineup do not affect the legality of the in-court identification provided that the prosecution establishes that the witness's in-court identification is based upon prior contact (the crime) and not based upon the tainted lineup. *U.S. v. Wade*, 388 U.S. 218 (1967).

**Answer (C) is incorrect.** Even if the defendant is in court as a result of an illegal arrest, he cannot have his face suppressed as the fruit of an illegal arrest to prevent an in-court identification. *U.S. v. Crews*, 445 U.S. 463 (1980).

**Answer (D) is incorrect.** The witness's in-court identification is admissible if the prosecution establishes that there was an independent source for the in-court identification. When the witness testified that she was able to identify the defendant as the robber based upon her observation of him at the time of the robbery, the prosecution argued successfully that the in-court identification was independent of the tainted lineup.

**135.**   **Answer (B) is correct.** The knock- and- announce- and- wait rule is part of the Fourth Amendment requirements. *Wilson v. Arkansas*, 514 U.S. 927 (1995). However, evidence seized during execution of a lawful search warrant is admissible even though police violated the knock and announce rule. *Hudson v. Michigan*, 547 U.S. 586 (2006). The Supreme Court said that "interests that were violated . . . have nothing to do with the seizure of evidence." It is very likely that the *Hudson* decision will doom the Fourth Amendment requirement that police knock and announce and wait prior to entering to execute a search warrant. However, informing people in the house that the police seek entry may serve to protect both police and the inhabitants of the house.

**Answer (A) is incorrect.** Police may request a no-knock authorization in a search warrant. But even if they do not have such a provision in a search warrant, events may give rise to the existence of exigent circumstances between the time the warrant is issued and the search takes place, a fact which justifies a no knock entry even without court authorization.

**Answer (C) is incorrect.** There was no evidence of exigency to justify the no knock entry. However, evidence seized during execution of a lawful search warrant is admissible even though police violated the knock and announce rule. *Hudson v. Michigan*, 547 U.S. 586 (2006).

**Answer (D) is incorrect.** The Fourth Amendment does require police to knock and identify themselves and wait before entering a dwelling to execute a search warrant. Wilson v. Arkansas, 514 U.S. 927 (1995).

**136.** Justice Oliver Wendell Holmes, in (*Silverthorne Lumber Co. v. U.S.,*) 251 U.S. 385 (1920), allowed that if knowledge of the derivative evidence is gained from an independent source, rather than from the government's own illegality, the derivative evidence may be used. In actuality, the independent source exception is not an exception at all. The secondary evidence is not derivative because it was not obtained as a result of the initial police illegality. was. In Segura v. U.S., 468 U.S. 796 (1984), the Supreme Court held admissible items not discovered during the illegal entry "and first discovered . . . the day after the entry, under an admittedly valid search warrant" for which there was an independent source. The independent source rule has been significantly expanded in the last decade so that the independence of the source is not quite as clear as it once was.

In *Murray v. U.S.*, 487 U.S. 533 (1988), the Supreme Court held that evidence observed by police during an illegal entry need not be excluded if such evidence is later discovered during the execution of a valid search warrant issued on information wholly unconnected to the prior entry. The Court said the government must establish that: (1) no information presented in the affidavit for the warrant was seen during the initial entry; and (2) the agents' decision to seek the warrant was not prompted by what they had seen during the initial entry. Since the same agents who had illegally entered and searched sought the subsequent warrant, it is incredible that their decision to seek the warrant was not influenced by what they observed. At the very least, the initial illegal entry was confirmatory, which destroys the claim of independence. Had the initial entry not confirmed the presence of the contraband would the agents still have sought the warrant?

The problem case is very similar to *Murray*. The police had probable cause to obtain a search warrant for Coca Mary's house prior to authorizing the informant to break and enter to confirm the presence of the drugs. The likely reason for the initial illegal entry was to ensure the presence of the marijuana so as not to expend the effort to obtain a warrant unless the agents were sure to find what they sought when they came back with the warrant. While it should then be impossible to meet the Court's second condition in *Murray.*, it is likely that the court, in reliance on *Murray*, would deny the motion to suppress. Some courts have held that *Murray* does not impose an explicit requirement that an officer seeking a warrant must disclose the prior illegal entry. *See, e.g., State v. Krukowski*, 100 P.3d 1222 (Utah 2004).

**137.** **Answer (C) is correct.** Inevitable discovery is a limitation on the derivative evidence rule; some courts even treat it as an exception to the exclusionary rule, itself. The inevitable discovery limitation seeks to put the prosecution in the same position, not a worse position, than it would have been if no police error or misconduct had occurred. Under the limitation, evidence that was obtained illegally is admitted, nonetheless, if it would have been obtained lawfully without the constitutional violation. *Nix v. Williams*, 467 U.S. 431 (1984).

In the problem, the defendant's vehicle was stopped to determine if the defendant was driving under the influence. Subject to such a stop, police may conduct a limited pat-down search for weapons of the suspect (and the interior of the vehicle) if the police have reasonable suspicion to believe that the suspect may be armed. There are no facts even to justify a *Terry*-frisk in this case; nor is there any alternative theory which would allow the police to search the trunk of the vehicle. The arrest in this case is incident to the unlawful search of the vehicle. There was no probable cause to search the vehicle under the automobile search. Nor may police impound a vehicle incident to a traffic citation. There is no alternative legal theory to justify the state's claim that the drugs would have been inevitably discovered.

**Answer (A) is incorrect.** Police may search the interior compartment of a vehicle, not the trunk, incident to the custodial arrest of an occupant of the vehicle. The Supreme Court has said that the underlying reasons which justify the search of the vehicle incident to arrest are not applicable incident to the issuance of a traffic citation. *Knowles v. Iowa*, 525 U.S. 113 (1998).

**Answer (B) is incorrect.** Although it sometimes seems that police can find some justification for stopping any vehicle, that is not true for the search of a vehicle. The facts in this problem do not fall within any of the exceptions allowing a warrantless search of a vehicle. Consequently, the inevitable exception limitation is inapplicable.

**Answer (D) is incorrect.** If the police had probable cause to arrest the defendant, they would likely have been permitted by their department policies to impound the vehicle and conduct an inventory search. Thus, the evidence would have been inevitably discovered during the inventory. However, in the problem, the arrest was the product of the illegal search of the trunk; impounding the vehicle would have been derivative of the illegal search and the illegal arrest.

138.  **Answer (D) is correct.** The exclusionary rule does not invariably bar the testimony of a witness whose identity is revealed to the authorities as the result of an illegal search. Exclusion is dependent upon the degree of attenuation between the illegal search and the testimony. A number of considerations, including that (1) "the testimony given by the witness was an act of her own free will in no way coerced or even induced by official authority," (2) "substantial periods of time elapsed between the time of the illegal search and the initial contact with the witness . . . and between the latter and the testimony at trial," and (3) the identity of the witness and her relationship with the defendant "were well known to those investigating the case." *U.S. v. Ceccolini*, 435 U.S. 268 (1978).

The fact that Stewart and Ellison elected to plead guilty, presumably with the assistance of counsel, helps to establish the attenuation from the illegal search. The length of time between the illegal search and their in-court testimony is another factor weighing in favor of allowing the testimony. In determining that the testimony of both witnesses was properly admitted at trial, the court will focus on the length of time between the illegal search and the testimony and the willingness of both witnesses to testify as a result of their plea agreements. *U.S. v. Akridge*, 346 F.3d 618 (6th Cir 2003).

**Answer (A) is incorrect.** Although their testimony (at least Stewart's testimony) likely resulted from the illegal search, the Supreme Court has expanded the limitations on the derivative evidence rule. The court will apply the attenuation doctrine to determine whether the police came "upon the evidence by exploitation of [the initial] illegality or instead by means *sufficiently distinguishable* to be purged of the primary taint."

**Answer (B) is incorrect.** The Supreme Court majority rejected an absolute rule that live witness testimony cannot be the fruit of the poisonous tree, although there is almost a presumption in favor of admitting live witness testimony. *U.S. v. Ceccolini*, 435 U.S. 268 (1978). In applying an attenuation analysis, courts will focus on the length of the road between the illegality and the discovery of the witness, as well as the willingness of the witness to testify. These principles are inapplicable to a police officer's testimony about a defendant's inadmissible statement.

**Answer (C) is not the best answer.** The argument for inevitable discovery would be that the identity of Ellison and Stewart and their relationship to the defendant would have become known independently of the illegality. Some courts require that the alternative route to the evidence (here the identities and their later testimony) be in motion prior to the illegality.

**139.**   **Answer (A) is the best answer.** At one time, evidence seized as a result of a Fourth Amendment violation could not be used by the government for any purpose. However, the Supreme Court now strongly supports the view that the exclusionary rule should only be used as a "shield," preventing the government from using the evidence in its case-in-chief, but may not be used by the defendant as a "sword." Therefore, when the defendant was called as a witness and testified that he never possessed more than a small quantity of marijuana, the prosecution could rebut the defendant's testimony during cross-examination by asking him about the evidence seized during the illegal search. The rule allows the prosecutor "to work in . . . evidence on cross-examination (as it would) in its case in chief." *U.S. v. Havens*, 446 U.S. 620 (1980). The jury must be instructed that it only may consider that evidence in determining the defendant's credibility as a witness and not in determining whether the prosecution has proven its case beyond a reasonable doubt. That is almost an impossible task for a jury.

     **Answer (B) is not the best answer.** Theoretically, the defendant's lie on the witness stand opens the door for the prosecutor to question him about what was found on his person during the illegal search. The prosecution can question the defendant about matters that are plainly within the scope of the defendant's direct examination.

     **Answer (C) is not the best answer.** Allowing the prosecutor to question the defendant about the illegal search permits the government to profit by the illegal conduct of the police officer. It puts the defense in the very difficult position of determining whether to call the defendant as a witness or to keep him off the witness stand altogether. It is very difficult to limit the direct examination of the defendant so that it does not open the door for the prosecutor to question him about the illegal search. The prosecutor may question the defendant about the illegal search as long as the cross-examination is "reasonably suggested" by the defendant's direct examination. *U.S. v. Havens*, 446 U.S. 620 (1980).

     **Answer (D) is not the best answer.** The suppression of the evidence from the prosecution's case-in-chief does not determine whether it may be used on cross-examination when the defendant elects to testify in his own behalf.

**140.**   **Answer (B) is the correct answer.** The Supreme Court in *Miranda* said that a confession secured without compliance with the warnings is not admissible for any purpose. Later cases have distinguished between use of the confession in the prosecution's case-in-chief and in use during cross-examination of a defendant who elects to testify. Consequently, statements secured in violation of the *Miranda* rules (as well as those in violation of a defendant's Sixth Amendment rights) may be used by the prosecution to impeach the defendant's credibility as a witness. Harris v., New York, 401 U.S. 222 (1971); *Michigan v. Harvey*, 494 U.S. 344 (1990); *Kansas v. Ventris*, 129 S. Ct. 1841 (2009).

Therefore, the defendant controls the outcome. If she does not testify, the confession cannot be used for any purpose. In the problem, however, the confession was not used only to impeach the defendant's credibility. The prosecutor used the confession in final argument to help prove the state's case. The trial judge should have instructed the jury to limit its use to determining whether to believe the defendant's testimony, not for any other purpose. Here, that purpose was muddied, and the conviction must be reversed.

**Answer (A) is incorrect.** A confession, although inadmissible to prove the charge, may be used during cross-examination to impeach the credibility of a defendant who elects to testify to impeach her credibility.

**Answer (C) is incorrect.** It was not used in the prosecution's case-in-chief because of the *Miranda* violation, and it was not used until Maria took the witness stand and lied. However, the prosecutor used her confession in his final argument to strengthen the state's proof on the charge. If the prosecutor had merely used the confession to argue that the jury should not believe Maria's testimony, the conviction would not be reversed.

**Answer (D) is incorrect.** The confession was not used only to impeach Maria's credibility. The prosecutor improperly used it to bolster the state's case. The judge should have instructed the jury to use the confession only for the permissible limited purpose.

**Author's note.** The impeachment exception to the exclusionary rules may not be used to impeach the testimony of defense witnesses other than the defendant. If Maria not been indicted but called as a defense witness at Danny's trial, the state could not have used her confession to impeach her credibility.

141.   **Answer (D) is the best answer.** There are strong policy reasons to permit a prosecutor to use inadmissible evidence to impeach a defendant's testimony, and there are strong policy reasons not to permit such use. Allowing the defendant to take the witness stand without concern for her prior statement, which was inadmissible in the prosecution's case-in-chief, would allow her to lie with impunity. On the other hand, allowing the prosecutor to use the inadmissible confession to impeach the defendant's testimony allows the state to profit from the police illegality.

In this case, there is no technical or inadvertent *Miranda* violation; it is an intentional violation of *Miranda* for the purpose of obtaining a statement for the sole purpose of impeaching a defendant who takes the witness stand. The practice operates on the theory that the officer has nothing to lose. If the defendant elects to remain silent and the officer does not proceed with interrogation, no statement will be forthcoming. If the defendant invokes the right to counsel and a lawyer is provided, no statement will be forthcoming, either. Here, however, if the officer ignores the invocation of the right, there may be a statement forthcoming which may be usable for the limited purpose of impeachment. Despite the problems with allowing this practice, the Supreme Court held that a statement that is the result of an intentional violation of *Miranda* that is otherwise voluntary is admissible for impeachment purposes. Oregon v. Hass, 420 U.S. 714 (1975).

**Answer (A) is incorrect.** The admissibility of the statement for impeachment purposes does not turn on whether the officer intentionally chose to violate the *Miranda* rules. If the statement is voluntary, it does not matter if the *Miranda* violation was intentional and blatant. This kind of *Miranda* violation is intended to secure an inadmissible statement and to keep the defendant from testifying because of the threat of the use of that statement for impeachment purposes.

**Answer (B) is incorrect.** The statement was secured in violation of Maria's *Miranda* right to counsel. Her Sixth Amendment right to counsel would not attach until the beginning of formal adversary proceedings, evidenced by a first court appearance. However, statements secured in violation of an accused Sixth Amendment right to counsel may also be used to impeach the accused's credibility at trial.

**Answer (C) is incorrect.** The *Miranda* rules are violated when during custodial interrogation the police fail to advise an accused of her *Miranda* rights. The violation exists even if it could be proven that the accused was already aware of those rights. Requiring the officer to recite the *Miranda* warnings is designed to reaffirm that the police officer is prepared to respect those rights.

142. **Answer (B) is correct.** Maria's confession is involuntary and may not be used for any purpose. The Supreme Court has always distinguished between the impeachment use of statements secured in violation of *Miranda* which are otherwise "trustworthy" and involuntary statements which violate due process. Coerced statements are violations of the Fifth Amendment and may not be used for any purpose. *Mincey v. Arizona*, 437 U.S. 385 (1978). The reason for the different treatment of statements that are the product of *Miranda* violations and those that are "coerced or involuntary" stems from the Court's analysis that *Miranda* violations are not Fifth Amendment violations (even though the warnings are constitutionally required), but "merely" violations of rules intended to protect Fifth Amendment rights. Since the Fifth Amendment contains within its language an exclusionary rule, any statement that is coerced or otherwise involuntary is a violation of a Fifth Amendment right and may not be used for any purpose. Here, Detective Madden shouted at Maria, frightened her, and threatened her until he overcame her ability to resist, and she confessed. The officer's conduct violated her Fifth Amendment right to be free from compelled self-incrimination.

**Answer (A) is incorrect.** The confession may not be used to impeach the defendant's testimony because the statement was the product of actual coercion, violating the defendant's right to due process. If the statement was voluntary but secured without compliance with the *Miranda* rules, the statement could be used on cross-examination for the limited purpose of impeaching Maria's credibility.

**Answer (C) is incorrect.** By her taking the witness stand and denying involvement in the illegal enterprise, the prosecutor could use Maria's statement, if it were voluntary, for the limited purpose of impeaching her credibility. It could not be used in the prosecution's case-in-chief. In the problem, however, the statement was involuntary and violated the defendant's Fifth Amendment rights and may not be used for any purpose.

**Answer (D) is incorrect.** Coerced statements are violations of the Fifth Amendment and may not be used for any purpose. *Mincey v. Arizona,* 437 U.S. 385 (1978). The statement may not be used even for the limited purpose of impeaching Maria's credibility.

143.    **Answer (D) is correct.** It is permissible for the prosecutor to ask the defendant about his failure to come forward and tell police that he shot in self-defense before and after arrest until such time as the defendant is read his *Miranda* rights. Once the defendant is given *Miranda* warnings, his silence from that moment on may not be used for impeachment purposes. An accused's silence following receipt of the *Miranda* warnings may not be used because of its inherent ambiguity and the impossibility of determining whether that silence is the product of reliance on the *Miranda* warning. *Doyle v. Ohio,* 426 U.S. 610 (1976). Any erroneous reference to a defendant's silence following issuance of *Miranda* warnings requires reversal unless the state can show that the error was harmless.

**Answer (A) is incorrect.** Whether a defendant's silence, which may be inconsistent with his in-court explanation, may be used for impeachment purposes depends on when the silence occurs and whether the accused was given *Miranda* warnings. An accused's silence following receipt of the Miranda warnings may not be used because of its inherent ambiguity and the impossibility of determining whether that silence is the product of reliance on the *Miranda* warning. Answer (A) does not put any time limits on the use of silence for impeachment purposes, and is wrong.

**Answer (B) is incorrect.** A defendant's silence at the time of an arrest may be used for impeachment purposes. The state also may use the defendant's silence following the formal arrest, until such time as he is read the *Miranda* warnings.

**Answer (C) is incorrect.** A defendant's silence at the time of arrest and at the police station following an arrest may be used for impeachment purposes. The location is not the critical factor. The cut-off is the reading of *Miranda* rights: "It is fundamentally unfair to promise an arrested person that his silence will not be used against him and thereafter to breach that promise by using the silence to impeach his trial testimony." *Wainwright v. Greenfield,* 474 U.S. 284 (1996).

144.    **Answer (C) is correct.** Under Rule 8(a), joinder of offenses, of the Federal Rules of Criminal Procedure, crimes may be joined together if they are of the "same or similar character, or are based on the same act or transaction, or are connected with or constitute parts of a common scheme or plan." The important thing to remember here is the "common scheme or plan" requirement. Cooter possesses specialized knowledge that he shares with customers and mechanics so they can run their own insurance scams.

**Answer (A) is incorrect** because at the very least I and III can be joined.

**Answers (B) and (D) are incorrect** because defrauding insurance companies and illegal dumping of waste do not meet the 8(a) test. Note that regardless of your answer you should have ignored the language in II, which identifies dumping of hazardous waste products as a misdemeanor. Under Rule 8(a), crimes can be joined together regardless of whether they are felonies (ordinarily defined as crimes punishable by imprisonment for a year or more) or misdemeanors (crimes punishable by imprisonment for less than a year).

145.    Under Rule 14(a) of the Federal Rules of Criminal Procedure, the trial court has the discretion to order separate trials on validly joined counts within an indictment or information if it feels that the prosecution or defense would be prejudiced by the joinder. Here the defendant is charged with four homicides, but each one is unique in some respects, yet there are strong similarities in them.

Joinder may be prejudicial in several respects. A jury may find it extremely difficult to consider each individual count on its own set of circumstantial facts. This is unfairly prejudicial to the defendant's right to have a jury find beyond a reasonable doubt that she is guilty of each individual count. Thus, if the evidence of guilt for several homicides is quite strong, but that for another one is very weak, the jury may convict of all three without adequate individual consideration of each offense.

The case against joinder is even stronger if, under the Federal Rules of Evidence, evidence of one homicide would be inadmissible in the trial for the others. Joinder would permit the jurors to hear evidence of all homicides even though some of that proof is not to be considered in resolving some of the cases. At the least, this could be quite confusing to jurors and is unlikely to be cured by jury instructions directing the jurors how to use certain evidence.

146.    **Answer (A) is correct.** This question requires an analysis under the joinder of offenses provision of Rule 8(a), Federal Rules of Criminal Procedure. Rule 13

permits a *trial* joinder if Rule 8(a) permits a joinder of *offenses* in an indictment. Rule 8(a) permits joinder of offenses which are of the same or similar character or "based on the same act or transaction" or on "two or more acts . . . connected together or constituting part of a common scheme or plan."

Because the gun in question was found with the defendant who was also in possession of the drugs, this qualifies for joinder under Rule 8(a) since there is a strong connection between possessing a gun and the transportation of illegal drugs. The two are based on the "same act or transaction" and are part of a "common scheme or plan." Drug dealers often carry guns in order to protect their money, drugs, and personal safety. *See United States v. Mason*, 658 F.2d 1263 (9th Cir. 1981). If the gun had been found at Max's home some time later, arguably the two offenses could not be properly joined in one trial. United *States v. Terry*, 911 F.2d 272 (9th Cir. 1990).

**Answer (B) is incorrect** because Federal Rule of Criminal Procedure 8(a) allows joinder of only some offenses, not all offenses with which a person is charged. Answer B is too broad to be correct. The criteria of Rule 8(a) must be satisfied before joinder of offenses is permitted.

**Answer (C) is incorrect** because the court is allowed to consider the entire scheme or transaction or plan, even though the crimes are of a different character.

**Answer (D) is incorrect** because Rule 8 joinder does not involve discretionary relief from joinder because of prejudice. Rule 14, on the other hand, specifically authorizes relief from prejudicial joinder and would be the proper rule to seek a severance on this ground. Presumably Max would still have a chance with a Rule 14 motion.

147.    **Answer (A) is the best answer.** This question requires analysis under Rule 8(b), Federal Rules of Criminal Procedure. Rule 8(b) provides that offenders may be joined together if they participated in the "same act or transaction, or in the same series of acts or transactions." (Rule 8(a) deals with joinder of *offenses* rather than *offenders*.) The rule also provides that not all defendants need be charged together in each count of the indictment.

In this case, Answer (A) is the best answer because it puts Sarah and Ken together possibly discussing both computer crimes and gives prosecutors justification to charge them jointly for each crime. The two computer theft offenses may be part of the "same series of acts" since *modus operandi* was so sophisticated and similar. Moreover, the eyewitness may have seen Sarah and Ken discussing their method of hacking into the computers, rendering it more possible that the two bank jobs were part of the same "series of acts" under Rule 8(b).

**Answers (B) incorrect** because it is insufficient to show that the two defendants shopped in the same stores or knew each other. Neither fact is much help to the prosecutor in establishing under Rule 8(b) "the same series of acts or transactions."

**Answer (D) is not the best** answer though it carries a strong suggestion that Sarah and Ken might have conspired in planning the second credit card information theft, but there is no direct evidence linking the two. Similarity in methodology is very weak evidence of the necessary link required by Rule 8(b) to join offenders.

148. Based solely on the facts presented in this question, there are no reasonable grounds for the court to order separate trials. Rule 8(b), which deals with joinder of defendants and is the applicable rule, would appear to be satisfied since Herb and Donald clearly participated in the "same act or transaction" as shown by the arrest situation and the neighbor's identification. Rule 13 permits a joint *trial* if Rule 8 permits a joint *indictment*.

A slight possibility is a severance under Rule 14, which provides a discretionary remedy for prejudicial joinder. If Donald has confessed, implicating Herb, and the prosecution will use Donald's confession against Herb (but not against Donald pursuant to an agreement with Donald), perhaps a severance would be appropriate under Rule 14 because the joint trial could prejudice Donald. But in the facts presented, it is not even clear that Donald even gave a statement to the police. Herb might want to try to get information about any statements Donald made. To obtain this information, Herb's counsel could ask the judge to hold an *in camera* inspection of Donald's statement under Rule 14(b), ask the prosecutor to provide the statement informally, or use permissive or mandatory discovery rules. But with the facts in the question, joinder is very likely.

149. **Answer (C) is the best answer.** For Rule 14 prejudicial joinder motions, the movant has the burden of proving prejudice and courts set the bar fairly high. In *Zafiro v. United States*, 504 U.S. 534, 539 (1993), the United States Supreme Court described the standard of proof as presented in Answer (C).

**Answers (A) and (B) are incorrect** because the defendant makes the motion to sever and thus has the burden of proof. Under Rule 14, the trial judge ultimately has a hefty amount of discretion in determining joinder and severance issues.

**Answer (D) is not the best answer.** The language in Answer (C) is taken from *Zafiro v. United States*, 506 U.S. 534, 539 (1993), and is a more accurate choice than the lower "reasonable possibility" standard stated in Answer (D). The difference between Answers (C) and (D) illustrates that severance under Rule 14 requires the movant to make a substantial showing of prejudice.

150. **Answer (C) is the best answer,** though not a strong one. Rule 8(a) requires that for joinder of offenses the charges must be of the "same or similar character," "based on the same act or transaction," or "connected with or constitute parts of a common scheme or plan." Although the court may still deny a severance motion, Answer (C) shows that the bombs, evidencing significant technical differences, might not have been part of some common scheme, though admittedly the argument is not strong. Joinder is very likely in this case.

**Answer (A) is incorrect** because Rule 8 motions for improper joinder do not hinge on questions of fairness; that is the realm of Rule 14, which authorizes a severance to avoid prejudice to either party.

**Answer (B) is a trick answer** and not the best answer. The site of mailing is not important if the offenses were of the same or similar character or based on the same act or transaction or part of a common scheme or plan. Rule 8(a). The fact that the bombs were mailed from different locations may well indicate a plan to send the bombs while avoiding apprehension.

**Answer (D) is incorrect** because Rule 8 specifically states that felony and misdemeanor charges can be joined together.

**151.** This question concerns the elements of a valid complaint under Rule 3 of the Federal Rules of Criminal Procedure. The elements are: made under oath before a federal magistrate judge or, if a federal magistrate judge is unavailable, state judge. Case law adds an additional requirement: that the statement be signed by a U.S. Attorney.

**Answer (C) is correct.** Rule 3 requires a written statement made under oath of the essential facts and the charged offense(s), signed by a U.S. Attorney (case law). All these elements are satisfied in the scenario.

**Answer (A) is incorrect.** Rule 3 requires that the written statement must contain the "essential facts constituting the offense charged." This general statement lacks sufficient specificity to satisfy the "essential facts" standard. It also must have been signed by a U.S. Attorney, according to case law.

**Answer (B) is incorrect.** Rule 3 requires that the written statement be made under oath. No one swore to the validity of the information in the statement.

**Answer (D) is incorrect.** Rule 3 requires that the written statement of essential facts be made under oath, which did not occur in this case. It can be issued by a state or local judicial officer.

**152.** Rule 5(a)(1)(A) of the Federal Rules of Criminal Procedure states clearly that an officer arresting a person under a warrant must take that person "without unnecessary delay" before the nearest available federal magistrate judge or, in some cases, a state or local judicial officer for an initial appearance. This means that you must locate a judge and have Martin brought before that person without too great a delay. The vague "without unnecessary delay" tests of Rule 5(a) does allow some flexibility in the time of this process.

In addition to the timeliness of the initial appearance, you must also comply with the location requirement in Rule 5. Since Martin was arrested in the same federal district where the crime occurred, under Rule 5(c)(1), Martin should be brought to a judge in that district for the initial appearance.

**153.** Under the new facts, the crime occurred in the Eastern District of State A but Martin was arrested in the Western District of State A. Under Rule 5(c)(2), the initial appearance may be in the district of arrest (Western District) or in an adjacent district if the initial appearance could occur more promptly there.

**154.** If the arrest were made without a warrant, *Gerstein v. Pugh*, 420 U.S. 103 (1975), requires that the defendant be given a judicial hearing to assess probable cause for detention. This may be — and often is — combined with the initial appearance. *Gerstein* and later cases also mandate that the *Gerstein* probable cause hearing be held in timely fashion. *County of Riverside v. McLaughlin*, 500 U.S. 44 (1991), says ordinarily the *Gerstein* hearing should be held within 48 hours of arrest. After that time, the government bears the burden of showing why the excessive delay occurred.

**155.** **Answer (D) is correct.** There are several doctrines that come into play that make Answer (D) the correct answer. Courts are extremely reluctant to interfere with prosecutorial discretion. The separation of powers doctrine is cited frequently as the basis for this "hands-off" approach. In *Inmates of Attica v. Rockefeller*, 477 F.2d 375 (2d Cir. 1973), the leading case, the Second Circuit held that courts would not order prosecutions, even if a state investigation of inmate grievances showed strong evidence of criminal wrongdoing and even if a statute "required" prosecution.

**Answer (A) is not the best answer.** The *Attica* court and many others refuse to require the prosecution to make these discretionary decisions in good faith.

**Answer (B) is also not the best answer.** Courts virtually never interfere with the grand jury's discretion. In some jurisdictions a grand jury may return an indictment without the prosecutor's approval, and in a few states the state attorney general or governor may appoint a special prosecutor, but even in these jurisdictions the prosecutor may subsequently end the case by refusing to bring it to trial.

**Answer (C) is incorrect.** Some states have a mechanism to transfer responsibility of certain cases from local prosecutors to specially appointed prosecutors. This, however, is ordinarily an executive branch function, one that the courts rarely interfere with and that is beyond the scope of this question. Therefore, Answer (D) is the best answer.

The only situation where the courts may intervene in a prosecutor's decision not to prosecute is where there is some indication that the prosecutor was involved in selective prosecution on the basis of an unconstitutional criterion, such as race, religion, or other arbitrary classification. *See United States v. Armstrong*, 517 U.S. 456 (1996). To obtain discovery to establish this claim, *Armstrong* would require the defense first to make a "credible showing of different treatment of similarly situated persons." In the hypothetical above, there is no evidence that the prosecutor used an unconstitutional criterion.

**156.** **Answer (B) is correct.** If Claudio uses a bail bonding company, he will have to pay its fee, which is usually about ten percent of the total bond (*i.e.* $250 on a $2500 bond). Sometimes the bonding company also is permitted to charge various administrative fees as well. If Claudio shows up for all court appearances, he is not entitled to a refund from the bonding company. The ten percent fee is kept by the company.

**Answer (A) is incorrect** because if Claudio posts a cash bond of $2500, when he appears as required he will ordinarily get back all or most of the entire sum he deposited with the court.

**Answer (C) is incorrect** because the property bond means that Claudio's real property will be released from any lien after he appears for court proceedings. The property bond means simply that if he does not appear, the property he uses for the bond could, in theory, be sold to satisfy his obligations for the bond. If he does appear, his property interests remain intact.

**Answer (D) is incorrect** because an unsecured bond is simply a promise to pay a certain amount (here $2500) if Claudio does not appear at the required proceedings. When Claudio does appear, he will not pay any sums.

**157.** **Answer (B) is correct.** Under 18 U.S.C. § 3142, in the usual case the first choice is release on personal recognizance (or unsecured appearance bond).

**Answer (A) is incorrect** because release on conditions is to be used only if release on personal recognizance will not assure the appearance of the person or the safety of the community. 18 U.S.C. § 3142(c).

**Answer (C) is similarly incorrect** because release on a secured bond is a release condition that is disfavored by the priority rule in Answer (A) above.

**Answer (D) is incorrect** because temporary detention is authorized for someone on release from another offense, on probation or parole, or in the country illegally. 18 U.S.C. § 3142(d). Golda fits in none of the categories for which temporary detention is authorized.

**158.** **Answer (C) is correct** because the Bail Reform Act of 1984, 18 U.S.C. § 3142(f), requires that the judicial officer "by clear and convincing evidence" that no conditions will assure the safety of a person or the community.

**Answers (A), (B), and (D) are incorrect** because the standard is clear and convincing evidence rather than probable cause (Answer (A), preponderance of the evidence (B), or beyond a reasonable doubt (D)

**159.**    The Federal Bail Reform Act of 1984 contains authority to detain an offender until trial. This could occur if the judge finds that no condition or combination of conditions will reasonably assure the appearance of the person as required and the safety of any other person and the community. 18 U.S.C. § 3142(e). In some cases this Act creates a rebuttable presumption that the above test mandates detention. The exact criteria for this presumption are complicated and we will have to obtain more information about Merrriweather before the presumption applies.

One category of rebuttable presumption cases that could be relevant to Merriweather involves people charged with a crime of violence, serious drug offense, or with two previous convictions if they have a former conviction for a serious offense. They must have committed that offense while on release pending trial for still another offense. The former conviction must have occurred within the last five years since the date of conviction or release from imprisonment for that conviction. The second category of cases where there is a rebuttable presumption involves people charged with serious drug offenses or using a firearm during commission of a felony.

**160.**    You should reject defense counsel's argument. In *United States v. Salerno*, 481 U.S. 739 (1987), the United States Supreme Court upheld the Bail Reform Act's provision authorizing pretrial detention if no release conditions will reasonably assure the safety of any other person and the community. The Court rejected the argument that detention was only permissible for fear of flight. The *Salerno* opinion stressed that detention was regulatory, not punitive. The opinion also noted that the government's interest in preventing crime by arrestees is legitimate and compelling and may be more weighty than an individual's interests in pretrial freedom. Therefore, according to *Salerno*, the Due Process Clause does not bar the pretrial detention.

*Salerno* also held that pretrial detention does not violate the Eighth Amendment's excessive bail provision since the detention is not excessive when balanced against the evil of individual or community harm.

**161.**    **Answer (A) correct.** The Eighth Amendment states, "Excessive bail shall not be required. . . ."

**Answer (B) is incorrect.** It is well accepted that the Eighth Amendment does not create any right to release on bail and certainly does not bar the denial of bail.

**Answer (C) is incorrect** because the Eighth Amendment does not require that the poor cannot be incarcerated because of their inability to post money bail.

**Answer (D) is incorrect.** The Eighth Amendment also does not deal with the administration of the bail system. Thus, it does not deal at all with the use of professional bail bonding companies or with their power to apprehend people who abscond while on bail.

**Answer (E) is incorrect.**

**Answer (F) is incorrect** because the Eighth Amendment does not create any right to release on bail, so Answer (B) is incorrect.

162.  **Answer (A) is the best answer.** I, III, and IV are all appropriate actions in most jurisdictions that use a grand jury.

**Answers (B), (C), and (D) are therefore incorrect.** The grand jury procedure is controlled by the prosecutor who may resubmit a case to the same grand jury or a different grand jury. Like other constitutional rights, the right to a grand jury can be waived by the defendant. Thus, Mr. Farrell may waive the grand jury and agree to have the case prosecuted by information. In such an instance, the prosecutor would file an information which has the same legal status as an indictment or presentment returned by a grand jury.

**Answer (D) is incorrect** because jeopardy does not attach at the grand jury stage.

163.  **Answer (B) is correct.** Under Federal Rule of Criminal Procedure 6(f), a grand jury may indict only with the concurrence of at least twelve jurors. Therefore, **Answers (A), (C) and (D) are incorrect.**

164.  **Answer (D) is the only correct answer.** Under Federal Criminal Rule 6(a)(1), a federal grand jury must have 16-23 members.

Therefore, **Answers (A), (B) and (C) are incorrect.**

165.  The challenge will likely be unsuccessful. Although grand jury proceedings are, in general, considered to be conducted in secret, Federal Rule of Criminal Procedure Rule 6(d)(1) recognizes that some people other than grand jurors may be present to facilitate the orderly work of the grand jury. These include the federal prosecutor, a language interpreter when needed to assist the witness, and a court reporter.

166.  **Answer (C) is correct.** The defendant's request for a jury trial does not bar a preliminary hearing.

Under Federal Rule 5.1(a)(1) a federal defendant charged with an offense other than a petty offense is entitled to a preliminary hearing before a magistrate judge unless the defendant waives the hearing, the defendant is indicted, the government files an information charging the defendant with a felony or misdemeanor, or the defendant is charged with a misdemeanor and consents to a trial before a magistrate judge.

**Answers (A) is incorrect** because an indictment precludes a preliminary hearing.

**Answer (B) is incorrect** because a defendant is not entitled to a preliminary hearing if he or she waives it.

**Answer (D) is incorrect** since a valid information replaces a preliminary hearing.

167.    **Answer (A) is correct.** Rule 6(e)(2) of the Federal Rules of Criminal Procedure imposes a general obligation of secrecy on a list of people involved with a federal grand jury. Grand jury witnesses are not included in this list and are not subject to any duty of secrecy.

    **Answers (B), (C), and (D) are incorrect** because each of these categories of grand jury participants is specifically subjected to a general obligation of secrecy under Rule 6(e)(2).

168.    **Answer (D) is correct.** Under Federal Rule of Criminal Procedure 6(e), grand jury secrecy is not absolute. Disclosure is permitted to a number of people. Answer (D) is the best answer because the Rule does not authorize the indicted person to penetrate grand jury secrecy, although Rule 6(e)(3)(E)(ii) does permit the court to order disclosure to defense counsel upon a showing that grounds may exist for a motion to dismiss the indictment because of matters occurring before the grand jury.

    **Answers (A), (B), and (C) are incorrect.** Rule 6(e) specifically permits disclosure to an attorney for the government for use in performing her duties (Answer (A)), an investigator assisting that government lawyer (Answer (B)), and a state government official who is enforcing state law (Answer (C)).

169.    **Answer (C) is correct** (*i.e.*, it is untrue). It is the only answer that is untrue; all other responses are true. Rule 6(e) mandates that all grand jury proceedings must be recorded by a court reporter or other suitable recording device.

    **Answer (A) is incorrect** (*i.e.*, it is true) because the Federal Rules of Evidence do not apply to grand jury proceedings. See *Costello v. United States*, 350 U.S. 359 (1956); Federal Rule of Evidence 1101(d)(2) (Federal Rules of Evidence, other than privileges, do not apply in grand jury proceedings). Evidence inadmissible under the Federal Rules of Evidence may be heard and considered by grand jurors.

    **Answer (B) is incorrect** (*i.e.*, it is true) because Rule 6(e)(4) of the Federal Rules of Criminal Procedure specifically authorizes a sealed indictment.

    **Answer (D) is incorrect** (*i.e.*, it is true). Grand jury proceedings must not be recorded when the grand jury is deliberating or voting. Rule 6(e)(1).

170. **Answer (C) is correct.** Under Rule 7(f) of the Federal Rules of Criminal Procedure and similar rules in many jurisdictions, a Bill of Particulars is sought by defense counsel in order to obtain more information about a vague indictment.

**Answer (A) is incorrect** because this "bill" has nothing to do with money or a quantitative measure of professional services.

**Answer (B) is incorrect** because the Bill of Particulars is a request by the defense, not the prosecution.

**Answer (D) is incorrect** because a Bill of Particulars is only designed to assist the defense in preparing for trial, not for assisting the judge in his or her scheduling.

171. **Answer (B) is correct.** A federal felony (other than contempt) must be initiated by indictment. Rule 7(a).

**Answer (A) is incorrect** because an information may only be used in such cases if the offender waives indictment in open court. Rule 7(b). This would be impossible because of your goal of initiating proceedings without alerting Vito.

**Answers (C) and (D) are incorrect** since under Rule 58(b)(1) a complaint may be used to begin a misdemeanor prosecution and a citation is appropriate for a petty offense; neither is authorized for a felony.

172. **Answer (C) is correct.** A federal indictment need not be signed by defense counsel.

**Answers (A), (B), and (D) are incorrect.** Under Federal Rule of Criminal Procedure 7(c)(1), an indictment must be in writing (Answer (A)), cite the statute allegedly violated (Answer (B)), and be signed by an attorney for the government (Answer (D)).

173. A defendant who wants more detailed information than provided in the indictment may file a timely motion for a Bill of Particulars. Pursuant to Rule 7(f) of the Federal Rules of Criminal Procedure, the defendant may move for a Bill of Particulars before arraignment, within 10 days of arraignment or any time later that the court permits.

The primary function of the Bill of Particulars is to inform the defendant of the nature of the crimes against him or her. Specifically, it informs the defendant about the essential facts of the crimes for which the defendant has been indicted. The situation described in the question is a good illustration since the charges are so general that the defense does not know which specific acts are alleged to have violated federal criminal laws.

Additional helpful functions of the Bill of Particulars include enabling the defendant to prepare a defense, avoid double jeopardy, and lessen surprise for the defendant at trial.

174.  You will probably be unsuccessful. In *United States v. Williams*, 504 U.S. 36 (1992), the United States Supreme Court held that a prosecutor had no duty to provide the grand jury with exculpatory statements about the alleged crime. The Court noted that the grand jury's responsibility is not to determine guilt or innocence, but rather to assess whether the evidence provides an adequate basis to bring criminal charges. Neither the grand jury guarantee of the Fifth Amendment nor the Supreme Court's supervisory power mandates that prosecutors must disclose exculpatory evidence to the grand jury. The law in a few state, however, does obligate the prosecutor to share exculpatory information with grand jurors.

175.  **Answer (C) is clearly correct.** An indictment is not mandatory for prosecution of a crime punishable by a prison sentence of one year or less, making Answer (C) the correct choice. Federal Rule of Criminal Procedure7(a)(1)(B).

      **Answers (A) and (B) are incorrect.** Under Federal Rule of Criminal Procedure 7(a), an indictment, unless waived, is required for the prosecution of a crime punishable by death or imprisonment for more than one year.

      **Answer (D) is not the best answer.** Though it is true that virtually all federal felonies must be initiated by an indictment (unless waived), the yardstick is the maximum *punishment*, not whether the crime is a felony or misdemeanor. If the punishment — irrespective of the category of the crime — is more than one year in prison, an indictment is needed.

176.  The success of your challenge will depend on state rather than federal law. The United States Supreme Court in *Hurtado v. California*, 110 U.S. 516 (1884), held that the Fifth Amendment's grand jury guarantee does not apply to the states. Therefore, states do not have to utilize a grand jury and a large number have rejected this procedure.

      As a matter of state constitutional or statutory law, however, a number of states have retained the right to a grand jury, at least in felony cases. The challenge to the use of an information rather than an indictment for your client will hinge on whether state law mandated an indictment in this particular type of case. The facts in the question suggest that your state has not adopted the grand jury as part of its criminal justice process.

**177.** **Answer (D) is correct.** Federal Rule 47(b) indicates that a motion must ordinarily be in writing unless made during a trial or hearing or excused by the trial judge. Thus, **answer (B) is incorrect** since an in-trial motion may be oral and not a reason to deny the oral motion. Similarly, **Answer (C) is incorrect** because a motion necessitated by in-trial events need not be filed pretrial.

**Answer (A) is not correct** because it is a viable reason to have the motion denied since both the defendant and public have a right to attend a trial, subject to exceptions for a strong public interest.

**178.** Rule 12, Federal Rules of Criminal Procedure, provides a list of motions that must be filed pretrial.

**Answer (A) is correct** because Rule 12 does not establish a time limit for a Motion to Admit Victim's Prior Criminal Records. The judge, of course, may use his or her inherent authority to impose a time limit for filing such motions.

**Answers (B), (C), and (D) are incorrect** because Federal Rule of Criminal Procedure 12(b) specifically says that a Motion to Suppress Evidence (Answer (B)), Motion to Sever Charges (Answer (C)), and Motion to Dismiss Indictment (Answer (D)) must be raised prior to trial.

**179.** To: Judge Neophyte

From: Law Clerk

Re: Motions

Dear Judge,

Motion practice in criminal cases is very different from those filed in civil cases. There are no specific lists of available motions spelled out in the Federal Rules of Criminal Procedure. Criminal lawyers are generally free to use whatever caption and motion text best serves their needs that adequately states the relief they seek.

With that being said, it would be impossible to prepare a short list of the exact motions that you will be asked to rule on because such a list would be bounded only by the creativity of the local criminal bar. In general, however, you can expect exclusionary motions (to exclude confessions, searches, etc.), bail motions, motions to modify or dismiss indictments, motions to compel discovery, and, most frequently, motions for a continuance. You can also expect many motions that embrace several or none of these broad categories.

**180.** One option, of course, is to spend the weekend preparing to argue against the Motion to Suppress. This would please the judge but could compromise your case if you are unable to prepare adequately over the weekend.

Another option is to request a total continuance or at least a continuance of the hearing on the confession issue. This would give you time to prepare your response to the new motion, but might well anger the judge who does not like continuances. Under the second option, you would have to present the judge with the facts and convince him or her that you were not in any way at fault in needing more time to respond to the Motion to Suppress. Perhaps the judge would need to know that your case could be seriously weakened if the confession were suppressed. You might also suggest that the defense counsel was at fault in not preparing and submitting the Motion in time for you to prepare to meet it.

**181.** **Answer (C) is correct.** A motion in limine is a pre-trial motion that allows the court fully to adjudicate likely "hot button" issues at trial. Since this motion is filed and may be resolved before trial, both parties are on notice about the court's ruling on the issue and, if the ruling excludes the evidence, may be required to instruct their witnesses that they may not talk about the excluded issue.

**Answer (A) is incorrect.** This approach might not work because even the most attentive lawyer may not rise to object before the opposing party or a witness begins to discuss a sensitive topic in front of the jury.

**Answer (B) is incorrect** because the arrest may well be brought up by prosecution witnesses, such as the investigating officer, on direct examination. Accordingly, defense counsel's decision to avoid such questions will not necessarily prevent the issue from being raised.

**Answer (D) is incorrect** because such questions of law are ultimately for the court to decide and you have a duty to zealously defend your client and bring to the court's attention any tactically wise motion that could assist your client and is ethically permissible.

**182.** **Answer (A) is correct.** The movant, in this case the trial-level defense attorney, has the duty not only to file a motion but also to demand that the court act on it. In reality, a defendant may file many motions, some of which may be overlooked or ignored by the court. Therefore a party must bring to the court's attention any motion that it would like the court to resolve. Appellate courts generally will not rule on matters not originally considered by the trial judge.

**Answer (B) is incorrect** because there is no error in this case on the part of the court. Each party must see to it that its motions are heard.

**Answer (C) is incorrect** because the issue was waived when it was not taken up originally in the trial court. However an appellate court could very well order this in the interests of fundamental fairness or upon a showing of ineffective assistance of counsel at trial. The appellate court could also deem it "plain error" under Federal Rule of Criminal Procedure 52(b) and consider the issue despite trial counsel's failure to request a ruling on the unresolved motion.

**Answer (D) is incorrect** because an appellate court in virtually all instances will not consider an issue until it is fully adjudicated at the trial court level. Of course the court could consider it under plain error, as described above.

183. **Answer (D) is correct.** Obviously the outcome to this situation may very somewhat between jurisdictions and individual courts. However, in the absence of a local rule to the contrary, under the Federal Rules of Criminal Procedure (which are silent on the issue) prosecutors are generally free to offer only oral responses to defense motions. Given a typical prosecutor's large caseload, many do not respond in writing to every filed motion when most defendants will end up pleading guilty anyway. Naturally some trial courts in certain cases will encourage and even require written responses in especially complex matters.

**Answer (A) is incorrect** because the Federal Rules of Criminal Procedure do not give any restrictions on the timeliness of objection and rebuttal. Again, a local judge or the local court rules may impose such restrictions but the Federal Rules of Criminal Procedure do not.

**Answer (B) is incorrect** because there does not appear to be any nonfeasance on the part of the prosecutor's office, absent a local rule requiring a written response to defense motions.

**Answer (C) is also incorrect** because the Federal Rules of Criminal Procedure impose no requirement to file a timely written objection to a motion. Again, local court rules may require a written response to all or certain motions.

184. Under Federal Rule of Criminal Procedure 29, a Motion for Judgment of Acquittal (formerly known as a motion for directed verdict) may be made virtually any time during the trial. Rule 29 states that it may be made after the evidence for either side is closed, after the jury returns a guilty verdict or is discharged without having returned a verdict, or even within seven days after the jury is discharged or a guilty verdict is rendered.

Rule 29(b) gives the judge significant latitude in when there must be a ruling on a Motion for Judgment of Acquittal. The court may rule on the Motion when it is made or may reserve decision until before the jury returns a verdict. The judge also has the option of resolving the Motion after the jury returns a verdict of guilty or is discharged without having returned the verdict.

185. **Answer (C) is correct.** Rule 33(a) specifically authorizes the trial judge to vacate a conviction and grant a new trial "if the interest of justice so requires."

**Answers (A), (B), and (D) are incorrect.** Although the violations listed in Answers (A), (B), and (D) may well convince a court to vacate a judgment "in the interest of justice," those answers do not correctly describe the vague standard adopted in Rule 33(a).

186. **Answer (C) is correct.** Federal Rule of Criminal Procedure 33(b) establishes two specific time limits for filing a Motion for New Trial. If the Motion is based on newly discovered evidence, as in the above question, the Motion must be filed

within three years after the verdict or finding of guilty.

**Answers (A), (B), and (D) are incorrect** because they misstate Rule 33(b)'s three-year limit. It should be noted that Rule 33(b) sets a far shorter time limit for filing a Motion for New Trial for reasons other than newly discovered evidence. For these other grounds, the Motion must be filed within seven days after the verdict or finding of guilty, unless the court sets another time limit.

187.   The Motion for Judgment of Acquittal (Rule 29) is granted when the evidence at trial was insufficient to sustain the conviction. Thus, it involves ending a trial or second-guessing the jury's decision after a guilty verdict is given.

The Motion for a New Trial (Rule 33) is permitted "if the interest of justice so requires." The grounds are open-ended, but may include newly discovered evidence.

The Motion in Arrest of Judgment (Rule 34) narrowly authorizes a judgment to be "arrested' (1) if the indictment or information does not charge an offense or (2) if the court does not have jurisdiction over the crime.

**188.** Terence has a Sixth Amendment right to have "compulsory process for obtaining witnesses in his favor." While this right is subject to reasonable limits, the one subpoena rule probably violates it in the context of Terence's case. *Washington v. Texas*, 388 U.S. 14 (1967), and other Supreme Court cases provide that an accused has a right to present witnesses to establish a defense. In *Washington* the defendant was unconstitutionally denied the right to call a codefendant as a witness who would testify that the defendant was not present when the fatal shot was fired.

**189.** **Answer (C) is correct.** Under Rule 17(a) of the Federal Rules of Criminal Procedure, a subpoena is issued by the court clerk, under the seal of the court.

**Answers (A) and (B) are incorrect.** A judge or prosecutor may also order a subpoena, but, once again, the subpoena is actually issued by the court clerk as part of the clerk's administrative duties.

**Answer (D) is incorrect.** Even though the defense lawyer may have the subpoena served on a defense witness, the subpoena is still issued by the court clerk.

**190.** **Answer (C) is correct.** Under Federal Rule of Criminal Procedure 17(a) the clerk must issue the subpoena in blank. The prosecutor would fill in the name of the person subpoenaed and the clerk's office would not have a record of that name.

**Answer (A) is not the best choice** since the prosecutor may have a subpoena issued in blank which will protect the identity of the witness who is subpoenaed.

**Answers (B) and (D) are incorrect** because the clerk's office does not maintain a record of the people who are subpoenaed. The subpoenas are issued in blank.

191.    **Answer (C) is correct.** Under Federal Rule of Criminal Procedure 25, if a judge becomes disabled during a federal trial, another judge may proceed with the trial "upon certifying familiarity with the record of the trial."

       **Answers (A) and (B) are incorrect** because the trial may continue with or without the consent of the lawyers or the accused.

       **Answer (D) is incorrect** because Rule 25 specifically permits the rest of the trial to be conducted by a substitute judge.

192.    **Answer (A) is correct.** Under Rule 25(b) of the Federal Rules of Criminal Procedure, after a defendant is found guilty another regularly sitting judge may handle the remaining judicial responsibilities in the case if the judge who presided in the trial is absent, dead or otherwise disabled.

       **Answer (B) is incorrect** since under Rule 25(b) a new judge may complete the sentencing part of the trial even though he or she did not preside over the trial.

       **Answer (C) is incorrect.** Judge Al-Haftiri does not have to handle the sentencing; another judge may do so under Rule 25(b).

       **Answer (D) is incorrect.** There is no limit on the sentence that the new judge could impose.

| TOPIC 64 | ANSWERS |
|---|---|
| **PLEAS AND PLEA BARGAINING** | |

193.   A criminally accused person may want to plead no contest (also called a nolo contendere plea) to avoid prejudice in a subsequent civil or criminal case. The no contest plea does not affect the sentence in the instant criminal case since it has the same effect as a guilty plea. The primary advantage of a no contest plea is that in most jurisdictions such a plea or the resulting conviction would not be admissible in a later civil or criminal case to prove liability. Federal Rules of Evidence 410 and 803(22).

Some states do not allow nolo contendere pleas at all and the rest give the judge broad discretion in agreeing to accept or reject a nolo contendere plea.

194.   **Answer (D) is correct** because Rule 11(f) provides that: "[t]he admissibility or inadmissibility of a plea, a plea discussion, and any related statement is governed by Federal Rule of Evidence 410," which renders a nolo contendere inadmissible in a subsequent trial but admits an accepted plea of guilty as evidence.

**Answer (A) is incorrect** because, when withdrawing either a guilty plea or nolo contendere after the court accepts the plea but before sentencing, the defendant is required to "show a fair and just reason for requesting the withdrawal" pursuant to Rule 11(d)(B).

**Answer (B) is incorrect** because Rule 11(b)(2) states: "[b]efore accepting a plea of guilty or nolo contendere, the court must address the defendant personally in open court and determine that the plea is voluntary and did not result from force, threats, or promises (other than promises in a plea agreement)."

**Answer (C) is incorrect** because Rule 11(c)(1) states: "[t]he court must not participate in [plea agreement] discussions." Thus, the court cannot inform the defendant of the benefits of a nolo contendere plea during plea negotiations.

195.   **Answer (B) is correct.** Under Federal Rules of Criminal Procedure 11(c)(3)(A) and 11(c)(5), the court may accept or reject the plea agreement. It may not accept the guilty plea but then reject the plea agreement that induced the plea. Accordingly, Kimberly is free to withdraw his guilty plea if any part of the plea agreement is disapproved by the court. Moreover, such a withdrawal of a guilty plea is generally not admissible in any civil or criminal court. Federal Rule of Criminal Procedure 11(f) indicates that the admissibility of a plea is determined by Federal Rule of Evidence 410, which makes it clear that a withdrawn guilty plea is inadmissible, against the defendant who made the plea, in any civil or criminal proceeding.

**Answer (A) is incorrect** because it indicates, incorrectly, that the attempted guilty plea is admissible.

**Answer (C) is incorrect** because the plea may be withdrawn if the plea agreement is not accepted by the court.

**Answer (D) is incorrect** because trial judges do not have to accept any plea agreement. But if a court rejects a plea agreement of the type offered Kimberly, it must allow the accused to withdraw the plea made pursuant to the rejected agreement.

196.    **Answer (A) is correct.** The general rule is that the prosecution must live up to its plea agreements. *Santobello v. New York*, 404 U.S. 257 (1971). If Fred fully adhered to his end of the bargain, the prosecutor must live up to her part. Since the facts in this hypothetical do not indicate clearly whether or not Fred "fully cooperated," the court should make a factual inquiry to resolve the issue. If Fred did satisfy his responsibilities, the prosecutor must recommend the lower sentence or, if the prosecutor refuses to do so, the court must sentence Fred to the lower term.

**Answer (B) is incorrect** because plea agreements are generally viewed as contractual-type arrangements. If Fred met his duties under the plea agreement, the prosecutor must meet hers.

**Answer (C) is incorrect** because courts can and often do inquire into the nature of a plea agreement and interpret it if need be. The court can also reject an offered plea agreement. A court, however, normally cannot become a part of the plea negotiation process. Federal Rules of Criminal Procedure 11(c)(1) (the court must not participate in plea agreement discussions).

**Answer (D) is incorrect** because it is not clear whether the prosecutor lived up to the letter of the plea agreement. Moreover, even if the prosecution violated the agreement, the remedy is not dismissal of the case. It would be either enforcement of the agreement or allowing Fred to withdraw his plea. However, if Fred has already complied fully with his part of the deal, the remedy of specific performance may be most appropriate.

197.    **Answer (B) is correct.** The United States Supreme Court has held there is no constitutional prohibition against having criminal defendants who face a jury serve longer prison sentences. *Brady v. United States*, 397 U.S. 742 (1970).

**Answer (A) is therefore incorrect.**

**Answers (C) and (D) are incorrect.** Although Answers (C) and (D) are good arguments, Answer (B) is the best answer because it explains the legal justification for this effect.

198.    **Answer D is correct.** Courts have long recognized that co conspirators do not necessarily have to be convicted of consistent verdicts or outcomes. In this case, Bobby made a fair bargain that avoided any possibility of a long prison sentence. He will, therefore, be held to the bargain he made regardless of how other trials come out.

**Answer A is incorrect** because inconsistent convictions are allowable.

**Answer B is incorrect** because the fundamental fairness doctrine would not apply here. Bobby voluntarily entered a plea to avoid the risk of a harsh sentence. Fundamental fairness was not violated.

**Answer C is incorrect** because the plea bargain process does not require knowledge of the ultimate result of all proceedings. All it requires is that the plea was made knowingly, intelligently, and voluntarily under the circumstances

199.  **Answer (B) is correct.** Chances are this is merely harmless error. Most courts are very skeptical about allowing defendants to change their mind once a plea is accepted. This case would be decided under the two-part *Strickland* test. *Strickland v. Washington*, 466 U.S. 668 (1984). The court will first determine if the lawyer's assistance fell below an objective standard of reasonableness. If it did, the court will then determine if any deficiencies on the part of counsel might have actually produced a different outcome.

In this case the court is likely to conclude that there would not have been a different outcome. Jack would have pled guilty even had he been informed of the new registration and publicity rules. The relatively lenient probation sentence balanced against the real risk of a thirty-year sentence and a hostile jury would probably have overcome any concerns about the new law.

**Answer (A) is incorrect** because a lawyer should advise a client about all foreseeable consequences before recommending a course of action, regardless of whether they have anything to do with sentencing itself or not. Jack's ignorance of this law, by itself, will not bar his efforts to allege his lawyer should have informed him about the new law.

**Answer (C) is incorrect** because a court is not obligated to inform the defendant of every negative consequence of a guilty plea. Federal Rule of Criminal Procedure 11(b) provides a list of topics the court must address with the defendant. The new law involving sex offender registration and publicity is not included in that list. That is the job of the defense attorney. The court is required to inform the defendant only about the most noteworthy rights that he or she gives up when pleading guilty.

**Answer (D) is incorrect** because a criminal defense lawyer should apprize his or her clients about laws that will markedly affect the lives of their clients who plead guilty. Failure to do so, however, will not automatically establish ineffective assistance of counsel, as noted in the explanation of Answer (A) above.

200.  **Answer (D) is correct.** Despite the harsh result, the United States Supreme Court has held that prosecutors have virtually unfettered discretion to pursue any charges they choose to pursue. *See Bordenkircher v. Hayes*, 434 U.S. 357 (1978). The theory is that the trial court and the jury serve as a vital check on this authority and may refuse to convict or may convict on lesser charges if they so choose. Although a prosecutor has a great deal of power over what charges are brought, the defendant is protected because the prosecutor must still obtain a

conviction and the court must follow the law in setting the sentence. Both the trial and sentence may be challenged on appeal. Details of the plea bargaining process are generally irrelevant to appellate courts reviewing a particular case where no plea was entered and the case was resolved by a trial.

**Answers (A) and (C) are therefore incorrect.**

**Answer (B) is incorrect** because there is no legal ground to overturn the sentence and allow Kenny the opportunity to accept the original two year offer. Kenny had a chance to do so and turned it down. The prosecutor's decision to seek a three-strikes sentence was within his discretion even though his motives are less than admirable.

201.  **Answer (A) is correct** (it expresses an inaccurate standard). If the trial court has not yet accepted Marybeth's plea, under Rule 11(d)(1) she may withdraw it "for any reason or no reason." Thus, the standard of "a substantial reason that serves the interests of justice" is too high and incorrect.

**Answer (B) is incorrect** (because it expresses an accurate standard). Under Rule 11(d)(2)(A), if the plea is accepted but sentence has not yet been imposed, the defendant may withdraw the plea if the court rejects the agreement to dismiss charges in exchange for a guilty plea.

**Answer (C) is incorrect** (because it expresses an accurate standard). Under Rule 11(d)(2)(B), if the plea is accepted but sentence has not been imposed, the defendant may withdraw the plea if the defendant can show a "fair and just reason for requesting the withdrawal."

**Answer (D) is incorrect** (because it expresses an accurate standard). Under Rule 11(e), after the court accepts a plea and imposes sentence, the defendant may not withdraw the plea. He or she may only have it set aside on direct appeal or collateral attack.

202.  You should inform your judge that the defendant is seeking to enter an *Alford* or "best-interests" plea. According to the Supreme Court in *North Carolina v. Alford*, 400 U.S. 25 (1970), the judge has the discretion to accept or reject this type of plea.

If the plea is rejected, the court should schedule a trial to decide whether the defendant is guilty or innocent. If the court accepts the plea, the judge could follow Rule 11, particularly with regard to establishing a factual basis for the plea.

203.  In a minority of American courts, such as that in the question, a defendant will have to either plead guilty and admit to the crime under oath or go to trial. In these locales a defendant may not plead guilty and deny guilt at the same time.

States are free to set their own requirements for permitting a trial court to accept a guilty plea, including the requirement to waive the Fifth Amendment and admit guilt. There is no federal constitutional right to enter an *Alford* or "best interests" plea where the defendant pleads guilty but denies being guilty. *See North Carolina v. Alford*, 400 U.S. 25 (1970).

**204.** **Answer (C) is correct.** Dora wants to enter an *Alford* or "best interests" plea. This plea was approved by the United States Supreme Court in *North Carolina v. Alford*, 400 U.S. 25 (1970). Though the defendant denies guilt, the plea is a guilty plea and authorizes the court to impose sentence as with any other guilty plea.

**Answer (A) is incorrect** because an *Alford* plea leads to a conviction that may be admissible later.

**Answer (B) is incorrect.** A defendant whose *Alford* plea is accepted by the court is convicted, and the plea has the same effect and consequences as any other kind of guilty plea.

**Answer (D) is incorrect** because an *Alford* plea is not a no contest or nolo contendere plea.

**205.** **Answer (A) is correct.** The rule of *caveat emptor* applies (let the buyer beware). The prosecutor should never have offered a deal not knowing whether the children were dead or alive. Viktor appears to have complied with his part of the bargain.

**Answer (B) is incorrect** because of the vague "offer" Viktor was not required to indicate whether the victims were living or deceased. Viktor accepted the offer that was put out on the table.

**Answer (C) is incorrect** because there is a valid offer and acceptance, the necessary elements of a plea.

**Answer (D) is incorrect** because the deal is not voidable error. The defendant has fully complied with his part of the deal and the government must do so as well.

**Answer (E) is incorrect.** Even though the deal had not been accepted by the court, the defendant fully complied with his part of the deal and the government must as well.

**206.** **Answer (C) is correct.** Even though there may be some deviation from the most recent local guilty plea script, a plea entered in federal court will be valid if it complies with Federal Criminal Procedure Rule 11 and other federal law. There is no independent legal significance to the particular script a court chooses to use. Conversely, the plea entry is not necessarily insulated from future challenge even if an approved local script is used verbatim. Furthermore, a plea entry may be valid even if the wrong script or no script is used, if the rules of criminal procedure are actually followed.

**Answers (A) and (D) are incorrect** because noncompliance with a local rule or custom will not automatically invalidate an otherwise valid plea proceeding.

**Answer (B) is incorrect** because the proceeding using the outdated script may have involved reversible error in the text of the unapproved script. The question contains no facts indicating whether or not the error was harmless.

**207.** **Answer (C) is correct.** A guilty plea does not waive the defendant's Sixth Amendment right to the effective assistance of counsel.

**Answers (A), (B), and (D) are incorrect.** A guilty plea, however, routinely involves a waiver of jury trial (Answer (A)), confrontation (Answer (B)), and self-incrimination (Answer (D)). *See* Federal Rule of Criminal Procedure 11(b)(1).

208.    **Answer (D) is correct.** Rule 11 of the Federal Rules of Criminal Procedure does not mention a reserved plea as an option, although some federal courts use their inherent authority and permit defendants to reserve the plea. This essentially postpones the entry of the plea until a later date, perhaps to allow plea bargaining between the defense counsel and the prosecutors. If the accused who reserved a plea later chooses to enter one, he or she must choose between those authorized by Rule 11(a)(1).

**Answers (A), (B), and (C) are incorrect.** Rule 11(a)(1) specifically authorizes a guilty plea (Answer (A)), not guilty plea (Answer (B)), and nolo contendere plea (Answer (C)).

209.    **Answer (C) is correct.** Under Rule 11(a)(2) of the Federal Rules of Criminal Procedure, an accused may enter a conditional guilty plea, reserving the right to appeal an adverse determination by the trial court. The court and government must consent to this.

**Answer (A) is incorrect** because the guilty plea effectively waives the search issue, rendering it highly unlikely the appellate court would reverse on this ground.

**Answer (B) is incorrect** because it deprives Kyle of the favorable plea offer and exposes him to a potential sentence far harsher than that offered in plea negotiations.

**Answer (D) is incorrect** because it deprives the accused of the possibility that an appellate court will suppress the drugs. If the drugs are ruled inadmissible, Kyle could possibly have the charges dropped, win an acquittal at trial, or at least get an especially favorable plea deal from a prosecutor who has lost the use of critical evidence.

210.    **Answer (A) is correct.** Under Rule 11 of the Federal Rules of Criminal Procedure, the court has many obligations during plea proceedings. Answer (A) is correct, however, since the court does not have to ensure that defense counsel thoroughly worked up the case.

**Answer (B) is incorrect** because the court must ensure that the plea is voluntary. Rule 11(b)(2).

**Answer (C) is incorrect** because the court must ensure that there is a factual basis for the plea. Rule 11(b)(3).

**Answer (D) is incorrect** because the court must inform the defendant of the maximum possible penalty, even if the maximum exceeds that agreed on by the parties as part of the plea deal. Rule 11(b)(1)(H).

211.    **Answer (C) is correct.** Under Federal Criminal Procedure Rule 11(a)(2), the government must consent if the accused is to be permitted to enter a conditional

plea.

**Answers (A), (B), and (D) are incorrect** because, under Rule 11(a), the accused may enter a guilty, not guilty, or nolo contendere plea irrespective of the presence of absence of the government's consent. The court, though not the prosecuting attorney, must consent before a nolo plea is entered. Rule 11(a)(1).

212.   A criminal accused who pleads guilty waives many important constitutional rights. These rights are outlined in Federal Rule of Criminal Procedure 11(b), where the accused must be apprized of the rights waived by the plea.

The rights include the rights to: plead not guilty, have a trial, impanel a jury, be represented by effective counsel at the trial and during appeal of many issues, confront and cross-examine adverse witnesses, issue compulsory process to obtain witnesses at a trial, assert a Fifth Amendment right not to be compelled to testify at trial, testify in his or her own defense and present evidence at a trial, and, with the exception of a few issues, the right to appeal the conviction or sentence.

**213.** **Answer (C) is correct.** Though the order of proceedings in federal criminal cases does not necessarily follow a consistent pattern (for example, the defendant may be indicted, *then* arrested, etc.), if all procedures are followed the grand jury routinely considers a case *after* the preliminary examination, arrest, and initial appearance.

**Answer (D) is incorrect.** The preliminary examination is held ordinarily 10-20 days after the initial appearance, according to Rule 5.1(c), making it the third event in the sequence. The grand jury is held after the preliminary examination.

**Answer (A) is incorrect** because an arrest would occur first.

**Answer (B) incorrect.** The initial appearance ordinarily occurs shortly after an arrest according to Federal Rule of Criminal Procedure 5, but before the preliminary examination and the grand jury.

**214.**    To: Boss

From: Law Clerk 1

1. Failure to satisfy Rule 12.2 of the Federal Rules of Criminal Procedure may bar us from raising the insanity defense. Rule 12.2(a).

2. To satisfy Rule 12.2, at the time for filing pretrial motions (unless this deadline is changed by the court), we must notify the prosecutor in writing (with a copy filed with the court clerk) of our intention to rely upon an insanity defense. Rule 12.2(a).

3. Similarly, if we plan on using expert testimony relating to a mental condition bearing upon guilt, we must also provide notice similar to that outlined above. Rule 12.2(b).

4. After this notice is filed if the government so moves, the court may order our client to be examined by certain mental health professionals. Rule 12.2(c). Our client must submit to the exam or we may be barred from introducing our own expert testimony on our client's mental status. Rule 12.2(d). Although this procedure will subject our client to a mental evaluation that might not support an insanity defense, the process has the advantage of providing us with a free mental evaluation. The expert conducting the evaluation may not testify about any statements made by the defendant during the examination, except on an issue concerning mental condition on which our client has introduced testimony.

5. If we change our mind and withdraw either the notice to use an insanity defense or the notice to use expert testimony, the notice we originally gave is not admissible against our client. Rule 12.2(e).

**215.**    **Answer (D) is correct.** Rule 12.1 does not require the government to show the defense its entire investigative file whenever the defense offers an alibi defense. Of course under *Brady v. Maryland* the prosecution must provide the defense with information about witnesses who will support the alibi defense.

**Answer (A) is incorrect.** Rule 12.1(a)(1) requires that the government request in writing notice of the defendant's intent to present an alibi defense.

**Answer (B) is incorrect** because Rule 12.1(a)(1) states that the government's request for notice of an alibi defense must include a statement of the time, date, and place of the carjacking.

**Answer (C) is incorrect.** Rule 12.1(b)(1) requires the government, after the defense has provided notice of an intent to use an alibi defense, to inform the defendant of the names, address, and telephone number of government witnesses to be called to establish the defendant's presence at the carjacking.

216.    **Answer (B) is correct.** One of the primary reasons for disclosure is to prevent surprises and surprise tactics at trial. Both Rules 12.1(f) and 12.2(e) prevent the admissibility of a withdrawn notice against the party withdrawing it.

**Answer (A) is incorrect.** Rule 12.2 on the insanity defense is initiated by the defense, while Rule 12.1 is initiated by the prosecution.

**Answer (C) is incorrect.** Again, choice (II) is not correct for the alibi defense, which is triggered by the government, not the defendant.

**Answer (D) is incorrect.** Choices (I) and (IV) are correct, rendering answer (D) incorrect.

217.    The failure to comply with Rule 12.1, notice of alibi defense, depends on which side did not comply and at what stage the noncompliance occurred. Since Rule 12.1 is triggered by a government written request for notice of an intent to offer an alibi defense, if the government fails to make the request, the defense is not obligated to provide alibi information in advance of trial. If the defense fails to respond adequately to the government request, under Rule 12.1 it is not entitled to have the government disclose the names and addresses of its own location witnesses. Similarly, if either party does not comply with its obligations under Rule 12.1, the court is authorized to exclude the testimony of the undisclosed witness.

For Rule 12.2, if the defendant fails to provide notice of an intent to use an insanity defense under Rule 12.2(b) or to submit to an examination under 12.2(C), the court may exclude expert evidence on the issue of the defendant's mental disability and may even exclude an insanity defense itself if there is a failure to notify of an intent to present this defense.

**218.**    **Answer (B) is correct.** In the federal system and that of many states, the prosecutor actually makes two closing arguments. Federal Rule of Criminal Procedure 29.1 states clearly that the prosecution gives the first closing argument, then defense counsel gives her closing, then the prosecutor is given a chance to rebut the defense's closing argument.

   **Answers (A) and (C) are not the best answers,** although neither is totally incorrect. Under Rule 29.1 the prosecutor does address the jury before the defense closing and then again after the defense closing.

   **Answer (D) is incorrect** because it is unlikely that a court would permit a prosecutor to make a jury argument when the jury returns to the courtroom to have a question resolved.

219. Rule 30 of the Federal Rules of Criminal Procedure prescribes the steps necessary to present a proposed jury instruction. First, Colon must request the instructions in writing. The request should indicate the exact language Colon wants the judge to use.

Second, the request must be timely. Rule 30(a) provides that the request must be made at the close of evidence, unless Judge Huang has established an earlier, reasonable time.

Finally, Colon, as the requesting party, must provide every other party with a copy of her written request.

220. **Answer (C) is correct.** Rule 30(b) requires Judge Huang to rule on the request and so inform the parties before their closing arguments. This will enable the parties to use the ruling in fashioning their closing arguments.

**Answers (A) is incorrect** since a ruling on jury instructions could not be given as early as during a pretrial evidentiary hearing.

**Answer (B) is incorrect** because jury instructions are not finalized until after the evidence is presented by both sides. Developments during the defense case may have to be dealt with in the jury instructions.

**Answer (D) is incorrect** since Rule 30(b) requires a ruling before closing statements so the parties may use the actual jury instructions in their closings.

221. Rule 30(d) states that a party objecting to any portion of the jury instructions or, as in this case, a failure to give a jury instruction must inform the court of the specific objection and the grounds for the objection. In order to give the judge an opportunity to correct any error, the objection must be made before the jury retires to deliberate.

To protect the jury from being confused and to avoid any possible prejudice to the parties, Rule 30 further says that Judge Huang must give Colon an opportunity to make this objection out of the jury's hearing and, upon her request, the jury's presence. A failure to follow this procedure will ordinarily bar appellate review of the jury instruction issue.

222. **Answer (A) is correct.** An "Allen charge" (sometimes referred to as the "dynamite charge"), named after the Supreme Court's decision in *Allen v. United States*, 164 U.S. 492 (1896), is a jury instruction given to a deadlocked jury. Designed to encourage the jurors to reach a decision, it instructs the jurors that it is their duty to decide the case and it tells jurors to listen to the opinions of others and give those opinions appropriate deference. More particularly, it urges jurors holding a minority position to reassess the correctness of their views. [Some jurisdictions reject the concept or wording of the federal Allen charge, characterizing it as coercive. *E.g., State v. Howard*, 537 N.E.2d 188 (Ohio 1989)]

**Answer (B) is incorrect** because an *Allen* charge has nothing to do with allowing lawyers to address the jury.

**Answer (C) is incorrect** because the *Allen* instruction mandates more deliberation. It is not a fine imposed on jurors who prevent a unanimous verdict.

**Answer (D) is incorrect** since the *Allen* charge concerns resolving a deadlock rather than dealing with an impropriety.

223. **Answer (A) is correct.** The primary criticism is that it coerces the minority into agreeing with the minority, thus, in practice, increasing guilty verdicts, decreasing hung juries, and depriving people with minority views of the full measure of their independence.

**Answer (B) is incorrect** because the real brunt of *Allen* is to coerce the minority jurors, not the majority ones.

**Answer (C) is incorrect** because an *Allen* charges produces more convictions than acquittals. The minority jurors asked to reconsider their votes are routinely holdouts for acquittal rather than conviction.

**Answer (D) is incorrect** since the *Allen* charged is designed to reduce the number of hung juries, not increase their number.

**224.** **Answer (C) is correct** (*i.e.*, it is untrue). No jury participates in a preliminary examination; the judge alone conducts the hearing and decides all questions of fact.

**Answers (A), (B), and (D) are incorrect** (*i.e.*, they are all true). A federal preliminary examination is an adversary hearing (Answer (A)), during which the accused has the right to testify (Answer (B)), and to cross-examine prosecution witnesses (Rule 5.1(e)(Answer (D))).

**225.** **Answer (A) is correct.** Rule 5.1(e) states: "may introduce evidence but may not object to evidence on the ground that it was unlawfully acquired." Therefore, the defendant cannot challenge the constitutional legality of the evidence during the preliminary examination.

**Answer (B) is incorrect.** The evidentiary rules apply in trial situations, and are relaxed for the preliminary examination proceedings.

**Answer (C) is incorrect.** Rule 5.1(f) states: "[i]f the magistrate judge finds no probable cause to believe an offense has been committed or the defendant committed it, the magistrate judge must dismiss the complaint and discharge the defendant." As such, the judge must discharge the defendant when there is no probable cause.

**Answer (D) is incorrect.** Rule 5.1(c) states: "[t]he magistrate judge must hold the preliminary hearing within a reasonable time, but no later than 10 days after the initial appearance if the defendant is in custody and no later than 20 days if not in custody." As such, a 30-day delay violates this provision.

**226.** **Answer (A) is correct.** Under Rule 5.1(e) of the Federal Rules of Criminal Procedure, the standard of proof in a preliminary examination is whether the evidence made it appear to the judge that there is probable cause to believe that an offense was committed by the defendant.

**Answer (B) is incorrect** because the beyond-a-reasonable-doubt standard is for the trial, not the preliminary examination.

**Answer (C) is incorrect** because the defense does not have to prove the defendant's innocence; the prosecution must satisfy the probable cause standard.

**Answer (D) is incorrect** because the prosecution need not use its best witnesses at a preliminary examination; it need only satisfy the probable cause standard. The judge is to consider the witnesses actually presented at the preliminary examination, not those that the prosecution could have produced had it chosen to do so.

**227.** Unfortunately for you, under Rule 5.1(e) of the Federal Rules of Criminal Procedure and Rule 1101(d)(3) of the Federal Rules of Evidence, the rules of evidence in a preliminary examination differ markedly from those of a criminal trial.

In the federal system, evidence seized in violation of the Constitution may be admitted at a preliminary examination since the exclusionary rule does not apply to that proceeding, according to Rule 5.1(e).

In addition, Rule 1101(d)(3) of the Federal Rules of Evidence provides that the rules of evidence do not apply to a preliminary examination. This means that hearsay evidence may be admitted at a preliminary examination. Some states take a different approach, applying their constitutional exclusionary rules and ordinary evidence rules to preliminary examinations.

**228.** **Answer (D) is correct.** Even though Joe may well have lost a chance to prove his innocence, the case will not be dismissed. Under *Arizona v. Youngblood*, 488 U.S. 51 (1988), due process does not require the police to preserve all evidence in a criminal case. Answer (D) is correct because Youngblood held that unless "a criminal defendant can show bad faith on the part of the police, failure to preserve potentially useful evidence does not constitute a denial of due process of law."

**Answers (A) and (B) are incorrect.** The police have no duty to preserve all relevant evidence. They may destroy evidence even if it compromises the defendant's possible defense as long as they do not act in bad faith.

**Answer (C) is incorrect.** Police bad faith is the key; therefore Answer (C) is not the best answer. The speculative possibility that the evidence may have assisted the defendant is not dispositive since this uncertainty may be present irrespective of good or bad faith actions by the police. *Brady* is not dispositive since the investigating officer thought the criminal on the tapes looked like Joe; thus, the video did not present evidence covered by *Brady v. Maryland*.

**229.** You should turn this over to the defense for two reasons. First, in *Brady v. Maryland*, 373 U.S. 83 (1963), the United States Supreme Court held that due process requires the government to give the accused any evidence, favorable to the accused on guilt or punishment, that is in the government's possession. Although it is unclear whether this evidence will actually help the defense since it may well be inadmissible (problems with hearsay, lack of personal knowledge, and authentication), the safe course is to give the evidence to the defense and let defense counsel decide whether and how to use it. Perhaps defense counsel will be able to identify the handwriting on the note and then locate the anonymous author. Failure to disclose the document could lead to appellate reversal if the defendant is convicted. *See United States v. Bagley*, 473 U.S. 667 (1985).

The second reason for giving the document to the defense is Federal Rule of Criminal Procedure 16(a)(1)(E), which mandates government disclosure of documents that are in the government's possession and are material to preparing the defense. Since the defense has made a formal request under Rule 16 for this kind of evidence, the government should assume that this strange document may be material to the preparation of the defense and disclose it to defense counsel.

**230.** **Answer (C) is correct.** Rule 16(a)(2) specifically exempts "internal government documents made by an attorney for the government or other government agent in connection with investigating or prosecuting the case" except as specified in the statute.

**Answers (A), (B) and (D) are incorrect** because Rule 16 requires the government, upon the defendant's request, to turn over the defendant's statements to the police in response to interrogation if the government intends to use them at trial, under Rule 16(a)(1)(A) (Answer (A)); the defendant's prior criminal record, under Rule 16(a)(1)(D) (Answer (B)); and any mental or physical examination of the defendant that the government intends to use at trial, under Rule 16(a)(1)(F) (Answer (D)).

231.   **Answer (A) is correct.** Several answers could provide the defense with helpful information, but Answer (A) is the best answer. Under Rule 7(f), the court may direct the prosecutor to file a Bill of Particulars, which will provide the accused with more information about the facts of the case.

   **Answer (B) is incorrect.** Answer (B) is not the best answer because under Rule12.1, a Notice of Alibi is begun by a written demand *by the government*, not the defense. However, if this demand is made and the accused provides the necessary information about his or her whereabouts, the prosecution must provide the accused with information about the witnesses to the offense. Therefore, the Notice of Alibi could provide the defense with helpful information about the details of the offense.

   **Answer (C) is incorrect** because the insanity defense process under Rule 12.2 will provide the accused with relatively little information about the offense.

   **Answer (D) is not the best answer** because depositions are allowed in criminal cases only in "exceptional cases" under Rule 15(a)(1) of the Federal Rules of Criminal Procedure.

232.   **Answer (C) is correct.** Under Rule 12.1(a), Notice of Alibi processes are begun when the prosecutor makes a written demand on the defense, stating the time, date, and place of the alleged offense. The defense must then inform the prosecution of an intent to use an alibi defense.

   **Answer (A) is incorrect** because under Rule 12.2(a) the defendant has the responsibility for first informing the prosecution of an intent to rely upon an insanity offense.

   **Answer (B) is similarly incorrect** because Rule 12.2(b) provides that the accused must first inform the government of an intent to use expert testimony on the defendant's mental condition bearing upon the issue of guilty.

   **Answer (D) is incorrect** because Rule 12.3 requires the defendant to first notify the government of an intent to use a defense involving public authority.

233.   **Answer (B) is correct** (*i.e.*, the statement is not accurate). Rule 15(c) specifically provides for the defendant's presence at the deposition.

   **Answer (A) is incorrect** (*i.e.*, the statement is accurate) because under Rule 15(a) a deposition may be ordered only due to "exceptional circumstances" of the case.

   **Answer (C) is incorrect** (*i.e.*, the statement is accurate). Under Rule 15(a), a deposition in a criminal case is permissible only if the court so orders. This is a significant difference from depositions in civil cases.

**Answer (D) is incorrect** (*i.e.*, the statement is accurate) because Rule 15(f) indicates that the deposition may be admissible at trial; indeed, that is the reason the deposition under Rule 15 is taken.

234. **Answer (D) is the best answer.** All the previous answers are correct, making Answer (D) the most accurate choice.

**Answer (A) is correct but not the only answer.** Rule 15(a)(2) provides that a detained material witness may file a written motion requesting a deposition.

**Answer (B) is correct but not the only answer.** Rule 15(a)(2) provides that a detained material witness must sign a deposition transcript before being released from detention.

**Answer (C) is correct but not the only answer.** Rule 15(a)(2) provides that a detained material witness may be discharged after being deposed.

235. **Answer (B) is correct.** Rule 16 does not mandate pretrial discovery of statements by (non-expert) witnesses.

**Answer (A) is incorrect** because Rule 16(a)(1)(B) does require the government to give the defense a copy of the defendant's written statement.

**Answer (C) is incorrect** because Rule 16(a)(1)(D) obligates the prosecution to give the defense a copy of the defendant's criminal record.

**Answer (D) is incorrect** because Rule 16(a)(1)(E) mandates disclosure of documents within the government's possession which are material to the preparation of the defense.

236. **Answer (A) is correct.** Rules16 (a)(1)(A) and 16(a)(1)(B) require the prosecution to turn over written or recorded statements of the defendant, but the Rule does not require the defense to turn over such statements to the prosecution.

**Answer (B) is incorrect** because Rules 16(a)(1)(F) and 16(b)(1)(B) require exchange of information of examination and tests.

**Answer (C) is incorrect** because Rules 16(a)(1)(E) and 16(b)(1)(A) mandate mutual disclosure of documents and tangible objects.

**Answer (D) is incorrect** because Rules 16(a)(1)(G) and 16(b)(1)(C) provide for the exchange of summaries of the testimony of experts intended to be used at trial.

237. **Answer (C) is correct.** Rule 16(b)(a)(B) requires Siegel to give the government access to file reports she intends to use in her case-in-chief at trial.

**Answer (A) is incorrect.** Siegel need only provide information that she intends to use at trial; the test is not whether it is material to the prosecution's trial preparation.

**Answer (B) is incorrect.** *Brady v. Maryland* is not reciprocal. Siegel, as defense counsel, need not turn over items merely because the items would be helpful to the prosecution.

**Answer (D) is incorrect.** When Siegel requests information under Rule 16, she effectively waives any objection to providing the government with reciprocal materials that would be detrimental to the defense. Siegel can avoid such disclosure by simply not requesting that type of information under Rule 16, which comes into play only upon the "request" by the defense.

238.   **Answer (D) is correct.** Rule 26.2 does not apply in grand jury proceedings. Rule 26.2(g).

       **Answers (A), (B), and (C) are incorrect.** Rule 26.2 does apply in a sentencing hearing (Answer (A)), preliminary hearing (Answer (B)), and suppression hearing (Answer (C)).

239.   **Answer (B) is correct.** Under Rule 26.2(a), the defense is entitled to see statements by a prosecution witness after the witness has testified on direct examination, but only if the defense makes a motion to produce the statement.

       **Answer (A) is incorrect** because the work product doctrine does not protect against disclosure under Rule 26.2.

       **Answer (C) is incorrect** because disclosure does not depend on whether or not the statement appears to be helpful. The defense will make this determination when it decides whether or not to use the statement during cross-examination.

       **Answer (D) is incorrect** because Spotter's wishes are not dispositive. Rule 26(c) does permit the court to excise portions of the statement that contain matters that are privileged or unrelated to the subjects of the direct examination.

**240.** Based on the facts in the question, you should deny the motion to compel, though the case is not clear. The decision depends on a balance between the interests of the government, the informant, and the criminal accused.

"What is usually referred to as the informer's privilege is in reality the Government's privilege to withhold from disclosure the identity of the persons who furnish information of violations of law to officers charged with enforcement of that law." *United States v. Roviaro*, 353 U.S. 53, 59 (1957), citing *Scher v. United States*, 305 U.S. 251, 254 (1938).

"The purpose of the privilege is the furtherance and protection of the public interest in effective law enforcement. The privilege recognizes the obligation of citizens to communicate their knowledge of the commission of crimes to law-enforcement officials and, by preserving their anonymity, encourages them to perform that obligation. . . . "*United States v. Roviaro*, 353 U.S. at 59. Where the informant and law enforcement purposes would not be harmed by revelation of the informant's identity, the privilege ceases. "A further limitation on the applicability of the privilege arises from the fundamental requirements of fairness. Where the disclosure of an informer's identity . . . is relevant and helpful to the defense of the accused, or is essential to a fair determination of a cause, the privilege must give way." *Roviaro*, 353 U.S. at 60-61.

In this case, the government asserts the informant's very life would be in jeopardy if his or her identity were released, plus future assistance by this informant would be compromised. The defense could counter with the fact that the defense needs the information to attack the warrant (not based on adequate probable cause) and to help it locate witnesses and discover motives for the prosecution.

On balance, the defense has not offered any compelling need for disclosure of the informant's identity and the prosecution has suggested, though without any proof, that the informant's health would be jeopardized by disclosure. Absent more compelling reasons by the defense, disclosure of the informant's identity should be denied because of the informant's privilege.

241. **Answer (B) is correct.** The Fifth Amendment states that "No person shall . . . be subject for the same offense to be twice put in jeopardy of life or limb. . . . " The precise language is important because it is so vague that it does not clearly resolve many issues about the reach of this provision. It does make clear, however, that the concept of "same offense" is pivotal to any interpretation. Similarly, it must be decided what constitutes being in "jeopardy."

**Answer (A) is incorrect** because the Fifth Amendment does not specifically mention "conviction."

**Answer (C) is similarly incorrect** because the phrase "double jeopardy" does not appear in the amendment.

**Answer (D) is incorrect** because the word "trial" is not in the amendment.

242. **Answer (C) is correct.** Double jeopardy does not bar a second trial for a mistrial following a hung jury. In *United States v. Perez*, 22 U.S. 579 (1824), the Supreme Court held that a mistrial caused by a hopelessly deadlocked jury does not bar a retrial since there has been no final verdict and society has an important interest in giving the prosecution one complete opportunity to convict persons who have violated laws. *See also Arizona v. Washington*, 434 U.S. 497 (1978).

**Answers (A), (B), and (D) are incorrect** because they represent the three categories of results traditionally barred by the double jeopardy guarantee. *See North Carolina v. Pearce*, 395 U.S. 711, 717 (1969).

243. Under the Double Jeopardy Clause, when the defense objects to a mistrial, a retrial is still permitted if there was "manifest necessity" for the mistrial. of if the ends of justice would be defeated by a retrial. *United States v. Dinitz*, 424 U.S. 600 (1976).

In a case such as this where the defendant did not request a mistrial and objected to it, the key concept is whether there were effective alternatives to the mistrial. Here, the judge did not appear to explore fully the many possible alternatives to declaring a mistrial. This may suggest that there was no manifest necessity and, therefore, retrial is barred. Another consideration is whether the prosecution acted in bad faith in causing the mistrial. Here, there is no evidence of prosecutorial bad faith.

244. When the defense requests the mistrial, reprosecution is usually allowed under the Double Jeopardy Clause. In *United States v. Dinitz*, 424 U.S. 600 (1976), the Supreme Court held that when the defendant asks for the mistrial, he or she has essentially made a decision whether to continue with the trial, despite the errors, or to surrender the right to have the matter resolved by the original jury.

The primary exception is when the defendant is provoked into requesting a mistrial because of the intentional misbehavior by the prosecution. Perhaps the prosecutor is motivated by a desire to gain an advantage by starting anew or by a desire to harass the accused by forcing a second trial. *See also Oregon v. Kennedy*, 456 U.S. 667 (1982). In the instant case there is no hint that the prosecution intentionally provoked the defense into requesting the mistrial.

245. **Answer (B) is correct.** Under *Blockburger v. United States*, 284 U.S. 299 (1932), the Supreme Court announced the test for determining whether two crimes are the "same offense" for purposes of double jeopardy analysis. The *Blockburger* test, often referred to as the same element or same evidence test, is whether "each provision requires proof of a fact which the other does not." This means that if transportation of a firearm across state lines is proved every time alien in possession of a firearm is proved, the two crimes are the "same offense."

**Answer (A) is incorrect.** Answer (A) is not the best answer because *some* common elements: are ordinarily insufficient to satisfy *Blockburger*.

**Answer (C) is similarly incorrect** because the legislature's intent is irrelevant for determining whether double jeopardy would be offended by a second *trial* for the same offense.

**Answer (D) is incorrect.** Whether or not the two crimes occurred during the same transaction or time period is irrelevant under *Blockburger*, which focuses on elements and proof rather than time periods.

246. In *Ashe v. Swenson*, 397 U.S. 436 (1970), the United States Supreme Court held that collateral estoppel applied to criminal cases pursuant to the double jeopardy guarantee. The prosecution may not relitigate issues already resolved in the defendant's favor in a prior prosecution. In the facts of the question, it is possible, though unlikely, that collateral estoppel will bar the second trial. The record of the first case will have to be reviewed carefully to ascertain exactly what issue the first jury resolved when it acquitted the defendant.

If the proof showed that only one person committed both rapes and the jury acquitted the defendant because he was not the person who committed the first rape, collateral estoppel could bar the second prosecution. On the other hand, if the acquittal in the first case was not based on identity or if different people could have committed the two rapes, collateral estoppel would not bar the second trial. Even if the jury found that an element of rape, such as penetration, was not proven in the first trial, that element may have been present during the second crime. Similarly, even if Jamison was not the person who raped the victim at the earlier time, he may have been the rapist at the second offense.

247. **Answer (C) is correct.** This case involves the reach of double jeopardy in a single trial. Unlike the situation where there are multiple trials, in the case of a single trial the double jeopardy test is not *Blockburger*; it is one of statutory construction. A court asks whether the legislature intended for there to be cumulative punishment for the two applicable criminal statutes. *See Missouri v. Hunter*, 459 U.S. 359 (1983).

**Answer (A) is incorrect** because the double jeopardy test has nothing to do with the timing of the two events.

**Answer (B) is incorrect** because similarity of elements is not a dispositive issue. The key is what the legislature intended.

**Answer (D) is incorrect** because the *Blockburger* test does not apply to multiple punishments in the same trial. It applies only to sequential proceedings.

248. **Answer (D) is correct.** In *North Caroline v. Pearce*, 395 U.S. 711 (1969), the United States Supreme Court held that due process prohibits a state from imposing a harsher sentence on retrial for the purpose of punishing the defendant who successfully appeals a conviction. But an increased sentence is permissible, according to *Pearce*, if the record reflects objective information that the defendant's conduct since the new trial merited the increased sanction. This will overcome the presumption of vindictiveness triggered by the harsher penalty. Here, the defendant's new arson conviction could merit an increased punishment after the retrial.

**Answer (A) is incorrect** because *Pearce* clearly held that double jeopardy does not bar an increased sentence after retrial in some circumstances.

**Answer (B) is incorrect** because *Pearce* also held that equal protection was not violated since the defendant could receive exactly the same sentence after each trial.

**Answer (C) is incorrect** because *Pearce* places some limits on the sentence after a retrial.

249. **Answer (C) is correct.** In a jury trial, the double jeopardy guarantee attaches once the jury is sworn in. It does not apply to any prior proceedings. *Crist v. Bretz*, 437 U.S. 28 (1978). Here, the jury was not sworn (it had not even been selected) when the judge stopped the proceedings and rescheduled the trial.

**Answers (A) and (B) are incorrect.** because double jeopardy does not attach at such early stages as the defendant's arrest or after the indictment is signed.

**Answer (D) is incorrect** because in a jury trial jeopardy has already attached before the first witness takes the stand. *See Crist v. Bretz*, 437 U.S. 28 (1978).

250. **Answer (D) is correct.** In non-jury cases, jeopardy attaches when the first witness for the prosecution is sworn. *See Crist v. Bretz*, 437 U.S. 28 (1978).

**Answers (A), (B) and (C) are incorrect** because they are all at later stages, after the first witness is sworn.

**251.**    **Answer (D) is correct.** Double jeopardy bars a retrial if the appellate court reversed because the government's evidence at trial was insufficient. *See Burks v. United States*, 437 U.S. 1 (1978). The government had a fair opportunity to present its best case and the Double Jeopardy Clause bars giving the government a second opportunity to obtain a conviction.

**Answer (B) is incorrect.** By way of contrast (and not necessarily clear logic), if the reversal was based on dissatisfaction with the *weight* of evidence rather than the sufficiency of the evidence, retrial is permissible. *See Tibbs v. Florida*, 457 U.S. 31 (1981).

**Answers (A) and (C) are incorrect.** When the appellate reversal is because of a trial error, retrial is ordinarily permitted. The defendant has chosen to take an appeal and has a legitimate interest in a readjudication free from judicial error. Answers (A) and (C) are incorrect because these "trial error" grounds do not bar retrial. If the Supreme Court cannot tell whether the reversal was for trial error or insufficient evidence, it may remand for clarification. *Greene v. Massey*, 437 U.S. 19 (1978).

**252.**    This question raises the so-called "separate sovereign doctrine" that allows more than one jurisdiction to prosecute a person for the identical conduct.

**Answer (D) is correct** because state and local governments are considered the same sovereign for double jeopardy purposes. Thus, Union City, located in State Y, may not pursue charges for the same crimes as prosecuted by State Y. The two are not considered separate sovereigns under the double jeopardy clause.

**Answers (A), (B), and (C) are incorrect.** Under the "separate sovereign" or "dual sovereign" doctrine, double jeopardy does not bar prosecution by different government entities. The underlying theory is that a crime is an offense against the sovereignty of each governmental unit having jurisdiction over a criminal act. *See Heath v. Alabama*, 474 U.S. 82 (1985). The federal government and each state are considered separate sovereigns and may each prosecute crimes over which they have jurisdiction. Thus, Connecticut and New York State (Answer (B)); the United States and New York State (Answer A); and the United States and New York City (Answer (C) are all considered separate sovereigns and may each pursue a prosecution of Solicit.

**253.** The Sixth Amendment to the United States Constitution guarantees an adult criminal defendant charged with a serious offense the right to be tried by a jury. Whether an offense is "serious" in the constitutional sense is assessed by looking at the maximum *available* penalty for conviction of that offense. Any offense with a potential penalty of more than six months' imprisonment is a serious offense, and any offense with a maximum penalty of six months or less is presumed to be petty and not implicate the right to a jury trial. *Duncan v. Louisiana*, 391 U.S. 145 (1968); *Baldwin v. New York*, 399 U.S. 66 (1969). Here, the maximum prison term is six months, one day under the sanction triggering the right to a jury trial under the sixth amendment.

However, an offense carrying a maximum sentence of six months or less may still be a serious offense if additional authorized penalties are so severe that they clearly reflect a legislative determination that the offense is a serious one. A fine of $10,000 in conjunction with a six-month term of imprisonment is not sufficiently serious as to entitle a defendant to a jury trial. *Blanton v. City of North Las Vegas*, 489 U.S. 538, 543 (1989). Here, the $700 fine is obviously insufficient to trigger the defendant's right to a jury trial.

The restitution obligation is irrelevant because for purposes of the right to a jury trial, restitution does not impose an additional obligation on the defendant; rather it recognizes the debt that the defendant already owes.

Under the U.S. Constitution, the defendant was not entitled to a jury trial.

**254.** **Answer (B) is correct.** Whether a defendant is entitled to a jury trial is determined by examination of the maximum authorized penalty, not the "felony" or "misdemeanor" classification noted in Answer (A). See discussion for Answer (D) below.

**Answer (A) is therefore incorrect.**

**Answer (C) is incorrect.** Any offense carrying more than six months' imprisonment is a "serious" offense, implicating the Sixth Amendment right to be tried before a jury. *Baldwin v. New York*, 399 U.S. 66 (1969). Any crime with a maximum sentence of six months or less is presumed to be a "petty" offense.

**Answer (D) is incorrect.** In such a case, the defendant is only entitled to a jury trial if he or she can demonstrate that any additional statutory penalties, viewed in conjunction with the prison term, are so severe that they clearly reflect a legislative determination that the crime is a "serious" offense. In performing this analysis, only penalties resulting from state action, *e.g.*, those mandated by statute or regulation should be considered, because nonstatutory consequences are speculative in nature, incapable of a consistent determination of when and if they will occur. *Blanton v. City of North Las Vegas*, 489 U.S. 538 (1989).

Since the state statute authorizes only a six-month maximum prison term, the legislature is presumed to have determined domestic violence assault to be a "petty" offense. The consequence of losing one's right to bear arms is not authorized in the state statute, but rather in a federal law. That collateral effect cannot be interpreted to clearly indicate the state legislature's determination about the level of seriousness, since Congress, not the state legislature, considered and imposed that additional consequence. *Accord United States v. Chavez*, 204 F.3d 1305, 1314 (11th Cir. 2000). The state legislature's determination is not altered; therefore, Answer (D) is incorrect. [This question is based on *State ex rel. McDougall v. Strohson*, 945 P.2d 1251 (1997).]

255.    **Answer (C) is correct.** The majority opinion in *Duncan* focuses almost exclusively on the historical reasons for the inclusion of a jury trial right in the United States Constitution.

[T]he jury trial provisions . . . reflect a fundamental decision about the exercise of official power – a reluctance to entrust plenary powers over the life and liberty of the citizen to one judge or to a group of judges. Fear of unchecked power, so typical of our State and Federal Governments in other respects, found expression in the criminal law in this insistence upon community participation in the determination of guilt or innocence. *Duncan v. Louisiana*, 391 U.S. 145, 156 (1968).

Thus, finding that the right to a jury was among those "fundamental principles of liberty and justice which lie at the base of all our civil and political institutions," the *Duncan* Court ruled that it was applicable to the states through the Due Process clause of the Fourteenth Amendment.

**Answers (A) is incorrect.** Accuracy in factfinding was not the primary reason *Duncan v. Louisiana* found a Sixth Amendment right to a jury trial in serious cases and specifically recognized that a bench trial is not necessarily unfair.

**Answer (B) is incorrect.** While jury participation may increase public respect for a verdict, the opinion of the court in *Duncan* did not focus on or discuss this as a rationale for recognizing the right to a jury trial. The Court did not rule that a jury would be more accurate in its ability to determine fact, but that it would be less susceptible to corruption or caprice.

**Answer (D) is incorrect** because the Court was not focused on educating the public, but rather whether the jury was fundamental to a defendant's right to a fair trial.

256.    **Answer (C) is correct.** Under the Sixth Amendment to the United States Constitution, an offender is entitled to a jury trial if the sentence carries more than six months' imprisonment. *Baldwin v. New York*, 399 U.S. 66 (1969). The defendant's age is irrelevant.

**Answers (A) and (D) are incorrect.** A defendant in juvenile proceedings is not entitled to a jury trial under the Sixth Amendment, as such hearings are different in nature from normal criminal trials. A jury would tend to introduce an adversarial nature to the proceedings and hinder the cooperative, protective goals of juvenile proceedings. *McKeiver v. Pennsylvania*, 403 U.S. 528 (1971).

**Answer (B) is incorrect** because the maximum sentence falls below the six-month "seriousness" threshold set by *Duncan v. Louisiana*, 391 U.S. 145 (1968), and *Baldwin v. New York*, 399 U.S. 66 (1969).

257.  In *Batson v. Kentucky*, 476 U.S. 79 (1986), the United States Supreme Court held that purposeful racial discrimination in jury selection violates the defendant's right to equal protection as well as rights of the excluded group and those of the entire community. In *Davis v. Minnesota*, 511 U.S. 1115 (1994), the Court held that *Batson*, also barred exercising a peremptory challenge on the basis of a religious classification. *Davis*, however, did not bar all considerations of religion. A potential juror's religion may be a permissible ground for exclusion if the faith is relevant to an issue in the case.

In *Purkett* v. *Elem*, 514 U.S. 765 (1995), the Court may have made it easier for you to use your peremptory challenge to exclude jurors for religion-based reasons. *Purkett* held that the exercise of a peremptory challenge is permissible if the prosecutor can establish a race-neutral explanation of the challenge. According to *Purkett*, this explanation does not have to be "persuasive, or even plausible."

In this case, it is unlikely that the juror's religion *per se* is relevant to an issue in the bribery case, but the juror's faith may be relevant if her familiarity with the defendant or sympathy toward him would bias the potential juror. If the potential juror knows the defendant or believes she has a duty to support other members of the their common faith, the challenge may be permitted.

258.  **Answer (D) is correct** (*i.e.*, it states an erroneous legal conclusion). While in many states the prosecutor does have the power to demand a jury trial and thereby "veto" a defendant's waiver, this is not a *federal* constitutional right, but is derived from state status or practice. That power does not conflict with a defendant's right to a jury trial, since:

**Answer (C) is therefore incorrect** (*i.e.*, it is a legally valid argument). Donnie's rights are not violated by the state procedure.

**Answer (A) is similarly incorrect** (*i.e.*, it is also a legally valid argument). The three requirements for a valid waiver are that it must be knowing, intelligent, and voluntary. *See e.g.*, *Schneckloth v. Bustamonte*, 412 U.S. 218 (1973). You seemed satisfied that Donnie knew what he was doing, but there is no indication that you asked him any questions about whether he had been pressured or coerced in any way to make a waiver. Not did you ask about his reasons or try to determine at all whether it was an intelligent decision for him to make in this case and whether he had carefully considered the risks and advantages of a waiver. These inquires are all the more important since Donnie is representing himself and does not have the advice of counsel in this decision. So, Answer (A) is legally valid, and thus does not correctly answer the question asked.

**Answer (B) is incorrect** (*i.e.*, it is a legally valid argument). The question ask you to identify the faulty argument. Under Federal Rule of Criminal Procedure 23(a), a defendant's waiver of jury trial must be made in writing to be recognized.

259. **Answer (A) is correct.** A defendant's Sixth Amendment right to a jury trial does not guarantee a twelve-member jury in state court-. The Supreme Court has approved the use of a jury as small as six-members in *Williams v. Florida*, 399 U.S. 78 (1970).

**Answer (B) is incorrect** according to *Williams v. Florida*.

**Answer (C) is incorrect** because juries smaller than twelve people were used even before the Bill of Rights was ratified. More importantly, the Supreme Court has not based the determination of jury size on historical figures, but rather on whether a specific jury size would adequately achieve the reasons for which the right to trial by jury was guaranteed. Some of those reasons are to prevent oppression by the government by promoting group deliberation, insulating members from outside intimidation, and providing a representative cross-section of the community. *Ballew v. Georgia*, 435 U.S. 223 (1977).

**Answer (D) is incorrect** as well. A jury of six people is capable of achieving this purpose. *Williams v. Florida*, 399 U.S. 78 (1970).

260. **Answer (B) is correct.** A defendant's right to a jury trial does not necessarily guarantee a twelve-member jury. The Supreme Court has approved the use of a jury even as small as six persons. *Williams v. Florida*, 399 U.S. 78 (1970). However, a jury of four is too small to satisfy the Sixth Amendment.

**Answer (A) is incorrect.** The Supreme Court has also held, however, that a jury of five persons or smaller is not sufficiently large to achieve the reasons for which the right to trial by jury was guaranteed. Some of those reasons are to prevent government oppression by promoting group deliberation, insulating members from outside intimidation, and providing a representative cross-section of the community. *Ballew v. Georgia*, 435 U.S. 223 (1977).

**Answers (C) and (D) are incorrect.** Answer (D) is incorrect because juries smaller than twelve people were used even before the Bill of Rights was ratified. More importantly, the Supreme Court has not based the determination of jury size on historical figures, but rather on whether a specific jury size would adequately achieve the reasons for which the right to trial by jury was guaranteed. Nor is the question of whether a larger jury would have convicted the defendant the appropriate determination; therefore Answer (C) is incorrect, as well.

261. Assuming your state's constitution does not mandate a unanimous jury verdict in criminal cases (as many state constitutions do), there is also no federal constitutional impediment to reducing the jury verdict requirement from unanimous to 10-2 in non-capital cases. In *Apodoca v. Oregon*, 406 U.S. 404 (1972), the United Stares Supreme Court upheld an Oregon law that permitted a criminal

conviction by jury vote of 10-2. The less-than-unanimous rule, according to *Apodoca*, does not violate the cross-section requirement, since there is no guarantee that any particular jury would have members constituting a cross-section of the community, and it does not unconstitutionally impair the jury's functioning.

The wisdom of the non-unanimous verdict is another matter. It dilutes the impact of minority participants who no longer have a veto over the verdict. Moreover, it increases the likelihood that an innocent person will be convicted since the number of convictions will increase and the lone juror with doubts about guilt may well be ignored since his or her vote may be rendered irrelevant. On the other hand, it will result in fewer mistrials since 11-1 and 10-2 verdicts that formerly resulted in a hung jury will not result in a conviction or acquittal.

262. **Answer (C) is correct.** "[The] purpose of the jury trial . . . is to prevent oppression by the Government. 'Providing an accused with the right to be tried by a jury of his peers gave him an inestimable safeguard against the corrupt or overzealous prosecutor and against the compliant, biased, or eccentric judge.' Given this purpose, the essential feature of a jury obviously lies in the interposition between the accused and his accuser of the commonsense judgment of a group of laymen, and in the community participation and shared responsibility that results from that group's determination of guilt or innocence." *Williams v. Florida*, 399 U.S. 78, 100 (1970), *citing Duncan v. Louisiana*, 391 U.S. 145, 156 (1968) (emphasis added).

**Answer (A) is incorrect.** The Constitution is violated if there is a jury selection system in place that systematically under represents a distinctive group. "This prophylactic vehicle is not provided if the jury pool is made up of only special segments of the populace or if large, distinctive groups are excluded from the pool." *Taylor v. Louisiana*, 419 U.S. 522, 530 (1975). Therefore, "the selection of a petit jury from a representative cross section of the community is an essential component of the sixth amendment right to a jury trial. . . . the fair-cross-section requirement [is] fundamental to the jury trial guaranteed by the sixth amendment. . . . " *Id.* at 528, 530.

**Answer (B) is incorrect.** This ethnic group obviously meets the requirements that (1) it is a "distinctive" group; (2) the statistical disparity is not fair and reasonable; and (3) this under representation is due to a systematic exclusion of the group in the jury-selection process." *See Duren v. Missouri*, 439 U.S. 357 (1979). So, Daisy's Sixth Amendment right to a trial by jury was infringed, and she should have the right to be retried by a satisfactory jury, but not for the reason given in Answer (B). Whether the right is violated depends not on the final, actual composition of the *petit jury*, but on the systematic and unfair exclusion of a distinctive group from the jury selection process. *Taylor*, 419 U.S. at 530.

**Answer (D) is incorrect.** The right to a jury selected from a representative cross-section of the community is enforceable by the defendant, even though the exclusion might also involve a violation of the rights of members of the excluded segment of the community. Thus, the Supreme Court in *Taylor* allowed the defendant, a male, to challenge the exclusion of women from the Louisiana jury pool.

263. **Answer (A) is correct.** Rule 43 of the Federal Rules of Criminal Procedure (which codifies case law on some of the defendant's rights of confrontation and due process) states that the trial will proceed to completion and the defendant will be considered to have waived the right to be present whenever a defendant, initially present at trial, is voluntarily absent after the trial has commenced (whether or not the defendant has been informed by the court of the obligation to remain during the trial). Since for Answer (A) the defendant's absence began *before* the trial commenced rather than afterward, the court must postpone the trial and wait for the defendant to be present at the beginning of trial. *Crosby v. United States*, 506 U.S. 255 (1993).

**Answer (B) is incorrect** because in this scenario, the defendant Corrigan was present at the commencement of the trial, and by absconding, she waives the right to be present at trial, which may proceed in her absence. *Taylor v. United States*, 414 U.S. 17 (1973).

**Answer (C) is incorrect** because the hearing from which the defendant was excluded did not interfere with the defendant's due process right or with the opportunity or ability to cross-examine at trial. The defendant's attorney was present, and the defendant will have a full opportunity to hear, confront, and cross-examine the witness in open court during the trial. A defendant's presence is not necessary for every part of a criminal proceeding, such as those involving only minor questions of law.

**Answer (D) is incorrect** because a defendant need not be present: . . . when represented by counsel and the defendant is an organization. Fed. R. Crim. Pro. 43(b)(1)

264. Yes, the criminal defendant does have a right to testify at the defendant's own trial, although the Construction contains no specific language recognizing this right. Nevertheless, in *Rock v. Arkansas*, 483 U.S. 44 (1987), the United States Supreme Court recognized that the right to testify and be heard in one's own defense is one the fundamental rights protected by Due Process clauses of the Fifth and Fourteenth Amendments, and by the Compulsory Process Clause of the Sixth Amendment.

The Court reasoned that the Compulsory Process Clause gives the accused the right to call helpful witnesses, including even the accused, who may be the most important defense witness to testify. A related source cited by *Rock* is the Sixth Amendment's guarantee of the right of the accused personally to make his or her defense, which includes the right personally to call favorable witnesses, including the defendant himself or herself. Still another source is the Fifth Amendment's guarantee against self-incrimination. The *Rock* Court expansively read this right as guaranteeing both the right to remain silent and the right to testify.

265. **Answer (A) is correct.** Every criminal defendant has the right to remain silent and not testify at his or her criminal trial. The right is guaranteed by the Fifth Amendment and is applied to the states by the Fourteenth Amendment. Allowing the prosecutor to comment at all on the defendant's choice to remain silent would allow the prosecutor to penalize the defendant for exercising the constitutional right. The clear intent would be to induce the defendant not to take the stand. Such an effect would be even more severe if the court instructed the jury that the defendant's choice reflected on the evidence. *Griffin v. California*, 380 U.S. 609 (1965).

**Answer (B) is incorrect.** The judge may instruct the jury not to consider the defendant's choice to exercise the defendant's Fifth Amendment rights. A different conclusion would require the assumptions that (1) the jurors did not notice the fact that the defendant kept silent, and (2) they will ignore the judge's instructions and hold against the defendant the very thing they were told to disregard. "Federal constitutional law cannot rest on speculative assumptions so dubious as these." *Lakeside v. Oregon*, 435 U.S. 333, 340 (1978).

**Answer (C) is incorrect** because the prosecutor may comment on the defendant's opportunity to conform the defendant's testimony to that of other witnesses. According to the Supreme Court, such an argument would be a comment upon the defendant's credibility as a witness, not a suggestion that the exercise of the defendant's right not to testify is evidence of guilt. *Portuondo v. Agard*, 529 U.S. 61 (2000).

**Answer (D) is incorrect.** The prosecutor's statements about Quiet would be unconstitutional. Since Answer (A) reflects an unconstitutional statement by the prosecution, Answer (D) is incorrect.

266. A trial judge has a considerable degree of discretion in dealing with a disruptive defendant. Since Weiser was highly disruptive the judge clearly warned her and told her she could return if she acted in an appropriate manner, the judge should deny Weiser's motion for a mistrial. *Illinois v. Allen*, 397 U.S. 337, 343-44 (1970).

267. **Answer (D) is correct.** A jury instruction to use the defendant's trial conduct in assessing guilt is not one of the options approved in *Illinois v. Allen*, 397 U.S. 337 (1970).

**Answers (A), (B), and (C) are incorrect.** Each represents one of the three options that *Illinois v. Allen* held was permissible in some situations.

**268.** The Sixth Amendment guarantees a defendant that "in all criminal prosecutions, the accused shall enjoy the right to a . . . public trial." This establishes a strong presumption in favor of openness and free access to criminal trials. Therefore, any party seeking to close the courtroom "must advance an overriding interest that is likely to be prejudiced, the closure must be no broader than necessary to protect that interest, the trial court must consider reasonable alternatives to closing the proceeding, and it must make findings adequate to support the closure." *Waller v. Georgia*, 467 U.S. 39, 48 (1984). The courtroom in *Waller* was closed to prevent the public and press from hearing tapes of wiretaps, because the state feared that persons other than the defendant would have their privacy invaded.

Here, however, the courtroom was not actually closed. There was no motion or order to prevent the public and press from attending. There was no attempt to restrict the flow of information to the press or shield the proceedings from public scrutiny. The public, as a whole, was present. Surely limiting the number of observers is reasonable considering the possible fire hazard involved. Since the courtroom was never actually closed, Daniel's right to a public trial was not violated. [Based on *Wilson v. State*, 814 A.2 1 (Md. App. 2002).]

**269.** **Answer (D) is correct** (*i.e.*, it is not a legitimate reason). Closing court proceedings to the public would not be justified by the goal of protecting the defendant from what the press or public might say about the defendant or the alleged crime. In fact, discussion of such matters is necessary both to a healthy political body and to ensuring that the defendant receives a fair trial. If the press coverage or public discussion goes too far, the defendant has recourse by way of claims for libel or invasion of privacy.

**Answer (A) is incorrect** (*i.e.*, it is a legitimate reason) because court proceedings sometimes may be closed or limited as necessary to protect the identity of an undercover agent's identity, both for the agent's physical safety and for the benefit of future operations.

**Answer (B) is incorrect** (*i.e.*, it is a legitimate reason). A judge may also close or limit access to the courts in order to protect a witness, defendant, or victim from threats that may have been made. Similarly, it may be necessary in some instances to protect a particular crime victim from public exposure when the nature of the crime, the victim's age, and the psychological condition of the victim are highly sensitive. *Globe Newspaper Co. v. Superior Court*, 457 U.S. 596, 608 (1982).

**Answer (C) is incorrect** (*i.e.*, it is a legitimate reason). Court proceedings may be closed when national security dictates keeping certain matters confidential and when opening the proceedings would violate that need. *Richmond Newspapers, Inc. v. Virginia*, 448 U.S. 555, 598 n.24 (1980).

270.   **Answer (A) is correct.** "[T]he First Amendment guarantees of speech and press, standing alone, prohibit government from summarily closing courtroom doors which had long been open to the public at the time that Amendment was adopted. . . . [T]he right [of the public] to attend criminal trials is implicit in the guarantees of the First Amendment. . . . Absent an overriding interest articulated in findings, the trial of a criminal case must be open to the public." *Richmond Newspapers, Inc. v. Virginia*, 448 U.S. 555, 576, 580-81 (1980). Here, the judge's blanket order violates the First Amendment, and Answer (A) is a valid argument. Therefore, Answer (D) is incorrect.

**Answers (B) and (C) are incorrect.** The newspaper cannot, however, argue the Sixth Amendment in support of its injunction. The right to a public trial under the Sixth Amendment is a right personally possessed by the defendant alone. *Gannett Co., Inc. v. DePasquale*, 443 U.S. 368, 379-80 (1979).

**Answer (D) is incorrect.** for the reason stated above.

271. **Answer (B) is correct.** The Due Process Clause of the Sixth Amendment, as applied to the states by the Fourteenth Amendment, guarantees that a defendant may only be convicted "upon proof beyond a reasonable doubt of every fact necessary to constitute the crime with which [the defendant] has been charged." *In re Winship*, 397 U.S. 358, 364 (1970). By creating a presumption about the defendant's intent that the jury is required to apply, the instruction would relieve the state of the burden of proving the element of intent. *Francis v. Franklin*, 471 U.S. 307 (1985). Therefore, Proposed Jury Instruction #2 is unconstitutional.

   **Answer (A) is incorrect** because it is constitutionally permissible to require the defendant to prove "affirmative" defenses such as self defense. Thus, Answer (D) is incorrect, as well.

   **Answer (C) is incorrect** because the instruction does not require the jury to apply a presumption about the defendant's intent. The instruction affirms a "permissive inference," clarifying that the jury may find intent based upon circumstantial evidence, just as it may do with any other element.

   **Answer (D) is incorrect because Answer (B) is correct.**

272. **Answer (C) is the best answer.** While the United States Supreme Court has held that the state has the burden of persuasion on each element of the crime, it has not provided specific guidance on the burdens for defenses. In *Patterson v. New York*, 432 U.S. 197 (1977), the Supreme Court indicated that states are free to allocate the burden of persuasion and the standard of proof for traditional defenses as they see fit. Accordingly, since **Answers (A) and(B) are all correct** and states are free to adopt any of them, answer (C), embracing (A) and (B), is the best answer.

   **Answer (D) is incorrect** since both Answers (A) and (B) are permissible options for states to choose in allocating the standard of proof and burden of persuasion for an insanity defense.

**273.** **(D) is the most accurate answer** because prosecution could be held in any of the three jurisdictions.

**Answer (A), which is correct,** is not the best answer. The general rule is that criminal court jurisdiction is in the area where the crime occurred. For federal cases, Federal Rule of Criminal Procedure 18 mandates that the prosecution occur in the judicial district where the offense was committed unless a statute or other rule provides otherwise. This would include the federal district court with jurisdiction over federal crimes in Ware County.

**Answers (B) and (C) are also correct,** but neither is the best answer. In state systems, the rule that prosecution may occur where the crime occurs means that the prosecution may be in Ware or Selle County, since the merchandise possession occurred in both counties.

**274.** The general rule is that jurisdiction in a criminal case is where the crime occurred. Here two states are involved. The State of Dickerson may try Michelle since the baby died there. The fact that a part of the conduct that resulted in the baby's death occurred in another state is ordinarily irrelevant in assessing Dickerson's jurisdiction.

The State of Jefferson may also have jurisdiction. Many states have adopted a rule that gives a state jurisdiction for a crime either that begins ("commences") or ends ("consummates") in that state or when criminal acts occurred in that state. Here, when Michelle shook and struck the baby in the State of Jefferson, she inflicted serious harm on the child and therefore "began" the crime in that State, giving the State of Jefferson jurisdiction over the homicide, even though the death actually occurred in another state.

It should be noted that the separate sovereign doctrine of double jeopardy would permit both states to try Michelle for the murder. *See Heath v. Alabama,* 474 U.S. 82 (1985).

**275.** **Answer (B) is correct.** Rules 20 and 21 are triggered by a defense motion, not a government one. This is because venue is a right of the defendant who must consent to any change.

**Answer (A) is incorrect.** since Rule 21 specifically authorizes a venue change to obtain a fair and impartial trial.

**Answer (C) is incorrect.** Rule 20 specifically permits a motion to change venue for plea and sentence.

**Answer (D) is incorrect.** because Rule 20 states that both federal prosecutors must approve in writing a venue change for plea and sentence.

276.    **Answer (A) is correct.** Rule 21 does not mandate the consent of the government as a prerequisite to the court's granting the transfer for convenience. Of course, the court will ordinarily ask the government for its views on the matter.

**Answer (B) is incorrect.** A transfer for convenience is given only upon the defendant's motion. Rule 21(b).

**Answer (C) is incorrect.** Rule 21(d) says that the motion for transfer should be filed before arraignment "or at any other time the court or these rules prescribe."

**Answer (D) is incorrect.** Of course the court's consent is required since the transfer requires a formal court order.

**277.** The Sixth Amendment to the United States Constitution provides that "in all criminal prosecutions, the accused shall enjoy the right to a speedy . . . trial. . . . " In *Barker v. Wingo*, 407 U.S. 514 (1972), the Supreme Court refused to set specific parameters on this right and adopted a flexible, factor approach to resolving the issue of when the accused's speedy trial rights have been violated.

The first factor is the length of the delay between the initiation of criminal proceedings (the arrest or indictment) and the criminal trial. The length of this delay is considered to be a "triggering mechanism" and is "presumptively prejudicial" as it approaches a year. *Doggett v. United States*, 505 U.S. 647 (1992). Here, Solan was tried and convicted (July 16th this year) more than three years after she was arrested (March 15th, three years ago) ago, a length of time surely triggering a possible Sixth Amendment claim.

The second *Barker* factor is the reason for the delay. In the instant case, the first trial was scheduled in December, three years ago and was postponed six times. The first (Dec. 1st, three years ago) and sixth (Oct. 18th, last year) postponements were because of defense needs (defendant's new lawyer needed time to prepare; defendant ill); the second (May 1st, two years ago) was because of the judge's heart attack and not for any reason related to either party. The third (Sept. 1st, two years ago) and fourth (Jan. 15th, last year) postponements specifically were to aid the prosecution when the prosecutor had too many cases to handle and when a key government witness disappeared.. The fifth postponement (April 15th, last year) was because the court house caught fire, again a reason not attributed to either party. Since two of the delays were to assist the government in presenting its best case, it may be that this factor will be so decisive that it will cause a Sixth Amendment violation. Delays by defense counsel are attributed to the defendant. *Vermont v. Brillon*, ___ U.S. ___ (2009).

The third *Barker* factor is whether the accused demanded a speedy trial. The defendant specifically objected to postponements three (Sept. 1st, two years ago), four (Jan. 15, last year), and five (April 15th, last year). Thus, the defendant consistently demanded a speedy trial (other than when there was a heart attack or court house fire) and this *Barker* factor is satisfied.

The fourth *Barker* factor is prejudice to the accused. Defendant Solan must establish that the delay somehow prejudiced her ability adequately to prepare the case for trial. Based on the facts in the question, there is no obvious prejudice.

278.  **Answer (C) is correct.** In *Smith v. Hooey*, 393 U.S. 374 (1969), the United States Supreme Court held that the Sixth Amendment speedy trial guarantee protects prisoners incarcerated in a state other than one that has issued an indictment against the prisoner. Upon that prisoner's demand, the jurisdiction that issued the indictment must make a "diligent, good faith effort" to bring the prisoner before its courts for trial. American jurisdictions have signed the Interstate Compact on Detainers that facilitates this interstate cooperation.

      **Answers (A) and (B) are incorrect** because *Smith v. Hooey* held that the speedy trial guarantee does apply to persons charged with crimes who are incarcerated in another jurisdiction.

      **Answer (D) is incorrect** because *Smith* does not mandate a trial in the State of Boerum (where he is incarcerated) of the homicide charges pending in the State of Brooke.

279.  **Answer (B) is correct.** Under 18 U.S.C. § 3161(b), ordinarily an indictment must be filed within 30 days of arrest if the federal grand jury is in session. If the federal grand jury is not in session, an additional 30 days is permitted.

      **Answers (A), (C), and (D) are incorrect** because they state inaccurate time periods in which an indictment must be filed.

280.  **Answer (B) is correct.** Under 18 U.S.C. § 3161(c) ordinarily trial should commence within 70 days from the filing of the indictment or information. If the accused is indicted and then taken before a judicial officer, the date the accused appears before the judicial officer begins the 70–day time limit.

      **Answers (A) and (C) are incorrect** because each states an inaccurate time period.

      **Answer (D) is incorrect** because the Federal Speedy Trial Act establishes time limits that differ markedly from the vague ones protected by the constitutional speedy trial guarantee. *See Barker v. Wingo*, 407 U.S. 514 (1972).

281.  **Answer (D) is correct** because the time it took the government to relocate missing evidence is not an exception under 18 U.S.C. § 3161(h).

      **Answers (A), (B), and (C) are incorrect.** (because they are exceptions). The time it took the government to respond to any pretrial motion is excluded under 18 U.S.C. § 3161(h)(1)(D) (Answer A); the time to resolve the interlocutory appeal is excluded under 18 U.S.C. § 3161(h)(1)(E) (Answer B); and the time to conduct a mental examination of Kenneth is also excluded under 18 U.S.C. § 3161(h)(1)(A) (Answer C).

282.  Two limits exist with respect to setting criminal cases too quickly. First, the defendant has a Due Process right to a fair opportunity to prepare a defense. This may also be part of the accused's Sixth Amendment right to the effective assistance

of counsel. Scheduling a case too promptly may well violate these important rights.

Second, the Federal Speedy Trial Act of 1974, 18 U.S.C. § 3161(c)(2), provides that absent the defendant's consent in writing, a trial shall not commence less than 30 days from the date the defendant first appears through counsel.

| TOPIC 79 | ANSWERS |
|---|---|
| **STATUTE OF LIMITATIONS** | |

283.  **Answer (A) is correct.** The statute of limitations begins to run from the time of the crime and ordinarily ends at arrest or indictment. Sometimes this is difficult to establish if the precise date of the offense is uncertain.

**Answers (A), (B), and (C) are incorrect** because these dates do not determine when the statute of limitation begins to run. Some of these dates may be important in assessing when the statute of limitations *stops* running. Typically, the statute of limitations ceases to run when the defendant is arrested or indicted.

284.  **Answer (C) is correct.** When a statute of limitations is tolled, it stops running. The period during which it is tolled does not count in assessing whether the statute was violated. For example, often the statute of limitations is tolled during the time the defendant is out of state. Thus, if the defendant commits a crime on January 1st and immediately leaves the state to avoid apprehension, the statute of limitations does not run during the defendant's absence from the state.

**Answers (A) is incorrect** because tolling deals with an interruption in the running of the statute of limitations, not in the fact that it was exceeded.

**Answer (B) is incorrect** since tolling means the running of the statute is interrupted, not that it has started to run.

**Answer (D) is incorrect** since tolling means that the running of the statute is interrupted. By definition, the initial event starting the statute has occurred.

285. **Answer (B) is correct.** A federal prisoner challenging a federal conviction by a collateral attack ordinarily would file a Motion to Vacate Sentence under 28 U.S.C. § 2255.

**Answer (A) is incorrect** because ordinarily federal habeas corpus is used by a state prisoner. Federal prisoners challenging federal convictions ordinarily use the Motion to Vacate Sentence, § 2255.

**Answers (C) and (D) are incorrect** because state remedies are not used to argue that a federal constitutional right was violated in a federal criminal trial.

286. **Answer (D) is correct.** A federal habeas corpus petition may be filed in the federal district where the petitioner is "in custody." If the state has more than one federal judicial district, the habeas corpus petition may also be filed in the federal district where the state trial occurred. 28 U.S.C. § 2241(d).

**Answer (A) is incorrect** because the initial federal habeas corpus petition is filed in the federal district court where the petitioner is in custody (or was tried); the matter would be filed later in Washington if the U.S. Supreme Court is ultimately asked to review the matter.

**Answer (B) is incorrect** because a federal habeas corpus petition is filed in federal, not state, court.

**Answer (C) is incorrect** because the location of the state supreme court is irrelevant in assessing where a federal habeas corpus petition is filed.

287. **Answer (A) is correct.** A second federal habeas corpus application is barred if the identical claim was presented in a prior application. 28 U.S.C. § 2244(b)(1).

**Answer (B) is incorrect** because completion of service of the conviction being challenged in the habeas corpus petition would not bar the habeas corpus petition; indeed, a reason for filing the petition is to obtain release from that sentence.

**Answer (C) is incorrect.** The statute of limitations for federal habeas corpus for someone in state custody is generally one year, not six months, after the state judgment becomes final by the expiration of the time for seeking direct appellate review of that judgment. 28 U.S.C. § 2244(d)(1).

**Answer (D) is incorrect** because federal habeas corpus is specifically designed to permit an attack on a state conviction obtained in violation of the United States Constitution. 28 U.S.C. § 2254(a). It is not an appropriate remedy for violation of a state constitutional guarantee.

**288.**   **Answer (D) is correct.** None of the suggested items would be helpful. Federal habeas corpus law strongly encourages a habeas corpus applicant to file only one petition that brings out all grounds for reversing a conviction. If, as in the instant case, the first habeas corpus petition did not mention a particular ground, 28 U.S.C. § 2244(b)(2) establishes the general rule that the court should dismiss a second petition alleging the new ground. However, this provision also establishes three exceptions where the second petition will not be dismissed.

**Answer (A) is incorrect.** The fact that the issue was actually presented in the first petition effectively bars reconsideration in the second, absent several statutory exceptions not present in this case. 28 U.S.C. § 2244(b)(1).

**Answer (B) is incorrect** because a failure to present the issue in an earlier petition is specific grounds for a federal court to disallow it in a second petition unless the failure to raise the issue earlier is excused because the factual predicate for it could not have been discovered through due diligence. 28 U.S.C. § 2244(b)(2)(B).

**Answer (C) is incorrect** because the fact that the case law on point had been in existence over twenty years makes it hard to establish that the issue could not have been discovered by due diligence.

**289.**   **Answer (A) is correct.** 28 U.S.C. § 2244 (b)(1) specifically provides that a claim presented in a second habeas petition that was presented in a prior application shall be dismissed.

**Answer (B) is incorrect.** A second petition may be permitted by a three-court panel of court of appeals judges; a single appellate judge lacks the authority to approve the second petition. 28 U.S.C. § 2244(b)(3)(B).

**Answer (C) is incorrect.** A federal court may issue a stay of state proceedings pending against the habeas corpus petitioner. 28 U.S.C. § 2251.

**Answer (D) is incorrect** since Answer (A) is correct.

**290.**   **Answer (C) is correct.** A prerequisite to appealing a dismissed federal habeas corpus petition is a "certificate of appealability." 28 U.S.C. § 2253(c)(1). The certificate may be obtained from a judge of the appropriate federal circuit. This often cumbersome procedure was instituted to minimize frivolous appeals in habeas corpus actions. The applicant for the certificate must make a "substantial showing of the denial of a constitutional right." 28 U.S.C.§ 2253(c)(2).

**Answer (A) is incorrect** because the Supreme Court's permission is not necessary to appeal a dismissed habeas corpus petition.

**Answer (B) is incorrect** because filing a brief in the circuit court does not perfect the appeal, though a brief may be necessary if the appeal is permitted.

**Answer (D) is incorrect.** A notice of appeal filed in the district court is not a prerequisite to filing an appeal of a dismissed habeas corpus petition.

**291.**   Federal habeas corpus petitioners must satisfy the so-called "exhaustion of remedies" requirement in 28 U.S.C. § 2254(b)(1), which in general, means that the applicant must have exhausted available state remedies or have a satisfactory reason for not doing so. In reviewing the file, you must ascertain whether your client has "exhausted the remedies available in courts of the State." 28 U.S.C. § 2254(b)(1).

Federal habeas corpus law specifically provides: "[A]n applicant shall not be deemed to have exhausted the remedies available in the courts of the State, within the meaning of this section, if he has the right under the law of the State to raise, by any available procedure, the question presented." 28 U.S.C. § 2254(c). This provision will require you to determine what issues were appealed in state court and whether there are any available state remedies to raise the issues you want to address in your habeas corpus petition.

Federal habeas corpus law also recognizes that the exhaustion rule need not be satisfied in two situations, both of which you may have to investigate if your review of the file and state law suggests the issue has not been "exhausted." First, no exhaustion is necessary if there is an "absence of available State corrective process." 28 U.S.C. § 2254(b)(1)(B)(I). What remedies are still available in state courts to raise the issues you want to pursue?

The second excuse for not exhausting state remedies is that "circumstances exist that render such [available state] processes ineffective to protect the rights of the applicant." 28 U.S.C. § 2254(b)(1)(B)(ii). This difficult standard requires you to determine whether the existing state procedures are somehow ineffective in protecting your client's rights.

**292.**   Federal habeas corpus law makes it difficult to relitigate an issue that was already litigated in state court: "An application for a writ of habeas corpus on behalf of a person in custody pursuant to the judgment of a State court shall not be granted with respect to any claim that was adjudicated on the merits in State court proceedings unless. . . . " 28 U.S.C. § 2254(d). If the same issue about the illegal confession was raised and resolved in the state appellate court, the federal petition may be dismissed for that reason alone.

But federal law also recognizes some exceptions where a prior state adjudication on the issue is not dispositive. The first exception is where the state decision was "contrary to, or involved an unreasonable application of, clearly established Federal law, as determined by the Supreme Court of the United States." 28 U.S.C. § 2254(d)(1). You will have to review the state appellate court decision as well as U.S. Supreme Court precedents to see whether the state ruling on the confession satisfied this high standard.

The second exception is when the state decision "was based on an unreasonable determination of the facts in light of the evidence presented in the State court proceeding." 28 U.S.C. § 2254(d)(2). You will have to review the trial to ascertain whether the "unreasonable" standard was met when the state court determined the facts underlying your illegal confession issue.

**293.**   **Answer (B) is correct.** In *Anders v. California*, 386 U.S. 738 (1967), the Supreme Court held that counsel should not leave an indigent defendant unrepresented on appeal even when appellate counsel is convinced the appeal has no merit. The Court prescribed what is now called an *Anders* brief which requires appellate counsel to file a document briefly referring to anything in the record that might arguably support an appeal. Counsel may request to withdraw from the case after the brief is filed. The indigent client should be given a copy of the *Anders* brief, which the appellate court will consider in deciding whether to allow counsel to withdraw and to dismiss the appeal.

**Answer (A) is incorrect.** Informing your client that you will file no documents may violate your indigent client's right to be represented by counsel. The better procedure is for counsel to file an *Anders* brief described above.

**Answer (C) is incorrect.** A letter to the appellate court is inadequate to satisfy the indigent client's right to be represented by counsel. An *Anders* brief should be filed instead of a letter.

**Answer (D) is incorrect.** Filing a serious brief arguing issues you know are frivolous is not consistent with the requirements that counsel be both candid and not misleading. An *Anders* brief is the better choice.

**294.**   **Answer (A) is correct.** *Furman* was based on the Eighth Amendment's Cruel and Unusual Punishment Clause.

   **Answers (B), (C), and (D) are incorrect** since *Furman* was based on the Eighth Amendment, not the Fourteenth (Answers (B) and (C)), or the Supremacy Clause (Answer (D)).

**295.**   **Answer (D) is correct.** The three categories in Answers (A) — (C) are barred from being executed for murder.

   **Answer (A) is incorrect.** The Supreme Court held in *Roper v. Simmons*, 543 U.S 1 (2005), that the Eighth Amendment bars executing people who were under age 18 when they committed a murder.

   **Answer (B) is incorrect.** The Court in *Atkins v. Virginia*, 536 U.S. 304 (2002), held that the mentally retarded may not be executed.

   **Answer (C) is incorrect.** *Ford v. Wainwright*, 477 U.S. 399 (1986), holds that the insane may not be executed consistent with the Eighth Amendment.

**296.**   **Answer (D) is correct.** The Supreme Court has severely limited the types of criminal activity for which the death penalty may be imposed. It has specifically approved that penalty for major participation in a felony combined with reckless indifference to human life. *Tison v. Arizona*, 481 U.S. 137 (1987).

   **Answers (A) and (B) are incorrect.** The Court has specifically rejected the death penalty for rape of an adult (*Enmund v. Florida*, 458 U.S. 782 (1982)) or child (*Kennedy v. Louisiana*, 128 S. Ct. 2641 (2008)).

   **Answer (C) is incorrect.** *Tison v. Arizona*, 481 U.S. 137 (1987), approved the death penalty for *major* participation in a felony murder (accompanied by reckless indifference to human life) but not to *minor* participation in the felony.

   **Answer (E) is incorrect** because Answers (A), (B), and (C) are not valid crimes for the death penalty.

**297.**   The Supreme Court has held that states have great latitude in formulating their aggravating and mitigating factors in capital cases, but there are some limits. One such limit, bottomed on the Eighth Amendment's Cruel and Unusual Punishment Clause, is that the state must permit the jury to take an "individualized" approach that involves considering virtually anything relevant to mitigation. This includes information about the defendant's background, character, and details about the crime that could convince the jury to impose a sentence other than death. *See, e.g.,*

*Johnson v. Texas*, 509 U.S. 350 (1993)(jury must be permitted to consider youth of defendant as mitigating factor); *Penry v. Lynaugh*, 492 U.S. 302 (1989)(jury must be permitted to consider mitigating evidence about defendant's retardation and childhood abuse).

The instant defendant's childhood abuse by the priest would surely qualify as relevant to an individualized approach to mitigation and should be admitted.

298.     **Answer (B) is correct.** In *Ring v. Arizona*, 536 U.S. 584 (2002), the Supreme Court held under the Sixth Amendment a jury (unless waived) must decide any fact that increases the maximum punishment. In *Ring*, state law authorized the jury to decide guilt or innocence but the judge decided the presence or absence of any aggravating factors.

     **Answer (A) is incorrect.** The Supreme Court in *Ring* held that a jury, not judge (unless waived), must resolve factual issues increasing the maximum sentence.

     **Answer (C) is incorrect.** A state may constitutionally allow a victim's impact statement to be introduced as evidence in the sentencing phase of a capital case. *Payne v. Tennessee*, 501 U.S. 808 (1991).

     **Answer (D) is incorrect** since all of the above are not true. Answers (A) and (C) are not true, as explained above.

299.    **Answer (A) is correct.** Retribution is not designed to prevent future conduct; its focus is on punishing someone because the person deserves to be punished for violating the criminal law.

**Answer (B) is incorrect.** Deterrence is designed to prevent (deter) future conduct by having the offender not recidivate because of fear of punishment.

**Answer (C) is incorrect.** Rehabilitation attempts to change the offender's values/opportunities so he or she will not reoffend.

**Answer (D) is incorrect.** Incapacitation seeks to make it impossible for the offender to reoffend by removing the defendant from society (prison) or otherwise taking away the opportunity for continued criminal activity.

**Answers (E) and (F) are incorrect.** since only one of the above answers (Answer (A)) is correct.

300.    **Answer (C) is correct.** At allocution, the defendant may address the court concerning his or her views about the sentence.

**Answer (A) is incorrect.** Of course defense counsel may address the issue of sentence, but this is not considered "allocution."

**Answer (B) is incorrect.** Allocution refers to a statement by the defendant, not by the jury.

**Answer (D) is incorrect.** The prosecutor may express sentiments about the appropriate sentence, but allocution refers to a statement by the defendant, not the prosecutor.

301.    **Answer (D) is correct.** This is an accurate summary of the *Apprendi* holding.

**Answer (A) is incorrect.** *Apprendi* refers to factual findings, not to setting the exact sentence that will actually be imposed based on the facts found by the jury. The judge still sets the precise sentence under *Apprendi*.

**Answer (B) is incorrect.** *Apprendi* is based on the Sixth Amendment and the Due Process Clause. The Equal Protection Clause is not the basis for *Apprendi*.

**Answer (C) is incorrect.** *Apprendi* made it clear that a jury must find many facts related to sentencing, but need not find the fact of a prior conviction.

302.    The primary argument is that the sentence is so excessive that it violates the proportionality standard in the Eighth Amendment. Though the United States

Supreme Court has rendered a number of fractured decisions on the issue, the Court has made it clear that a sentence that is grossly disproportionate to the gravity of the crime would violate the Eighth Amendment. *Harmelin v. Michigan*, 501 U.S. 957 (1991).

Defense counsel's argument that this particular sentence is grossly disproportionate will be rejected since the Court has upheld even longer sentences for lesser crimes. Thus, in *Lockyer v. Andrade*, 538 U.S. 63 (2003), the Supreme Court upheld two consecutive sentences of 25-years to life for thefts of five videotapes worth $85 by a person with three prior felony convictions for violent felonies. The Court held the sentence was not grossly disproportionate so as to constitute cruel and unusual punishment.

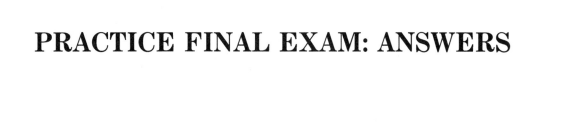

# PRACTICE FINAL EXAM: ANSWERS

**303.** This question pits a black letter rule against the fundamental Fourth Amendment principle that our homes are entitled to the highest protection of Fourth Amendment privacy interests. *Kyllo v. U.S.*, 533 U.S. 27 (2001). The black letter rule is that a dog sniff in general is not a search. Nothing indicates that the officer had any factual predicate — reasonable suspicion or probable cause — to believe that any tenant had drugs. A dog sniff in a public place which alerts police to the presence of drugs is not a search. *U.S. v. Place*, 462 U.S. 696 (1983). The Court's reasoning in exempting a dog sniff from the reasonableness standard of the Fourth Amendment was based upon three factors: a dog sniff is a minimal intrusion, a dog only sniffs for the presence of contraband, and a drug dog is highly accurate. That *dicta* in *Place* was unsupported by any data, and all three pillars have subsequently been challenged If the dog sniff, here, is not a search, the dog's positive alert provided probable cause to secure the search warrant.

There are competing interests which will determine the validity of the search warrant. Does a tenant have a protected privacy interest in the common hallway of an apartment house? At most, there is a limited privacy interest in the hallway. One has no expectation of privacy in the sounds and smells emanating from one's apartment which fellow-tenants may perceive. Does that mean that the limited expectation of privacy gives way to no privacy and there are no limits to police presence and surveillance in the hallway? There is no expectation of privacy in the common hallway. By disclosing sounds and smells to fellow tenants, one has no retained privacy protection in those sounds and smells. More important, though, is whether the dog sniff is of the air outside the threshold of the apartment or does the dog allow police to discover intimate behavior from within the apartment?

Courts are divided over whether a dog sniff of the hallway outside an apartment is a search. The uncertainty surrounding this issue developed as a result of a Florida prosecution. Twice, a Florida Court of Appeals held that a dog sniff around a home is a search. The state appealed two times to the U.S. Supreme Court. The first time, the Supreme Court granted certiorari and summarily reversed the Florida court's decision. After the Florida Court of Appeals pushed back and reaffirmed its original ruling that a dog sniff outside of a home is a search, the U.S. Supreme Court backed off and denied the state's petition for certiorari. Obviously, the issue is not resolved. *See State v. Rabb (Rabb II)*, 920 So.2d 1175, cert. denied, 127 S. Ct. 665 (2006).

Detective Roberts submitted an application for a search warrant based upon information received from a confidential unnamed informant. After considering the affidavit, the magistrate informed Roberts that the probable cause section was insufficient. The magistrate administered the oath to Roberts and asked him questions to fill out the probable cause. The magistrate recorded Robert's supplemental testimony. After hearing Roberts' additional information, the magistrate told Roberts and the assistant prosecutor that she was not convinced that the informant really existed. The magistrate ordered Roberts and the assistant prosecutor to produce the informant in chambers the next morning.

304.    **Answer (A) is correct.** The solution to this question lies along the divisions of power in the criminal justice system. The judge's authority is to issue the search warrant or deny the application. The prosecutor determines what type and how much evidence to present in the affidavit to the issuing judge. The judge may demand additional evidence, including information about the informant, as a condition of issuing the warrant. At that point, the prosecutor must decide whether to produce the additional evidence or forgo the warrant.

　　　　**Answers (B) and (C) are incorrect.** There is an "informant's privilege" that allows the prosecutor to use information from an informant without disclosing the informant's identity in most situations. The justification for the privilege is two-fold. Certain crimes cannot be prosecuted without inside information. Such information is usually supplied by someone involved in the illegal enterprise or a purchaser of contraband offered for sale by the illegal enterprise. The lives of informants would be placed in danger if the source of the information becomes known. The safety concerns of ordinary witnesses who are not involved in the enterprise also may need to be protected. While the privilege may allow the prosecution not to disclose the identity of the informant, it does not require a judge to issue a warrant without such disclosure. Therefore, it is up to the prosecutor to produce the witness, or in some cases provide just the informant's identity, or not pursue the warrant. *McCray v. Illinois*, 386 U.S. 300 (1967). The informant's privilege is not absolute. If the informant's testimony is relevant to questions of guilt or innocence at trial, the defendant has the right to know the identity of the informant and have the opportunity to cross-examine the informant at trial. *Roviaro v. United States*, 353 U.S. 53 (1957). In most cases where an informant's information is used to obtain a search warrant, the subsequent prosecution will be based upon evidence found during the execution of the search warrant, and the informant will never have to testify, nor will the informant's identity have to be disclosed.

　　　　**Answer (D) is incorrect.** In most jurisdictions, the prosecutor's office could submit the application to another judge (judge shopping). The judge does have the right to demand the information and can enforce the order by refusing to issue the warrant if the information is not forthcoming.

305.    **Answer (C) is correct.** A warrant must specify the place to be searched. Where the search involves a multi-unit building, the warrant must describe the specific unit to be searched. The specificity required in a warrant must control police during execution of the warrant. Although there was an error in the description of the apartment to be searched, the warrant contained sufficient specificity to direct police to the correct unit. The warrant correctly specified a unit on the second floor belonging to Angel Smith whose name was on the door plate. The error — front or

back unit — did not lead police to the wrong unit. A requirement of greater specificity would exceed the constitutional standard of reasonableness. The federal constitutional requirement is satisfied "if the description is such that an officer with a search warrant can, with reasonable effort, ascertain and identify the place to be searched." *Steele v. U.S.*, 267 U.S. 498 (1925).

**Answers (A) and (B) are incorrect.** The purpose of the specificity requirement is to limit the discretion of officers executing a warrant and to ensure that the search is limited to the place where probable cause existed to believe that evidence would be found. A minor error in the number of the house or apartment will not necessarily be fatal to the search, if the place to be searched is otherwise sufficiently described in the warrant and readily identifiable. The Fourth Amendment standard is reasonableness. A mistake in the identification of the premises to be searched will not necessarily invalidate the warrant so long as the mistake is reasonable. Even where an investigation led police to believe that the entire third floor of a house was one apartment and this belief continued during execution of the warrant until they discovered incriminating evidence in a second apartment, not occupied by the original suspect, the mistake was held to be reasonable and the search upheld. *Maryland v. Garrison*, 480 U.S. 79 (1987).

**Answer (D) is not the best answer.** If the error in the warrant proved to be fatal, the good faith exception to the warrant requirement would save the evidence and insure its admissibility. *U.S. v. Leon*, 468 U.S. 897 (1984). A hearing court may apply the good faith exception without first determining the validity of the search warrant. The best approach is to rule on the search warrant first; otherwise, there is no future guidance for police and magistrates.

306. The motion to suppress should be denied; the drugs and the necklace are admissible. A search warrant is more than just an admission ticket; it also regulates the scope of the search. During the execution of a lawful search warrant, police may seize other objects in plain view in the course of a lawful search. Those objects must be found while the police are lawfully searching. Police discovered drugs while searching for the necklace. The fact that police had probable cause to look for drugs does not expand the lawful scope of the search. The failure to include that evidence in the affidavit and its absence from the warrant precluded them from searching for anything beyond the necklace listed in the warrant. As long as they were searching for the necklace, what they discovered in plain view may be admissible. If the police had discovered the necklace early in the search, they would have had to terminate the search immediately, even though they had probable cause to look for drugs. Since a necklace could be hidden anywhere, the search for the necklace could extend to any area, room, and container within the house. Once they had the item specified in the warrant, they had no authority to search for anything else. Here, the police lucked out because the necklace was not discovered until they had completed the search of the first floor. *Horton v. California*, 496 U.S. 128 (1990).

307. **Answer (A) is the best answer.** Absent exigent circumstances, a search warrant is required to enter a home to arrest a non-resident. *Steagald v. U.S.*, 451 U.S. 204

(1981). However, the illegal entry of the home does not render Tom's arrest illegal. A magistrate issued an arrest warrant based upon probable cause, and the arrest, itself, is legal notwithstanding the illegal entry. Even if the entry tainted the arrest, the arrest would become legal as soon as the police removed Tom from his girlfriend's home. *New York v. Harris*, 495 U.S. 14 (1990).

**Answer (B) is not the best answer.** Even if Tom's mother had warned him that the police were on the way, there are no facts to support a reasonable belief that Tom is armed or dangerous or a flight risk. Consequently, exigent circumstances did not exist to justify an entry without a search warrant.

**Answers (C) and (D) are not the best answers.** Ordinarily, entry of a home to arrest a non-resident without a search warrant and without consent or exigent circumstances violates the Fourth Amendment. However, the entry does not make the arrest illegal. A magistrate issued an arrest warrant based upon probable cause. The police violated the residents' privacy, not the defendant's privacy. Even if the entry tainted the arrest, the arrest would become legal as soon as the police removed Tom from his girlfriend's home.

308.    **Answer (D) is correct.** The Fourth Amendment standard governing the scope of an intrusion following a custodial arrest is reasonableness. In order to determine the reasonableness of such an invasive procedure as a strip search, the court balances the need against the invasion that the search entails. Presumably, the governmental interest is to prevent smuggling of contraband into the jail. The facts indicate that Piersall would not at any time have been integrated into the jail population. D.U.I. defendants are isolated in individual holding cells until such time as they are released. In order to justify a search under these circumstances the police would have to have facts and circumstances giving rise to a reasonable belief that the detained individual has contraband hidden on her person. There was no such evidence in this case, and the strip search violated the defendant's Fourth Amendment rights. *Way v. County of Ventura*, 445 F.3d 1157 (9th Cir 2006); *Clements v. Logan*, 455 U.S. 942 (4th Cir 1981).

**Answer (A) is incorrect.** Controlling police discretion is only one of two purposes served by the Fourth Amendment. The other purpose protects individual privacy. In this case, the absence of police discretion ensured that every detainees' rights were violated. D.U.I. arrestees are not introduced into the jail population in the facts. Consequently, a strip search could only be justified if there was cause to believe that the defendant had contraband hidden on her person.

**Answer (B) is incorrect.** Police may incident to a custodial arrest conduct a full search of an arrestee's person. Strip searches are not treated like ordinary incidental searches. If the arrestee is to be integrated into a jail's general population, the policy is likely to be upheld. Where the arrestee is not integrated into the jail population, there must be specific cause to believe that the arrestee has contraband on her person.

**Answer (C) is incorrect.** The scope of a search incident to arrest is not limited by the offense for which the person is arrested. A police officer may conduct a full search of an arrestee's person without cause to believe that the person has a weapon or contraband. Strip searches are treated differently and require separate justification.

309. The statute authorizing warrantless record inspections will be upheld. The Supreme Court upheld a statute authorizing warrantless administrative searches of automobile junkyards. The Court found that junkyards are pervasively regulated businesses. Those businesses are regulated because of the societal interest in tracking down stolen vehicles. The same interest justifies regulation of second-hand dealers that may serve as a market for stolen goods. Even though administrative searches originally focused upon health and safety issues, expansion to other public interests did not cause the Supreme Court even to hesitate. *New York v. Burger*, 482 U.S. 691 (1987).

The issue turns upon the lawfulness of warrantless inspections of such records. Just as with traditional search warrants, the pressure has been on the courts to sanction warrantless administrative searches. The thrust for warrantless inspection systems has focused on regulated businesses. The Supreme Court in *See v. City of Seattle*, 387 U.S. 541 (1967), stated that challenges to such programs could only be resolved on a case-by-case basis under the Fourth Amendment standard of reasonableness.

In *Burger*, the Supreme Court majority upheld the warrantless inspection scheme because junkyards are a closely regulated business. Thus, Police do not need exigent circumstances to excuse the normal warrant requirement when inspecting a highly regulated business. A closely regulated business is apparently any business that has a long history of governmental regulation in a number of states. Of course, the statutory scheme here is aimed specifically at finding evidence of criminal violations. The whole concept of administrative searches focused on the existence of a critical governmental interest, such as health and safety, which justified excusing traditional Fourth Amendment requirements such as a warrant and probable cause. Thus, historically, even though criminal prosecution could follow upon an administrative search, the primary purpose for the administrative search served a different governmental interest. In *Burger*, the Court upheld a state regulatory inspection scheme, like the statute in this Question, that was intended solely to uncover evidence of criminal acts. This statute falls within the *Burger* holding expanding the scope of warrantless administrative searches.

310. **Answer (C) is correct.** A thorny issue arises when a third person holds out to police that he has authority to consent when in fact he never did or no longer has such authority. Police may rely upon third party consent when they erroneously, but reasonably, believe that the third party possesses common authority over the premises. An objective standard is used when testing whether facts available at the moment would warrant a reasonably cautious police officer to believe that the consenting party had authority. *Illinois v. Rodriguez*, 497 U.S. 177 (1990).

The issue most often arises when police rely upon the consent of a temporary worker in a home, such as a babysitter, to enter and conduct a search. Ordinarily, one would not expect such persons to have authority over the premises to grant consent to search. Even though the temporary worker may have the run of the house, that authority does not generally extend to allowing strangers into the house, including the police, except in emergency situations. The rules pertaining to apparent authority provide that police may not rely upon the consent of a third person when facts and circumstances would alert the reasonable person to question the third-party's authority. Here, the facts should have put the police on notice that Craig did not have unlimited access to every room in the house, except for the very limited purpose of making repairs.

**Answer (A) is incorrect.** The issue surrounding consent by a third person is to be resolved by determining the authority of the consenting person. The question should not be resolved under an agency theory. A third person may not waive another person's Fourth Amendment rights. The question comes down to whether Craig had sufficient access to the house and the daughter's bedroom to waive his own Fourth Amendment rights. He did not have unlimited authority; his authority was limited to making necessary repairs.

**Answer (B) is incorrect.** Although police were investigating a potentially serious threat to public safety, the facts do not present the type of urgency and immediate need that would qualify under exigent circumstances. Their investigation might have sufficiently ripened, given public concern with school shootings, to allow a judge to issue a search warrant to investigate the potential threat to public safety. The claim of exigency would fail.

**Answer (D) is incorrect.** Police may seek third-party consent. They do not have to seek the consent of the target of the search. They may even seek third-party consent, in certain circumstances, after the target has refused consent. *Cf. United States v. Matlock*, 415 U.S. 164 (1974). The issue turns on whether the person consenting has an adequate personal privacy interest in the premises to grant consent. A temporary worker in a home does not have a sufficient privacy interest.

311. **Answer (C) is correct.** The area immediately surrounding a home is within the curtilage of the house and is accorded the same Fourth Amendment protection as the house. *U.S. v. Dunn*, 480 U.S. 294 (1987). If the police officer could have seen the patio from the driveway or from the street, there would be no Fourth Amendment protection. The Fourth Amendment protection of the curtilage and areas around the home, where the Court recognizes the greatest protection of privacy, is limited or non-existent if the homeowner fails to take steps to protect the privacy of those areas from the view of persons on the street. However, "open fields" are not subject to the same protection as the home or curtilage, even where the field is fenced, locked and posted, in other words, where it is not open and the officer is trespassing under state law. *Oliver v. United States*, 466 U.S. 170 (1984).

**Answer (A) is incorrect.** While an anonymous tip cannot by itself provide probable cause, police are free to investigate such tips. Entry onto an "open field" requires no factual predicate, whether probable cause or reasonable suspicion. Officer 1 was not free to enter the curtilage of Glass's home without a warrant; probable cause without a warrant would not have sufficed to justify the entry of the backyard.

**Answer (B) is incorrect.** Officer 2 did not violate Glass's protected privacy interest by entering the open field and walking around. However, Officer 1 did violate Glass's Fourth Amendment rights by entering the backyard attached to Glass' house.

**Answer (D) is incorrect.** The protected privacy interest in a home, backyard and the curtilage of a home does not extend to "open fields," even those that are fenced, locked and posted. "The special protection accorded by the Fourth Amendment to the people in their persons, houses, papers, and effects is not extended to open fields. The distinction between the latter and the house is as old as the common law." *Hester v. U.S.*, 265 U.S. 57 (1924).

312.   **Answer (D) is correct.** In most jurisdictions, speeding is not an arrestable offense, and a police officer may not conduct a search incident to an ordinary traffic stop for a non-arrestable offense. The dangers to a police officer ordinarily associated with the custodial arrest of a motorist are not the same when the motorist is not under arrest and will receive only a traffic ticket. *Knowles v. Iowa*, 525 U.S. 113 (1998). However, it is up to the states to determine whether an offense is an arrestable offense; a state law that authorizes custodial arrests for minor traffic offenses does not violate the Fourth Amendment. *Atwater v. City of Lago Vista*, 532 U.S. 318 (2001).

**Answers (A) and (C) are incorrect.** Whether or not speeding is an arrestable offense in the jurisdiction, the officer had already decided to issue a traffic citation and not arrest the defendant. An officer may not search incident to the issuance of a traffic citation.

**Answer (B) is incorrect.** Incident to any lawful stop of a motor vehicle, a police officer may order the motorist and any other occupants of the vehicle out of the car. The officer need not articulate any reason for ordering the occupant out of the vehicle. *Pennsylvania v. Mimms*, 434 U.S. 106 (1977); *Maryland v. Wilson*, 519 U.S. 408 (1997). However, absent an arrest, the authority over the motorist does not extend beyond ordering the motorist to get out or stay inside the vehicle. Any further intrusion, such as a frisk for weapons, must be based upon articulable facts and circumstances creating a reasonable suspicion that the motorist is armed or otherwise poses a danger to the police officer. No such factual basis was presented in this case.

313.   **Answer (B) is correct.** Incident to a valid non-custodial traffic stop, a police officer may order the motorist out of the car and may conduct a limited search — frisk — of the motorist's outer clothing for a weapon if facts support a reasonable suspicion that the motorist is armed or poses a threat to the officer. The supplemental facts in the question support such an inference. *Terry v. Ohio*, 392 U.S. 1 (1968). In fact, Abby's conduct justified the officer's decision to have her sit in the police car so that she would be under control. Moreover, a police officer may conduct a limited search of the interior of a vehicle for weapons under the same justification that gives rise to a frisk of the motorist's person. *Michigan v. Long*, 463 U.S. 1032 (1983).

**Answer (A) is incorrect.** Although the motorist was validly stopped for speeding, there was no custodial arrest until after the officer found the gun under the driver's seat in the vehicle.

**Answer (C) is incorrect.** Reasonable suspicion that the motorist is armed or dangerous will support a limited search of a vehicle for weapons. Probable cause is not required.

**Answer (D) is incorrect.** The decision to issue the traffic citation and release the motorist does not negate the authority to conduct a limited search for weapons. In fact, some courts have held that a limited search of the vehicle for weapons is not permissible until the officer has definitely decided to allow the motorist to return to the vehicle and depart the scene.

314.    **Answer (C) is correct.** The evidence is inadmissible. The bullet would not have been lost if the procedure was delayed while a court order or warrant was sought. Therefore, there was no justification for the warrantless intrusion. If the object sought was evanescent and might have dissipated if the procedure was delayed, such as blood alcohol count in a drunk driving investigation, exigent circumstances would justify a warrantless intrusion. A simple blood test, though, is far less intrusive than a surgical intrusion involving anesthetic. Even if one could imagine such a procedure that might have been necessary to proceed without judicial authorization, the facts of this case do not come close to creating exigent circumstances to justify bypassing prior judicial authorization. Prior judicial authorization is not required if the procedure is medically necessary for Dunn's health and safety.

**Answer (A) is incorrect.** While the state's need for the evidence in this particular case would weigh heavily in favor of allowing such a procedure, there was no exigency to justify bypassing prior judicial authorization.

**Answer (B) is incorrect.** Incident to arrest, a defendant is subject to a full search of his or her person, including physical tests. However, the authority to conduct a warrantless search incident to arrest does not extend to surgical procedures, especially one that involves administration of a general anesthetic. For a surgical intrusion, even a warrant is probably insufficient. A defendant would be entitled to an adversary proceeding at which the defendant is entitled to representation by counsel. Whether a court will order a surgical intrusion must be decided by balancing the state's need for the evidence versus the nature of the intrusion and the risk it poses to the defendant. *Winston v. Lee*, 470 U.S. 753 (1985).

**Answer (D) is incorrect.** Although the Fourth and Fifth Amendments were originally deemed to provide complementary protection, the United States Supreme Court separated the two guaranties by holding that the Fifth Amendment privilege against compelled self-incrimination applies only to testimonial evidence, not physical evidence. *Schmerber v. California*, 384 U.S. 757 (1966). In this case, then, the issue comes down solely to whether the surgical intrusion to retrieve the bullet complied with the reasonableness command of the Fourth Amendment.

**315.** The evidence is inadmissible. There are multiple exceptions to the warrant requirement which allow for a search of an automobile. The search in the problem does not fit under any of the exceptions.

Incident to the arrest of a motorist or another occupant of a vehicle, a police officer may search the interior compartment of the vehicle. *New York v. Belton*, 453 U.S. 454 (1981). The *Belton* search allows for a search while the arrestee remains at the scene of the arrest and not in a police car. *Arizona v. Gant*, 129 S. Ct. 1710 (2009). Lush had already been removed from the scene before the officer searched the car. Moreover, a *Belton* search does not extend to the trunk of the vehicle where the prescription drugs were found.

A police officer may search the entire vehicle, including the trunk, under the automobile exception, whether or not the arrestee is still on the scene. However, the automobile exception requires independent probable cause to believe that contraband or other evidence is located in the vehicle. *Carroll v. U.S.*, 267 U.S. 132 (1925). There was no probable cause to search the vehicle. Police may search the area around the driver's seat for a weapon if there is reasonable suspicion to believe that the motorist is armed or dangerous. *Michigan v. Long*, 463 U.S. 1032 (1983). However, a frisk of the vehicle is not permitted absent reasonable suspicion nor if the motorist is arrested and will not be permitted to drive the car away.

An alternative theory that might allow for a search is the inventory exception to the warrant requirement. An inventory search is not a search for evidence; it is an administrative procedure, comparable to booking at the police station, which permits police to inventory the contents of a vehicle in order to protect the owner's property and to insulate police from false claims of loss. *South Dakota v. Opperman*, 428 U.S. 364 (1976); *Colorado v. Bertine*, 479 U.S. 367 (1987). Authorization to conduct an inventory, however, rests upon a lawful impoundment. If the car is impounded, police may conduct an inventory of its contents and inventory the contents of closed containers provided it is part of the standardized procedure. *Florida v. Wells*, 495 U.S. 1 (1990). Here, there was no valid reason to impound the vehicle. It was not damaged, and Lush's girlfriend was prepared to take possession of the car. If there is no lawful impoundment, there is no lawful inventory. The search of the car fails under all of the exceptions to the warrant requirement.

**316.** **Answer (D) is correct.** An ordinary traffic stop does not trigger the need for *Miranda* warnings. It is short in duration, and its purpose is the issuance of a traffic citation. Moreover, it is done in full view of the public, and police are thus naturally restrained. The test for whether a police-citizen encounter is custodial is an objective one: whether a reasonable person in the suspect's position would have believed that he was in custody. The officer's subjective intent and the suspect's subjective understanding, while helpful, are not dispositive. Here, the detention was lengthy, the suspect's ride was sent away, and the suspect was asked to sit in the police car. While the latter factor is not dispositive by itself, coupled with the others, it helps to show that the suspect was in custody when Officer Dogood asked Stout how much he had drunk that evening. He should have been advised of his *Miranda* rights before being asked the question. *Berkermer v. McCarty*, 468 U.S.

420 (1984).

**Answer (A) is incorrect.** This was not an ordinary traffic stop for the purpose of issuing a citation. It matured into a custodial arrest fairly quickly requiring warnings prior to any questioning.

**Answer (B) in incorrect.** Stout was in custody before he was told he was under arrest.

**Answer (C) is incorrect.** Ordinarily a traffic stop is not custodial and does not require police to administer *Miranda* warnings prior to questioning a suspect. Traffic stops, like all *Terry*-stops, could be custodial depending upon the conduct of the officers.

317.    **Answer (B) is the correct answer.** There was no valid reason for the state to have the pretrial identification take place outside the presence of defendant's attorney. It was the day of trial, and counsel was present in the courtroom. The final out-of-court identification took place for either or both of two reasons: a final check to make sure that the defendant was the right one or an effort to bolster the witness' testimony and provide her with a live opportunity to see the defendant in order to make her in-court identification more certain. Considering there was no reason whatsoever for excluding the defense attorney from the holding cell identification, the state raised unnecessary uncertainty about its own witness' testimony. However, so long as the standard is not beyond a reasonable doubt, courts will hold that the witness' in-court identification was independent of the tainted holding cell viewing because of the victim's description of Big and her ability earlier on two occasions to identify him.

**Answer (A) is incorrect.** Big's Sixth Amendment right to counsel was violated when his attorney, who was present, was excluded from the holding cell viewing. However, the prosecution may demonstrate that the in-court identification is not the fruit of the constitutional violation. Here, the witness gave a strong description of the defendant shortly after the crime and identified him twice before the tainted holding cell viewing. *U.S. v. Wade*, 388 U.S. 218 (1967).

**Answer (c) is incorrect.** The violation of the defendant's Sixth Amendment right to counsel was purposeful. However, that is not the end of the inquiry. The witness may identify the defendant in court if the state proves that the in-court identification is not the result of the tainted identification.

**Answer (D) is incorrect.** Although it could be argued that the show-up was a lineup, it does not matter. The Sixth Amendment right to counsel is equally applicable to show-ups and confrontations where the accused is not in a lineup but presented individually in a pretrial court appearance or out of court. *Moore v. Illinois*, 434 U.S. 220 (1977).

**318.** The motion to suppress the evidence found in George and Laura's suitcases should be denied. Ordinarily, passengers do not have standing to challenge the search of a car in which they are riding because they are not deemed to have a protected privacy interest in items stored within the car. That is a fairly extreme rule arising in a case that involved the search of a passenger compartment. *Rakas v. Illinois*, 439 U.S. 128 (1978). However, a credible argument can be made that passengers have standing to challenge the search of their individually labeled luggage in the trunk of the vehicle. They have a privacy expectation in such luggage, so the reasonableness of the search is at issue. No probable cause focused on George and Laura prior to the search, nor did they seek to avoid the police (they voluntarily stayed around to take the car).

When police believed that Abner and Lisa, arrested near the border, were attempting to leave the country and were suspected of taking the mortgage business records, there was probable cause to believe that the missing business records were with them in the car. Once probable cause focuses on the entire vehicle, police may search any compartment, including the trunk, and any container in the vehicle that could contain the objects sought. Therefore, the search may extend to a passenger's possessions in the trunk even though probable cause has not focused on the passenger. *Wyoming v. Houghton*, 526 U.S. 295 (1999). The drugs were in plain view once the police searched the various containers in the trunk.

**319.** The motion to suppress statements made by Laura to her cellmate should be denied. At the time Laura was arrested and placed in a cell, she had not been read *Miranda* rights. However, that is not material to the outcome of the question. Although Laura was in custody and was essentially interrogated by the police through the cellmate-informer, her rights were not violated. *Miranda* rights are intended alleviate the inherent coerciveness associated with custodial interrogation when a police officer is asking questions. The absence from the equation of the police officer changes the equation. Laura did not know that she was being interrogated by or on behalf of the police; she was not under the same pressure that exists when an arrestee is questioned by a police officer. Consequently, there is no *Miranda* violation here, and Laura's statements to the cellmate are admissible. Illinois v. Perkins, 496 U.S. 292 (19990).

**320.** The motion to suppress Lisa's statements about the drug charges should be denied. Lisa, like Laura, does not have a *Miranda* claim since she did not know that the cellmate was a police informant. However, she was in court on the original bank fraud charges, so her Sixth Amendment right to counsel had attached. Under the

Sixth Amendment right to counsel, Lisa has the right not to be interrogated by the police without the presence of her attorney. While the cellmate's questioning does not constitute police interrogation under *Miranda*, it does fulfill the Sixth Amendment definition of interrogation — the deliberate elicitation of incriminating statements. However, the Sixth Amendment right is offense-specific and is limited to the offense for which Lisa was indicted and arraigned — mortgage fraud. It is not applicable to the drug charges where formal charges had not yet been filed, and Lisa had not been arraigned on the drug charges. Since the facts indicate only that she made statements about the narcotics, these revelations are admissible because she did not know that she was being questioned by a police agent. *United States v. Henry*, 4447 U.S. 264 (1980); *McNeil v. Wisconsin*, 501 U.S. 171 (1991).

The outcome is understandable once the purposes behind the different rules are understood. The Sixth Amendment rights are trial rights assuring a fair trial. Once a defendant is formally charged and arraigned, the full protections of the adversary process are activated, and the prosecution may not seek to discover the defendant through interrogation without the presence of the defendant's attorney. The Sixth Amendment protection is limited to offenses where the adversary process has been initiated. *Miranda* rights exist to ensure that statements made by an accused are voluntary by neutralizing the inherent coerciveness of custodial interrogation. *Miranda*/Fifth Amendment rights and the Sixth Amendment rights protect different interests.

**321.** The motion to suppress Abner's statements about mortgage fraud should be granted, and the motion as to statements about drug trafficking should be denied. The Sixth Amendment right to counsel attached to the bank mortgage fraud charges because of the prior arraignment, where Abner had counsel. Any statements made during the interrogation about the mortgage fraud charges (even if not in response to specific questions) would be inadmissible under the Sixth Amendment right to counsel unless Abner waived the Sixth Amendment right. A valid waiver of the Sixth Amendment right to counsel may be accomplished through the giving of *Miranda* warnings and a subsequent valid waiver of *Miranda* rights. Here, however, Abner did not waive his offense-specific Sixth Amendment right as to the mortgage fraud charges because it was not the subject of interrogation. *Maine v. Moulton*, 474 U.S. 159 (1985); *Patterson v. Illinois*, 487 U.S. 285 (1988). His statements about the drug trafficking operation would be resolved solely under *Miranda*. Abner was in custody and was interrogated by the detective; since he waived his *Miranda* rights, his incriminating statements about the drug trafficking operation are admissible. His Sixth Amendment right to counsel was not implicated because he had not been charged with a drug offense, and the Sixth Amendment right to counsel attaches when the adversary process begins. *Brewer v. Williams*, 430 U.S. 387 (1977).

**322.** The motion to suppress George's statements should be granted. Following his arrest a week earlier, George had exercised his *Miranda* right to counsel, and, at that time, questioning ceased. Once an arrestee exercises the *Miranda* right to counsel, police may not initiate questioning until such time as the arrestee has the opportunity to consult with a lawyer. The *Miranda* right to counsel also includes the right to have the lawyer present during interrogation. Only if the arrestee initiates discussion about the charge may a court look into whether the arrestee, then, waived the previously invoked right to counsel. *Edwards v. Arizona*, 451 U.S. 477 (1981); *Minnick v. Mississippi*, 498 U.S. 146 (1990). George had been released after invoking his *Miranda* right to counsel. The facts of this Question are different from when police try to question an arrestee shortly after he or she invoked the right. Here a week had passed, and George was arrested on other (drug) charges. However, the same detective attempted to question George. George did not initiate the discussion about the charges. Invocation of the *Miranda* right to counsel is taken to signify that the defendant feels unable to field police questions on any subject without the assistance of a lawyer; the *Miranda* right to counsel is not offense-specific as is the Sixth Amendment right. Even though time had elapsed and George was arrested again, the police should not have initiated interrogation, and George's waiver is not valid. It is possible that the Supreme Court, in the future, would consider the break in custody, when he presumably consulted with a lawyer, sufficiently significant to allow police to begin questioning George following his second arrest on new drug charges.

323. **Answer (C) is correct.** The Equal Protection Clause of the Fourteenth Amendment protects against discrimination based on heritage.

**Answer (A) is incorrect** because entrapment would be close to impossible to prove since O'Madigan approached the officer, an act which shows a predisposition to commit the gambling offense and would essentially preclude a successful entrapment defense.

**Answer (B) is incorrect.** The First Amendment's guarantee of freedom of expression does not protect speech involved in accepting an illegal wager.

**Answer (D) is incorrect.** While both substantive and procedural due Pprocess may well be a defense in some cases, here neither will be. Substantive due process, to the extent it still exists, does not render gambling laws unconstitutional since there is a defensible policy-based rationale for the existence of such laws. Procedural Due Process sets parameters on many facets of criminal procedure, but does not affect whether a crime, such as gambling, is constitutional.

324. **Answer (A) is correct.** The arraignment, occurring after the indictment, is where the defendant is asked to plead to the indictment. Fed. R. Crim. P. 10.

**Answer (B), (C), and (D) are incorrect.** The complaint occurs early in the criminal procedure, representing the first formal charges. Fed. R. Crim. P. 3. The indictment (Answer (C)) ordinarily comes after the preliminary examination but before the arraignment, which is where the defendant enters a plea, such as not guilty, to the indictment.

325. **Answer (D) is correct.** In *Gerstein v. Pugh*, 420 U.S. 103 (1975), the United States Supreme Court held that a person arrested without a warrant must have a hearing before a judge to assess whether there is probable cause to hold the person in jail. Since Fagan was arrested without a warrant and no judge has determined whether there is probable cause to detain him, he must be given a *Gerstein* hearing, ordinarily within 48 hours of arrest. *County of Riverside v. McLaughlin*, 500 U.S. 44 (1991).

**Answers (A), (B), and (C) are incorrect** since none is triggered by a warrantless arrest. An initial appearance (Answer (A)) is required after every arrest, whether with or without a warrant. Fed. R. Crim. P. 5. The grand jury (Answer (B)) and preliminary hearing (Answer (C)) have nothing to do with the status of the arrestee.

326.    **Answer (A) is correct.** In *United States v. Salerno*, 481 U.S. 739 (1987), the United States Supreme Court upheld the federal Bail Reform Act's provisions permitting pretrial detention to protect the safety of a person. Neither the due process nor excessive bail provision was violated by the so-called "preventive detention" rule. State laws authorizing detention for similar grounds also do not violate the United States Constitution.

   **Answer (B) is incorrect.** *Salerno* held that preventive detention to protect the life of a potential government witness does not offend the Eighth Amendment.

   **Answer (C) is incorrect.** Equal protection is not violated by a classification scheme permitting pretrial detention of persons who have threatened the lives of government witnesses.

   **Answer (D) is incorrect.** The Bail Reform Act of 1984 regulates pretrial release of persons facing charges in federal court, not state court.

327.    **Answer (D) is correct.** At a preliminary examination (or hearing) under the Federal Rules of Criminal Procedure and the similar rules in many other jurisdictions, the judge decides whether there is probable cause to believe that a crime was committed and that the defendant committed it. Fed. R. Crim. P. 5.1(e).

   **Answers (A), (B), and (C) are incorrect.** The standard for a preliminary examination is relatively low: probable cause. Fed. R. Crim. P. 5.1(e). It is not beyond a reasonable doubt (Answer (A))(which is the standard for guilt or innocence), or clear and convincing evidence (Answer (B))(a standard rarely used in criminal law, but is present under the Federal Bail Reform act for release pending appeal), or preponderance of the evidence (Answer (C))(which is the standard used in civil cases and for criminal defenses in some locales).

328.    **Answer (D) is correct.** Since Answers (A), (B), and (C) are all true, the best response is Answer (D), all of the above. Under the Federal Bail Reform Act, 18 U.S.C. § 3143(b), a defendant who seeks release pending appeal must establish by clear and convincing evidence that he or she is not likely to flee (Answer (A)) or pose a danger to the safety of the community (Answer (B)) and that the appeal raises a substantial question of law likely to result in reversal or a new trial (Answer (C)).

329.    **Answer (B) is correct.** The United States Constitution does not mandate a grand jury and states are free to eliminate the procedure. *Hurtado v. California*, 110 U.S. 516 (1884).

   **Answers (A), (C), and (D) are incorrect** since under the United States Constitution states are free to adopt or reject in whole or part the use of grand juries. Some states have used this latitude and have eliminated the grand jury and substitute prosecution based on an information or complaint.

330.    **Answer (B) is correct.** The prosecutor has no constitutional duty to share exculpatory evidence with a grand jury. *United States v. Williams*, 504 U.S. 36

(1992). Many commentators and a few jurisdictions disagree with this approach and argue that the prosecutor should provide known exculpatory information with the grand jury so the grand jurors have the data needed to perform their important screening function.

**Answer (A) is incorrect.** Due process does not mandate that exculpatory evidence be given to the grand jury. Due process is satisfied if the defense has a chance to provide this evidence to the petit jury at trial.

**Answer (C) is incorrect.** The Fifth Amendment does not require the government to give the grand jury exculpatory information. Indeed, the grand jury itself is not even required in state criminal procedures.

**Answer (D) is incorrect.** The defendant's right to present exculpatory evidence to a grand jury does not exist. It does not matter whether the exculpatory evidence was presented to the prosecutor or to the trial judge.

331.    **Answer (C) is correct.** Under federal law, an indictment does not have to provide, on its face, information to assess whether there is probable cause. The grand jury should have been presented with this quantum of evidence during the grand jury hearing, but the indictment itself may be conclusory and does not have to list the underlying information used to find probable cause.

**Answers (A), (B), and (D) are incorrect** (*i.e.* they are required for a valid indictment). According to the Supreme Court, a federal indictment must contain the elements of the offense (Answer (D)), fairly inform the defendant of the charge to be defended (Answer (A)), and be sufficient to enable the accused to plead double jeopardy if the same charges are pursued in a later proceeding. (Answer (B)) *Hamling v. United States*, 418 U.S. 87, 117-118 (1974).

332.    **Answer (A) is correct.** Under Rules 8(b) and 13, Federal Rules of Criminal Procedure, joinder of defendants is permissible if each is alleged to have participated in the same act or transaction, or series of acts or transactions constituting an offense or offenses. Here, Jayne and Tyrone, operating as a team, engaged in exactly the same transaction: putting their joint account numbers on deposit slips. Joinder is permissible.

**Answer (B) is incorrect** because joinder under the Federal Rules of Criminal Procedure does not depend on violation of the same statute but on participation in the same act or transaction constituting the offense. Two people who totally separately violate the same criminal statute may not, because of the common violation, be indicted or tried together.

**Answers (C) and (D) are incorrect** because a person does not have a right to a separate trial. Joinder is permissible if the standards in Rules 8 and 13 are satisfied, irrespective of the wishes of the accused persons, who may seek a severance under Rule 14.

333.    **Answer (D) is correct.** Under *Brady v. Maryland*, 373 U.S. 83 (1963), the Due Process Clause of the Fourteenth Amendment requires the prosecution to disclose to the defense evidence that would be favorable to the accused on either guilt or sentence. This rule is based on the principle that a fair trial is more likely if such evidence is provided.

**Answer (A) is incorrect.** As noted above, *Brady v. Maryland* requires the government to provide the defense with certain helpful evidence. The defense need not reciprocate. Thus, the discovery rules are not identical for both sides and the Constitution does not require such parity.

**Answer (B) is incorrect.** This answer is similar to Answer (A) and is wrong for almost the same reason. Due Process, in general, does not mandate that the rules not be tilted against the defense, though at some point it may be that incredibly one-sided procedures that considerably disadvantage the defense could violate Due Process. Some criminal procedure rules requiring the defense to provide pretrial notice to the prosecution of certain defenses, such as alibi and insanity, may be viewed as tilted against the defense but are nevertheless constitutional. But a rule that rejected all discovery would not be constitutional because of the failure to follow *Brady v. Maryland*, irrespective of whether the end result was tilted in favor of or against the defendant.

**Answer (C) is incorrect.** Due Process does not mandate reciprocal discovery. Its minimal requirements are that the prosecution provide the defense with *Brady* materials that are helpful on sentence or guilt.

334.    **Answer (D) is correct.** None of the theories in Answers (A)–(C) is likely to lead to a reversal of the conviction.

**Answer (A) is incorrect** because a one year delay in itself would not support a due process violation absent more compelling information. The government has no duty to investigate a case and bring charges. *United States v. Lovasco*, 431 U.S. 783 (1977). Perhaps the due process argument would succeed if it could be shown that the defendant suffered actual prejudice from the delay and that the delay was caused by the government's desire to obtain a tactical advantage.

**Answer (B) is incorrect.** Though speedy trial protects against delays between the arrest or formal charges and trial, it does not reach the period between arrest and indictment. In addition, a six month delay is neither unusual nor a violation of due process absent far more compelling circumstances.

**Answer (C) is incorrect.** The statute of limitations regulates the period between the crime and formal charges, not the time between an indictment and trial. The latter is covered by speedy trial.

335.    **Answer (A) is correct.** The usual rule is that the venue for a crime is where the crime occurred.

**Answer (B) is incorrect.** Venue is not based on where the defendants live; it is based on the location of the crime.

**Answer (C) is incorrect.** Venue is not based on where the victim lives, but rather on where the crime occurred.

**Answer (D) is incorrect** since Answers (B) and (C) are incorrect.

336. **Answer (C) is correct.** According to *Richmond Newspapers, Inv. v. Virginia*, 448 U.S. 555 (1980), the First and Fourteenth Amendments give the press and the public a right to attend a criminal trial. This right is not absolute, however, and may be denied for important, specific reasons and only to the extent that is necessary to further the important interests mandating closure. In the exam question, no such reasons are given, no findings have been made, and no limited disclosure options have been explored.

**Answer (A) is incorrect.** Though the defendant does have a due process right to a fair trial, no case has been made that a fair trial is not possible without removing the press from the court room. Other options will assure a fair trial, such as sequestering the jury or limiting their access to the media.

**Answer (B) is incorrect.** Though the defendant may attempt to waive a public trial, both the public and the press also have a right to a public trial and the defendant's desire to waive that right is not dispositive and does not automatically override the interests of the public and the press.

**Answer (D) is incorrect** because the government does not have an absolute right to a public trial. For important, articulated reasons, a judge may totally or partially close a trial to the extent necessary to serve those interests.

337. **Answer (B) is correct.** Since the state constitution mandates a jury of twelve, the new statute lowering that to ten is unconstitutional in violation of the state constitution.

**Answer (A) is incorrect.** The United States Constitution's Sixth Amendment does not bar a jury of ten in a state felony case. *Williams v. Florida*, 399 U.S. 786 (1970). Therefore, the state's reduction in the number of jurors does not offend the United States Constitution.

**Answer (C) is incorrect.** Since answer (A) is incorrect, answer (C) is also incorrect.

**Answer (D) is incorrect.** A state constitution routinely trumps a state statute that conflicts with the constitutional provision. Here, the state constitution dictates a jury of twelve and a state statute may not override that constitutional provision. The proper way to accomplish this is to amend the state constitution, often a difficult procedure.

338. **Answer (A) is correct.** A judge in most locales may give a deadlocked jury a jury instruction, called an *Allen* or dynamite charge, urging the jurors to continue deliberation but give weight to the views of other jurors. The charge is named after the federal case, *Allen v. United States*, 164 U.S. 492 (1896), which approved it.

**Answer (B) is incorrect** since the accused is entitled under state law to a unanimous verdict before a conviction is valid. Giving the decision to the side with an "overwhelming majority" would not satisfy the unanimity requirement.

**Answer (C) is incorrect.** Though the court has the discretion to declare a mistrial, this decision would not accomplish Judge Nobuku's goal of having the jury continue deliberations and possibly reach a verdict in the case.

**Answer (D) is incorrect.** The court may not replace sitting jurors with alternates simply because the sitting jurors could not reach agreement. The defendant has a right to have the case decided by the jury that was selected to hear it.

339. **Answer (D) is correct.** In *Missouri v. Hunter*, 459 U.S. 359 (1983), the United States Supreme Court held that double jeopardy does not prevent a state from imposing multiple punishments in a single trial if the state legislature authorized the multiple punishments. Here the state legislature clearly intended for the penalty for an aggravated assault of an elderly person to be enhanced by five years.

**Answer (A) is incorrect** because, as noted above, the Double Jeopardy Clause does not bar multiple punishments in a single trial when authorized by the state legislature.

**Answer (B) is incorrect.** The Double Jeopardy Clause does not deal with the severity of punishment. The Eighth Amendment's Cruel and Unusual Punishment Clause would address this issue, but would surely not be violated by a 20 year sentence for a severe assault on an elderly person.

**Answer (C) is incorrect.** Double Jeopardy protects the accused in single as well as sequential trials, though the focus is different in the two situations.

340. **Answer (A) is correct.** Even though a potential juror's exposure to pretrial publicity may merit further inquiry to ascertain whether the juror could be unbiased because of the information, that exposure by itself will not ordinarily result in the person being excluded for cause.

**Answer (B) is incorrect.** If a potential juror is being prosecuted for a criminal offense, that person will ordinarily be excused for cause. The potential juror's possible bias against the prosecution (anger at being prosecuted) or against the defendant (desiring to please the prosecution) is seen as so strong that the juror will be excused for cause.

**Answer (C) is incorrect.** A potential juror who is in a marriage-like relationship with the accused will be excluded for cause as unable to be unbiased in the case.

**Answer (D) is incorrect.** A potential juror who is close to the victim will be excused for cause as unable to be unbiased in the case. Here the juror is the victim's Sunday school teacher and could hardly be expected to be unbiased.

341. **Answer (C) is correct.** Under Rule 15, Federal Rules of Criminal Procedure, the court must approve a deposition in a criminal case. No other person's approval is necessary.

**Answers (A) and (B) are incorrect.** Rule 15 requires the court's approval for a criminal deposition, but does not mandate that either the person deposed or the prosecuting attorney must also approve the deposition.

**Answer (D) is incorrect.** Under Rule 15, the court must approve each deposition in a federal criminal case. This is unlike a deposition in a civil case where the parties themselves schedule the deposition without judicial involvement or the approval of either the other side or the person to be deposed.

342.   **Answer (D) is correct.** The defendant's presence or absence at the time the hearsay statement was made does not affect its admissibility under the Confrontation Clause.

**Answers (A), (B), and (C) are incorrect** because all are needed for the statement to be covered and admissible under the Confrontation Clause. Under *Crawford v. Washington*, 541 U.S. 36 (2004), a testimonial statement is admissible against an accused if the declarant is unavailable (Answer (A)), was subject to cross examination about the statement (Answer (B)), and the statement is hearsay (Answer (C)). Of course if the statement is not hearsay, it also would not be barred by the Confrontation Clause, which reaches only statements that satisfy the test of hearsay.

343.   **Answer (B) is correct.** Statutes or procedure rules routinely limit the number of peremptory challenges available to each side. For example, under federal law, each side in a capital case gets 20 peremptory challenges and in a felony case the government has 6 challenges while the defendants collectively have 10 challenges. Fed. R. Crim. P. 24(b).

**Answers (A), (C), and (D) are incorrect.** The law does not impose a numerical limit on the number of challenges for cause (Answer (A)), trial objections (Answer (C)), or motions *in limine* (Answer (D)).

**344.** Under the Double Jeopardy Clause of the Fifth Amendment, "no person shall . . . be subject for the same offense to be twice put in jeopardy of life or limb." This means that if a person is convicted of a crime, he or she may not be convicted of the "same offense" in a subsequent prosecution by the same jurisdiction.

Whether two crimes are the "same offense" is determined by the *Blockburger* test, stemming from *Blockburger v. United States*, 284 U.S. 299 *(1932)*. This test asks whether "each provision requires proof of a fact which the other does not." In the instant case, attempted murder and sending a destructive device are not the "same offense" since each crime contains elements not present in the other. For example, attempted murder requires an act designed to take human life, while sending a destructive device requires that the offender use the postal system to send a destructive device, whether or not the object is to take human life. Attempted murder may be accomplished without any involvement of the postal service, but section A-46 mandates the use of the mail but does not require the intent to kill.

The motion should be denied since the current prosecution does not offend the Double Jeopardy Clause.

**345.** A guilty plea involves the waiver of many constitutional rights. Accordingly, it must be handled in a way that documents that the plea and waiver were knowing, intelligent and voluntary. *Brady v. United States*, 397 U.S. 742 (1970). Compliance with Rule 11, Federal Rules of Criminal Procedure ordinarily satisfies this test.

In the exam problem, Rule 11 was virtually ignored and the plea should be overturned since there is no record that it was entered knowingly, intelligently, and voluntarily. There are many obvious problems under Rule 11. First, the court did not place the defendant under oath. Second, the court did not personally advise the defendant of the many constitutional rights (such as the right to a trial, to confront adverse witnesses, and to have a jury trial) available and that would be waived if the defendant entered a guilty plea, and of such procedural requirements as the maximum and minimum possible sentence. Third, the court did not ensure the plea was voluntary. Fourth, no factual basis was determined.

**346.** The court should reject the prosecution's *Batson* claim. *Batson v. Kentucky*, 476 U.S. 79 (1986), bars purposeful use of race-based peremptory challenges. Which violate the Equal Protection Clause. While subsequent decisions have extended the *Batson* rationale to intentional discrimination on the basis of gender and other identifiable or ethnic groups, none has extended it to bar the use of peremptory challenges to exclude better educated people or similar groups. If better educated people are entitled to any protection, it would be analyzed under the rational basis test. In *J.E.B. v. Alabama*, 5212 U.S. 127 (1994), the Supreme Court applied *Batson* to gender-based peremptory challe4nge, but said the parties may still exercise peremptory challenges to remove members of a group subject to rational basis analysis. Here, the challenges are based on a history of involvement with moonshine, not on any racial or other suspect classification or even directly on affluence. The *Batson* challenge will fail.

**347.**   The Supreme Court has held that the government has no Due Process duty to preserve evidence, but cannot destroy or lose the evidence in bad faith. *Arizona v. Youngblood*, 488 U.S. 51 (1988). Here, if you could establish that the government lost the alleged drugs in bad faith, you could make a serious Due Process argument that the government lab report should be suppressed. Your effort will be hurt by the fact that the drugs may have not had any "apparent" exculpatory value, as noted in a footnote in *Youngblood*, since the drugs had already been tested and the results were incriminatory, not exculpatory. Apparent exculpatory value is evidence of bad faith.

You should try to find out how the drugs were lost and whether there was every any doubt by the police as to the accuracy of their own lab reports. While establishing bad faith is difficult, it is not impossible but far more facts are needed than are presented in the exam question.

**348.**   This question raises two discovery issues. First, the defense is entitled to access to the government forensic tests if they would be helpful to the defense on guilt or sentence. *Brady v. Maryland*, 373 U.S. 83 (1963). This means that if the government lab tests show that the bullet did not come from Davies' pistol, the government must give the defense the lab report. Your boss should make a specific request under *Brady* for any lab results.

The other issue is Rule 16, which creates a structure for reciprocal discovery of certain items. Rule 16 is triggered by a defense request. If the defense requests lab reports under Rule 16(A)(1)(F) and the government complies, the defense must then give the government copies of defense lab tests that the defense intends to introduce at trial. Since it is likely that the defense will want to introduce its favorable lab tests but does not want to disclose them to the prosecution before trial, the defense should consider not requesting lab reports from the government under Rule 16. Of course even if no such defense request is made, the defense is still entitled to helpful lab reports under *Brady*.

# INDEX